Graveyard Gothic

Manchester University Press

Graveyard Gothic

Edited by

Eric Parisot, David McAllister
and Xavier Aldana Reyes

MANCHESTER UNIVERSITY PRESS

Copyright © Manchester University Press 2024

While copyright in the volume as a whole is vested in Manchester University Press, copyright in individual chapters belongs to their respective authors, and no chapter may be reproduced wholly or in part without the express permission in writing of both author and publisher.

Published by Manchester University Press
Oxford Road, Manchester, M13 9PL

www.manchesteruniversitypress.co.uk

British Library Cataloguing-in-Publication Data
A catalogue record for this book is available from the British Library

ISBN 978 1 5261 6631 9 hardback

First published 2024

The publisher has no responsibility for the persistence or accuracy of URLs for any external or third-party internet websites referred to in this book, and does not guarantee that any content on such websites is, or will remain, accurate or appropriate.

Typeset by Newgen Publishing UK

Eric would like to dedicate this book to John and Michael Parisot, for proving that horror is a tie that binds.

David would like to dedicate this book to Francis McAllister Jordan, aged 9 and already a fan of tales that make the flesh creep.

Xavier would like to dedicate this book to Verónica Páez, Mar Albadalejo and Sara Sánchez. Four for the road.

Contents

List of figures	ix
List of contributors	xi
Acknowledgements	xv
Introduction: Graveyard Gothic – Eric Parisot, David McAllister and Xavier Aldana Reyes	1
1 The Gothic churchyard in graveyard poetry: cultural remains and literary beginnings – Eric Parisot	18
2 Graveyard pleasures: visiting (and revisiting) the burial site in late eighteenth-century Gothic fiction – Yael Shapira	32
3 The last days of the urban burial ground: horror, reform and Gothic fiction – Roger Luckhurst	47
4 De-Gothicising the Victorian Gothic graveyard – David McAllister	61
5 Relics and ruins, photographs and fellowship – Corinna Wagner	77
6 The colonial Australian Gothic and the grave – Ken Gelder	96
7 Weirding the Gothic graveyard – James Machin	111
8 Graveyards in Western Gothic cinema – Xavier Aldana Reyes	125
9 The ventriloquised corpse and the silent dead: Gothic of the British First and Second World Wars – Sara Wasson	140
10 Home among the headstones: graveyards in Western Gothic television – Stacey Abbott	155
11 The graveyard in neo-Edwardian fiction: refashioning the Victorian death space – Emma Liggins	169
12 Unstable coordinates: textures, *tehkhana* and the Gothic in the horror films of the Ramsay brothers – Vibhushan Subba	183
13 Conversations with spectres: Mexican graveyards and Gothic returns – Enrique Ajuria Ibarra	196

14 Monsters of history: a tour of the cinematic Slavic cemetery
 – Agnieszka Jezyk and Lev Nikulin   208
15 Indian burial grounds in American fiction and film
 – Kevin Corstorphine   223
16 Adolescent existence and resistance: graveyards as a Gothic chronotope in twenty-first-century fiction for young people
 – Debra Dudek   238
17 The graveyard level: anachronism, Anglo-Japanese semiotics and the cruel nightmare of resurrection in early horror video games – James T. McCrea   252

Coda: the futures of graveyard Gothic – Eric Parisot, David McAllister and Xavier Aldana Reyes   268

Index   279

Figures

2.1 Engraving in James Gillray, *Tales of Wonder* (1802). (Yale Center for British Art, Paul Mellon Collection.)   39
2.2 Frontispiece to Anon., *Tales of Terror* (1801). (Sadleir-Black Collection of Gothic Novels, Albert and Shirley Small Special Collections Library, University of Virginia.)   40
5.1 Corinna Wagner, *Resurrection* (2022). (Copyright © Corinna Wagner.)   78
5.2 Corinna Wagner, *Roadside Memorial* (2021). (Copyright © Corinna Wagner.)   82
5.3 Corinna Wagner, *Seaside Memorial* (2020). (Copyright © Corinna Wagner.)   83
5.4 Corinna Wagner, *Shout* (2020). (Copyright © Corinna Wagner.)   84
5.5 Corinna Wagner, *Hardy Tree* (2022). (Copyright © Corinna Wagner.)   87
5.6 Corinna Wagner, *Grave of Rose Pinsky* (2022). (Copyright © Corinna Wagner.)   90
8.1 Henry profanes a grave under the watchful eye of a *memento mori* in *Frankenstein* (1931).   126
8.2 Repressive ideologies rise from the tomb in *La noche del terror ciego* (1972).   131
8.3 In *Nightbreed* (1990), a necropolis is the gateway to Midian, a sanctuary for persecuted monsters.   135
10.1 Family home overlain with graveyard *mise en scène* in *The Addams Family* (1964).   158
10.2 Concealing the horrors of death and loss beneath a carefully manicured lawn in the credit sequence for *Six Feet Under* (2001–5).   163
10.3 The horror of the cemetery from the perspective of the dead in *Buffy the Vampire Slayer* (2001).   167

13.1 The protagonist and the mysterious woman locked inside
the mausoleum in *Cien gritos de terror* (1965). 200
13.2 The spirits of the deceased visit the graveyard in *Coco* (2017). 206
15.1 The supernatural burial ground in *Pet Sematary* (1989). 226
15.2 Not an old Indian burial ground! The cemetery in
Poltergeist (1982). 228
17.1 Early horror video games like *Ghosts 'n Goblins* (1985)
feature upright tombstones resembling modern graveyard
architecture despite their medieval settings. 254
17.2 The skeletal enemies in *Castlevania II: Simon's Quest*
(1987) populate graveyards, adding a sinister element
to an environment formerly associated with piety and
ancestor worship. 256
17.3 Tombstones permeate the world of *Dark Souls III* (2016),
depicting a universe reliant on death and resurrection
replete with corpse-like foes. 263
17.4 Skeletal enemies resurface in *Elden Ring* (2022),
reinforcing the graveyard's agency in warping
negotiations between the living and dead. 265

Contributors

Stacey Abbott is Professor in Film and Television at Northumbria University, UK. She is the author of *Celluloid Vampires* (University of Texas Press, 2007), *Angel: TV Milestone* (Wayne State University Press, 2009), *Undead Apocalypse* (Edinburgh University Press, 2016), and *Near Dark* in the BFI Film Classics series (Bloomsbury, 2020). With Lorna Jowett, she co-authored *TV Horror* (I. B. Tauris, 2012) and co-edited *Global TV Horror* (University of Wales Press, 2021). She is currently co-writing a book, with Jowett, on *Women Creators of TV Horror* (Liverpool University Press) and researching a monograph on horror and animation (Edinburgh University Press).

Enrique Ajuria Ibarra is Senior Assistant Professor at Universidad de las Américas Puebla, Mexico. He has published several articles and book chapters on Mexican Gothic and horror cinema. He is the editor of the peer-reviewed online journal *Studies in Gothic Fiction* and is currently exploring Gothic in Archie Comics, as well as continuing to work on Mexican Gothic.

Xavier Aldana Reyes is Reader in English Literature and Film at Manchester Metropolitan University and a founding member of the Manchester Centre for Gothic Studies, UK. He is the author of *Body Gothic* (University of Wales Press, 2014), *Horror Film and Affect* (Routledge, 2016), *Spanish Gothic* (Palgrave Macmillan, 2017) and *Gothic Cinema* (Routledge, 2020), the editor of *Horror: A Literary History* (British Library Publishing, 2016) and co-editor, with Maisha Wester, of *Twenty-First-Century Gothic: An Edinburgh Companion* (Edinburgh University Press, 2019). Xavier is co-president of the International Gothic Association.

Kevin Corstorphine is Programme Director in American Studies at the University of Hull, UK. His research interests lie in horror and Gothic fiction, with a particular interest in representation of space and place, the environment and haunted locations. He has published widely on authors such as Bram Stoker, H. P. Lovecraft, Ambrose Bierce, Shirley Jackson, Stephen King and Clive Barker. He is co-editor, with Laura R. Kremmel, of *The Palgrave Handbook to Horror Literature* (Palgrave Macmillan, 2018).

Debra Dudek is Associate Professor in English at Edith Cowan University, Australia. Her research analyses visual and verbal texts for young people and how these texts represent ethics and social justice issues. She wrote *The Beloved Does Not Bite: Moral Vampires and the Humans Who Love Them* (Routledge, 2017).

Ken Gelder is Emeritus Professor of English at the University of Melbourne, Australia. His books include *Reading the Vampire* (Routledge, 1994), *Popular Fiction: The Logics and Practices of a Literary Field* (Routledge, 2004) and *New Vampire Cinema* (Routledge, 2012), as well as the co-authored *Uncanny Australia: Sacredness and Identity in a Postcolonial Nation* (Melbourne University Press, 1998), *Colonial Australian Fiction* (Sydney University Press, 2017) and *The Colonial Kangaroo Hunt* (Miegunyah Press, 2020). He is a Fellow of the Australian Academy of the Humanities.

Agnieszka Jezyk specialises in the Polish avant-garde poetry of the interwar period and Slavic horror studies. She has published in *The Polish Review*, *Canadian Slavonic Papers*, *Slavic and East European Journal* and *Ab Imperio*, among others. She is co-editor, with Lev Nikulin, of the volume *Slavic Horror across the Media: Cursed Zones*, forthcoming from Manchester University Press. She has worked at the University of Illinois at Chicago, the University of California Los Angeles and the University of Toronto, Canada. Since January 2024, she has been appointed as Assistant Professor of Polish Studies at the Slavic Department of the University of Washington, Seattle.

Emma Liggins is Reader in English Literature in the Department of English and Co-Director of the Long Nineteenth-Century Network at Manchester Metropolitan University, UK. Her recent publications include *Odd Women? Spinsters, Lesbians and Widows in British Women's Fiction, 1850–1939* (Manchester University Press, 2014) and *The Haunted House in Women's Ghost Stories, 1850–1945: Gender, Space and Modernity* (Palgrave Macmillan, 2020). Her research interests include ghost stories, haunted heritage and Victorian cemeteries.

Roger Luckhurst is Geoffrey Tillotson Chair of Nineteenth-Century Studies at Birkbeck, University of London, UK. He is the author of *The Invention of Telepathy* (Oxford University Press, 2002), *Science Fiction* (Polity,

2005), *The Trauma Question* (Routledge, 2008), *The Mummy's Curse: The True Story of a Dark Fantasy* (Oxford University Press, 2012), *Zombies: A Cultural History* (Reaktion, 2015) and *Corridors: Passages of Modernity* (Reaktion, 2019).

James Machin is an Honorary Research Fellow at Birkbeck, University of London, UK. He is the author of *Weird Fiction in Britain, 1880–1939* (Palgrave Macmillan, 2018) and editor of *British Weird: Selected Short Fiction 1893–1937* (Handheld Press, 2020). He has been editor and co-editor of *Faunus: The Journal of the Friends of Arthur Machen* since 2013. He is currently working on a new scholarly edition of Arthur Conan Doyle's 1895 novel *The Stark Munro Letters* for Edinburgh University Press.

David McAllister is Senior Lecturer in Victorian Literature at Birkbeck, University of London, UK, and Director of the Birkbeck Centre for Nineteenth-Century Studies. He is the author of *Imagining the Dead in British Literature and Culture, 1790–1848* (Palgrave Macmillan, 2018) and has published articles on a range of Victorian and Romantic writers, including Dickens, Carlyle, Wordsworth and Gaskell.

James McCrea is an interdisciplinary art historian with trans-historical thematic interests in funerary art, death iconography and materialities of human remains. He was educated in art history at the University of North Carolina Wilmington, funerary archaeology at the University of York and Gothic studies at Manchester Metropolitan University.

Lev Nikulin is an independent scholar, originally from Novosibirsk, Russia, and now based in Philadelphia. He is an educator, translator of Russian and academic specialising in Slavic studies. He works on Slavic horror, Nikolai Gogol, and LGBT narratives in late Soviet culture. He previously taught Slavic culture and Russian at Swarthmore College and at Princeton, where he also defended his dissertation on Nikolai Gogol as a horror writer.

Eric Parisot is Associate Professor in English at Flinders University (Adelaide, Australia). His primary interests lie in British eighteenth-century literature and culture, especially related to death (and cognate themes), the Gothic and the history of emotions. He is also the author of *Graveyard Poetry* (Ashgate, 2013) and *Jane Austen and Vampires* (Palgrave Macmillan, 2024).

Yael Shapira is Senior Lecturer in the Department of English Literature and Linguistics at Bar-Ilan University in Israel. She is the author of *Inventing the Gothic Corpse: The Thrill of Human Remains in the Eighteenth-Century*

Novel (Palgrave, 2018). Her current research focuses on the forgotten 'trade Gothic' of the Romantic period.

Vibhushan Subba is Assistant Professor in the School of Arts and Aesthetics, Department of Cinema Studies, Jawaharlal Nehru University. His research interests include South Asian screen cultures, cult/exploitation cinema and fandom. His works have appeared in the journals *Bioscope: South Asian Screen Studies* and *Studies in South Asian Film and Media*, the collection *The Routledge Companion to Cult Cinema* (Routledge, 2020) and UNESCO publications.

Corinna Wagner is a photographer and Professor of Visual and Literary Arts at the University of Exeter, UK. Recent exhibitions focus on ruins and the environment. Her publications include *The Oxford Handbook of Victorian Medievalism*, co-edited with Joanne Parker (Oxford University Press, 2020), *A Body of Work: An Anthology of Poetry and Medicine*, co-edited with Andy Brown (Bloomsbury, 2015), *Gothic Evolutions: Poetry, Tales, Context, Theory* (Broadview Press, 2014) and *Pathological Bodies: Medicine and Political Culture* (University of California Press, 2013).

Sara Wasson is Reader in Gothic Studies at Lancaster University, UK. Her research specialties are Gothic, science fiction and medical and environmental humanities. Her research is concerned with ethical witness in response to individual and collective suffering. Her books, *Urban Gothic of the Second World War* (Palgrave Macmillan, 2010) and *Transplantation Gothic: Tissue Transfer in Literature, Film and Medicine* (Manchester University Press, 2020), both won the Allan Lloyd Smith Memorial Prize from the International Gothic Association. Sara co-edited with Emily Alder the collection *Gothic Science Fiction, 1980–2010* (Liverpool University Press, 2011).

Acknowledgements

The editors would like to thank the editorial team at Manchester University Press for their assistance, especially Matthew Frost for his unfailing belief in, and support of, this collection from day one. We are also very grateful to the anonymous readers of our original proposal for their helpful suggestions and endorsement of the volume. Finally, we would like to express our immense gratitude to the contributors to this book for their goodwill and patience throughout its gestation over the past four COVID-affected years. To say these have been unprecedented times is likely an understatement, and we really appreciate everyone's commitment to seeing this project through to publication, or from the cradle to the grave, one might say.

Introduction: Graveyard Gothic

Eric Parisot, David McAllister and Xavier Aldana Reyes

The development of the Gothic – an artistic mode that relies, among other things, upon imbrications of past and present and the affective power of significant locations – was enabled by the custom of burying the dead and marking their graves. It was this practice that initiated both the temporality of human history and the institution of the places in which human lives are lived. For Robert Pogue Harrison, these connections are axiomatic. '[W]e cannot understand the early institution of places on the earth independently of the institution of burial,' he suggests. 'For what is a place if not its memory of itself – a site or locale where time turns back upon itself?' (2003: 23). This new temporality first emerges at the graveside because a location where the dead are buried 'marks a site in the landscape where time cannot merely pass through, or pass over. Time must now gather around the [grave] and mortalize itself' (2003: 23). It was here that our ancestors first inhabited a temporality that was separate from the cycles of the natural world. Burial thus began both the 'mortalization of time' and the differentiation of human spaces from the wilderness: the grave gave 'place its articulated boundaries, distinguishing it from the infinity of homogeneous space' (2003: 23). When viewed in this light, every Gothic location, from the ruined castle to the flickeringly strip-lit psych ward, is ultimately founded upon and authorised by the place-making power of the grave, as is every Gothic reckoning with inheritance, which begins with the grave's original declaration of human finitude and generational interconnection. The graveyard, as the space in which these temporal markers have most often been located in Western cultures, can therefore be read as the foundational Gothic location: the ground from which all Gothic ultimately derives its specific and distinctive character.

Even without the perspective offered by this deep history of the buried dead, the graveyard has long been recognised as a key site and symbolic topos of Gothic written culture and the later varieties of media that adapted and visualised it. Its significance has endured through time and extended across cultures, its imagery endlessly appropriated and reappropriated in texts that span both centuries and geographies. The essays in this collection demonstrate the graveyard's past and ongoing centrality to Gothic literature and film, identifying it as one of the mode's most important sources of affect, solace, identity, oppression and resistance. It is a space whose meaning is both historically and culturally contingent as well as being significantly overdetermined. For William Wordsworth, writing in the first of his *Essays upon Epitaphs* (1810), the country churchyard was 'a visible centre of a community of the living and the dead; a point to which are habitually referred the nearest concerns of both' (Wordsworth, 1974: 56). Yet Gothic poems, novels, film, television and games repeatedly alert us to the fact that the concerns of these two groups are often conflicting: that the living can choose to break faith with the dead, while, as Karl Marx famously observed, the '[t]radition from all the dead generations weighs like a nightmare on the brains of the living' (Marx, 2002: 19), using an image that was itself drawn from the rich storehouse of the Gothic graveyard. The graveyard is a key symbolic location in which the living struggle to shake off unwanted inheritances, to fashion themselves as they see fit, to supplant their ancestors as prime actors in the scene. In Chris Baldick's well-known formulation, the 'Gothic effect' requires the combination of 'a fearful sense of inheritance in time with a claustrophobic sense of enclosure in space' (1992: xix), both of which combine to generate a sense of decay. The efficiency of inheritable spaces such as castles and stately homes in generating these effects has long been a staple of Gothic criticism. But where better to find this mix of inheritance, enclosure and disintegration than in the graveyard?

Wordsworth's sense of the graveyard as the 'visible centre of a community' describes a churchyard that is geographically situated at the heart of a settlement, and thus necessarily integrated into the daily lives of its inhabitants. Yet the buried dead were not always so central to the communities in which they had lived. It is all but impossible to accurately recreate the patchwork of localised belief systems that existed in pre-Christian Europe, but the archaeological record suggests that while the graves of the dead were marked for commemoration they were also typically separated from the community of the living, reflecting tensions between the small group of those who happened to be living at any one time and the invisible crowd of the dead who vastly outnumbered them (Binski, 1996: 11–12). A fragile peace between the two groups was established through ritual; one of the main aims of ancient funeral rites was to prevent the deceased from returning to disturb the living, and this truce was maintained with regular offerings to placate the dead and ensure that they did not return to ruin crops or affect fertility (Ariès, 1974: 14). The hostile and inexplicable acts of the natural world were often figured as the work of dissatisfied ancestors, while periods of calm and plenty were signs that the terms of this transmortal contract were being fulfilled: that the dead were satisfied with the behaviour of the living, who nevertheless kept them at a safe distance.

It was the spread of Christianity that caused the first radical reformulation of this separation of graves from houses by placing death and resurrection at the centre of its message (Binski, 1996: 11). The fifth century Byzantine historian Eunapius of Sardis was one of the first writers to comment on the unusual closeness of early Christians to their dead:

> [T]hey collected the bones and skulls of criminals who had been put to death for numerous crimes ... made them out to be gods, and thought that they became better by defiling themselves at their graves. 'Martyrs' the dead men were called, and ministers of a sort, and ambassadors with the gods to carry men's prayers.
>
> (Quoted in Binski, 1996: 11)

Veneration of the remains of saints and martyrs made bones and other bodily relics into valuable commodities, which were housed either in or close to the altars of churches. This, in turn, made it desirable to be buried as near to the altar as possible. Churches were built with subterranean crypts that gradually filled with coffins; churchyards housed those who lacked either the money or status to be buried inside. By the time Gothic fiction emerged in the mid eighteenth century, almost all of Britain's dead were clustered into graves that surrounded the parish church, or on land that it owned, and these graveyards, around which communities had grown, were now 'probably the oldest feature of a very old landscape' (Lacquer, 2015: 123). Here was a space in which statuary and stonework from long-gone centuries sat next to newer gravestones with deeper, more recent inscriptions: a contrast that provoked the living to consider their own mortality, sometimes in pensive neoclassic melancholy, but at other times with anxious trepidation. The graveyard mingled past, present and future more visibly, and recognisably, than any other location; any writer drawn by the emerging Gothic looking for an evocative setting thus found one ready-made at the heart of their communities, in a space that felt uncannily familiar yet always slightly threatening, still the terrain of the capricious, never-quite-assuageable dead.

Graveyard representations in early Gothic fiction focused upon two principal threats: a fear of what might emerge from the grave in the shape of revenants, ghosts and other supernatural manifestations, and a gloomy recognition of its inescapability as our ultimate destination. The former takes priority in Horace Walpole's *The Castle of Otranto* (1764), where both the materiality and spatiality of Alfonso's tomb play significant roles in restoring social order and resolving issues of inheritance and political legitimacy. The novel begins with the son of Manfred, prince of Otranto, being crushed by a supernatural replica of a helmet from the tomb of the former ruler Alfonso the Good, who had been usurped by Manfred's grandfather; it effectively concludes at Alfonso's tomb, where Manfred accidentally murders his daughter Matilda in the crypt's sepulchral darkness. The tomb itself is thus directly implicated in curtailing Manfred's bloodline, ending his reign and restoring Alfonso's family to power through supernatural interventions that seem to proceed from the grave. Here, at the origin of Gothic fiction, the grave's centrality is established by a plot in which the archetypal Gothic antagonist is 'pursued by an avenging grave monument until his bloodline is expunged' (Quinn, 2016: 41). In other first-wave texts the grave's connection to the supernatural is invoked so that it can explicitly be denied. A paradigmatic example of Ann Radcliffe's 'explained supernatural' in *The Mysteries of Udolpho* (1794) involves what appears to be a disinterred corpse, which Emily St Aubert finds hidden behind a veil on the wall of a chamber in the castle of Udolpho. Emily swoons when she pulls back the veil, and although what she sees is initially withheld from the reader, we later learn that it is a waxen 'human figure ... dressed in the habiliments of the grave', with its face 'partly decayed and disfigured by worms' (1998: 662). This confrontation with what appears to be a displaced corpse, whose dissolution ought to have been hidden in the grave, rather than behind a veil, shapes Emily's sense of Udolpho as a threatening space in which normative behaviour is suspended and the supernatural is at work. The trauma she suffers echoes through the novel in numerous ways, from the repeated mention of the word 'veil' to her encounters with open graves (discussed in greater detail by Yael Shapira in Chapter 2). Both the seemingly displaced corpse and the yawning graves remind Emily of the threat that living in the castle poses to her survival, removing her ability to think clearly or act rationally as she indulges her emotions and allows them to overwhelm her. This repeated exposure to the grave shapes Emily's development and, as Jolene Zigarovich notes, it is only through repeatedly confronting her trauma that she quells her superstitious fears and 'learns to gradually control her sensibility and spectral imagination' (2023: 129).

Functioning as a wellspring of the supernatural, the graveyard quickly became a recognisable marker of the Gothic, and a principal source of its affects. Its ubiquity made it an easy target for satirists who engaged in parodic 'double-coding', simultaneously condemning the public's appetite for Gothic narratives and participating in what had become a highly lucrative literary market (Hutcheon, 2003: 163; Dentith, 2000: 183). The ghostly narrator of James White's satirical *Earl Strongbow: or, the History of Richard de Clare and the Beautiful Geralda* (1789) explains graveyard hauntings as the product of a dearth of scandalous gossip in the afterlife: 'those apparitions which, during the gloom of night, are seen flitting in church-yards and other solitary places, to the vain terror of the timid and the foolish, are only scouts whom [the dead] have dispatched for the purpose of collecting terrestrial information' (White, 1789, vol. I: 67). Apart from their predilection for gossip, he explains, the dead are 'a harmless tribe' (1789, vol. I: 67). Despite this comically trivial explanation for graveyard haunting, we later learn that Strongbow is condemned to haunt Chepstow Castle because he has neglected to maintain the gravestone of a squire whom he killed, and until 'the honours of [his] grave' (1789, vol. II: 161) are restored there will be no peace for the troubled ghost. White simultaneously subverts and reinforces the graveyard's reputation as a site of Gothic and supernatural activity, which is so well established that when Henry Tilney invokes a typical Gothic novel in Jane Austen's *Northanger Abbey* (1817), he describes one that is published in 'three duodecimo volumes, two hundred and seventy-six pages in each, with a frontispiece to the first, of two tombstones and a lantern' (2003: 108). The graveyard's material culture is instantly legible as a metonym in Tilney's lampoon: a tombstone represents the genre in its totality and is deemed better able to summon its distinctive sensibility than any other trope, space or theme.

The essays gathered in this collection show how the graveyard's metonymic association with the Gothic has endured, deepened and become more wide-ranging and complex as it has developed through time, across cultural boundaries and within different media. They explore the plural roles the graveyard has taken across the Gothic's history, unpacking the symbolic role it has played for poets, writers, filmmakers and game designers, and identifying the cultural and iconic functions that have continued to accrue in graveyard spaces. What also emerges is a wide-ranging and transformative picture of how the Gothic graveyard has, despite its evolution across a wide array of political, national and historical spheres, continued to signify comparable notions about death, passing and the past. As the collection demonstrates, the fictional graveyard is as prone to transformation and update as any other chronotope, but its simultaneous stasis and polyvalence as a site of temporal and supernatural exchanges have ensured its constancy and relevance to the Gothic tradition and, indeed, to deeply human anxieties about mortality. As the Gothic mode developed over the decades and centuries, its graveyard entanglements moved beyond this narrow focus on graves and their occupants to encompass a perspective in which the space in its entirety is figured as 'other', as a site of transgression removed from the civility or surveillance of living communities, whether in the form of satanic ritual (Matthew Lewis's *The Monk* (1796), grave-robbing (from Mary Shelley's *Frankenstein* (1818) to Poppy Z. Brite's 'His Mouth Will Taste of Wormwood' (1990)), or teenage punk-rock tomfoolery (Dan O'Bannon's film *The Return of the Living Dead* (1985)) – let alone the countless hordes of the monstrous undead in all forms of Gothic culture. In his essay 'Of Other Spaces' (1967), Michel Foucault describes the graveyard as a 'heterotopia', his term for spaces that are discursively 'other' due to their disturbing and transformative qualities. For Foucault, heterotopias serve as 'counter-sites' to real sites of culture, and function 'to suspect, neutralize, or invert the set of relations that they happen to designate, mirror, or reflect' (1986: 24). As Fred Botting recognises, Foucault's notion of heterotopia is an apt lens through which to view the emergence of Gothic fiction in the eighteenth century: 'The main features of Gothic fiction, in neoclassical terms, are heterotopias: the wild landscapes, the ruined castles and abbeys, the dark, dank labyrinths, the marvelous, supernatural events, distant times and customs are not only excluded from the Augustan social world but introduce the passions, desires, and excitements it suppressed' (2012: 19). The graveyard is excluded from Botting's laundry-list of Gothic settings and locales – perhaps because of its neoclassical associations with philosophical contemplation – but is especially highlighted in Foucault's essay as a 'strange heterotopia', 'a place unlike' but reflective of 'ordinary cultural spaces' (1986: 25). In describing the gradual relocation of burial grounds from the heart of a society or village to outside city borders, as exemplified by the rise of the metropolitan cemetery in the nineteenth century, Foucault constructs the modern cemetery 'as *the other city* in which dead people reside, and which perversely imitates relationships within the living families as well as urban infrastructure' (Lukić and Parezanović, 2020: 1139, original emphasis). Viewed as such, the cemetery's strange, subversive heterotopian relation to the ordinary world around it has unbounded Gothic potential.

Foucault develops his notion of heterotopia through a series of characteristics and principles which usefully help to tease out its Gothic promise. As heterotopias, graveyards are culturally and historically contingent spaces, bound to specific times and places, and to specific rites of passage that vary between communities and over time. Ergo, as history unfolds, so too does the precise heterotopic function of the graveyard. Heterotopias are not, however, palimpsests – these varying functions operate simultaneously and accumulate over time. As Foucault describes, the heterotopia 'is capable of juxtaposing in a single real place several spaces, several sites that are in themselves incompatible' (1986: 25). This is patently evident in the evolving and oft contradictory functions of the graveyard, whether as a sanctified site of remembrance and consolation, as a hygienic repository of the dead, or as an imaginative site of Gothic *frisson* and horror. Foucault typically presents the juxtaposition of these varying functions as a comfortable one, but this accretion of purpose and meaning within the graveyard gives rise to other Gothic possibilities. Ideologies compete, are distorted and repressed, and breed discontents. Grinning corpses, reanimated zombies and fiendish vampires are but a few of the monsters that embody the graveyard's incompatible paradigms of life and death – and undeath (Davies, 2008: 397).

Accordingly, the graveyard is a space that transgresses traditional time by staging a tension between the past and the present that is – as already mentioned – typical of other Gothic chronotopes like the ruined abbey and medieval castle. Foucault highlights this in two ways. First, various functions of the cemetery are connected to different 'slices in time' – to what he terms 'heterochronies' (1986: 26). With the accretion of purpose and meaning, graveyards and cemeteries host several accumulated and incompatible timelines. This temporal accumulation, or 'heterochrony', is easily perceived in the graveyard, where corpses and tombstones old and new pile up to form something akin to a museum of death (1986: 26). For Foucault, however, heterotopic function peaks at an 'absolute break' with traditional time (1986: 26). As a space dedicated to 'the loss of life', the cemetery is inherently and 'highly heterotopic', a place where the individual is confronted with a 'quasi-eternity in which her permanent lot is dissolution and disappearance' (1986: 26). These temporal ruptures are marked by dates of death on gravestones, reifying the layering of time. Other forms of temporal accumulation and discontinuity emerge in the graveyard. Layers of circadian and ecological time ebb and flow around the static dead, changing perceptions of time, space and meaning (Deering, 2015: 185). The darkness of night, for instance, marks a break from the commotion of the day, but in depriving the senses also enervates the imagined past (2015: 195). The graveyard's affective and heterotopic potential is nocturnally enhanced, as recognised and exploited by eighteenth-century graveyard poets and, in turn, their literary descendants. Funeral rites also signify a break from ordinary reality, a liminal time and space where the dead are ushered from the living world and the bereaved can come to terms with their loss before resuming their lives (Van Gennep, 1960: 147; Ní Éigeartaigh, 2022: xi). In the graveyard, chronological time is suspended and warped, bringing pasts and present into uneasy collision, altering our grip on reality.

As a threshold, the graveyard also highlights the precarity of order. The liminal stage of rituals centred upon the dead often signal an alternative time and space, of opening and closing, of entry and exit, of existing in between, of temporary deviance from law, custom and convention (Turner, 1969: 95; Ní Éigeartaigh, 2022: xii). The graveyard also signals risk, a perilous moment when the shackles of normality are suspended and potentially seized by subdued menaces, or by those denied safe passage from one world to the next and left lingering in the interstices of metaphysical realms. For others, liminal deviance is a welcome state rendering both the physical and imagined graveyard a site of pleasure and respite. Indeed, the graveyard has become a popular destination for recreational tourism on this very basis, where ghosts and local legends are chased rather than doing the chasing.

Foucault's conception of heterotopia and its application to the graveyard and cemetery makes the necessity of this volume's transhistorical, multicultural and multimedia scope distinctly clear. As a space contingent upon its time, place and its surrounding culture, the graveyard is pregnant with meaning and bursting with multitudinous varieties of the restless past. What is more, it is a space where the imagined and the physical coalesce, a place that perpetually draws the functional capacity of stories to attempt to explain the troubling ambiguities of existence, and where layered narratives accumulate as blankets of moss upon stone.

The essays in this collection follow a rough chronology, moving from graveyard poetry of the eighteenth century to video games and YA fictions of the twenty-first. Their sequential arrangement showcases the accretion of cultural and symbolic functions over the centuries and their proliferating mutations across various forms of media. With this in mind, our introductory account of the collection's chapters, instead, eschews plotting a linear course in favour of unearthing some of the many buried links between and among them. Eric Parisot's tour of the graveyard, as imagined in eighteenth-century graveyard poetry, is our starting point in either case. In his opening chapter, Parisot draws a lexical distinction between the 'graveyard' – the nominal term used in this volume for burial sites – and its earlier iteration as the 'churchyard', for two significant purposes. For one, it highlights the consecrated authority of the co-located church, underscoring the import of religious piety in graveyard poetry's pursuit of eschatological and soteriological unease. But the chapter also invokes the churchyard as a composite *memento mori*, as a site of premodern sensibilities that have been eroded in modern times but simultaneously point the way forward to Gothic renditions. Graveyard poetry exemplifies the emergence of new ways of thinking, writing and living with the dead that can be tracked through the essays in this collection; in doing so, it helped to establish burial sites of all sorts as invariably Gothic locations.[1]

The enduring appeal of this location, along with its transnational and transmedia portability, is discussed by James T. McCrea in Chapter 17, the final essay in this collection, which focuses on graveyard representations in recent Japanese-designed video game series. As McCrea notes, Westernised graveyard spaces appear frequently in these games, offering a recognisably Gothic environment in which the gameplay can take place. The games themselves are typically set in what appears to be a medieval Europe of castles, knights in armour and pre-industrial weaponry, but feature a 'graveyard level' in which players do battle with assorted monsters that emerge from anachronistically post-medieval burial grounds. The graves here are derivatively 'Gothic' in appearance, indicating the graveyard's enduring ability to signify the Gothic, but also, as McCrea notes, signalling Japanese gaming culture's desire to attract Western audiences by incorporating easily legible, Westernised imagery. What, though, does it mean for a player to 'die' in such a level? Like the graveyard poetry with which the collection opens, this final chapter interrogates the role of graveyard representations in stimulating philosophical and religious contemplations of mortality in a safely liminal space.

The visual tropes upon which these games rely were established in twentieth-century Gothic and horror films, which both defined the iconography of the Gothic graveyard and radically expanded the range of its possible significations. For Xavier Aldana Reyes, in Chapter 8, the cinematic graveyard is 'an incongruent edgeland able to encompass everything from excitement to tongue-in-cheek gallows humour and sobering tragedy'. Aldana Reyes demonstrates this multiplicity with reference to a wide range of twentieth- and twenty-first-century cinema while focusing mostly on two aspects of the graveyard's cinematic depiction: as a source of revenants (in this case zombies) and as a 'hinge' connecting not just this life and the next but disparate communities, and particularly those that have been marginalised. As a result of their seclusion and their fundamental alterity to spaces dominated by the living, graveyards have often functioned as zones in which difference is not only tolerated but celebrated: where bonds within such communities can be established and nurtured and their relations to majority communities are reconfigured, often as resistance.

This liminality is central to a number of the essays in this collection. In Chapter 16, Debra Dudek considers the graveyard's role as a safe space in the often hostile environments of contemporary YA fiction. For Dudek, the graveyard's uncanniness and liminality offer analogies to the state of adolescence itself as it becomes a space of self-discovery, offering refuge to troubled teen protagonists as they grapple with the pressures of the move from the familiarity of childhood to the uncertainties of the adult world. In this account, the graveyard seems to inhabit a different temporality to the world outside, enabling YA protagonists time to fashion new identities and establish new friendships. By facilitating intersubjective communication and the alignment of pasts, presents and futures, the graveyard in these Gothic novels emerges as a site associated with love rather than sadness.

The narratives of becoming that typify contemporary YA fiction come with an expectation of closure; it may seem endless to all involved, but adolescence, like a novel, does eventually conclude. As Stacey Abbott notes in Chapter 10, this is not necessarily the case in television, where the seriality of long-running programmes with teen protagonists often mitigates against any such finality and makes it difficult for TV shows to bring about the sort of closure that characterises other Gothic texts. This, Abbott argues, has consequences for how protagonists (and viewers) experience the graveyard, and risks undermining the distinctive strangeness of the space by rendering it overly familiar or mundane. In Joss Whedon's *Buffy the Vampire Slayer* (1997–2003), the Hellmouth located in the local graveyard remains parted wide, unleashing vampires and all sorts of demons upon Sunnydale, a town seemingly caught in a liminal state of Gothic chaos. For Buffy and her gang, closure – both emotionally and of the gates of Hell – is inordinately delayed. And yet, as Abbott argues, this does not undermine the affective significance of graveyard narratives; while *Buffy* and other shows utilise the established Gothic significance of graveyards to create an unsettling atmosphere, they simultaneously reshape their Gothic inheritance by puncturing domestic space with uncanny explorations of grief and loss.

These televisual Gothic narratives identify benefits in living close to graveyard spaces, with Abbott reminding us that not only did the Addams family live at 1 Cemetery Lane, but they were also considerably more tolerant of difference than some of their neighbours and thus constituted a disruptively Gothic presence in American suburbia. However, the effects of living near graveyard spaces have not always been so positively construed. In the early nineteenth century, Roger Luckhurst argues in Chapter 3, the reality of many inner-city graveyards was more horrific than any literary representation could muster. Excavating some of the many non-fictional accounts of graveyards produced by sanitary reformers of the period, and discussing the horrifying images that they collated, Luckhurst argues that these scandalous texts stimulated the Gothic imagination, particularly in its emergent urban form: penny bloods and penny dreadfuls, and the sordid graveyards of Charles Dickens's London novels. The lurid accounts of burial reformers, in particular the London physician George Alfred Walker, emphasised the porousness of the tiny graveyard spaces into which the rapidly expanding population of London were crammed after death: the dead not only saturated the ground within the graveyard walls but spilled out to infect the city's air through miasma, and its waterways through effluvia. As Luckhurst shows, this excess of dead matter transforms the entire city into a Gothicised space: one vast graveyard where the dead were a constant presence, and which required biopolitical interventions to bring it back within the limits of reason, as defined and understood by a generation of mid-nineteenth-century social reformers.

This campaign to reform the nation's burial practices, with its overt anti-Gothic rhetoric and focus on transforming graveyards from sites of horror and aversion to beautified spaces of aesthetic contemplation, is David McAllister's subject in Chapter 4. McAllister traces the anxiety that urban graveyards were causing not just physical but psychological damage to the nation in a process that, for reformers, was analogous to the harm caused by reading Gothic narratives. Graveyards, like ghost stories, weakened the nation's moral fibre, breeding psychological and moral disorders, spreading superstition and cultivating morbid thoughts. Graveyards emerged as a source of infection, both moral and physical. Reformers identified an antidote in the closure of London's old graveyards and the construction of new cemeteries, which were carefully planned on rational principles, and were subject to a cleansing and maintenance regime which sought to exclude the visible signs of decay, which they linked with the horror of bodily dissolution. Yet decay, as McAllister shows in a discussion of *Dracula*, is impossible to repress, and the attempt to do so became a source of terror: undeath can be as disturbing as decay. The failure of Victorian attempts to de-Gothicise the graveyard raises questions of cause and effect: does a culture's customary mode of thinking about the dead determine the aesthetic of its burial grounds, or does the influence flow in the opposite direction?

Enrique Ajuria Ibarra's account of graveyards in Mexican fiction, cinema and culture (Chapter 13) describes a death culture in which the graveyard functions as a point of joyful connection between the living and the dead, where familial networks can be extended through gift-exchange and conviviality in a space that is decorated with photographs and gifts and colourful tributes to the dead. A Gothic blurring of boundaries between the living and the dead works, in the texts considered, to police self-centred individualism and reassert communal values in which the dead are considered to have an enduring social role. Ajuria Ibarra's reading of Pixar's *Coco* lays out the connections between the graveyard and the family home as shared spaces in which sociality and community are forged through conversation, memory-making, and the curation of a material culture which sustains connections both among the living, through the promotion of community at the expense of individualism, and between the living and the dead beyond the grave. Living with the dead need not be a source of terror, Ajuria Ibarra suggests, and haunting need not be malign: the visual appeal of the Day of the Dead tradition and the graveyard space itself emerge as fundamental to this distinctive death culture.

Corinna Wagner also focuses on the disruptive effects of attempts to sanitise graveyard spaces in Chapter 5. Drawing on texts from across the nineteenth and twentieth centuries, Wagner argues that the sort of ruination associated with Gothic graveyard representations has often been a prerequisite for certain types of necessary encounter between the living and the dead, and that a modernity that ignores Gothic *Ruinenlust* risks severing vital links between the present and past. As Wagner demonstrates, graveyards are not benign spaces with static markers of our relationship with the dead: they are themselves subject to forces of organic impermanence, which effect slow transformations on everything that lies within the graveyard walls, including the inorganic materials we use to commemorate the dead. This process of ruination effectively mediates our relationship with the past and the dead and ensures that graveyards remain as repositories of memory and narrative that are never more needed than in a time of ecological, social and geopolitical crisis. The graveyard's role in enabling both memory and forgetting is similarly central to the neo-Edwardian Gothic novels discussed by Emma Liggins in Chapter 11. By discussing the effaced inscriptions and decaying ephemera on the graves of women in ageing churchyards, in novels by Susan Hill and Tracy Chevalier, Liggins shows how neo-Edwardian Gothic fiction works to reinstate occluded histories, which had been suppressed by cultures that sought to suppress scandalous historical voices and events from the collective memory. For Liggins, the cemeterial locus of these novels serves as a means of critiquing outmoded and oppressive understandings of sexuality, belonging and grief; its historic role in upholding these structures, through tactical omissions and occlusions, legitimates its artistic reinvention as a space of supernatural potential, uncanny encounter and reckoning with the past.

Such speaking encounters with the dead and the past are a central theme of Gothic scholarship both in this collection and elsewhere. The Gothic routinely gives voice to ghosts, often articulating the perspectives of others among the dead whose narratives may have been stilled during life by circumstance or social structure. In Chapter 9, however, Sara Wasson considers the silent dead of the First and Second World Wars: soldiers absorbed into battlefield mud and encrypted in trench walls; civilians buried beneath the rubble of bombed-out houses. These unspeaking corpses have proven themselves resistant to being incorporated into unifying narratives of national commemoration, such as those that influenced the construction of war cemeteries as quasi-national shrines, or in the poetic or fictional narratives through which historic wars have been mediated and are remembered. Using primarily memoir and poetry, Wasson considers how the complex physicality of their representation has contributed to their ongoing marginalisation in scholarship, and shows how Gothic's discursivity – its boundary-blurring ability to elide fictional with lived suffering – might help in their re-membering, and in reconstructing the chaos and suffering of war in opposition, perhaps, to national narratives of worthwhile sacrifice.

The graveyard's function as a site of memory and forgetting takes on a distinctive resonance at sites of colonial dispossession and extraction, where burial has often enabled settlers to occlude or overwrite indigenous narratives while seeking to construct their own fantasies of legitimacy and belonging. In Gothic texts set in colonised lands these acts of erasure often return to haunt both the original colonists and their descendants, as can be seen in the long history of the 'Indian burial ground' trope in US literature and film. In Chapter 15, Kevin Corstorphine casts new light on this familiar invention, returning to its origins in eighteenth- and nineteenth-century texts by Philip Freneau and Washington Irving before tracing it forwards, through a cluster of guilt-soaked horror novels and films in the aftermath of the Indian Self-Determination and Education Assistance Act (1975), which allowed individual tribes and nations to obtain restitution for broken land treaties in the past. The chapter suggests that this burial ground theme may finally have been killed off and considers some recent transformations and rejections of the trope in horror texts written by Native creators. In these, Corstorphine suggests, Native characters are de-romanticised, granted complexity and ambiguity, and represented without the distorting perspective of colonisation.

Ken Gelder, writing on graves in colonial Australian Gothic in Chapter 6, also notes progress in how Australia commemorates the dead of its colonial past, through the digital chronicling of the sites of Aboriginal massacres. Not only had these locations gone unmarked in the nineteenth century, but the victims of these massacres had often remained unburied. Conversely, settler graves were typically not only marked but used to construct the narrative of settlement, and Gelder contrasts this 'necronationalism' (using the dead to construct a fantasy of nationhood) with the necropower being exercised in the genocidal transformation of landscape into deathscape.

Reckonings with colonial pasts also feature in Vibhushan Subba's contribution (Chapter 12), which considers the Bombay horror films of the Ramsay brothers as key texts in South Asian Gothic cinema. Subba focuses on the subterranean space of the *tehkhana* – vast basements that lie beneath Mughal palaces and which repeatedly function for the Ramsays as both ad hoc burial sites and the repositories of other secrets. Subba's analysis of these overlooked spaces goes beyond postcolonial critique, identifying the *tehkhana* as a site of submerged feudal tensions, post-emergency anxieties, asynchronous temporalities and monstrous or ghostly bodies. Like Corstorphine's and Gelder's, this chapter exposes the lingering ghosts of those brutalised by violence, of men and women denied safe exit to an afterlife, caught between worlds in both life and death. Left to loiter in resentment, the monstrosity of their deaths is often returned and reciprocated upon the living.

Agnieszka Jezyk and Lev Nikulin point to a different kind of graveyard reckoning with national history in their chapter on late-Soviet and post-Soviet Polish and Russian Gothic film (Chapter 14). Jezyk and Nikulin read the cemeteries of films directed by Marek Piestrak, Oleg Teptsov, Andrzej Żuławski and Aleksandr Itygilov collectively as a Bakhtinian chronotope, a liminal site of spatial and temporal fusion that encases histories of traumatic violence, fear of social change and political uncertainty under Soviet rule. This cemetery is a place where old regimes come to die but are never quite obliterated. Their residue and waste are not so easily discarded, forming veritable wastelands of history that are difficult to escape. One consequence is the rendering of the cemetery as a distinctly anti-aesthetic Gothic space that nevertheless serves a crucial function in mediating post-Soviet reality with its troubled past. These chapters point to the graveyard's complex role in commemorating both official and alternative histories, and the ways in which Gothic texts seek to trouble the criteria by which these accounts of the past determine who and what should be remembered, and why.

While the graveyard has long been recognised as a site of potential haunting, the chapters in this collection suggest that it is the living who choose to spend their time among the tombs, persistently devoting fictional, cinematic, poetic, televisual and ludic space to its representation, and valuing those texts that linger in its precincts. Unlike the dead, the living are not compelled to remain in, or return to, this space: we do so because we enjoy it. Graveyard visitation has a long association with pleasure, as Yael Shapira reminds us in Chapter 2, arguing that this pleasure is discernible both on the part of those who choose to consume graveyard texts and, at times, among the characters who populate them. Focusing on canonical Gothic novels of the late eighteenth century, Shapira shows how protagonists value crypt spaces for the privacy that allows them to pursue their often illicit or transgressive desires. The prominence of similar vault scenes in the numerous 'trade Gothic' books that followed in the wake of Lewis's and Radcliffe's success indicates that readers took pleasure in narrative developments set in close proximity to graves: supernatural intrusions, the airing of long-hidden family secrets and the sudden revelation of a hero or heroine's true identity. The graveyard, in these first Gothic texts, is no longer a site of gloomy didactic instruction but rather a cultural pleasure-space, a site of play and affective encounter. James Machin also identifies the disruptive pleasures of graveyard visitation in Chapter 7, which focuses on H. P. Lovecraft's stories, in which the graveyard begins as a site of decadent melancholy before eventually becoming something weirder, less human, more difficult both to comprehend and to represent. The nature of this weirding is characteristically Lovecraftian: Machin shows how his early stories feature gleeful revels in graveyards that are described in the most concrete terms, while the graveyards in his later fiction contain non-Euclidean spaces that may house some unnameable and ungraspable 'thing' towards which his prose can only gesture. For Machin, this most resolutely human of spaces becomes, or is becoming, post-human in the hands of an author who was engaging with the avant-gardes of the early twentieth century. As a site of pleasure, philosophical speculation, aesthetic experimentation and reckoning with the past, the graveyard's range of possible signification, as identified in these essays, is capacious.

This collection begs the question: what can the Gothic imaginary tell us about our real relationship with graveyards, cemeteries and other burial sites? Surprisingly, there has been little systematic research into the practice of visiting graveyards and cemeteries in the twenty-first century (Bachelor, 2019: 49–50; Colombo and Vlach, 2021: 219). What compels people in this secular age to visit, whether practical, spiritual or cultural? When visiting, what do they think, feel or perceive? In this regard, graveyard Gothic can offer some insight by way of its tendency to seize upon and embellish persistent and evolving personal and social anxieties about our relationship with the dead, the past they embody, and the place they occupy – physical, but also psychological, allegorical and even ethical through their passive interaction in processes of individual, community and national mourning. Collectively, the chapters in this volume expose how the graveyard locale serves to mediate concerns about personhood, nationhood, memorialisation and grief, and how the Gothic animates these concerns, both affectively and aesthetically, as a mode uniquely positioned to articulate and innervate its anxieties, tensions and ambiguities. In other words, the Gothic has shown an expansive capacity to articulate our multifarious relations to burial sites that has arguably escaped expression by other means.

Viewing the Gothic itself through the lens of the graveyard reaffirms the primacy of the dead in the Gothic imagination (Smith, 2016; Davison, 2017). If one of the fundamental concerns of the Gothic is how the past comes to haunt the present, then graveyard Gothic reminds us that every past leaves a cadaverous trace, one that we are often forced to reckon with. By its intense focus on mortality, graveyard Gothic also reminds us that we, too, will one day shuffle off this mortal coil, prompting questions of not only our metaphysical or eschatological prospects in death but perhaps of our own future role as revenants of the past. What anxieties might we one day serve to articulate and embody, whether to loved ones, to a nation, or even – crossing over to the EcoGothic – to other species? The graveyard locale itself forces us to confront the materiality of life, decay and death, whether in the form of erected monuments, commemorative photos or even the freshly dug earth. We often speak of a graveyard site in the singular, but, as this volume shows, commemorative and burial sites are far more ubiquitous than we perhaps care to believe; the chapters of this collection alone point to unmarked graves, roadside memorials, domestic substructures and video games, amongst other more recognisable iterations of the graveyard setting. The dead might appear to have their demarcated space separate from the living, but in reality the presence of the dead is almost everywhere: on our streets, in our homes, online and in our memories and thoughts. If, as stated at the beginning of this introduction, the temporality of human history central to the Gothic was initiated by the custom of burying and remembering the dead, then the history of the Gothic extends well before Walpole's *Castle of Otranto* or the graveyard poets that preceded him, and will continue long into the dark, unknown recesses of the future. Indeed, graveyard Gothic is a human history in itself.

Note

1 The terms 'graveyard' and 'cemetery' are used interchangeably elsewhere in the collection, as there is little difference in the representational use of these sites in the texts under analysis. As has been noted, 'graveyard' is favoured over 'cemetery' due to its association with the Gothic tradition via graveyard poetry.

References

Ariès, Philippe (1974) *Western Attitudes toward Death: From the Middle Ages to the Present*, trans. Patricia M. Ranum (Baltimore: The Johns Hopkins University Press).

Austen, Jane (2003) [1817] *Northanger Abbey*, ed. Marilyn Butler (London: Penguin Classics).

Bachelor, Philip (2019) *Sorrow and Solace: The Social World of the Cemetery* (Abingdon: Routledge).

Baldick, Chris (1992) 'Introduction', in Chris Baldick (ed.), *The Oxford Book of Gothic Tales* (Oxford: Oxford University Press), pp. xi–xxiii.

Binski, Paul (1996) *Medieval Death: Ritual and Representation* (London: The British Museum Press).

Botting, Fred (2012) 'In Gothic Darkly: Heterotopia, History, Culture', in David Punter (ed.), *A New Companion to the Gothic* (Malden: Wiley Blackwell), pp. 13–24.

Colombo, Asher D. and Eleonora Vlach (2021) 'Why Do We Go to the Cemetery? Civicness, and the Cult of the Dead in Twenty-First Century Italy', *Review of Religious Research*, 63, 217–43.

Davies, Ann (2008) 'Guillermo del Toro's Cronos: The Vampire as Embodied Heterotopia', *Quarterly Review of Film and Video*, 25:5, 395–403.

Davison, Carol Margaret (ed.) (2017) *The Gothic and Death* (Manchester: Manchester University Press).

Deering, Bel (2015) 'In the Dead of Night: A Nocturnal Exploration of Heterotopia in the Graveyard', in Maria-José Blanco and Ricarda Vidal (eds), *The Power of Death: Contemporary Reflections on Death in Western Society* (New York: Berghahn), pp. 183–97.

Dentith, Simon (2000) *Parody* (London: Routledge).

Foucault, Michel (1986) [1967] 'Of Other Spaces', trans. Jay Miskowiec, *Diacritics*, 16:1, 22–7.

Hutcheon, Linda (2003) *The Politics of Postmodernism*, 2nd edn (London: Routledge).

Laqueur, Thomas (2015) *The Work of the Dead: A Cultural History of Mortal Remains* (Princeton: Princeton University Press).

Lukić, Marko and Tijana Parezanović (2020) 'Heterotopian Horrors', in Clive Bloom (ed.), *The Palgrave Handbook of Contemporary Gothic* (Cham: Palgrave Macmillan), pp. 1137–51.

Marx, Karl (2002) [1852] *The Eighteenth Brumaire of Louis Bonaparte*, in Mark Cowling and James Martin (eds), *Marx's 'Eighteenth Brumaire': (Post)modern Interpretations* (London: Pluto Press), pp. 19–109.

Ní Éigeartaigh, Aoileann (2022) 'Editor's Introduction', in Aoileann Ní Éigeartaigh (ed.), *The Graveyard in Literature: Liminality and Social Critique* (Newcastle upon Tyne: Cambridge Scholars Publishing), pp. xi–xxi.

Pogue Harrison, Robert (2003) *The Dominion of the Dead* (Chicago: Chicago University Press).

Quinn, Vincent (2016) 'Graveyard Writing and the Rise of the Gothic', in Dale Townshend and Angela Wright (eds), *Romantic Gothic: An Edinburgh Companion* (Edinburgh: Edinburgh University Press), pp. 37–54.

Radcliffe, Ann (1998) [1794] *The Mysteries of Udolpho*, ed. Bonamy Dobrée (Oxford: Oxford University Press).

Smith, Andrew (2016) *Gothic Death 1740–1914: A Literary History* (Manchester: Manchester University Press).

Turner, Victor (1969) *The Ritual Process: Structure and Anti-Structure* (London: Routledge and Kegan Paul).

Van Gennep, Arnold (1960) *The Rites of Passage*, trans. Monika B. Vizedom and Gabrielle L. Caffee (Chicago: University of Chicago Press).

White, James (1789) *Earl Strongbow: or, the History of Richard de Clare and the Beautiful Geralda*, 2 vols (London: J. Dodsley).

Wordsworth, William (1974) [1810] 'Essays upon Epitaphs', in W. J. B. Owen and Jane Worthington Smyser (eds), *The Prose Works of William Wordsworth*, vol. II (Oxford: Oxford University Press), pp. 45–119.

Zigarovich, Jolene (2023) *Death and the Body in the Eighteenth-Century Novel* (Philadelphia: University of Pennsylvania Press).

1

The Gothic churchyard in graveyard poetry: cultural remains and literary beginnings

Eric Parisot

Towards the end of the eighteenth century, in her 'Invocation: To Horror' (1788), Hannah Cowley summons Horror 'from the mould'ring tower, / The murky church yard, and forsaken bower', where 'morbid Melancholy' and 'phantoms of Despair' conjured by Horror's 'grisly labours' dwell (Voller, 2015: 205, lines 16–17, 21, 26). Cowley's derivative homage to graveyard poetry of the early to mid eighteenth century draws, in shorthand, upon a myriad of well-established conventions of the poetic mode – such as the mounds of turf and epitaphic memorials that mark the presence of the dead; the skulls and worms that occupy and spill from the graves; the squawking ravens and silent yews that keep watch; and the necessarily nocturnal setting to heighten the terrified imagination. The poem is a small testament to the import of this poetic mode on much grander literary traditions that emerge late in the eighteenth century, namely, the Gothic and the Romantic. But as Ian Ousby observes, by the time of Cowley's invocation '[t]he cults of the tomb, the churchyard and the ruin, all characteristic of late eighteenth-century culture, blend easily and at times indistinguishably with one another' (1990: 98). Barring the deft assonance applied to Cowley's description of the churchyard, there is little distinction between these settings in her invocation and other poems of a similar vein of the period, often merged by virtue of their common affective ends. This chapter attempts to redress this creative (and critical) homogeneity by differentiating the poetic setting of the churchyard from a range of similar settings popular in the eighteenth century. Through historical and lexical intervention, it will concentrate intently on the churchyard as a proto-Gothic poetic locale, focusing on how the interrelation of nature, the church and the buried dead was carefully managed to produce a spectrum of emotions ranging from pensive melancholy to religious awe, existential and eschatological anxiety and deathly horror. Doing so helps to reveal more explicitly how graveyard poetry is both the last literary gasp of a fading mortuary culture and a harbinger of the Gothic's expansive and transformative engagement with the dead.

In recent criticism the taste for graveyard poetry has been subject to contextualisation within broader cultural and historical patterns. Roger Luckhurst (2021), under the banner of 'Necropolitan Gothic', places graveyard poetry at the head of a transitional period in the cultures and practices of burial and mourning, one most visibly indicated by the necrogeographical shift from the churchyard to the suburban garden cemetery of the nineteenth century and beyond. Similarly, Carol Margaret Davison (2021) situates graveyard poetry at the forefront of a collision between pre-Enlightenment and Enlightenment beliefs surrounding death, dying, mourning and memorialisation. As Davison astutely frames it, graveyard poetry is a crucial source for the Gothic's 'necropoetics – its death-centred symbols and tropes, including spectrality and the concept of *memento mori*,' even if the Gothic's 'necropolitics – its foregrounding of intergenerational power dynamics between the (un)dead and the living' – marks a shift from the devotional and compensatory function of graveyard poetry (2021: 276–7). This chapter will attempt to furnish these cultural and historical patterns with detail by focusing explicitly on the churchyard as a poetic locus for a remarkably persistent cultural and emotional regime. In centuries past, developing communities were often centred upon the burial grounds that would develop into churchyards; in Thomas Laqueur's terms, 'the dead came first', with altars and churches erected near the dead functioning as founding landmarks for the peoples and villages that followed (2015: 112). The churchyard is typically a place with deep historical roots, where the dead are doubly bestowed with local and religious authority. This necrogeography remained unchallenged in Western Christendom for almost a millennium, until communities demanded new work of the dead in the early nineteenth century, post-Enlightenment, and a new segregation of the dead from the living. What follows, then, pays tribute to the premodern sensibilities exhibited in the literary churchyard, in some ways acknowledging the poetic locale as a remnant of a bygone era while still attesting to its enduring imaginative potency beyond the tradition it emblematises.

To achieve this, a lexical intervention is required. The term 'churchyard' was the dominant term for a burial ground for centuries and into the eighteenth century, reflecting the long-standing cultural hegemony described above (Laqueur, 2015: 113). The term 'graveyard' is a lexical derivative. Although the *OED* cites a 1773 source as the first incidence of the term, its history can be traced back to a 1691 letter by Quaker Robert Barrow reporting upon the funeral of George Fox at Bunhill Fields, described in the latter as a 'graveyard'. Bunhill Fields – a derivative of the more macabre 'Bone-Hill' (Arnold, 2007: 70) – was established by the Quakers as an explicit expression of their disbelief in consecrated ground. All ground was

God's ground, according to the Quakers; hence, churches were replaced with meeting houses, and churchyards replaced by unconsecrated burial grounds such as Bunhill Fields. These new grounds provided Quakers and other Nonconformists with 'Burying places Convenient' and, in George Fox's terms, stood testimony 'against the Superstisious Idolizing of those places Cal[l]ed holy grownd [sic], formerly used to that purpose' (Stock, 1998: 129). In short, the term 'graveyard' originates linguistically and theologically from the rejection of the concept of a sanctified church and churchyard. The appellation of 'graveyard poetry' – a critical term adopted in the late nineteenth century (Parisot, 2013: 1–2) – is, then, problematic in that it lexically understates the holy presence of the consecrated church and churchyard (and the theology they embody) in favour of a macabre fixation upon the dead as a source of secular *frisson*. It is also an anachronism: at the time this poetry was published, the term 'graveyard' – unlisted in Samuel Johnson's 1755 *Dictionary* – signifies a nascent necrogeography and funerary culture that had yet to gain ascendancy. Accordingly, a critical examination of the churchyard as a premodern and proto-Gothic literary locale needs to reinstate the affective import of the church and its consecrated surrounds. As the 1712 Church of England form for the consecration of churches, chapels and churchyards proclaims, the sanctified ground of the churchyard is a 'peculiar' space assigned, amongst other things, to 'learn and seriously consider how frail and uncertain our Condition here on Earth is, and so number our Days, as to apply our Hearts unto Wisdom' (Lewis, 1719: 128–9). It is the historical, lexical and religious peculiarity of the churchyard that I wish to restore here.

Thomas Parnell's 'A Night-Piece on Death' (1721), with its neat tripartite movement through the natural landscape to the church and finally to the surrounding dead and the inevitability of death, serves as an exemplary churchyard poem for this stated purpose. In churchyard poetics each of these interrelated necrogeographical elements contribute to the spectrum of emotions that James Hervey courts in his prose *Meditations among the Tombs* (1746) as an apt demonstration of reverential piety – 'calm Attention', 'profound Awe' and 'godly Fear' (10–11). These affective states constitute an emotional trajectory primarily designed to inculcate Christian faith, but one readily adaptable to less instructional aims.

The natural environment

Ecologically, ancient churchyards represent spaces of continuous, relatively undisturbed natural habitats. Both St Giles in Stoke Poges and St James the Great in Kilkhampton, for instance – whose respective churchyards inspired Gray's *Elegy Written in a Country Churchyard* (1751) and Hervey's *Meditations* – bear evidence of pre-existence as Saxon burial grounds before Norman churches were built on site (Bude Tourist Information Centre, 2022; McDowell, 2018). Such cultural, spiritual and geographical hegemony lends itself to deep ecological history. When set in this context, the role of the natural environment in churchyards – flora, fauna and terrain – as local and extra-human historical witness should not be understated, nor its contribution to the reverential solemnity of the place.

Early in Parnell's 'Night-Piece', before our introduction to the churchyard and its macabre accoutrements, the poetic speaker is confronted with a scene of natural beauty:

> How deep yon azure dyes the sky!
> Where orbs of gold unnumber'd lye,
> While thro' their ranks in silver pride
> The nether crescent seems to glide.
> The slumb'ring breeze forgets to breathe,
> The lake is smooth and clear beneath,
> Where once again the spangled show
> Descends to meet our eyes below.
>
> (Voller, 2015: 21, lines 9–16)

This is a contemplative nocturnal scene without yet a hint of death and the dead. The glimmering crescent moon sheds a soft, comforting light across the picturesque setting, bestowing a visual acuity that is not always present in later, more bleak poetic renditions of the churchyard. The stillness of the night does little to foretell the arresting, howling winds of poems to come, such as Blair's *The Grave* (1743). The starry night sky 'descends' to reflect in the still waters of the lake, a symbolic reminder of the translation of divine revelation to accommodate our lowly human capacities. The absence of sound is telling, too, so often used to harrowing effect in other literary churchyards. Parnell's initially silent landscape bespeaks a tranquillity that in isolation appears anything but Gothic, but this solemn, attentive ease – encouraged by the poem's unchanging couplets of iambic tetrameter – is a transitory state, a necessary precursor to more extreme feelings.

Gray's country churchyard, imbued with understated natural agency, is likewise not the proto-Gothic scene that we might find in other grisly poems of the period, but it does induce more than just pastoral serenity. Where Parnell's churchyard is a space of human habitation clearly demarcated from the natural landscape that surrounds it, the dead that inhabit Gray's churchyard are forever entwined with, and indebted to, the natural guardians that provide sanctuary for them. This is evinced by the churchyard's 'complain[ing]' owl, an avian sentinel alert to intruders (Voller, 2015: 145, line 10). The owl has long been associated with wisdom as the companion of the Greek Athena and Roman Minerva; as a bird of ill omen, it also has deep literary connections to death, perhaps owing to its nocturnal habits and its mournful cries (Ferber, 2003: 146–7). Both of these figurative contexts apply in Gray's *Elegy*, but are perhaps less important than the local authority with which the resident owl is imbued as *genius loci*. Necrobotany also makes its presence felt in the *Elegy*, where 'rugged elms' and the 'yew-tree's shade' shelter the 'many a mould'ring heap' where the 'rude Forefathers of the hamlet sleep' (Voller, 2015: 145, lines 13–16). The yew tree is renowned for its longevity, with many living for more than a millennium (Hageneder, 2013: 64–81). Age bestows the yew tree with an authority well beyond human years, and in Gray's *Elegy* with a commanding stature as a resolute, evergreen guardian of the dead. Other symbolic associations reinforce the tree's dominion over the local dead: the tree's poisonous berries and foliage might suggest a protective, altruistic relationship with the dead they traditionally accompany, warding off the overly curious; this is also reflected in Blair's description of the 'trusty yew' as a 'Chearless, unsocial plant!' (Voller, 2015: 46, lines 21–2). Superstition also suggests that yews prevent the appearance of ghosts and keep the devil at bay (Hageneder, 2013: 158–9; Laqueur, 2015: 133–5) – a belief contradicted, this time, in Blair's *The Grave*, where the yew tree enjoys the 'merriment' of 'light-heel'd ghosts' and 'visionary shades' (Voller, 2015: 46, lines 27, 24). Certainly, there are no hints of diabolic supernaturalism in Gray's poem. Instead, we encounter an elegiac melancholy, a pensive grief for what has been lost, forgotten and unfulfilled – to which the local flora and fauna can attest. The poetic speaker is all too alive to the rustic obscurity for which he too is destined. This melancholy, in the words of friend and poetic imitator William Mason, is a sorrow of a 'softer kind' ('Ode: On Melancholy' (1756), in Voller, 2015: 167, line 52), but one that nevertheless demands the consolation of religious faith and hope for union with God.

Young's *Night Thoughts* (1742–5), so often discussed as a key example of graveyard poetry, occupies a more problematic position when considering the churchyard setting. This is because Young's rapturous, verbose and idiosyncratic poetic meditation on death and salvation rarely situates itself in a terrestrial setting, least of all a traditional churchyard. Come the ninth and final instalment, 'The Consolation', Young ultimately turns towards the divine sublimity of the night sky as his temple of devotion:

> ... how I bless *Night*'s consecrating shades,
> Which to a *Temple* turn an *Universe*;
> Fill us with great Ideas, full of Heaven,
> And antidote the pestilential Earth?
> In every Storm, that either frowns, or falls,
> What an Asylum has the Soul in Prayer;

And what a Fane is *This*, in which to pray?
And what a GOD must dwell in such a fane?
(1989: 292, book 9, lines 1349–56; original emphasis)

Here, night reigns as an analogue to the absent churchyard, enclosing the poet in holy sanctuary (Parisot, 2013: 14). The divinity of nature supersedes the church and its hallowed grounds: '*Nature* all o'er is consecrated Ground', Young asserts, as a somewhat more rapturous version of the Quaker's refusal to believe in sanctified land reserved for God's purpose (1989: 305, book 9, line 1885). Furthermore, Young's sublime, natural church is not a depository of the dead, but instead is one 'Teeming with Growths Immortal' (1989: 305, book 9, line 1886). Typical of Young's oxymoronic inversions, *Night Thoughts* invests in the holy divinity of nature itself as a source – as we see in the ultimate instalment – of profound awe, the kind of reverence that is more typically awakened by the presence of the church in other graveyard writing (as discussed in the next section).

The iterations of nature that we see in the poems of Parnell, Gray and Young all contribute significantly to their affective range. Nature is presented variously here as a source of beauty and solemnity, as an austere and steadfast witness to human mortality and as divine in itself. All of these constructions complement the serious, religious function of graveyard poetry as *memento mori*. What is more, they all serve to call the poetic speaker to attention: each alike is moved by the natural elements of the churchyard and its surrounds to states of heightened awareness and to a renewed receptivity to the otherworldly. In the Gothic such enhanced states of alertness are often exploited for the pursuit of *frisson* and horror. In churchyard poetics this precondition is directed to a more holy purpose. These two ends, however, are not always mutually exclusive.

The church

In churchyard poetics the contemplation of nature is often supplanted by the sovereignty of the local church, a sacred presence signalled by sight and sound. Returning to Parnell's 'Night-Piece', we find the poetic speaker positioned between two landscapes: the grounds on the right which rise into the darkness, and the churchyard on the left surrounding the 'steeple that guides thy doubtful sight' (Voller, 2015: 21, line 21). The verb 'aspire', used by Parnell to describe the ascending hills, aurally resembles the implied 'spire' of the church, as if to suggest direct comparison (line 17); nature may be imbued with divinity, but the reader's gaze is directed elsewhere here. And by this stage of the poem it *is* the reader's gaze – the singular first-person pronouns of the opening stanza cede, firstly, to the first-person plural of 'our' (line 16), and then to the second-person possessive 'thy' (line 21). These shifts signal the transference of moral obligation from speaker to reader, as reaffirmed shortly afterwards:

> And think, as softly-sad *you* tread
> Above the venerable dead,
> 'Time was, like *thee* they life possest,
> And time shall be, that *thou* shalt rest.'
>
> (Voller, 2015: 22, lines 25–8, emphasis added)

But it is the church's steeple that guides our steps towards the churchyard – once over 'There' (line 23), but now beneath our feet – to meditate upon the varied lives and fates of the dead. Our sight, once blessed with acuity, is here 'doubtful', perhaps to reflect the growing darkness, the precarity of religious faith or even the diminished capacities of our fallen human state (line 21). Parnell's church does not quite elicit the swelling profundity or reverential awe that others do – the poem's steady rhythm and rhyme manage to contain any mounting religious enthusiasm – but it plays a key symbolic role as an architectural beacon guiding the direction of the poetic speaker's excursion and our imaginary gaze, and subsequently the Christian contemplation of death and the afterlife.

Blair's *The Grave* also engages our imaginary sight when drawing our attention to the nearby church, albeit far more emphatically: 'See yonder hallow'd fane!' (Voller, 2015: 46, line 28). Blair also has a penchant for using sound to activate states of dread, and before long the chapel is aurally brought to life in combination with other non-human elements. The wind soon howls through the aisles: 'hark! … / … I never heard a sound so dreary' (lines 32–3); 'Doors creak, and windows clap' (line 34); the resident owl in the spire is not the benign sentinel of Gray's *Elegy*, but 'night's foul bird', whose shrieking assaults the imaginary ear and jolts the reader into involuntary fear (line 34); and finally these fiendish cries resound among the low vaults, 'the mansions of the dead' (line 39). *The Grave* rarely dabbles with aching melancholy; as argued elsewhere, Blair instead prefers to frighten his reader into piety by sheer panic and horror (Parisot, 2021). Blair's church, then, is not a solemn contemplative space but an echo chamber, where a dissonant cacophony resounds to both provoke and articulate our most dreaded fears. It is a clamour to arouse the imagination and to rouse the dead, as a 'grim array' of 'grizly spectres' pass eerily (and contrastingly) in silence (line 40). But this procession is a momentary diversion: 'Again! the screech-owl shrieks: ungracious sound! / I'll hear no more, it makes one's blood run chill' (lines 43–4). Both Parnell and Blair use their respective churches as a visible signpost to guide their poetic excursions, but where Parnell's church benevolently summons the speaker and reader,

Blair's church is an unsympathetic arena confronting fallen humanity with a discomfiting theatre of death.

Young, like Gray after him, chooses to actuate the contemplative mind acoustically through the tolling of bells. Admittedly, the first bells we hear early in *Night Thoughts* are not necessarily church bells; at this point, Young has not established a physical setting, save the sensory privation of silence and darkness that works as a blank canvas for his affective imagination. But in the 'solemn Sound,' 'heard aright' by Young as the articulation of time lost, he apprehends 'the *Knell* of [his] departed Hours' (1989: 38, book 1, lines 58–9, original emphasis). The conceit is drawn upon throughout *Night Thoughts*, as Young hears the imaginary death knell that fuels his anxious complaint. The bell's 'Iron tongue / Calls daily for his Millions', provoking Young's unease, all too aware that 'the Knell / Calls for our Carcases to mend the Soil' (1989: 41, book 1, lines 172–3; 133, book 5, lines 664–5). Young's humility, which ultimately extends to his personal and artistic submission before God, is in this moment uncharacteristically terrestrial; the tolling of the bell foreshadows his return to *humus*. Young's use of the imaginary bell as an existential prompt is a more elaborate rendition of David Mallet's 'slow sad bell' in 'The Funeral Hymn' (1763), which 'In holy musings wrap[s] the mind', and 'Strikes mute instruction to the heart' (Voller, 2015: 32, lines 13–14, 20).

It is, however, in the prose of James Hervey that we find the fullest expression of the affective potential of the church. Hervey's *Meditations* are grounded in an actual physical setting, stemming from an excursion to the church of St James the Great in Kilkhampton, Cornwall. The meditation, unlike the poems mentioned above, does not merely rely on an imagined topography as a literary device to spur contemplation of death and salvation, but is instead deeply rooted in personal, physical and emotional experience. Hervey observes the 'regular Range of the Pillars' and the 'magnificent Plainness of the whole', which are 'rendered more affecting, by a certain Air of Solemnity peculiar to places of this kind' (1746: 2). Animated with feelings of gratitude, repentance and humility, he remarks that 'We are apt to be struck with Admiration at the beautiful Grandeur of a masterly Performance in Architecture' such as the 'antient Sanctuary' within which he rests (1746: 6). This is a space that 'should more sensibly affect our *Hearts*, than ... delight our *Eyes*', for its capacity to speak to the '*Condescension* of the Divine' through Jesus Christ, and to God's grace in permitting 'sinful Mortals to approach his Majesty' in this 'House of Prayer' (1746: 6, original emphasis). The ensuing lessons of the dead to be found in the surrounding churchyard in Hervey's *Meditations* are only of instructional value within this consolatory framework, and within a redeeming faith in Christ. Without the solace of heavenly salvation, the ensuing imagined deaths of the innocent infant, the youth on the verge of maturity and the man in his prime on the cusp of nuptial joy threaten to overwhelm the pensive traveller with feelings of unconquerable grief, anxiety and existential dread (Parisot, 2014). Hervey plays on this Gothic potential, at one point describing the grave as a predatory 'Pit [that] shuts its Mouth' upon the blooming youth, but, like Parnell before him, ultimately comforts the frightened soul with the promise of heavenly bliss for the repenting sinner (1746: 17). In such examples of churchyard poetics the contemplation of the buried dead is a devotional practice guided by the sanctified presence and authority of the church. It is God, through his son Jesus Christ, that remains the spirit of the place. Deferring consolation, however, opens poetic opportunities to exploit the monstrous, proto-Gothic potential of the buried dead.

The dead

The final phase of Parnell's 'Night-Piece' brings the reader to the churchyard proper, and within closer proximity to the dead. Our imaginary sense of sight gradually deteriorates as the pale moon fades, casting a dark pall over the scene. It is this visual privation – such a key feature of Young's *Night Thoughts*, for instance – that enables the affective imagination room for play. Foreshadowing Blair's method, Parnell triggers the frightful imagination with the startled exclamation of the poetic speaker: 'Ha!' (Voller, 2015: 22, line 47). The supernatural scene that follows is the poem's first encounter with the dead inhabitants of the yard, as 'All slow, and wan, and wrap'd with shrouds, / They rise in visionary crouds', imploring in 'sober accent[s]' to 'Think, mortal, what it is to die' (lines 49–52). The terrifying discord that we encounter in Blair's church is reserved by Parnell for the burial ground, displacing the calm, contemplative mood of earlier lines; the poetic speaker thinks he hears a disembodied voice amidst the 'croaking din' of the cawing ravens and the pealing bells which resound as if 'hollow groans' from the bones of the dead (Voller, 2015: 23, lines 56, 59). Here, the affective potency of nature, the church and the dead are combined as the poetic narrator relinquishes his position to a new, final speaker: Death. But the self-anointed 'King of Fears' (line 62) is anything but – instead, he reassures that he is merely the product of a frightened imagination:

> Fools! if you less provok'd your fears,
> No more my spectre-form appears.
> Death's but a path that must be trod,
> If man wou'd ever pass to God.

(Lines 65–8)

Death denounces the ceremonies, superstitions and accoutrements of death, burial and mourning, reminding the poetic speaker and the reader that death is the necessary and triumphant occasion upon which body and soul must part. The departing soul experiences a joy 'far transcending sense' that renders grief redundant as it wings its way towards the heavenly 'blaze of day' (lines 83, 90). In the end, the darkness of death and the poetic locale are expunged in Parnell's poem by the inextinguishable light of God on high. The remnant corpse mired in churchyard gloom, cannot know the 'forms of woe' that the living attach to the moment of death and that serve a function to which it is oblivious (Voller, 2015: 24, line 78). Only the living can feel, and it is through living emotion that the pious work of the proximal dead is achieved. Parnell briefly flirts with fear as a godly emotion, but subsequently disarms the terrors of the tomb. It is an affective strategy that prefigures the explained supernaturalism of Radcliffe's novels later in the century; Parnell is limited by the brevity of lyric verse, while Radcliffe exploits the longer form to defer the reassurance of reasonable explanation.

Parnell's consolation is implicitly contingent upon faith and piety. But what of the doubtful and wicked? Other minor poems of the period claim that it is sin and the burden of guilt that accentuates the terrors of the churchyard. Only those 'sunk by guilt and sad despair' succumb to the 'tort'ring fears' of death, according to Elizabeth Carter's 'Ode to Melancholy' (1739), for it is 'The mist of error, whence our fears / derive their fatal spring' (Voller, 2015: 37, lines 61, 65, 56–7). Jane Timbury's 'Reflections in a Church-Yard' (1787) likewise claims the churchyard as 'A scene of terror to the guilty heart / For conscious guilt alone created fear' (Voller, 2015: 201, lines 11–12). But as Samuel Johnson attests, who can ever be sure of their salvation? The 'most rational' believer, knowing 'salvation as conditional … never can be sure that they have complied with the conditions' (Boswell, 1998: 1280). Such assurances are withheld from the living, and it is such insecurities that Blair exploits with his ghastly visions of the exhumed.

Blair's *The Grave* has been well identified as the example of graveyard poetry that most closely approaches the Gothic (Parisot, 2021). It is also a poem deeply imbued with a Calvinist rejection of all earthly things, wholly directing its reader to salvation by faith alone (Parisot, 2013: 64–74). From Blair's perspective, the two are not mutually exclusive; fear is a religiously endorsed affective strategy. Blair follows the lead of Isaac Watts (1674–1748), a prominent Nonconformist preacher, hymnist and poet whom Blair greatly admired, who once claimed that some 'are best frighted from Sin and Ruin by Terror, Threatening and Amazement; their Fear is the properest Passion to which we can address our selves, and begin the Divine Work' (Watts, 1709: xvii–xviii). But where Watts's own churchyard meditation, 'The Church-Yard' (1734), invokes a vision of Burkean sublimity built upon the vast multitude of the dead, where 'the Hillocks of Mortality arise all around' as 'Monument[s] of Death', where 'Ten Thousand Pieces of Human Nature, Heaps upon Heaps, lie buried' to teach the 'sinful and thoughtless mortal' of death (Watts, 1734: 107–8), Blair takes a distinctly different aesthetic approach. Blair's churchyard vision is immediate, arresting and seemingly tangible: it is a nightmarish fantasy of religious horror. It is one that stems not from any psychological guilt of the individual sinner but from his theological insistence that we, as fallen humans in a desolate world, are utterly incapable of attaining salvation without Christ's succour.

Blair's churchyard is alive with the dead. '[L]ight-heel'd ghosts' are purportedly seen to 'perform their mystick rounds' (Voller, 2015: 46, lines 24, 26); 'Wild shrieks', according to neighbours, announce the spirits of the dead that roam at the 'witching time of night' (Voller, 2015: 47, lines 51, 55); and, as mentioned earlier, silent 'grizly spectres' move in 'grim array' as their fleshless 'Grin' belies their 'obstinately sullen' nature (lines 40–1). Yet the poem places a heavier emphasis on the many scattered corpses underfoot, imaginatively exhumed for the reader's instruction. The youthful jester, the mighty conqueror, the proud noble, the artist, the vain beauty, the scholar, the orator, the physic, the miser – all are summoned from their dank graves and castigated in heavy strains of *ubi sunt*. The conqueror of lands far and wide is now vanquished, 'cramm'd into a space we blush to name' (Voller, 2015: 49, line 131); the 'surfeited', 'high-fed worm in lazy volumes roll'd, / Riots unscar'd' on the rouged cheek of the pretty belle (Voller, 2015: 53, lines 245–7); the 'tongue-warrior' is now 'gagg'd,' chopfallen and devoid of his organ of speech (Voller, 2015: 55, lines 297–8). Their putrid, decaying bodies, offensive to the eye and other senses, are said to be wisely concealed by the funerary arts of the undertaker: 'What would offend the eye in a good picture / The painter casts discreetly into shades' (Voller, 2015: 51, lines 175–6). But this conceit also serves to remind the reader of Blair's self-professed, opposing duty: 'To paint the gloomy horrors of the tomb' (Voller, 2015: 45, line 5). Blair unapologetically disinters the dead for full view, affronting the senses in order to petrify the reader with disgust and horror. As Victorian critic George Gilfillan testifies, the poem 'daguerrotypes its dreadful theme', a description that aptly evokes the poem's forensic examination of the gruesome scene (1854: 124). In this manner, the reader is brought within close proximity of the dead, crowding the reader's imaginative sphere like a horde of inanimate zombies, their immediacy and multitude heightening the horror. Some corpses are even imbued with a latent potential for reanimation. For example, Blair mercilessly castigates the imagined figure of Beauty for her former vanities, to the point of rousing her back into semi-consciousness:

> Look! how the fair one weeps! the conscious tears
> Stand thick as dew-drops on the bells of flow'rs:
> Honest effusion! The swoln heart in vain
> Works hard to put a gloss on its distress.
>
> (Voller, 2015: 53–4, lines 253–6)

The corpse remains motionless but not unmoved, restored momentarily as a sentient, emotional being. Similarly, the orator is reminded of the eloquent arts that have now disappeared with his fleshly tongue. He is mercilessly mocked, 'Enough to rouse a dead man into rage, / And warm with red resentment the wan cheek' (Voller, 2015: 55, lines 317–18). Indignant reanimation is hinted here, but ultimately unrealised. Above all other poetic depictions of the churchyard, it is *The Grave* that most artfully exploits the capacity of the dead to provide fearful instruction.

Unlike many of his contemporaries, Blair's macabre intent forces the reader's gaze downward. Hervey's likening of the church doors in his *Meditations* to the gates of heaven draws the imaginary eye upwards, towards the promise of salvation; likewise, both Parnell and Young direct our gaze towards the starry heavens, and ultimately to visions of rapture above. But Blair's fixation upon the dead below is unrelenting. What is more, his allusion to Shakespeare's *Hamlet* in line 55 – "Tis now the very witching time of night, / When churchyards yawn, and hell itself breathes out / Contagion to this world' – serves to remind the reader of the churchyard's imagined proximity to the gates of hell and its hordes of restless sinners (2008: 269). It is a poetic manoeuvre that brings into focus the churchyard as a horizontal, physical locale simultaneously situated within a vertical, metaphysical cosmos, comprising the earthly churchyard, heaven above and the abyss of hell below. As middling mortals, the churchyard, then, represents a spatial and teleological midpoint in the life of a pious Christian soul (Shuping, 2019: 120). But while the likes of Hervey, Young and Parnell reinforce the holy ascension from churchyard to heavenly bliss, Blair reminds his readers of the eschatological consequences of impiety; in Blair's churchyard, where the grave 'sustains / The keys of Hell and Death' (Voller, 2015: 45, line 9), hell seems unnervingly near, death presents as 'That awful gulf' (Voller, 2015: 57, line 372) and heaven seems a distant prospect. That Cowley's late-century poetic invocation might find Horror in the 'murky churchyard' and leave it seated on its 'native throne, amidst th' eternal shades of Hell' speaks to the symbolic relation between the literary churchyard and the Christian hell beneath it, one most forcefully affirmed by Blair's unholy dead (Voller, 2015: 205, line 17; 207, line 77).

Graveyard poetry is well established as a crucial tributary to the Gothic Revival, for a variety of reasons. In the poems under consideration, we can see foreshadows of the solemn, attentive melancholy characteristic of Radcliffean heroines; poetic precursors to Radcliffe's mode of explained supernaturalism; the consecrated church and churchyard as a fraught Gothic space of both sanctuary and superstition; and the disgust and horror of putrefying and/or animated corpses in Matthew Lewis and beyond (not to mention the ubiquitous Gothic paraphernalia of ravens, owls, epitaphs, skulls and worms). Moreover, at the birth of a new Gothic literary tradition, one that embraces culturally responsive heterogeneity as a hallmark of its endurance over the centuries, graveyard poetry has helped to establish burial sites – be they lonely graves, churchyards or cemeteries – as an invariably Gothic locale. But when we narrow our focus to the churchyard as a particular setting – that is, a sanctified space including a church and an adjoining burial ground typically including natural elements – we expose a specific set of premodern sensibilities that is eroded, or indeed lost, in the cosmopolitan necropolises of the modern era. The churchyard, as described here, is a composite *memento mori*, a hallowed devotional space set aside to reflect with seriousness upon death, salvation and the afterlife. It is a terrestrial midpoint in the Christian cosmos, a gateway to heaven and hell, where the living can observe the (typically) silent testimony of the dead. It is also a place of deep communal roots, rich with local history both human and non-human, a point of origin as well as of endings. It is, therefore, an apt literary emblem for a cultural tradition somewhat lost, as well as for a literary tradition gained.

References

Arnold, Catharine (2007) *Necropolis: London and Its Dead* (London: Pocket Books).
Barrow, Robert (1691) 'Letter to Lancashire Friends, 16 January', Friends House Library, Thirnbeck MSS 22.
Boswell, James (1998) [1791] *Life of Johnson*, ed. R. W. Chapman, intro. Pat Rogers (Oxford: Oxford University Press).
Bude Tourist Information Centre (2022) 'Church of St James the Great – Kilkhampton', www.visitbude.info/visit/bude-churches/church-of-st-james-the-great/ (accessed 18 February 2022).
Davison, Carol Margaret (2021) 'Death and Gothic Romanticism: Dilating in/upon the Graveyard, Meditating among the Tombs', in W. Michelle Wang, Daniel K. Jernigan and Neil Murphy (eds), *The Routledge Companion to Death and Literature* (New York: Routledge), pp. 276–87.
Ferber, Michael (2003) *A Dictionary of Literary Symbols* (Cambridge: Cambridge University Press).
Gilfillan, George (ed.) (1854) *The Poetical Works of Beattie, Blair and Falconer* (Edinburgh: James Nichol).
Hageneder, Fred (2013) *Yew* (London: Reaktion Books).

Hervey, James (1746) *Meditations among the Tombs* (London: Printed for J. and J. Rivington and J. Leake).

Laqueur, Thomas W. (2015) *The Work of the Dead: A Cultural History of Mortal Remains* (Princeton: Princeton University Press).

Lewis, Thomas (1719) *An Historical Essay upon the Consecration of Churches* (London: Printed for G. Strahan).

Luckhurst, Roger (2021) 'The Necropolitan Gothic', in Clive Bloom (ed.), *The Palgrave Handbook of Gothic Origins* (Cham: Palgrave Macmillan), pp. 263–80.

McDowell, Simon (2018) 'Restoration of St Giles' Church', Stoke Poges Church, www.stokepogeschurch.org/Publisher/File.aspx?ID=267955 (accessed 18 February 2022).

Ousby, Ian (1990) *The Englishman's England: Taste, Travel and the Rise of Tourism* (Cambridge: Cambridge University Press).

Parisot, Eric (2013) *Graveyard Poetry: Religion, Aesthetics and the Mid-Eighteenth-Century Poetic Condition* (Farnham: Ashgate).

Parisot, Eric (2014) 'The Work of Feeling in James Hervey's *Meditations among the Tombs* (1746)', *Parergon*, 31:2, 121–35.

Parisot, Eric (2021) 'Graveyard Poetry and the Aesthetics of Horror', in Clive Bloom (ed.), *The Palgrave Handbook of Gothic Origins* (Cham: Palgrave Macmillan), pp. 245–62.

Shakespeare, William (2008) *Hamlet*, ed. G. R. Hibbard (Oxford: Oxford University Press).

Shuping, Chen (2019) 'The Influence of Eighteenth-Century English Poetry on the Gothic Novels Written by Horace Walpole and Ann Radcliffe: the Aubade, the Nocturne and Graveyard Poetry'. PhD Dissertation, University of Macau, 2019.

Stock, Gwynne (1998) 'Quaker Burial: Doctrine and Practice', in Margaret Cox (ed.), *Grave Concerns: Death and Burial in England 1700 to 1850* (York: Council for British Archaeology), pp. 129–43.

Voller, Jack G. (ed.) (2015) *The Graveyard School: An Anthology* (Richmond: Valancourt Books).

Watts, Isaac (1709) *Horae Lyricae*, 2nd edn (London: Printed for N. Cliff).

Watts, Isaac (1734) *Reliquiae Juveniles: Miscellaneous Thoughts in Prose and Verse* (London: Printed for R. Ford and R. Hett).

Young, Edward (1989) [1742] *Night Thoughts*, ed. Stephen Cornford (Cambridge: Cambridge University Press).

2

Graveyard pleasures: visiting (and revisiting) the burial site in late eighteenth-century Gothic fiction

Yael Shapira

Why would anyone choose to go to the graveyard at night, when darkness, silence and solitude only heighten the fear of walking among the dead? By the middle of the eighteenth century, a cluster of 'graveyard poems' and similarly-minded prose pieces had offered one kind of answer to this question. In works such as Thomas Parnell's 'A Night-Piece on Death' (1721), Robert Blair's *The Grave* (1743) or James Hervey's *Meditations among the Tombs* (1746), clergyman-authors sent their textual alter egos into the dark, deserted churchyard in pursuit of a spiritual lesson. The time they spent among the dead was, in Eric Parisot's words, 'an elaborate memento mori', prompting both speaker and reader to consider the 'brevity and vanity of life' and using the fearful effect of the macabre setting 'strategically … as a spur to faith' (2019: 245). In the century's latter half, however, the literary graveyard visit migrated from religious verse into the Gothic novel, and its purpose – for both the visitor in the text and the reader outside it – became far less clear.

Authored primarily by men of the cloth, graveyard poems implied a reassuring analogy between the literary exchange and religious instruction. Novels, by contrast, were far more clearly produced at the intersection of art and commerce, a fact which drew hostile commentary all through the eighteenth century: novelists were accused of pandering to the audience's base desires for profit, just as readers were charged with gratifying those same desires through their reading, and both accusations only grew more vehement as Gothic novels flooded the market in the 1790s. In moving from the graveyard poem into Gothic fiction, then, the literary graveyard visit became part of a commercial-literary transaction in which the reader's gratification literally meant money in the bank. To return to my own opening question, when Gothic novels describe a visit to a burial site, it is often pleasure, not instruction, that seems to be at stake – our pleasure as readers, and sometimes also (as I will show) the pleasure of the characters themselves.

The idea that spending time among graves could be pleasurable was circulating long before Gothic fiction appeared on the scene. It was already acknowledged by Joseph Addison, who in *The Spectator* no. 26 (30 March 1711) describes a visit to Westminster Abbey as 'pass[ing] a whole Afternoon in the Church-yard, the Cloysters, and the Church, *amusing myself* with the Tomb-stones and Inscriptions that I met with in those several Regions of the Dead' (Bond, 1965, vol. 1: 109, emphasis added). The tombs evoke in Addison the same considerations of human folly and pride that centuries of *memento mori* art had expressed, and which the graveyard poets would reiterate. But he also refers to his stroll through the abbey as 'Entertainment', a chance to experience a pleasantly sombre cast of mind (1965: 111). Pleasure also seems to be the driving motive of his later excursion to an old abbey in the countryside (*The Spectator* no. 110, 6 July 1711). With its ruined walls, echoing vaults and old 'Graves and Burying-Places', the scene again provokes 'Seriousness and Attention' (1711: 453, 454); yet the feeling which dominates the account is that of mischievous enjoyment. '[V]ery much delighted' with the noise of the rooks and crows, Mr Spectator experiments with other auditory effects of the abandoned structure, stamping his feet to hear the 'Eccho among the old Ruins and Vaults' (1711: 454). His playful mood seems only enhanced by local rumours that the abbey is haunted; in fact, he deliberately ignores a servant's warning 'not to venture myself in [the abbey] after Sun-set' (1711: 453) and goes at night, as though seeking to make the experience more eerie. All this suggests less the solemn mindset of the spiritual seeker than the pleasure-oriented one of the tourist.

Graveyard poetry, too, likely aroused in its readers more than just high-minded religious fervour: the numerous editions of Blair's and Hervey's works, like the enormous popularity of Edward Young's *Night Thoughts* (1742–5) and Thomas Gray's *Elegy Written in a Country Churchyard* (1751), indicate a demand which probably cannot be attributed solely to strictest piety. Yet whatever pleasure readers may have taken in the gloom of graveyard poetry, its explicit, pronounced goal remained devotional. It would take a transitional poetic work such as Thomas Warton's *The Pleasures of Melancholy* (1747) to reiterate and amplify Addison's insight that the emotions experienced in the graveyard were rewarding in their own right, and therefore pursued for their own sake (Parisot, 2019: 256–5). And later still in the century, as this chapter will show, Gothic fiction both explored and exploited the link between pleasure and the burial site. In the novels I discuss below, characters move through the moonlit place of burial full of trepidation and horror – but also of curiosity, excitement, even pangs of delight. The history of Gothic publishing, moreover, bears out what the novels were acknowledging through their characters: as Gothic production leaped towards the century's end, the visit to the burial site became one of the expected, desired features of a successful literary product.

In what follows I consider the connection between pleasure and the Gothic graveyard – or rather, more commonly, the underground burial vault – from two complementary angles. I begin by looking at the role that one key characteristic of the burial vault – its privacy – plays in the two major Gothic masterpieces of the period, Ann Radcliffe's *The Mysteries of Udolpho* (1794) and Matthew Lewis's *The Monk* (1796). In both novels, the isolation of the enclosed burial space enables the pursuit of suspect thrills, whether these involve the excesses of sensibility or the more blatantly transgressive pleasures of sexuality. The chapter's second part will shift attention from the pleasure of the characters to that of the readers, focusing on the role that burial vaults play in 'trade Gothic' novels (Potter, 2005) – that is, lesser-known works produced in large numbers by commercial publishers such as the Minerva Press. The visit to the burial site – typically, the space beneath an old ecclesiastic structure – recurs so often in trade-Gothic novels that we can assume it was one of the pleasures readers sought in formulaic Gothic fiction. Trade-Gothic authors not only provide a sensationalist thrill through the graphic description of burial sites but use these sites as components in recurrent Gothic plot lines, so that their very presence comes to signal the imminence of a certain kind of much-loved, much-repeated story. Metonymies for Enlightenment Britain's lingering belief in ghosts, burial spaces are implicated in stories of suspected (if often debunked) supernatural visitation. Meanwhile, the vaults' historical function as the resting place of aristocratic families makes them a key component in suspenseful Gothic narratives of dynastic mystery.

Isolation, pleasure and the vault in Radcliffe and Lewis

The solitude of the visitor to the churchyard was an essential component of graveyard poetry. It allowed for the speaker's deep introspection, prompted by the reminders of death; readers, meanwhile, could be envisioned perusing the poem as part of their solitary devotional practice (Parisot, 2013: 10–15). In Gothic fiction, however, the solitude of the graveyard visit takes on a different valence, enabling experiences other than pious self-scrutiny. While remaining potent symbols of community, collectivity and social order (Laqueur, 2015: 107–363), burial sites are also recast in the Gothic as a space of potentially dangerous, if gratifying, privacy – a concept whose growing importance for eighteenth-century culture was haunted by fear of its potential misuses (see Spacks, 2003: 5). Retaining graveyard poetry's focus on the burial site as a trigger of intense response, Radcliffe and Lewis explore the dangerous potential of the vault's privacy when its function is no longer clearly dictated by religious discourse. In both novels, burial vaults allow for, and even enhance, private thrills that are questionable, if not criminal.

Radcliffe probes the link between the solitary tomb and suspect pleasure in a key scene of *The Mysteries of Udolpho*. When Emily St Aubert decides to visit her father's grave alone at night, the novel provides a seemingly plausible reason: she needs privacy in order to bid her beloved father farewell. Since M. St Aubert died in the course of their travels, Emily has been living at the Convent of St Clair in a paralysing state of grief, 'reluctant to leave the spot where [his] relics were deposited' (Radcliffe, 1998: 88). Finally ready to consider a journey back home, she senses that one last visit to his grave is needed. Unwilling to be interrupted, she defers her visit 'till every inhabitant of the convent ... should be retired to rest' (1998: 90). The nun who gives her the key offers to accompany her, but Emily, 'thanking her for the consideration, could not consent to have any witness of her sorrow' (1998: 90).

The solitude Emily craves can be seen as part of Radcliffe's psychologised, secularised view of mourning: 'True grief in Radcliffe occurs in clandestine isolation ... a private, even solitary activity ... that is contingent more upon the internal processes of memory than the trappings of ritual' (Townshend, 2008: 91). Indeed, after her vigil Emily sleeps well and wakes to find her mind 'more tranquil and resigned, than it had been since St. Aubert's death' (Radcliffe, 1998: 91). But the novel also proposes another reason for Emily's wish to avoid 'any witness of her sorrow': her father, who warned her on his deathbed against the excesses of sensibility, would not have approved. That even heartfelt grief should be contained within proper limits was already established at the beginning of the novel, when Emily was so distraught at the loss of her mother that her father gently chastised her, saying that 'even that sorrow, which is amiable in its origin, becomes a selfish and unjust passion, if indulged at the expence of our duties' (Radcliffe, 1998: 20). With her loss now doubled and her father gone, Emily must define the appropriate bounds of grief for herself. The measures she takes in order not to be 'interrupted, or observed in the indulgence of her melancholy tenderness' (Radcliffe, 1998: 90) suggest a guilty recognition that St Aubert would have seen her vigil as an equal failure of self-discipline.

I agree, therefore, with Carol Margaret Davison in seeing the scene at St Aubert's grave as diagnostic rather than curative, a moment which exposes excesses that Emily must learn to curb through the 'dual emotional self-regulation of love and grief' (Davison, 2015: 44). For Davison, the Gothic ambience of the scene – the moonlit church, the sound of a requiem, the open grave into which Emily almost falls – all reflect the particular form that Emily's emotional weakness takes: a 'raw, unadulterated terror' of death which the scene 'magnifies' rather than resolves (2015: 42). What I find intriguing, however, is that fear is only one emotion colouring Emily's progress through the church. While anxiety is surely central to the scene, so is the desire that literally propels Emily forward. She moves towards her father's grave as though in a trance, the pull of the tomb so powerful that it diminishes, rather than increases, the effect of her Gothic surroundings. The silence and darkness, which 'would at any other time have awed her into superstition' (Radcliffe, 1998: 91) go unnoticed; and although she was warned by the nun about the newly dug grave in her path, Emily is so focused on her own sensations and thoughts that she almost trips into it. Even then, she keeps moving: as the sound of the requiem revives the memory of her father's passing, the siren call of his burial place only intensifies; and 'turning aside to avoid the broken ground', she 'pass[es] on with quicker steps to the grave of St. Aubert' (1998: 91). When she finally reaches the marble marker bearing his name, the minute description of movements and perceptions abruptly halts, and hours of story time are suddenly contracted into a few words of narration: 'Emily remained at [her father's] grave till a chime, that called the monks to early prayers, warned her to retire' (1998: 91).

The shift in the pace of narration marks the moment when Emily, reaching the tomb, presumably sinks into the state of 'romantic self-absorption' that, according to Terry Castle, characterises mourning in *The Mysteries of Udolpho* (Castle, 1995: 125). Though rooted in a terror of death, the Radcliffean experience of mourning is strangely pleasurable, even addictive: 'so gratifying are the mind's consoling inner pictures, one becomes more and more transfixed by them – lost, as it were, in contemplation' (Castle, 1995: 132). Internal, private and (in Emily's case) somewhat guilty, this state of 'romantic reverie' is an experience that admits of no interruptions or witnesses: Emily needs privacy in order to sink fully into the painful pleasure of her memories (1995: 132). Radcliffe thus points to the potency of the graveyard setting in catalysing a heady internal mixture of agony and enjoyment, while framing the intense emotional reaction to the burial site as a self-indulgence that the heroine must learn to control.

If *The Mysteries of Udolpho* hints at a connection between the privacy of the burial vault and guilty pleasure, Lewis's *The Monk* no longer hints: it shouts. Emphasising his transgressive reworking of Radcliffe's Convent of St Clair by repeating its name with only a minor difference of spelling, Lewis adapts the 'subterraneous Vaults, where reposed the mouldering Bodies of the Votaries of St. Clare' into a key element in the monk Ambrosio's fall from grace (Lewis, 1998: 229). Each of the monk's three visits to the vaults increases his desire, holding out the promise of yet greater pleasure. He is first led there by his satanic seductress, Matilda, who is supposedly dying of a snakebite and needs the help of occult powers: 'Admit me into the burying-ground at midnight,' she tells Ambrosio. 'Watch while I descend into the vaults of St. Clare, lest some prying eye should observe my actions; Leave me there alone for an hour, and that life is safe which I dedicate to your pleasures' (1998: 225). Following her to the burial caverns on which his continued sexual gratification depends, Ambrosio is, like Emily, at once frightened and curiously compelled to advance. While Matilda descends, he remains at the top of the stairway, the eerie acoustics only heightening his senses: 'All was silent, except that at intervals He caught the sound of Matilda's voice, as it wound along the subterraneous passages, and was re-echoed by the Sepulchre's vaulted roofs' (1998: 232). Not merely a source of dread, the depths of the vault become a titillating secret, and Ambrosio is filled with the desire to 'penetrate into this mystery', though he ultimately heeds Matilda's warnings and remains in place (1998: 232). The equation of the vault's innermost depths with a longed-for ecstasy is confirmed when Matilda emerges triumphant: 'I shall live, Ambrosio, shall live for you! The step which I shuddered at taking proves to me a source of joys inexpressible!' (1998: 233).

In Lewis's hands, then, the burial place becomes a locus of forbidden knowledge that unlocks the door to 'joys inexpressible'. By the time he follows Matilda into the vault a second time, Ambrosio is looking for occult assistance of his own to gain access to his new erotic obsession, Antonia. As though to mark the parallel deepening of his desire and depravity, this time Ambrosio achieves the longed-for 'penetration' as he and Matilda move together through 'various narrow passages' into the vault's depths (1998: 275). Significantly, the vault at this point allows for the revelation of an even more secret desire than the one Ambrosio is pursuing: the suppressed homoeroticism that critics have traced in the novel (e.g., Haggerty, 2006). This desire surfaces when the demon Matilda summons appears in the form of a beautiful, 'perfectly naked' young man, who leaves the monk's 'faculties ... all bound up in pleasure, anxiety, and surprise' (2006: 277). Ambrosio's hinted-at longing for the naked youth thus blossoms briefly in the privacy of the vault, before disappearing again behind his criminal yet – in the terms of the novel, and of late eighteenth-century culture – more permissible lust for Antonia.

In leading his hero a third and final time into the vault, Lewis brings to its full, chilling expression the connection between the vault's privacy and criminal pleasure. Drugged so that she appears dead and laid to rest, Antonia is at last – Ambrosio thinks – 'absolutely in his disposal', and 'the gloom of the vault, the surrounding silence, and the resistance which He expected from her, seemed to give a fresh edge to his fierce and unbridled desires' (2006: 377, 380). Where Radcliffe had used the vault as the site of the heroine's loving (if overwrought) communion with the deceased, Lewis makes it the measure of a sexual predator's violent solipsism. While Antonia awakens and responds with understandable horror – 'Here are nothing but Graves, and Tombs, and Skeletons! ... Good Ambrosio, take me from hence' – Ambrosio can see only the private chamber that will enable him to gratify his lust: 'This Sepulchre seems to me Love's bower; This gloom is the friendly night of mystery which He spreads over our delights!' (2006: 381). Antonia's experience of the vault as a chamber of horrors does not diminish, and in fact amplifies, its appeal for Ambrosio as a libertine's boudoir, and he enforces the space's latter function through brute strength: Antonia's 'evident disgust, and incessant opposition ... inflame the Monk's desires', and he rapes and then murders her (2006: 383).

Lewis thus transforms the underground burial vault into a crucial part of what Peter Brooks calls the novel's 'psychic architecture', a topography laden with psychological insight (Brooks, 1973: 259). The sepulchre represents 'the interdicted regions of the soul, the area of the mind where our deepest and least avowable impulses lie' (1973: 258), and it serves as the space where these forbidden impulses are both revealed and consummated. The pleasures Emily finds by her father's grave in *The Mysteries of Udolpho* are, of course, of a different nature – psychological and emotional rather than carnal, unsalutary and self-indulgent rather than violent and criminal. Yet there is still a subtle, compelling commonality in the way both novels explore, in Brooks's words, 'the opening up of the sepulchral depths, the fascination with what may lie hidden in the lower dungeons of institutions and mental constraints ostensibly devoted to discipline and chastity' (1973: 259).

Readerly pleasures: vaults, stories and mysteries in trade-Gothic fiction

The connection between the Gothic vault and pleasure is not limited to the emotional or sexual thrills experienced by protagonists; it also lies in the way Gothic novelists use the burial site to offer pleasure to their readers. 'The merit of a novellist', Samuel Taylor Coleridge wrote in his review of *The Monk*, 'is in proportion ... to the *pleasurable* effect which he produces' (1797: 195, original emphasis). Though he admired some parts of Lewis's novel, Coleridge saw its gruesome scenes as an unpleasant imposition on the reader: to him, a writer who creates 'images of naked horror ... deserves our gratitude almost equally with him who should ... force us to sit at the dissecting-table of a natural philosopher' (1797: 195). Coleridge's puzzlement is understandable: why *should* a reader enjoy spending time amid the rotting cadavers, vividly present as well in the subplot of Agnes, who is buried alive in the vault as punishment for breaking her holy vows? What, exactly, is pleasurable about reading Agnes's description of how she awakens in the vault to 'a noisome suffocating smell' and, reaching out in the darkness, finds herself touching 'a corrupted human head' (Lewis, 1998: 403)?

Perplexing as this was to Coleridge, however, many readers evidently *did* enjoy the novel, grisly vault scenes and all, so much so that four editions of *The Monk* appeared within two years. Critics scoffed, but readers relished Lewis's gruesome brand of Gothic, as suggested by the mesmerised faces of the three society ladies reading *The Monk* in James Gillray's 1802 engraving (Figure 2.1). The skeletons cavorting with an exhumed corpse near an open grave in the frontispiece to *Tales of Terror* (1801; Figure 2.2) likewise imply that Lewis's lurid style was recognised as a crowd-pleaser. Lewis apparently did not write *Tales of Terror*, a collection of Gothic stories and parodies, but the book was clearly meant to be associated with him (Thomson, 2010: 34–6). It was issued by Lewis's own publisher, John Bell, shortly after Lewis's similarly titled Gothic ballad collection, *Tales of Wonder* (1801). Like the book's title, the frontispiece was a hint in Lewis's direction: vividly and visually echoing the sensationalist descriptions of graves and corpses in *The Monk*, the image implicitly promised more such pleasures awaiting readers inside *Tales of Terror*.

Radcliffe, too, wrote her vault scenes with the readers' pleasure in mind, though her strategy was famously different from Lewis's. Influenced by Edmund Burke's theories of the sublime, she sought to produce readerly

Figure 2.1 Engraving in James Gillray, *Tales of Wonder* (1802). (Yale Center for British Art, Paul Mellon Collection.)

Figure 2.2 Frontispiece to Anon., *Tales of Terror* (1801). (Sadleir-Black Collection of Gothic Novels, Albert and Shirley Small Special Collections Library, University of Virginia.)

delight of a specific kind – not the blunt reaction of horror, but the subtler effect of terror. Since terror required that the sources of fear be shrouded in 'uncertainty and obscurity' (Radcliffe, 1826: 150), her burial sites are spaces where perception is perpetually obstructed: what the eye cannot see, the imagination fills in, generating the *frisson* of terror. Between them, Radcliffe and Lewis thus identified various ways in which graveyard scenes could be pleasurable, whether they aroused a macabre thrill of shock or a more refined shiver.

That readers indeed enjoyed literary rambles among the graves is evident from the recurrence of similar scenes in 'trade Gothic' – i.e., many works by now obscure authors that were issued en masse by commercial publishers, foremost among them William Lane's Minerva Press. Recycling and adapting plot lines, images and character types, each new Minerva novel offered readers 'a new twist on a familiar pleasure' (Jacobs, 2000: 172). While these fictions' formulaic quality earned them a critical disdain that has only recently been re-evaluated (e.g., Hudson, 2019; Neiman, 2019; Shapira, 2020), it also makes them a helpful indication of what readers enjoyed. By all accounts a savvy businessman, Lane stocked his chain of libraries with reprints of old favourites alongside many new titles. His decision to republish Young's

Night Thoughts in 1793 and put out three new editions of Blair's *The Grave* in 1790, 1791 and 1793 reflects his understanding of the public's preferences; it is therefore not surprising to find that Minerva authors – perhaps guided by Lane, who is known to have offered his authors advice – identified the visit to the burial site as part of the formula for success.

Given that burial beneath ecclesiastical structures was one of the privileges of Catholic monastic life, subterranean burial sites became one of the expected features of the Gothic buildings frequently named in the titles of popular novels issued by Lane and others – e.g., Stephen Cullen's *The Haunted Priory* (1794), Isabella Kelly's *The Abbey of Saint Asaph* (1795) and *The Ruins of Avondale Priory* (1796), or Richard Warner's *Netley Abbey* (1795). Indeed, if readers chose any of the novels above hoping for a description of gloomy recesses full of decaying cadavers, *Netley Abbey* alone might have proved disappointing, as its vaults hold only a secret prisoner, not deceased monks. In all of the other examples, by contrast, the descent to the space beneath the eponymous structure becomes a de facto graveyard visit, as authors enhance the atmospheric effects of the setting – darkness, dampness, silence punctuated by eerie sounds – with graphic descriptions of the interred dead. The protagonists of *The Haunted Priory* find themselves in 'a large extensive cavern filled with dead bodies in various stages of dissolution, some mouldered to dust, some half consumed, and some again in a more offensive state of putrefaction, lying on their backs with crucifixes tied erect in their hands' (Cullen, 1794: 161). Jennet in Kelly's *Abbey of Saint Asaph* walks with 'reverential awe' among the 'ancient tombs' in the chapel when a staircase collapses under her step and she falls into 'a cold damp dungeon, involved in the most profound darkness' (Kelly, 1795, vol. 3: 5, 8). Though fearful, Jennet – like Emily before her, and Ambrosio after her – feels a 'desire of penetrating farther' (1795: 8–9). Advancing through a 'rugged cavern, gloomy and extensive', she comes upon 'innumerable coffins, ranged in melancholy order … The bodies appeared in different stages of decay, according to the length of time they had lain' (1795: 10, 11). Echoing the lingering influence of graveyard poetry, Jennet manages some 'deep and pious meditation' before her nerves give out and 'shrieking, she fl[ies], unheeding whither' (1795: 12, 13).

By the late 1790s, Gothic fiction's burial spaces had become the stuff of parody. Describing the abbey which serves as the setting of the Gothic spoof *More Ghosts!* (1798), the narrator notes that 'the account of this Gothic structure' cannot possibly omit 'the spacious and awful cymetery, where many an abbot and many a nun had mouldered into dust' ([Patrick], 1798, vol. 1: 16–17), while an anti-Gothic periodical piece from 1797 mocks the Gothic heroine who faints in a castle's underground recesses: 'when she awakes, the sun peeps through the crevices, for all subterraneous passages must have crevices, and shows her such a collection of sculls [sic] and bones as would do credit to a parish burying-ground' (Anon., 2000: 302). As repetitions of this scene proliferated, they became interestingly varied in tone. In the anonymously published 1799 novel *The Restless Matron,* a doctor and the eponymous ghost have a bizarrely matter-of-fact exchange over the doctor's visits to the family vault. 'I find a particular pleasure in contemplating the mouldering remains of the dead, and observing by what slow degrees the body is reduced to its original nothingness,' the doctor explains before describing his puzzlement at the late matron's failure to decay (Anon., 1799, vol. 2: 32). 'I often saw thee walk deliberately through the rows of coffins, stop at mine, take hold of my hand, remove the winding-sheet from my face, [and] attentively examine my features', the ghost replies companionably, going on to provide an account of the live burial which led to her current state as the spirit haunting the castle (1799, vol. 2: 34).

The pleasures of the Gothic burial site extend beyond the thrill of graphic description: if the naming of a medieval edifice in the novel's title created the reasonable expectation of a damp burial vault, the presence of the vault in turn suggested a high likelihood of certain beloved Gothic adventures. Burial places were obvious settings for one favourite kind of Gothic storyline, the tale of suspected haunting: Edward in *Netley Abbey* is interrupted during his reverie on the abbey's 'consecrated ground' by a spectral warrior in 'compleat armour', who, 'fixing his hollow eyes on the youth, heaved a most profound sigh' (Warner, 1795, vol. 1: 135–6, 137), while Kelly's heroine in *The Ruins of Avondale Priory* sees a mysterious figure 'gliding swiftly along an opposite gallery', lending credence to the local rumour that 'the old monkish tombs' are haunted (Kelly, 1796, vol. 1: 28, 12). Like the existence of the vault in a Gothic pile, the connection of burial place and ghost in Gothic narrative became so habitual that it lent itself to easy parody: the Gothic clichés mocked by *More Ghosts!* include not only the 'awful cymetery [sic]' full of 'mouldering abbots and nuns' but the active lives led by these deceased clerics, who, 'as thousands will affirm … are seen as regular as the owners themselves', wearing 'the same shrouds that enwrapped their clay-cold bodies' (Patrick, 1798, vol. 1: 15–16).

Gothic vaults hold not only the human remains but the secrets of aristocratic families. The privilege of burial beneath Catholic houses of worship, reserved for monks and priests until the eleventh century (Laqueur, 2015: 115), was later extended to their rich patrons, offering 'particular physical proximity to the prayers of the monks' while also being 'an expression of a layman's importance, wealth and standing in society' (Stoeber, 2012: 112, 113). When a family had a long-standing connection to a religious house, generations of its descendants could end up buried beneath it. The vault therefore held information about a family's history; in the hands of Gothic authors, it became a source of clues that both protagonists and readers could follow, gradually uncovering a dynasty's dark secrets and, often, the truth of the hero or heroine's own suppressed identity. For readers, the burial place thus became a key site in the unfolding riddle of the plot, offering the kind of enjoyment that would later come to be associated with the detective novel.

We already see a hint of this possibility in *The Mysteries of Udolpho*, where St Aubert's oddly specific request to be 'interred … near the ancient tomb of the Villerois' raises troubling questions about his past: was the late Marchioness de Villeroi his lover (Radcliffe, 1998: 87)? And might Emily – who bears an uncanny resemblance to her – be her daughter, born of their tryst? The suspense created by this question extends until the novel's denouement, when Emily discovers that the Marchioness was her father's sister. While minor next to some of the novel's other mysteries, the riddle posed by St Aubert's choice of burial place is thus resolved as well: tying up the final loose ends of the plot, the narrator takes care to note that the Marchioness's 'disastrous death' by poison 'may account … for [St Aubert's] request to be interred near the monument of the Villerois' (Radcliffe, 1998: 660).

Family tombs likewise combine eerie Gothic atmosphere with clues to dynastic riddles in Kelly's novels. In both *The Abbey of Saint Asaph* and *The Ruins of Avondale Priory*, Kelly places her crumbling monastic structures next to the ancestral castles of aristocratic families. The family tombstones found in the abbey and priory, respectively, offer important clues in the heroines' journeys towards their own identities. Before she falls from the chapel to the vault below, Jennet admires the 'plain black monument' commemorating Sir Eldred Trevaillon, former lord of the nearby castle, who is rumoured to have been murdered, as well as 'a superb monument … raised to the memory of Rodolpha', his infant daughter, who also came to a mysterious end (Kelly, 1795, vol. 3: 6, 4). As even a mildly experienced reader of formulaic Gothic would have been able to anticipate, the clues found on the tombstones above ground point to a mystery that will be resolved below it, in the vault's dark recesses. Jennet's fall underground leads her to the vault's secret prisoner, the still living Sir Eldred, and this discovery is followed swiftly by her own identification as Rodolpha, his daughter and the heiress to the castle. Evidently pleased with what she had devised, Kelly again used gravestones to anticipate dynastic discoveries in *The Ruins of Avondale Priory*. Ethelinde, too, walks in the chapel among the 'tombs … [which] inclosed the virtuous and warlike ancestors of the illustrious House of Avondale' and is filled with 'sacred gloom, and solemn contemplation' (1796, vol. 1: 23–4). But then she notices an 'arch erected in the Doric taste', beyond which lies an elaborate monument to the late Lord and Lady Avondale and their infant daughter, represented on top of their black marble tomb by an effigy 'of the purest alabaster' (1796, vol. 1: 24). The classical style of the arch signals a more recent addition to the crumbling Gothic structure, setting the last generation of dead Avondales off from their ancestors and hinting at their continued modern-day importance. The fact that the coat of arms engraved on the monument seems incomprehensibly familiar to Ethelinde already hints that what she faces in the chapel is not a standard-issue *memento mori*, but a piece of her own history. By the end of the novel, she will, of course, turn out to be the missing heiress of Avondale, who thus – without knowing it – sits in the chapel gazing in 'melancholy meditation' on the likenesses of her late parents and her own infant self (1796, vol. 1: 27).

Conclusion: fear and the pleasures of the Gothic vault

In taking pleasure as my subject, I have offered a perspective that diverges from, but ultimately complements, the common critical focus on Gothic scenes of death, burial and mourning as expressions of cultural anxiety (e.g., Castle, 1995; Davison, 2015; Trowbridge, 2017). Historian Philippe Ariès's (1981) well-known thesis about modernity's growing estrangement from death is certainly compelling, not least because our own death-phobic, death-denying present would seem to validate it. Yet anxiety and pleasure are not mutually exclusive; indeed, as the long success of popular horror suggests, under the right conditions what we fear becomes enjoyable precisely *because* we fear it. The emerging dread of death did not stop graveyard poems from becoming favourites of the reading public, any more than it kept eighteenth-century British tourists from visiting the catacombs in Rome and, later, publishing vivid accounts of their adventures there (Gaston, 1983). And – judging by the explosion of Gothic fiction at the century's end – it certainly did not prevent readers from seeking out novels in which characters spent eerie nights in damp, silent sepulchres surrounded by rotting cadavers.

In fact, Gothic fiction may have been an ideal vehicle for the vicarious graveyard visit thanks to the very characteristic which caused it to be denigrated almost as soon as it appeared: namely, its reliance on a set of recognisable, reproducible conventions. As John Cawelti writes in his now classic study of formula literature,

> In reading or viewing a formulaic work, we confront the ultimate excitements of love and death, but in such a way that our basic sense of security and order is intensified rather than disputed, because, first of all, we know that this is an imaginary rather than a real experience, and, second, because the excitement and uncertainty are ultimately controlled and limited by the familiar world of the formulaic structure.
>
> (1976: 16)

Without discounting deeper currents feeding the fictional fascination with burial sites, then, I have suggested that the Gothic's vault scenes might be considered part of the eighteenth century's emerging tradition of popular horror entertainment. Departing from the solemn, centuries-old use of macabre iconography as a tool of instruction, the Gothic assuaged the new fears of death by turning the same iconography into an object of play, replicating and trivialising it (see Shapira, 2018). The popularity of Gothic fiction, and the recurrence of vividly rendered burial sites within it, suggest that readers sought out the opportunity to perform their own graveyard visits – albeit from the safe remove of their position outside the text, and within the reassuring context of a repetitive, supposedly trivial literary pastime.[1]

Note

1 The research presented in this chapter was supported by the Israel Science Foundation, grant no. 178/19.

References

Anon. (1799) *The Restless Matron: A Legendary Tale*, 3 vols (London: William Lane).
Anon. (1801) *Tales of Terror* (London: Printed by W. Bulmer for J. Bell).
Anon. (2000) [1797] 'The Terrorist System of Novel Writing', in Rictor Norton (ed.), *Gothic Readings: The First Wave, 1764–1840* (London: Leicester University Press), pp. 299–303.
Ariès, Philippe (1981) *The Hour of Our Death*, trans. Helen Weaver (New York: Alfred A. Knopf).
Bond, Donald (ed.) (1965) [1711–12] *The Spectator* (Oxford: Clarendon).
Brooks, Peter (1973) 'Virtue and Terror: The Monk', *ELH*, 40:2, 249–63.
Castle, Terry (1995) *The Female Thermometer: Eighteenth-Century Culture and the Invention of the Uncanny* (Oxford: Oxford University Press).
Cawelti, John G. (1976) *Adventure, Mystery and Romance: Formula Stories as Art and Popular Culture* (Chicago: University of Chicago Press).
[Coleridge, Samuel Taylor] (1797) 'The Monk: A Romance', *The Critical Review; or, Annals of Literature*, 19 (February), 194–200.
[Cullen, Stephen] (1794) *The Haunted Priory: Or, the Fortunes of the House of Rayo* (Dublin: William James).
Davison, Carol Margaret (2015) 'Trafficking in Death and (Un)dead Bodies: Necro-Politics and Poetics in the Works of Ann Radcliffe', *The Irish Journal of Gothic and Horror Studies*, 14, 37–47.
Gaston, Robert W. (1983) 'British Travelers and Scholars in the Roman Catacombs 1450–1900', *Journal of the Warburg and Courtauld Institutes*, 46, 144–65.
Haggerty, George (2006) *Queer Gothic* (Urbana: University of Illinois Press).
Hudson, Hannah Doherty (2019) 'Sentiment and the Gothic: Failures of Emotion in the Novels of Mrs Radcliffe and the Minerva Press', in Albert J. Rivero (ed.), *The Sentimental Novel in the Eighteenth Century* (Cambridge: Cambridge University Press), pp. 155–72.

Jacobs, Edward (2000) *Accidental Migrations: An Archaeology of Gothic Discourse* (Lewisburg: Bucknell University Press).
[Kelly, Isabella] (1795) *The Abbey of Saint Asaph* (London: William Lane).
Kelly, Isabella (1796) *The Ruins of Avondale Priory* (London: William Lane).
Laqueur, Thomas W. (2015) *The Work of the Dead: A Cultural History of Human Remains* (Princeton: Princeton University Press).
Lewis, Matthew (1998) [1796] *The Monk,* ed. Howard Anderson (Oxford: Oxford World's Classics).
Neiman, Elizabeth (2019) *Minerva's Gothics: The Politics and Poetics of Romantic Exchange, 1780–1820* (Cardiff: University of Wales Press).
Parisot, Eric (2013) *Graveyard Poetry: Religion, Aesthetics and the Mid-Eighteenth-Century Poetic Condition* (Farnham: Ashgate).
Parisot, Eric (2019) 'Gothic and Graveyard Poetry: Imagining the Dead (of Night)', in David Punter (ed.), *The Edinburgh Companion to Gothic and the Arts* (Edinburgh: Edinburgh University Press), pp. 245–58.
[Patrick, Mrs F. C.] (1798) *More Ghosts!* (London: William Lane).
Potter, Franz J. (2005) *The History of Gothic Publishing, 1800–1835: Exhuming the Trade* (Basingstoke: Palgrave Macmillan).
Radcliffe, Ann (1826) 'On the Supernatural in Poetry. By the Late Mrs. Radcliffe', *New Monthly Magazine*, 16, 145–52.
Radcliffe, Ann (1998) [1794] *The Mysteries of Udolpho,* ed. Bonamy Dobrée (Oxford: Oxford World's Classics).
Shapira, Yael (2018) *Inventing the Gothic Corpse: The Thrill of Human Remains in the Eighteenth-Century Novel* (Cham: Palgrave Macmillan).
Shapira, Yael (2020) 'Isabella Kelly and the Minerva Gothic Challenge', *Romantic Textualities: Literature and Print Culture, 1780–1840*, 23, 168–84, www.romtext.org.uk/articles/rt23_n10/ (accessed 1 November 2021).
Spacks, Patricia Meyer (2003) *Privacy: Concealing the Eighteenth-Century Self* (Chicago: Chicago University Press).
Stoeber, Karen (2012) *Late Medieval Monasteries and Their Patrons: England and Wales, c.1300–1540* (Woodbridge: Boydell & Brewer).
Thomson, Douglass H. (2010) 'Introduction', in Matthew Gregory Lewis, *Tales of Wonder* (Peterborough: Broadview Press), pp. 13–36.
Townshend, Dale (2008) 'Gothic and the Ghost of *Hamlet*', in John Drakakis and Dale Townshend (eds), *Gothic Shakespeares* (Abingdon: Routledge), pp. 60–97.
Trowbridge, Serena (2017) 'Past, Present and Future in the Gothic Graveyard', in Carol Margaret Davison (ed.), *The Gothic and Death* (Manchester: Manchester University Press), pp. 21–33.
[Warner, Richard] (1795) *Netley Abbey: A Gothic Story* (Southampton: Printed for the Author).

3

The last days of the urban burial ground: horror, reform and Gothic fiction

Roger Luckhurst

James Whale's 1931 camp and lurid film adaptation of *Frankenstein* opens with three quick scenes. Henry Frankenstein and his sidekick Fritz are pictured waiting in the sound-stage wings for a graveyard burial to end so that they can steal the fresh corpse, which they do under cover of a heavy stylised German Expressionist night. Then they are seen at a roadside gibbet, where the criminal's body is declared useless because the neck is broken. And finally, Fritz breaks into the dissection room of the Goldstadt Medical College, where he fumbles and breaks a brain pickled in a specimen jar and so takes the one helpfully marked ABNORMAL BRAIN in big letters.

None of these scenes appear in quite these forms in Mary Shelley's original novel, which passes over the gruesome physiological necessity for body parts in a guilty rush: 'Who shall conceive the horrors of my secret toil, as I dabbled among the unhallowed damps of the grave?' Victor adds: 'The dissection room and the slaughterhouse have furnished many of my materials', but he evades providing any more detail with his own very physiological shiver of revulsion: 'My limbs tremble and my eyes swim with the remembrance' (Shelley, 1993: 36–7). The next time Victor picks up the graveyard shift, it is to assemble the monster's female companion in the wilds of Orkney. An even thicker veil is drawn over this 'filthy process': 'My eyes were shut to the horror of my proceedings.' All we know of this aborted commission is that Frankenstein is eventually so appalled that he 'tore to pieces the thing on which I was engaged' (1993: 137, 139). We hear no more about the brute fact of body parts.

Biographers often try to tie these scenes to Mary Shelley's childhood. The grave of her mother, Mary Wollstonecraft, in the Old St Pancras churchyard in London is given a heightened role in her traumatic early life. It was supposedly a notorious spot for grave-robbers and a little disreputable since it was one of the few grounds to take the Catholic dead. There, Mary Shelley learnt to spell her own name from the carved letters on the sepulchre her father William Godwin erected for her mother. Godwin later developed a theory of memorial politics in his 1809 *Essay on Sepulchres*, which included the injunction: 'let us erect a shrine to their memory; let us visit their tombs; let us indulge all the reality we can now have, of a sort of conference with these men [sic], by repairing to the scene which, as they are at all on earth, *they still inhabit*' (Godwin, 1809: 12, original emphasis). Godwin's proposal is one locus for what has since been called necromanticism (see Westover, 2009). Later, as a teenager, Mary declared her love for Percy Shelley at her mother's graveside. She also possibly conceived her first child under the cover of the weeping willow there (as Fiona Sampson (2018: 95) speculates). Yet, for all these grave matters, the novel *Frankenstein* (1818) insistently favours the elevated and metaphysical consequences of Victor's actions over the low-down and dirty physical matter of gravestones and bodies.

Whale's *Frankenstein* was a foundational horror film: the British film board classification 'H for Horrific' emerged partly as a result of its release (see Horton, 2014). And the opening triptych of scenes actually seems to depend less on Mary Shelley's source novel than on a long-embedded set of popular cultural memories. Henry Frankenstein, unlike the scholarly Victor in the novel, is framed first in the film as a grave-robber or resurrectionist, a career that seemed to start in the early eighteenth century with the commodification of dead bodies for supply to anatomy schools, but peaked in the 1810s and 1820s as the medical profession expanded in number. Since grave-robbing for dissection was popularly considered 'a gross assault upon the integrity and identity of a body and upon the repose of the soul' (Richardson, 1988: 76), local instances often produced violent social disorder, none more famously than the case of the Burke and Hare murders in Edinburgh in 1828, resulting in William Burke's hanging before a crowd of 25,000 and his posthumous dissection. The vengeful crowd that burns Henry and his creation to death at the end of the Universal Studio *Frankenstein* echoes these scenes of enraged popular sentiment from a century before.

Henry Frankenstein is then seen as a medical researcher frustrated by his dependence on the bodies of executed criminals: the gibbet offers meagre pickings. The Company of Barbers and Surgeons had been given a royal charter to dissect four bodies of criminals annually in 1540, a number that increased only to six a century later. This supply moved far more slowly than the demand from the rising profession of the surgeon. In 1752, judges were given the discretion to add the punishment of dissection to criminals given the death penalty by hanging, increasing the number of bodies for anatomy schools. However, this still did not alleviate the economy of scarcity that fuelled the body-snatching business. This restriction remained until the law was changed by the Anatomy Act of 1832, which allowed the use of pauper bodies unclaimed for burial – thus further embedding the popular fear and resentment of medical men and their power over the body and soul of the poor.

Finally, Fritz's raid on the dissection room for a suitable brain is meant to remind us of the callous reputation of anatomists themselves, who often kept a careful distance from their gruesome aiders and abetters in the burial grounds, even while depending on the illegal supply of bodies. This was a new cadre of medical professionals who, in the popular mind, murdered to dissect, introducing a discursive regime that morcellated the human body into 'functional segments' and forced the dead body mercilessly to speak its secular secrets (Foucault, 1994: xvii). A parliamentary investigation in 1828 took evidence from eminent medical men, such as Sir Astley Cooper, of the supply of bodies to the new, barely regulated private anatomy schools. Cooper denounced body snatchers as 'the lowest dregs of degradation' (Richardson, 1988: 71), and yet was himself supplied by numerous London gangs and even paid their legal fees if they were caught and tried. These vivisectors were seen as cold and immoral, irreligious desecrators of the integrity of the human being. They were already being depicted as demonic figures in the Gothic penny dreadfuls of the 1830s and 1840s, as Anna Gasperini documents, long before the National Anti-Vivisection Society, founded in 1875, fixed the image of the heartless, cruel experimental doctor in the public mind (Gasperini, 2019; French, 1975). They paved the way for the agonised and conflicted Victor Frankenstein to become H. G. Wells's monstrously deluded vivisector Doctor Moreau, splicing human and animal in the surgical torture cell of his 'House of Pain'. By the time of James Whale's adaptation of *Frankenstein*, the collection of skulls and brains had been embedded in the pseudo-scientific horrors of criminal anthropology and eugenics. The ABNORMAL BRAIN stolen by Fritz is less a gormless piece of crude sensationalism than a mockery of the confidence of reductive thinkers like Cesare Lombroso or Francis Galton, who affirmed that craniometry or study of the physical convolutions of the brain could determine innate, biological traits of the 'criminal man' (Gould, 1981).

Rather surprisingly, then, it is Whale's cinematic rendering of the *Frankenstein* myth more than Mary Shelley's novel that invites us to trace the deep roots of graveyard Gothic. In this chapter, however, I want to move beyond the relatively familiar Gothic contexts of body-snatching or anatomy schools and to focus more narrowly on the place where these horrors typically originated, at least in London: the inner-city graveyard. The urban Gothic, Sara Wasson argues, is the product of the city's accelerated modernity in the nineteenth century. By the 1830s, ceaseless transformation uprooted everything traditional or even notionally 'eternal' in the space of the city, including death itself. Resting places became disturbingly restless, temporary and commodified because of rising costs of burial and land values. Before the cemetery solution offered another way out, it was the city graveyard that was one of the privileged places for revealing 'the incorrigible fragility of modernity' (Wasson, 2014: 132). The jeremiads of 'Graveyard' Walker on the atrocious conditions of graveyards in London in the decade before the 1852 Burial Act will give us a guide to the rich loam from which the Gothic imagination leaked out of the boundaries of these graveyards.

The urban graveyard

Between about 1780 and 1850, the concentration of city populations, the quintessential transformation of modernity, started to produce an urban crisis through the sheer cumulative *number* of the dead. This oppressive and 'unwieldy majority', as David McAllister calls it (2018: 3), began to overwhelm any possibility of mournful, individualised pacifying elegy, as envisaged by Thomas Gray in his country churchyard in 1750, or even the 'deliberate graphic bluntness' in depicting the individual dead body in the boom in Gothic romance in the 1790s (Shapira, 2018: 10). It became instead an urgent matter of general public hygiene. As the piles of corpses were crammed into ever more saturated grounds, the dead increasingly threatened to overwhelm and menace the living.

In between the graveyard school of poets in the mid eighteenth century and the emergence of the suburban garden cemetery, typified by the Glasgow Necropolis (opened 1831) and London's 'Magnificent Seven' (from Kensal Green in 1832 to Tower Hamlets in 1841), the grim accumulation of the urban dead pushed the small city churchyard or burial ground into profound crisis. The toxic stench and leaking decay of the dead oozed into the public consciousness in a series of scandals that were exposed in London by the new Benthamites and metropolitan reformers in the 1830s and 1840s. It was the gruesome evidence collected by the Drury Lane doctor George A. Walker in pamphlets and government committee inquiries that led eventually to the 1852 Burial Act, which ended burials in city yards and enforced a change of funerary customs. Many of these graveyards had been closed off or entirely erased by the time Isabella Holmes wrote her survey *London Burial Grounds* in 1896. Holmes's survey was part of a campaign to preserve by law those grounds remaining as small parks, largely cleansed of their gloomy pestilential reputation and prettified as part of the programme of the Metropolitan Public Gardens Association. Yet these urban horrors underpin texts from *Frankenstein* to *Bleak House* (1852–3), and their afterlife has long influenced the popular Gothic imagination.

The early nineteenth century in Britain seems exemplary of the processes that Michel Foucault termed the birth of biopolitics in his 1975–6 lectures

(Foucault, 2004). It is an era in which government and its institutions commence the large-scale recording, measurement and statistical analysis of the population, the better to constitute, regulate and control a new social body (see Poovey, 1995). It is a period of a coordinated theory and practice of government; the emergence of a state police force; the extension of the civil service; the founding of government statistical offices; the rise of influential Utilitarian, dissenting and evangelical reformers who grounded changes in social policy through the accumulation of evidence to committees of inquiry; and the emergence of a network of funded public institutions (the workhouse, the hospital, the prison, the asylum, the school) that reached ever further into the body politic. This 'new microphysics of power' (Foucault, 1995: 139) aimed to extend its capillaries into each individual, dismantling the self and reassembling it as a subject or node through which pass multiple regulatory systems. In Britain, many elements of this agenda were knotted together in the new Poor Law of 1834, which reorganised public welfare around a punitive system to separate the shameful, indolent pauper from the productive citizen.

Foucault mentions only in passing 'the famous gradual disqualification of death' in the nineteenth century, drawing without much question on the conservative thanatology of the medieval historian Philippe Ariès's book *The Hour of Our Death* (Foucault, 2004: 247). Since 'power has no control over death' (2004: 248), Foucault argues that instead the networks of power focus on how to control mortality through biopolitical mechanisms of surveillance and regulation.

But there was also a necropolitics: one that refused death's negation of power and actively sought to appropriate even this.[1] The Utilitarian reformers around Jeremy Bentham, including his secretary Edwin Chadwick, who went on to become the architect of the 1834 Poor Law and much else besides, were frequently mocked as extremists of rationality, and particularly so in relation to their determination to make death 'useful'. In 1827, the medic Thomas Southwood Smith published in the flagship reformist journal *The Westminster Review* his essay 'Use of the Dead to the Living', a rational calculus in favour of the benefits of the dissection of human beings to aid the understanding of the body for the betterment of the living. This was an argument almost designed to enrage Christian believers and challenge the social rituals of burial. At least Bentham himself had the courage of his convictions: after his death in 1832, Southwood Smith undertook a public discourse and dissection of the eminent philosopher's body (published as an illustrated lecture). Bentham's body remains somewhat dubiously 'in use' as an 'Auto-Icon' – 'a man preserved in his own image' (Bentham, quoted in Marmoy, 1958: 78) – still sitting in a glass box in the dusty passageways of University College London, partly present in the corridors of the 'godless college' (as its enemies called it) as a counter-hex to the mysterious power that death was supposed to exert over the living.

It was the biopolitical concern with the health of the living population, though, that fostered urban burial reform. It was driven by the dissenting medical doctor George Alfred Walker, who had 'witnessed shocking mutilations and upturning of human remains' in the overcrowded graveyards of Nottingham as a child (Pinfold, 2022). Educated by Quakers, Walker then trained in medicine at the Aldersgate Street medical school, which stood near the large necropolitan network of Quaker, Irish Catholic, dissenting and pauper graveyards around the still surviving Bunhill Fields, just beyond the boundary of the City of London (for surveys of this complex space, see Holmes, 1896; Bard, 2008). Walker set up a medical practice in Drury Lane, serving some of the most notorious rookeries of London. These slums were often dotted with cramped pauper burial grounds or overspills from churchyards elsewhere, land purchased for cheaper interments. In these terrains, life and death were completely intertwined, offending Walker's moral principles almost as much as his medical ones.

In 1839, Walker published *Gatherings from Graveyards,* in which he denounced the condition of inner-city London burial grounds as menaces to public health and an outrage to Christian custom. Walker followed the predominant miasmatic theory of disease, in which putrefying effluvia rising from rotting organic matter produced toxic vapour (only sometimes trackable by its stench) that resulted in contagion or death. Walker repeated the stories of instances when gravediggers had died suddenly from the inhalation of toxic fumes when working in the worst of the overstuffed graveyards. Thousands of the poor crammed into the courtyards and cul-de-sacs of London. They lived and suffered in dangerous proximity to the dead, breathing in 'a vitiated atmosphere' through which the dead insidiously worked to bring the living quickly over to its majority (Walker, 1839: 1). The poor laid out the deceased in their own squalid rooms, often for days or even weeks at a time as the family observed communal customs, but also for the length of time it took for the family to raise the fees for burial. The graveyards themselves were often patches of ground in the same courtyards, many of them unregulated private speculative burial grounds that had emerged to undercut higher Church of England fees. Victims of cholera might die in a closed courtyard without much circulation of fresh, unpolluted air, and be buried just below their own windows, ready like vampires for their undead effluvia to infect their loved ones and pull them into the polluted earth in turn.

In these disregarded, unregulated spaces, the physical number of the dead was a constant problem, managed by burying paupers in communal graves (the poor in shrouds or cheap coffins stacked in precarious towers in deep pits), and by the night-time removal of bodies in varying states of decomposition, the remaining flesh and bone surreptitiously burnt, in violation of common custom, the coffin wood sometimes carried home for firewood by gravediggers as the only perk of the job. However, it was suspected that burning coffin wood was dangerous, and some believed that typhus fever could be caught from the smoke. That gravediggers could often only operate with large quantities of alcohol to blunt their senses was only the first of the moral outrages against Christian custom still centred on the belief in bodily resurrection. In this first damning account, Walker surveyed 149 individual grounds close to his practice: a catalogue of a city slowly being poisoned, in his view, by ground saturated in the grave mould of its own dead. Walker would discover, however, that church parishes proved resistant to any change in the use of city churchyards and burial grounds, holding out for another decade against reform, because they relied so heavily on burial fees paid to the church for interment and to the churchmen who conducted the burial service.

Walker's campaign, including a barrage of letters to the Home Secretary, Sir James Graham, led to a parliamentary Select Committee investigating specifically the 'effect of interment of bodies in towns' (Report, 1842). It was chaired by a sympathetic advocate for Walker's demand to put an end to interment in city graveyards and received testimony about places in London that Walker had already made notorious in his broadside.

A short walk from Walker's Drury Lane practice stood St Clement Danes church (long isolated by the traffic system feeding into the Strand from Fleet Street). Its crypt was stuffed with the intramural dead, often inhumed in expensive lead coffins that could burst with rotting effluvia, like corpse bombs. These were the most expensive burials – conforming to the medieval idea of being *in loco sancto*, closest to the holiest spaces of the church – but it meant that the congregation above was being slowly infused with gaseous emissions from the dead. The churchyard outside was overflowing; its overspill ground up Clement's Lane was even worse. The poor in Portugal Street had to put up with this graveyard and the slaughterhouses that clustered around Clare Market: human and animal offal seemed indistinguishable. The run-off from the meat market oozed through the street, through the warren of housing rented to the poor. James Lane, a local resident with a window no more than three feet above one of the graveyards, testified that he had seen gravediggers at night digging up coffins, breaking down the wood for burning, removing bones and shovelling 'soft substance' (Report, 1842: 32), or spreading quick lime to dissolve the bodies below (some of the poor favoured quick lime because it damaged bodies enough to save them from body snatchers). 'There is very little air attached to that quarter' (33), Lane told the Committee, and detailed health problems that confirmed the miasma premise. A gravedigger, John Eyles, reluctantly testified (in clear terror of his tyrannical sexton) that he had been obliged to dig up coffins at night from the shallow graves and break them up. He had even seen his own father's coffin dug up and broken down.

Enon Chapel was located in the same street. It was a Baptist dissenting chapel that had opened in 1823 as a speculative venture and began to offer cheap burial in its basement (there was no crypt as such) to the local residents. The congregation had to suffer a stench that was both 'abominable' and 'injurious' to health (Report, 1842: 8), and watched saprophagous corpse flies crawl sluggishly out of the cracks in the wooden floor during services or Sunday school. Some of the congregation had fainted from the smell; many left services with insidious, miasmatic headaches. When another reformist venture – the building of drains – required entry to the basement of Enon Chapel, it was discovered that perhaps twelve thousand corpses had been crammed into a space measuring just 50 × 30 feet.

This was not the end of the horror. The 'master carman' William Burn testified that he had helped remove some of the contents of the basement when the sewer was built, taking away over sixty loads of 'rubbish' by horse cart. Men repairing the road surface in Clement's Lane had asked for rubbish to fill potholes: 'they asked me to give them a few baskets of rubbish, which I did, and they picked up a human hand, and were looking at it, and there were crowds collected; it did not appear to have been buried probably a month; it was as perfect as my hand' (Report, 1842: 14). The bones, by contrast, got as far as Waterloo Bridge: they were used as landfill to shore up the construction of Waterloo Road (London literally building its infrastructure with the bones of its dead). Asked of his view of the neighbourhood, Burn declared: 'I consider it the most stinking, unhealthy place probably near London' (1842: 15).

Walker's own testimony also focused on the Clement's Lane complex of burial grounds, which had resulted in what he termed 'an infected district' (1842: 36). In the area around his practice in Drury Lane, he estimated that 'there are hundreds of tons of weight of human bodies', some in the disregarded overspill yard for St Martin-in-the-Fields (1842: 36, 38). Walker piled on the horrors, before offering his solution of rapid burial in suburban cemeteries dispersed around London, perhaps best reached by special necropolitan train services. He was doubtful about the location of some of the Magnificent Seven, but approved of the idea of the formal separation of the living from the dead and for this to be enforced by law. Later, Walker purchased the lease on the now abandoned Enon Chapel and paid personally for an estimated 20,000 bodies in the basement to be reinterred in a garden cemetery.

Edwin Chadwick followed this General Report with a *Supplementary Report ... into the Practice of Interment in Towns* a year later, focusing on the biopolitical effects on public health of 'morbific' matter spreading from city burial grounds, taking evidence from eminent doctors on the release of noxious gases. Chadwick also emphasised the detrimental effect on public morals, writing in the fashion of a 1790s terror novel: 'Neglected or mismanaged burial grounds superadd to the indefinite terrors of dissolution, the revolting image of festering heaps, disturbed and scattered bones, the prospect of the charnel house and its associations of desecration and insult' (Chadwick, 1843: 142). Mary Elizabeth Hotz suggests that in this extra report Chadwick was trying to break up the burial practices of the working classes, with their prolonged proximity to the corpse in the days after death, and impose instead the respectable norms of middle classes (see Hotz, 2008). The bourgeois relationship to death and burial was increasingly mediated and commodified by the undertaking profession (see Curl, 2000).

Burial reform was broadly supported, but soon stalled in negotiations with the Church of England, since many city churches survived only on their burial fees. Hence Walker used pamphleteering in the 1840s to maintain pressure. He had the perfect case when in 1845 the corpses moved to the bone house of another private burial ground, Spa Fields near Exmouth Market in Clerkenwell, were found to have been burning out of control for days. This large unconsecrated burial ground had been used for over fifty years and, at an estimate of 43,000 square feet, should have had a capacity for 1,361 adult burial plots. Instead, Walker suggested that upwards of 80,000 bodies were crammed into the site, sometimes with as many as eight bodies stacked in one grave. Walker calculated his numbers from the weekday burials (six to twelve a day) with up to thirty interments every Sunday, every year, all year round.

The respectable houses and businesses of the area had suffered the stench of decay for years, making it for Walker one of the worst 'reservoirs of pestilence' in the capital (1846: 9). 'Let my readers remember that *emanations from the dead* escaping in a pure and concentrated form *have caused the immediate loss of life*', Walker asserted (1846: 28, original emphasis). At the centre of the Spa Fields burial ground was a bone house. Walker's investigations turned up witnesses who noted that 'the custom ... was to disinter the bodies after they had been three or four days buried, chop them up, and burn them in this bone house' (1846: 12). The agitation of the middle-class businesses in the area forced this situation to a local magistrate court, since the parish of St James would not intervene, and the ultimate owner of the land, hidden behind a chain of managers, was revealed to be the Marquis of Northampton. The scandal then spilled into the national press. A gravedigger testified that disinterment soon after burial was common at Spa Fields, and 'the coffins were taken away and burnt with pieces of decomposed flesh adhering thereto'. 'I have been up to my knees in human flesh by jumping on the bodies so as to cram them in the least possible space at the bottom of the graves', the gravedigger continued (1846: 22). Graves could often only be reused if they were bailed out, the buckets full of 'a most sickening compound' (1846: 30). The disinterred sometimes then had hair cut off and 'rails' (teeth) removed for sale. Other grim details included using the small coffins of still-born children as firelighters, since their traditional deal wood coffins were more combustible than the elm used for adult coffins.

Walker was still agitating in 1851, twelve years after his first salvo, restating his basic premises again in *On the Past and Present State of Intramural Burying Places*. 'BULK MUST OCCUPY SPACE,' he began, bluntly, 'and nearly all the evils attendant on the system arise from the necessity of finding room for unlimited bulk in a limited surface' (1851: 3). There is a powerful sense of a continuing, dangerous 'necro-sociability' (Laqueur, 2015: 41), with London envisaged as a city stuffed with the dead, folded into every available nook and cranny: 'The bodies of the dead are crowded into every inch of available space ... myriads of bodies, in every stage of decomposition, have been, and continue to be, stowed away in subterranean receptacles in the streets, lanes, and blind alleys in this metropolis' (1851: 9). The beloved dead were committed to the earth, but not destined to stay there. London is envisioned as a city of the restless dead, its graveyards full of 'uncanny vitality' (Gasperini, 2019: 68).

A critical push for legislation had been given by the outbreak of cholera in London in 1848–9, with a growing understanding of modes of disease transmission that killed thousands (John Snow's famous resolution of cholera as a water-borne disease, rather than a product of miasma, arrived in 1854 in his investigation of an outbreak amongst the slums of Soho). The outbreaks prompted the Board of Health to push for the Metropolitan Interments Bill, yet vested interests still stalled negotiations, despite substantial compensation offered to the Church of England.

In 1852, the Burial Act was finally passed, announcing that 'for the Protection of the Public Health Burials in any Part of Parts of the Metropolis, or in any Burial Grounds or Places of Burial in the Metropolis, should be wholly discontinued' (1852: para. II). Local Burial Boards were established, fees fixed and inspection regimes formalised. Exceptions to the rule included the sites of national memorial, St Paul's Cathedral and Westminster Abbey, some family intramural vaults where resting places had long been purchased and judged healthy, and the Cemetery Companies set up for the Magnificent Seven and for the Jewish and Quaker populations of the city (cultures whose hygienic burial customs clearly passed muster). The suburban garden cemetery soon displaced the toxic inner-city grounds. These were quickly abandoned, sometimes boarded up and left to rot or the land informally occupied and repurposed as goods and storage yards. Isabella Holmes had to become an intrepid voyager through overlooked zones or appropriated private goods yards of London to try to document these lost burial grounds just forty years later.

Grave mould for the Gothic

It is hard to find in the fiction of this early Victorian period anywhere near the level of gruesome detail of Walker's campaigning pamphlets and the parallel testimonies in parliamentary reports. Isabella Holmes wrote that 'the revelations made to this committee are so revolting that they are best forgotten' (Holmes, 1896: 197). Yet the horror of the inner-city graveyards and their associated atrocities did feed the Gothic imagination, particularly in its emergent urban form. It is consistently there in the serial horrors of the penny dreadfuls, from *Manuscripts from the Diary of a Physician* (started in 1844) or *Sweeney Todd* (started in 1846, the Fleet Street address and basement murders being conducted only a few moments away from the horrors of St Clement Danes and Enon Chapel). In the vast labyrinthine text of *The Mysteries of London* (started by George Reynolds in 1844), the locale of Globe Town in East London is described as a place benighted by 'swamps of mire ... which exhale a nauseating and sickly odour, like that of decomposing dead bodies' (Reynolds, 2013: 833). It is a place that is bounded by the East London Cemetery, but also enfolded with 'two Jews' burial grounds, and two other places of sepulture' (2013: 834). These are 'so crowded with the remains of mortality, that it is impossible to drive a spade into the ground without striking against human bones' (2013: 834). This is serial fiction that weaves sensation melodrama with reportage.

Walker's horrors are also present in Charles Dickens's *Bleak House* (started in 1851), in which a pauper graveyard off a courtyard in Drury Lane (identified as a childhood memory by Dickens in a later letter (see Blount, 1963)) plays a central role in the life and death of Captain Nemo, Jo the corner-sweep and Lady Dedlock. The pestilential graveyard miasma is indifferent to social status, like the fogs that enclose London at the opening of the novel.

Dickens, the metropolitan sanitation advocate in the early 1850s, could afford to become nostalgic by 1860, writing in the chapter 'The City of the Absent' from *The Uncommercial Traveller* of the churchyards of the City of London as places overlooked and disregarded and collapsing in the 'contagion of slow ruin' (2015: 228). Dickens focuses first on the yard of Saint Ghastly Grim, with a spiked iron gate 'ornamented with skulls and cross-bones' (2015: 229), but goes on to catalogue an odd sense of timeslip in other City churchyards, spectral returns enacted in cramped, inaccessible quarters where anachronistic scenes of uncanny people (or just the shamefaced workhouse poor, allowed out for exercise) are glimpsed in rare shafts of prismatic sunlight striking through the gloom (for more detail, see Luckhurst, 2021).

In the 1870s, the concerted advocacy of Miranda and Octavia Hill began to secure the preservation of urban graveyards, leading to the reopening of the once gloomy retreat of Mary Shelley at the Old St Pancras church as a formal public garden in 1877, Mary Wollstonecraft's grave being one of the few older monuments to survive. The Metropolitan Public Gardens Association followed in 1882, a group that secured many survivals in law after campaigning for the Disused Burial Grounds Act in 1884 (see Thorsheim, 2011).

Just a few years later, Count Dracula's daily need to marinate in the earth and grave dust of his ancestral land marks out a crucial limit to his ability to adapt to the uprooted circulations or spaces of flow more typical of *fin de siècle* modernity. The band of Christian brothers must camp out in a graveyard (perhaps St Mary's churchyard or Hampstead Cemetery) to catch the unholy night-time flits of Lucy Westenra, who is first snared by Dracula in the old churchyard of Whitby's ruined abbey. Dracula's polluting boxes of grave mould are a fearful reversion to the insidious proximity of the living to the dead. It is an old-time pollution that had once been caught so luridly in the mid-century campaigns of George Alfred Walker.

Note

1 'Necropolitics' is a term used by Achille Mbembe, who puts Foucault's biopolitics into dialogue with Agamben's *homo sacer* to produce an analysis, particularly in the colonial context, of 'the creation of death-worlds, new and unique forms of social existence in which vast populations are subjected to conditions of life conferring upon them the status of the *living dead*' (2003: 40).

References

Bard, Robert (2008) *Graveyard London: Lost and Forgotten Burial Grounds* (London: Historical Publications).
Blount, Trevor (1963) 'The Graveyard Satire of *Bleak House* in the Context of 1850', *Review of English Studies*, 56, 370–8.
Burial Act (1852) 'An Act to Amend the Laws Concerning the Burial of the Dead in the Metropolis'. 15 & 16 Vict c 85.

Chadwick, Edwin (1843) *A Supplementary Report on the Results of a Special Inquiry into the Practice of Interment in Town* (London: Clowes).
Curl, James Stevens (2000) *The Victorian Celebration of Death* (Stroud: Sutton Publishing).
Dickens, Charles (2015) [1860–1] *The Uncommercial Traveller,* ed. Daniel Tyler (Oxford: Oxford World's Classics).
Foucault, Michel (1994) [1963] *The Birth of the Clinic: An Archaeology of Medical Perception,* trans. A. M. Sheridan Smith (New York: Vintage).
Foucault, Michel (1995) [1975] *Discipline and Punish: The Birth of the Prison,* trans. Alan Sheridan (New York: Vintage).
Foucault, Michel (2004) [1976] *'Society Must Be Defended': Lectures at the Collège de France, 1975–76,* trans. David Macey (London: Penguin).
French, Richard (1975) *Antivivisection and Medical Science in Victorian Society* (Princeton: Princeton University Press).
Gasperini, Anna (2019) *Nineteenth Century Popular Fiction, Medicine and Anatomy: The Victorian Penny Blood and the 1832 Anatomy Act* (Cham: Palgrave).
Godwin, William (1809) *Essay on Sepulchres: Or, A Proposal for Erecting Some Memorial of the Illustrious Dead in All Ages on the Spot Where Their Remains Have Been Interred* (London: Miller).
Gould, Stephen Jay (1981) *The Mismeasure of Man* (New York: Norton).
Holmes, Mrs Basil [Isabella] (1896) *The London Burial Grounds: Notes on Their History from the Earliest Times to the Present Day* (London: Fisher Unwin).
Horton, Robert (2014) *Frankenstein* (New York: Columbia University Press).
Hotz, Mary Elizabeth (2008) *Literary Remains: Representations of Death and Burial in Victorian England* (Albany: State University of New York Press).
Laqueur, Thomas W. (2015) *The Work of the Dead: A Cultural History of Mortal Remains* (Princeton: Princeton University Press).
Luckhurst, Roger (2021) 'Necropolitan Gothic', in Clive Bloom (ed.), *The Palgrave Handbook to Gothic Origins* (Cham: Palgrave), pp. 263–80.
Marmoy, C. F. A. (1958) 'The "Auto-Icon" of Jeremy Bentham at University College, London', *Medical History,* 2, 177–86.
Mbembe, Achille (2003) 'Necropolitics', *Public Culture,* 15:1, 11–40.
McAllister, David (2018) *Imagining the Dead in British Literature and Culture, 1790–1848* (Basingstoke: Palgrave).
Pinfold, John (2022) 'George Alfred Walker (1807–84)', *Oxford Dictionary of National Biography,* www.oxforddnb.com/view/10.1093/ref:odnb/9780198614128.001.0001/odnb-9780198614128-e-28484 (accessed 15 March 2022).
Poovey, Mary (1995) *Making a Social Body: British Cultural Formation 1830–64* (Chicago: University of Chicago Press).
Report from the Select Committee on Improvement of the Health of Towns (Effect of Interment of Bodies in Towns) (1842).
Reynolds, George W. M. (2013) [1844] *The Mysteries of London,* vol. I, fwd Louis James, annot. Dick Collins (Kansas City: Valancourt Press).
Richardson, Ruth (1988) *Death, Dissection and the Destitute* (Harmondsworth: Penguin).
Sampson, Fiona (2018) *In Search of Mary Shelley: The Girl Who Wrote* Frankenstein (London: Profile).

Shapira, Yael (2018) *Inventing the Gothic Corpse: The Thrill of Human Remains in the Eighteenth-Century Novel* (London: Palgrave).
Shelley, Mary (1993) [1818] *Frankenstein: 1818 Text*, ed. Marilyn Butler (Oxford: Oxford World's Classics).
Thorsheim, Peter (2011) 'The Corpse in the Garden: Burial, Health, and the Environment in Nineteenth-Century London', *Environmental History*, 16:1, 38–68.
Walker, George A. (1839) *Gatherings from Graveyards; Particularly Those of London, with a Concise History of the Modes of Interment among Different Nations* (London: Longman and Company).
Walker, George A. (1846) *Burial-Ground Incendiarism: The Last Fire at the Bone-House in the Spa-Fields Golgotha, or, the Minute Anatomy of Grave-Digging in London* (London: Longman, Brown, Green, and Longmans).
Walker, George A. (1851) *On the Past and Present State of Intramural Burying Places, with Practical Suggestions for the Establishment of National Extramural Cemeteries* (London: Longman, Brown, Green, and Longmans).
Wasson, Sara (2014) 'Gothic Cities and Suburbs, 1880–Present', in Glennis Byron and Dale Townsend (eds), *The Gothic World* (Abingdon: Routledge), pp. 132–42.
Westover, Paul (2009) 'William Godwin, Literary Tourism, and the Work of Necromanticism', *Studies in Romanticism*, 48, 299–319.

4

De-Gothicising the Victorian Gothic graveyard

David McAllister

Radically new graveyard aesthetics emerged in Britain in the middle decades of the nineteenth century. They were premised upon a belief that this enduringly Gothic space could have its traditional atmosphere of gloom scoured, cleansed and weeded out of existence: that the graveyard could be de-Gothicised, transformed from a site of introspection, superstition and terror into a place of leisure, learning and aesthetic delight; 'metamorphosed from a disgusting charnel-house into a delicious flower-garden', as the burial reformer John Strang argued (1831: 53). While Stephen Sowerby is right to observe that '[t]o the modern imagination nothing evokes a sense of the Gothic like the eerie romantic melancholy of a decaying Victorian cemetery' (2021: 467), this chapter points out that these spaces were designed with an explicitly anti-Gothic purpose, as part of a wider cultural attempt to sever fear and superstition from death and burial and engineer a more rational sensibility in which the Gothic had no place.

Nobody believed that this transformation could be brought about solely by reforming graveyard aesthetics: it would require the construction of a new, multiform death culture that also encompassed literary, material and visual texts; which aestheticised death in an attempt to normalise its presence in everyday life; and sentimentalised it by favouring the depiction of continuities between living and dead human bodies rather than acknowledging their difference. It typically represented the dead – in post-mortem photographs, sentimental deathbed narratives and hair jewellery, for example – as surviving in states of perfect preservation, captured before decay rendered them abject or terrifying (Lutz, 2015: 145). We often look back upon this culture as sentimental, kitsch, Gothic or weird, but it should also be understood as an attempt to reshape long-standing cultural attitudes by eliminating the disturbing affects of traditional death culture.

These were precisely the same affects that had long made graveyards and tombs such an attractive setting for Gothic writers. As Fred Botting argues, Gothic horror is often caused by 'a direct encounter with physical mortality, the touching of a cold corpse, the sight of a decaying body' (1996: 75), and these encounters often necessarily took place in or around graveyards. Eliminate such encounters, burial reformers argued, and the age-old horror of death could be eliminated too. This chapter focuses upon this audacious reformist project by first identifying the psychological theories that provoked its emergence, and which can be found in texts that argued for the closure of old graveyards and the construction of new cemeteries. It then shows how *Dracula* (1897) sets out the decline and failure of this de-Gothicising project as the graveyard was reclaimed both by, and for, the Gothic mode at the *fin de siècle*.

Associationist psychology and cemeterial aesthetics

The body horror found in nineteenth-century urban graveyards has been well documented elsewhere, along with the widespread anxiety that dead matter would seep out of London's burial grounds to infect the bodies of the living (see Luckhurst, 2021; Lacquer, 2015: 229–30). Yet the reformers who campaigned for the closure of these repulsive boneyards were concerned that graveyards were corrupting minds as well as infecting bodies and argued that the risk they posed was not just pathological, but psychological too. Edwin Chadwick claimed, in an unpublished memo probably written while he compiled his monumental 1843 report on urban burial, that 'the chief grounds' for burial reform were not physical, but 'moral and psychological' (Chadwick, n.d.). The reforms his report eventually proposed were designed to counteract the graveyard's tendency to 'pollute the mental associations ... of the population' (Chadwick, 1843: 195). John Claudius Loudon, perhaps the most influential cemetery designer of the century, claimed that urban graveyards were 'shunned and avoided' by mourners not because they feared for their physical health but because 'the associations which are generally attached' to them are too 'gloomy and terrific' (1843: 8). His Scottish compatriot John Strang described how graveyards produced 'sentiments of horror' in onlookers by generating a thought of bodily dissolution that 'forcibly presses itself on the mind'. In such a place, he notes, 'the only associations' we have with death 'are such as the imagination shrinks from contemplating' (1831: 49–52). As we can see, reform of graveyards was justified by identifying their Gothic affects – horror, gloom, terror – as causes of lasting psychological damage.

These critiques of the graveyard's Gothic affectivity are founded upon, and share the language of, associationist psychology, which was the most widely accepted model of mental development throughout much of the nineteenth century. Different models of mental association were favoured by different political and intellectual groups, but all stemmed from a belief that the mind begins as a *tabula rasa* and that ideas develop not from any innate or God-given knowledge but from an individual's sensory experiences. English associationism can be traced back to John Locke, who argued that experiences were inscribed and recorded on the mind, forming ideas which then became connected – depending on when and how the mind first encountered them – into 'trains of thought' (1700: 223). Some of these associations are natural, Locke suggests, while others are harmful, and once such 'wrong connexions' (1700: 223) are formed they can be difficult to remove, undermining later attempts to think rationally and act morally.

Locke's own example of how this process works highlights both the importance of fictional narratives to associationist thought and the belief that Gothic affects caused lasting psychological harm. There is no reason, Locke observes, why a child should necessarily associate darkness with 'Goblines and Sprights' (1700: 223), because the two ideas are not intrinsically connected. If, however, a child is told stories that yoke darkness with these frightening supernatural beings, then the concepts become associated in the child's mind, such that one thought will always accompany the other and '[d]arkness shall ever after bring with it those frightful *Ideas*' (1700: 223). Romantic-era educationalists were concerned about the harmful ways in which children first encountered the idea of death precisely because of the enduring nature of these unhealthy connections and their propensity to generate superstitious fears about death and the dead. To guard against this happening, many promoted depictions of death that minimised fear, pain or suffering in favour of sentimentalised narratives of happiness, peace and acceptance. Elizabeth Hamilton, for example, argued that children should be protected from the 'idea of apparitions, and winding sheets, and sable shrouds', which might establish 'early associations of terror' in their young minds. Instead, they should read texts that paint death 'in the most agreeable colours', making it seem 'not only familiar but pleasant' (1818: 44). It is within this anti-Gothic context that the identification of graveyards as a psychological danger must be understood. If an overstimulating bedtime story about a naughty goblin could permanently warp a young mind, what might be done by the sights and smells of a fetid urban graveyard?

Dale Townshend has recently discussed the emergence of a belief that architecture shaped individual psychology, describing an 'aesthetics of associationism' in eighteenth-century England. He recounts how Mark Akenside, Horace Walpole, Sir John Soane and others argued for 'the power and ability of architecture to move and inspire the conscious mind' (2019: 45) and developed an aesthetics to inspire fancy and the Gothic imagination. The associationist logic underpinning the drive to transform graveyards shows that this understanding of the link between built environments and the mind persisted into the mid nineteenth century, yet while the figures identified by

Townshend hoped to stimulate Gothic affects, their nineteenth-century successors wanted to do precisely the opposite, advocating for the construction of new burial grounds that were to be known as 'cemeteries', in which anything that suggested antiquity, decay or gloom would be eliminated. Their new cemeterial aesthetics was designed to stimulate reason rather than fancy, and to advance post-Enlightenment progress by eliminating superstition among a population that clung tenaciously to its inherited beliefs.

Reforming the graveyard's visual appearance was crucial to cemeterial aesthetics, as it was through the visual perception of a burial ground's 'neglected state' that psychological damage was believed to take place. Chadwick's claim that '[t]he images presented to the mind by the *visible* arrangements for sepulture are inseparably associated with the ideas of death itself to the greater proportion of the population' (1843: 142, original emphasis) outlines why the cemetery's appearance was so important to reformers, who believed that what people saw in a burial ground dictated how they thought about death. Strang identified what was wrong with the current 'visible arrangements' by observing that 'the chief characteristics' of graveyards are 'the noxious weed, the broken tombstone, and the defaced inscription' (1831: 24). The dominance of decay in this visual field meant the graveyard was neither 'the solemn and affecting shrine of devotion' nor 'the resort and consolation to weeping individuals', but 'little better than a disgusting charnel-house avoided by general consent, as if infected with a pestilence, and calculated ... to call forth rather the feelings of aversion and disgust, than of sympathy and sorrow' (1831: 24).

Yet, although associationist psychology stimulated the belief that graveyards caused psychic damage, it also suggested that a new type of burial ground could be its cure. Reformers believed that the graveyard need not be horrific at all: that it might just as easily be transformed into a site of pleasure, education and entertainment, a place that could contribute to the spread of joy and reason rather than fear and superstition. In a speech that circulated widely in Britain, the American Supreme Court justice Joseph Story asked why, if a 'tender regard for the dead be so universal ... do we not dispel from [the grave] that unlovely gloom, from which our hearts turn as from a darkness that ensnares, and a horror that appals our thoughts?' (1835: 92). Strang argued that it was 'the duty of every wellwisher to his species, to pour into the tomb the light of religion and philosophy, and thereby to dissipate the vain phantoms which the false gloom of the grave has tended to call forth' (1831: 61). The gloom here is false – a human addition which could be removed (as it had been constructed) by reforming the graveyard's aesthetics, because '[t]he decoration of the cemetery is a mean peculiarly calculated to produce these effects' (1831: 61). Chadwick agreed, arguing that '[c]areful visible arrangements, of an agreeable nature, raise corresponding mental images and associations which diminish the terrors incident to the aspect of death' (1843: 144). The equation, for burial reformers, was simple: more attractive graveyards will lead to more enlightened minds.

Reformers argued that to establish this 'agreeable' visual field would require the elimination of anything that connected death to decay, along with careful planting, regular cleaning and maintenance and stricter controls over the types of monuments allowed within its precincts (Loudon, 1843: 8). There was no place in the new cemeterial aesthetics for traditional gravestone carvings of skeletons and skulls, which were deemed to be too redolent of bodily decay. The journalist Charles Molloy Westmacott published a spoof prospectus for a cemetery company in which he outlined how the new space would tackle this problem:

> A *Committee of Taste* will superintend
> The designs and inscriptions to each latter end.
> Take notice: no *cross-bones* or *skulls* are allowed,
> Or naked young cherubims riding a cloud;
> In short, no allusions that savour of death
> Nor aught that reminds of a friend's parting breath.
> (1826: 115, original emphasis)

Westmacott's jibe was well founded; burial reformers pointed out that the power to remove this toxic visual pollutant lay within the hands of the current generation and argued for precisely the kind of close management that the spoof lampoons, favouring austere neoclassical monuments rather than the more traditional – and more Gothic – *memento mori*.

If this aesthetics were adopted, reformers claimed, the burial ground could be transformed into a place of learning and reason: 'the scene which now scares the schoolboy from its neighbourhood should be made to him a spot sacred to study', and 'the gay and the giddy should occasionally be induced to exchange the intoxicating pleasures and noisy revelry of the world for the beauty and the calm of a garden sepulchre, where they may more eloquently and more effectually learn than elsewhere, that to be virtuous is to be happy' (Strang, 1831: 53). It is this process that I identify as 'de-Gothicisation', while acknowledging that this was neither a term that reformers themselves deployed nor one they would easily comprehend given the shifting development of the 'Gothic' from a term denoting antiquity to one that signalled something closer to its current literary-critical meaning. Nevertheless, it is useful here because the characteristics of, and responses to, the traditional graveyard that reformers campaigned to eliminate are those that we typically identify with Gothic: gloom, decay and decrepitude.

De-Gothicisation did not have universal support, and contemporary critics of the project often mocked the sentimental language used by its advocates. Westmacott's spoof pokes fun at these de-Gothicising aims:

> To rob death of its terrors and make it delightful
> To give up your breath, and abolish the frightful
> Old custom of lying defunct in your shroud,
> Surrounded by relatives sobbing aloud[.]
> We've a scheme that shall mingle the "grave with the gay,"
> And make it quite pleasant to die, when you may.
> First, then, we propose with the graces of art,
> Like our Parisian friends, to make ev'ry tomb smart;
> And, by changing the feelings of funeral terrors,
> Remove what remain'd of old Catholic errors
> ...
> So novel, agreeable, and grateful our scheme,
> That death will appear like a sweet summer's dream;
> And the horrid idea of a gloomy, cold cell,
> Will vanish like vapours of mist from a dell.
>
> (1826: 115)

The poem's inappropriate diction and jaunty rhythm send up the reformers' pollyannish approach, while it points to the vagueness of hopes that such culturally entrenched ideas could simply be made to 'vanish like vapours of mist'. Similar doubts were expressed by the Gothic writer William Mudford, who published an account of his first trip to Kensal Green Cemetery in 1841. Mudford admits that he is a cemetery sceptic but had been convinced to visit by a friend 'in order that I might be converted' to this new mode of burial. Mudford, who is best remembered for 'The Iron Shroud' (1830), a tale of terror that first appeared in *Blackwood's Edinburgh Magazine*, rejects the aesthetics that informed the cemetery's design:

> Death and prettiness! Mouldering bones, shrouds, and coffins, associated with the ornamental! Beauty and the grave! What ill-assorted images! What a mockery of all that is, and pretends to be real, in broken hearts! What a violation of all those tender recollections of the departed, whose well-springs are gloom, and silence, and solitude!
>
> (1841: 92)

Where anti-Gothic writers had complained about the graveyard's dirt and decay, Mudford complains about the cemetery's cleanliness. Its 'ten thousand tombstones, in every fantastic variety of form' are too neatly maintained, he argues: they look 'so new and nice, that you fancy they must certainly be hearth-stoned once a week' (1841: 95).

Hearth-stoning was not a part of Kensal Green's stringent maintenance routine, but the cemetery did take great care over its appearance in the decades following its opening in 1832, and the ruthless exclusion of anything that might remind visitors of death or decay was essential to cemeterial aesthetics. The architectural historian William M. Taylor points out that 'garden cemeteries were perhaps the most regulated of nineteenth-century spaces', governed by 'sanitary laws and building codes governing tomb dimensions, path widths, drainage, fencings and funerary detail' (2018: 183). They also, as he notes, relied upon 'such seemingly pedestrian activities as trimming grass, removing weeds and the cleaning of headstones' to fulfil their self-stated function as sites of moral, psychological and educational improvement (2018: 192). Kensal Green invested huge sums in facing its buildings with stucco and Portland stone, reflecting a desire to build in smooth, impermeable surfaces that were more resistant to decay; it built colonnades and walkways to encourage pedestrians, planted shrubs that would flower all year round and hired teams of gardeners to tend them; imported cedars were planted, along with silver firs, ornamental chestnuts, evergreens and limes, all designed to draw the eye upwards, away from the grave itself and the unpleasantness that was rotting beneath (Curl, 2000: 103–4). As John MacNeill Miller has pointed out, this was a system 'designed to mask putrefaction' by distracting observers and giving pleasure (2017: 384). Some cemeteries were intended to help educate city-dwellers about the natural world (Abney Park, for example, was designed as an arboretum), but it was also widely believed that nature must always be visibly subject to human dominion in the cemetery, remaining always under the sign of culture. Weeds and creepers should be removed; shrubs must remain neatly trimmed in case their abundant growth spoke too loudly about the reclamation of the human body by the earth in which it was inhumed. 'Beneath the shade of a spreading tree,' wrote Strang, 'amid the fragrance of the balmy flower, surrounded on every hand with the noble works of Art, the imagination is robbed of its gloomy horrors – the wildest fancy is freed from its debasing fears' (1831: 61). Nature played a fundamental role in the cemetery's aesthetics and is thus allowed to 'spread', but it must always remain 'surrounded' by cultural productions wrought by human hands, which focused the minds of mourners on things beyond or above – but never within – the grave itself.

Even a sceptic like Mudford was forced to admit that garden cemeteries performed this task well. He may have found cemeterial aesthetics 'too garish, too artificial', but he also confessed that the graves are 'so symmetrically disposed, so clean, so neat in their appearance, that I think of anything *but* the grave while looking at them' (1841: 93, original emphasis). Tightly controlling the cemetery's visual field had successfully severed the link between the grave's status as aesthetic object and its function as receptacle for a rotting human body. The old associations governing Mudford's response to graveyards had seemingly been replaced without his acquiesence, even if new associations had not yet formed: the new cemetery aesthetics had successfully diverted his mind from thoughts of the grave, and what it contains, by offering multiple alternative appeals to aesthetic pleasure. The cemetery still generated an emotional response, but one 'which the GRAVE never should produce – PLEASURE', along with 'a lightsome, cheerful spirit' (1841: 93, original emphasis). That affects such as these were wholly new in graveyard literature suggests that the elimination of decay had succeeded, at least temporarily, in overturning the graveyard's longstanding Gothic associations.

Dracula, decay and the return of the Gothic graveyard

The rest of this chapter examines the progress of this project at the *fin de siècle* by tracking the graveyard's re-emergence as a Gothic space in Bram Stoker's *Dracula* (1897), a novel published sixty-five years after London's first garden cemetery had opened and at a time when sentimental Victorian death culture was in decline (Jalland, 1996: 372). It asks what the burial of Lucy Westenra, her undead escape from the graveyard and her enforced resumption of the natural processes of decay tell us about cemeterial aesthetics and the de-Gothicising project as the nineteenth century ended.

Dracula emerged in an intellectual and cultural climate that differed radically from that in which the attempt to transform graveyards had begun. New models of psychological development supplanted associationism and reinvigorated the Gothic, as Stoker and his peers exploited theories of degeneration, multiple personality, hypnotic influence and unconscious cerebration in one of the most productive eras of Gothic writing. Criminality was no longer widely believed to be caused by harmful associations established in childhood, but rather by inherited characteristics of the sort delineated by criminologists like Cesare Lombroso, or culturally influenced traits such as those identified as degenerate by Max Nordau. The literary sentimentalism of a few decades earlier had fallen into a critical disrepute from which it has only recently begun to emerge.

Dracula registers these cultural shifts in its depiction of graveyards and burial, most notably in the days after Westenra's death. Stoker shows cemeterial aesthetics still governing the disposal of the dead, shaping every aspect of the corpse's post-mortem treatment from the laying-out of the body to the incantatory recitation of sentimental poetry by the bereaved. At every turn, we see how the unpleasant facts of Lucy's death are disguised and overwritten by sentimental tropes: hedged round with pacifying texts that assert continuity between the living body and the lifeless corpse. Note the appeals to such continuity when John Seward confronts Lucy's dead body for the first time:

> Death had given back part of her beauty, for her brow and cheeks had recovered some of their flowing lines; even the lips had lost their deadly pallor. It was as if the blood, no longer needed for the working of the heart, had gone to make the harshness of death as little rude as might be.
>
> We thought her dying whilst she slept,
> And sleeping whilst she died.
>
> I stood beside Van Helsing, and said:–
> 'Ah well, poor girl, there is peace for her at last. It is the end!'
>
> (Stoker, 1986: 210)

Seward's attentiveness to the ways in which Lucy's corpse remains unchanged after death recalls the deathbed scene of Little Nell in Dickens's *The Old Curiosity Shop* ([1840–1] 1998), which remains the *locus classicus* of Victorian sentimentalism. Yael Shapira has shown that graphic depictions of dead bodies were fundamental to the Gothic mode in the long eighteenth century as 'a source of thrills' (2018: 2), but the sentimental treatment of the corpse favoured by Dickens (and echoed by Seward) sought different affects: as Maia McAleavey notes, such carefully aestheticised death scenes allowed a controlled release of emotion in a world where grief was often disciplined (2011: 135–7). Cleaving to this sentimentalist template in his descriptions of Lucy's corpse, Seward's response is clearly shaped by, and participates in, a death culture that draws its energy from the same forces underpinning cemeterial aesthetics.

His immersion in this culture is shown through his familiarity with sentimental Victorian poetry. Seward decorates his account with an unacknowledged quotation from Thomas Hood's poem 'The Death Bed' (1831), which describes a deathbed vigil in which the speaker recalls how he had 'watch'd her breathing through the night', with 'the wave of life … heaving to and fro' in her breast until the moment of her death. In the lines Seward quotes, the speaker describes the similarity of the as yet undecayed dead body to the living:

> Our very hopes belied our fears,
> Our fears our hopes belied–
> We thought her dying when she slept,
> And sleeping when she died.
>
> (Hood, 1846: lines 9–12)

Seward's rote repetition of this fragment shapes his own grieving utterance and brings Lucy's body into the domain of culture, connecting her 'real' death to Hood's poetic one. Perhaps it also offers Seward a distraction from trauma, with the pleasure of poetic language diverting his attention from the enforced contemplation of Lucy's phenomenal absence. As Alfred Lord Tennyson notes in the century's most famous elegy *In Memoriam A. H. H.* (1850), there is a 'use in measured language' which acts like an analgesic on the bereaved, functioning 'Like dull narcotics, numbing pain' for those with an 'unquiet heart and brain' (2004: canto V, lines 5–8).

Poetry functions in this way for Seward, both here and when he next encounters Lucy's corpse after the undertaker has prepared it for burial. Again, he lingers over the corpse's beauty while alluding to a poem that depicts death without decay:

> The undertaker had certainly done his work well, for the room was turned into a small *chapelle ardente*. There was a wilderness of beautiful white flowers, and death was made as little repulsive as might be. The end of the winding sheet was laid over the face; when the Professor bent over and gently turned it back, we both started at the beauty before us, the tall wax candles showing a sufficient light to note it well. All Lucy's loveliness had come back to her in death, and the hours that had passed, instead of leaving traces of 'decay's effacing fingers', had but restored the beauty of life, till positively I could not believe my eyes that I was looking at a corpse.
>
> (Stoker, 1986: 213)

The dead body is again hedged round with pleasure-giving cultural texts all working to make death 'as little repulsive as might be': the flowers, the candle, the winding sheet. Among them we should include the phrase 'decay's effacing fingers', which comes from the opening of Lord Byron's poem 'The Giaour' (1813) and which, like 'The Death Bed', denies the onset of decay and represents a beautiful corpse:

> He who hath bent him o'er the dead
> Ere the first day of Death is fled,
> The first dark day of Nothingness,
> The last of Danger and Distress,
> (Before Decay's effacing fingers
> Have swept the lines where Beauty lingers.
>
> (Byron, 1981: lines 68–73)

Seward's use of these poetic intertexts was by no means unusual: both extracts had circulated widely within Victorian culture, appearing frequently on mourning cards and in newspaper obituaries as well as in novels, poems, plays, sermons and periodical articles. Hood's poem had been so thoroughly absorbed into Victorian death culture that his daughter complained, after his death, that the poem was 'not generally known to be his' (Broderip, 1861: 5). Her claim is borne out in *Dracula*, where Seward not only fails to identify the source of the quotation but also misquotes it, replacing the original's 'when' with his own 'whilst'. It is a minor but revealing inaccuracy, suggesting the lines are not culled from a book but dredged up from memory. The misquotation might even be read as a reality effect, given that Seward's account is not written for publication but spoken into the phonograph on which he records the audio journal that will later be transcribed and woven into the novel's narrative: what could be more realistic than a trifling error, an inexact recall? These poetic allusions perform a similar task to the plants and sculptures in the garden cemetery, reinforcing an idea of continuity between living and dead by figuring the corpse as unchanged, and thus offering psychological comfort. Seward allows his grieving thoughts to be diverted by aesthetically pleasing texts which were routinely pressed into service by a culture that sought to avoid death's Gothic affects.

Stoker shows that every other facet of Lucy's burial is designed to perform a similar function and is governed by the same prevailing aesthetics. She is interred in the fictional Kingstead churchyard, which lies 'away from teeming London' (1986: 165) – a location that avoids any lingering association with the urban graveyards that had become so notorious earlier in the century. Stoker depicts it as an attractive place, where 'the air is fresh, and the sun rises over Hampstead Hill, and ... wild flowers grow of their own accord' (1986: 165). We learn that her body will remain above ground in the Westenra family tomb, encased within a lead sheet and placed within a wooden coffin whose fixtures and fittings are made with materials selected for their longevity: brass, iron, silver plate. The reader is never told why this lead lining was needed: to disguise and contain the corpse's liquefaction, which would otherwise become visible as it seeped through the coffin's wooden joints and dripped onto the stone floor of the tomb. Once again, the corpse's decay is denied and disguised.

Such a sight would risk undermining the aesthetic of the tomb itself, which is opulent to the point of extravagance: Seward describes it as a 'lordly death-house' (1986: 165), while Van Helsing reveals that it has been made from an impermeable stone when he refers to it as 'that so fine marble house' (1986: 164). We learn that it has been dressed with fresh flowers, which metonymically suggest the dead body's own resistance to decay. Stoker shows how the cemeterial aesthetic has developed into a much more complex and multivalent death culture, in which the dressing of Lucy's corpse, the elaborate diction of Seward's poetic intertexts, the peacefulness of the graveyard, the beauty of the family tomb and the multiple barriers of the layered coffin combine to protect the bereaved from a disturbing encounter with mortality. Even at the *fin de siècle*, this protection of the fragile psyche is still a principal objective in burying the dead. In what follows Lucy's burial, however, Stoker signals that this sentimental cemeterial aesthetics was no longer fit for purpose.

By the 1890s, death and decay were no longer seen as topics that had to be denied or beautified. This was the age of literary decadence, a movement that 'present[s] decay as a condition actively, wilfully sought' (Porter, 1997: 94), and which developed a heightened awareness of man's entanglement with a wider ecology (see Denisoff, 2022). Acknowledging that the human body was subject to ecological processes was no longer considered taboo, and campaigns for natural burial had emerged in Britain and elsewhere, with advocates calling for the introduction of open wickerwork coffins to allow decomposition to happen more quickly, and arguing that lead linings, such as Lucy's, ought to be banned (Hayden, 1875). Sentimental literary representations of death had become deeply unfashionable. Oscar Wilde's reputed quip about *The Old Curiosity Shop* (that 'one must have a heart of stone to read the death of little Nell without laughing' (Ellmann, 1997: 441)) is perhaps the most famous example of this shift in tone, but we might also cite D. H. Lawrence's inability to reconcile Hood's 'The Death Bed' with the reality of tending for his own dying mother in 1910:

> Mother is very bad indeed. It is a continuous 'We watched her breathing through the night–' ay, and the mornings come, snowy, and stormy ... and still she is here, and it is the old slow horror. I think Tom Hood's woman looked sad but beautiful: but my mother is a sight to see and be silent about for ever.
> (Lawrence, 2002: 192)

The dissonance Lawrence experiences when comparing his own experience to nineteenth-century literary accounts of mortality indicates sentimentalism's growing obsolescence in the early twentieth century – a process that already was under way in the 1890s, as *Dracula* suggests.

Like Lawrence, Seward finds that the reality of his mourning fails to correspond to the Victorian sentimental ideal. Burial reformers had insisted that mourners should be comforted by the signs of enduring culture that surrounded and disguised the corpse in the cemetery's landscaped acres and impermeable stone surfaces, but this is not what happens to Seward. Upon visiting Lucy's tomb, he finds that nature, in the form of decay, is beginning to reclaim the graveyard from culture, and that it is therefore becoming increasingly redolent of death. He notes that the fresh flowers in the tomb have wilted and hang 'lank and dead, their whites turning to rust and their greens to browns' (Stoker, 1986: 183). The lead coffin remains sealed, but the 'spider and the beetle' had 'resumed their accustomed dominance' (1986: 183) over the tomb's interior. Even the costly materials of tomb and coffin show signs of decay; grand stones are revealed in the candlelight to be 'time-discoloured', the silver plate 'clouded', the ironwork 'rusty' and the brass all 'tarnished' (183). Where earlier the graveyard air had been 'fresh', now Seward notes that the vault has a 'taint of death and decay' (183). Despite half a century of anti-Gothicisation, the burial ground still exhibits considerable Gothic potential.

Gothic has long been understood as a genre that stages the return of the repressed (Botting, 1996: 18–19). Here we see the reappearance of the decay that has so long been denied and obscured by cemeterial aesthetics and in sentimental literary depictions of the corpse, forcing Seward to acknowledge a gap between his initial response to Lucy's death and the messier, more confusing reality. Such evident signs of decay transform the graveyard's significance for Seward. 'It conveyed irresistibly the idea that life, animal life, was not the only thing that could pass away', he notes, and 'the effect' of this challenge to the tomb's pacifying symbolic function 'was more miserable and sordid than could have been imagined' (Stoker, 1986: 183).

Yet, although this evidence of decay initially disturbs Seward's mental equilibrium, it is not the decayed corpse that re-emerges as monstrous. Indeed, one of the debts *Dracula* owes to Decadence lies in its acceptance of decay as part of life, and its recognition of the monstrosity of anything that denies its value or restricts its agency. In this respect, *Dracula* corresponds perfectly to the division Andrew Smith identifies in Victorian Gothic between narratives in which 'the corruption of the body can be transcended (perhaps most clearly typified by the ghost story)' and those in which 'there is the horror of the dead undead body' such as vampire fiction (Smith, 2012: 159). This is a novel that falls squarely into the latter camp, in which preservation, not decay, is made horrific, and Seward is forced to recognise this inversion of the dominant death culture when he sees the vampiric Lucy and shudders 'with horror' (Stoker, 1986: 197). Her undead body manifests the promise of cemeterial aesthetics by remaining visually pleasing and undecayed. Yet, for Seward, her 'sweetness was turned to adamantine, heartless cruelty'; her eyes, while still Lucy's 'in form and colour', were 'unclean and full of hell-fire'; and her 'purity' was transformed into 'voluptuous wantonness' (1986: 196). Having previously vowed that Van Helsing should commit no 'mutilation of [Lucy's] dead body', and stating that he had a 'duty to do in protecting her grave from outrage' (1986: 192), Lucy's fiancé Arthur Holmwood now agrees to do both because he wishes there to be 'no horror like this ever any more' (1986: 198). It is Arthur who drives 'the mercy-bearing stake' (1986: 201) into Lucy's chest the next day in a hugely overdetermined scene which speaks to multiple different readings of the novel. Along with its obviously sexual, patriarchal and misogynistic significance, it also represents a violent overturning of Victorian sentimental notions about the preservation of the dead body and the sentimental idea of its continuity with the living. Once Lucy's heart has been staked, her head cut off and her mouth stuffed with garlic, there is no mistaking her for a living, but sleeping, woman.

Mary Elizabeth Hotz argues that Dracula gains a foothold in London because England has become a nation in 'denial about thanatological matters', unable to 'face the truth about death' (2009: 155, 156). I have shown that this denial was the result of de-Gothicising attempts to beautify death as a means of preventing psychological responses that were deemed harmful by associationist psychology. Stoker's novel recognises that this denial was no longer sustainable: that the graveyard's primary function is not to give pleasure to the living but to safely house the dead, and that it is therefore inseparable from its Gothic affects. This recognition is marked in the text when Seward notes a sudden change in the graveyard's appearance midway through his encounter with the undead Lucy. No longer does Kingstead churchyard seem like a pleasant or peaceful location:

> Never did tombs look so ghastly white. Never did cypress, or yew, or juniper so seem the embodiment of funeral gloom. Never did tree or grass wave or rustle so ominously. Never did bough creak so mysteriously, and never did the far-away howling of dogs send such a woeful presage through the night.
>
> (Stoker, 1986: 196)

The graveyard has been re-Gothicised, resembling once again those of the eighteenth and early nineteenth centuries, reinvested with all the gloom, unease and complex imaginative potential that sentimental cemeterial aesthetics had sought to efface. The attempt to strip graveyards of their Gothic affectivity was failing. Over the early decades of the twentieth century this process would accelerate as the grand Victorian cemeteries aged, their maintenance budgets were squeezed and they fell into increasing disrepair. *Dracula* recognised the inevitability of this process, accepting that decay cannot be excluded from the graveyard forever: that the blight in the petal and the beetle in the tomb need not be seen as unwanted intruders, encroaching upon a fantasy location of beauty and light, but that they existed as fellow inhabitants, with the dead, of a deeply and ineluctably Gothic space.

References

Botting, Fred (1996) *Gothic* (London: Routledge).
Broderip, Frances F. (1861) *Memorials of Thomas Hood*, vol. I (London: Edward Moxon).
Byron, Lord (1981) [1813] 'The Giaour: A Fragment of a Turkish Tale', in Jerome J. McGann (ed.), *Lord Byron: The Complete Poetical Works*, vol. 3 (Oxford: The Clarendon Press), pp. 39–82.

Chadwick, Edwin (1843) *A Supplementary Report on the Results of a Special Inquiry into the Practice of Interment in Towns* (London: W. Clowes).
Chadwick, Edwin (n.d.) 'Interment in Towns: Memoranda of the Chief Heads'. UCL Chadwick Papers, Box 48.
Curl, James Stevens (2000) *The Victorian Celebration of Death* (Stroud: Sutton Publishing).
Denisoff, Dennis (2022) *Decadent Ecology in British Literature and Art, 1860–1910: Decay, Desire, and the Pagan Revival* (Oxford: Oxford University Press).
Dickens, Charles (1998) [1840–1] *The Old Curiosity Shop*, ed. Elizabeth M. Brennan (Oxford: Oxford University Press).
Ellmann, Richard (1997) *Oscar Wilde* (Harmondsworth: Penguin).
Hamilton, Elizabeth (1818) *Letters on the Elementary Principles of Education*, 6th edn (London: Baldwin, Cradock and Joy).
Hayden, Francis Seymour (1875) *Earth to Earth: A Plea for a Change of System in Our Burial of the Dead* (London: Macmillan).
Hood, Thomas (1846) [1831] 'The Death Bed', in *Poems*, vol. 2 (London: Edward Moxon), p. 3.
Hotz, Mary Elizabeth (2009) *Literary Remains: Representations of Death and Burial in Victorian England* (Albany: State University of New York Press).
Jalland, Pat (1996) *Death in the Victorian Family* (Oxford: Oxford University Press).
Lacquer, Thomas (2015) *The Work of the Dead: A Cultural History of Mortal Remains* (Princeton: Princeton University Press).
Lawrence, D. H. (2002) 'To Arthur MacLeod, 5 December 1910', in James T. Boulton (ed.) *The Letters of D. H. Lawrence*, vol. 1. (Cambridge: Cambridge University Press), pp. 192–4.
Locke, John (1700) *An Essay Concerning Human Understanding* 4th edn (London: no publisher).
Loudon, John Claudius (1843) *On the Laying Out, Planting, and Managing of Cemeteries and on the Improvement of Churchyards* (London: Longman, Brown, Green, and Longmans).
Luckhurst, Roger (2021) 'The Necropolitan Gothic', in Clive Bloom (ed.) *The Palgrave Handbook of Gothic Origins* (Cham: Palgrave Macmillan), pp. 263–80.
Lutz, Deborah (2015) *Relics of Death in Victorian Literature and Culture* (Cambridge: Cambridge University Press).
McAleavey, Maia (2011) 'The Discipline of Tears in *The Old Curiosity Shop*', *Dickens Studies Annual*, 42, pp. 123–41.
Miller, John MacNeill (2017) 'Composing Decomposition: *In Memoriam* and the Ecocritical Undertaking', *Nineteenth-Century Contexts*, 39:5, 383–98.
Mudford, William (1841) 'Cemeteries and Churchyards – A Visit to Kensal Green', *Bentley's Miscellany*, 9, p. 92.
Porter, Laurence M. (1997) 'Decadence and the *fin-de-siècle* Novel', in Timothy Unwin (ed.), *The Cambridge Companion to the French Novel: From 1800 to the Present* (Cambridge: Cambridge University Press), pp. 93–110.
Shapira, Yael (2018) *Inventing the Gothic Corpse: The Thrill of Human Remains in the Eighteenth-Century Novel* (Cham: Palgrave Macmillan).
Smith, Andrew (2012) 'Victorian Gothic Death', in Clive. Bloom (ed.) *The Victorian Gothic: An Edinburgh Companion* (Edinburgh: Edinburgh University Press), pp. 156–69.

Sowerby, Stephen (2021) 'Victorian Gardens of Death', in Clive Bloom (ed.) *The Palgrave Handbook of Steam Age Gothic* (Cham: Palgrave Macmillan), pp. 467–508.

Stoker, Bram (1986) [1897] *Dracula*, ed. Roger Luckhurst (Oxford: Oxford University Press).

Story, Joseph (1835) 'Address at the Consecration of Mount Auburn', in *The Miscellaneous Writings: Literary, Critical, Juridical, and Political* (Boston: James Munroe and Company) pp. 88–99.

Strang, John (1831) *Necropolis Glasguensis; with Observations on Ancient and Modern Tombs and Sepulture* (Glasgow: Atkinson and Company).

Taylor, William M. (2018) *The Vital Landscape: Nature and the Built Environment in Nineteenth-Century Britain* (Abingdon: Routledge).

Tennyson, Alfred Lord (2004) [1850] *In Memoriam A. H. H.*, ed. Erik Gray (New York: W. W. Norton).

Townshend, Dale (2019) *Gothic Antiquity: History, Romance, and the Architectural Imagination, 1760–1840* (Oxford: Oxford University Press).

Westmacott, Charles Molloy (1826) *The English Spy*, vol. 2 (London: Sherwood, Gilbert and Piper).

5

Relics and ruins, photographs and fellowship

Corinna Wagner

Up he comes:
raised from his once-watery tomb
a Russian bomber last seen by long-dead witnesses in '45
a comet smashing though the thick ice of the Bzura River,
dry for the first time, this waterless summer.

Up he comes:
this modern-day Lazarus petrified in his sheepskin coat
identified by a muddied weapon engraved with mother tongue,
Cyrillic tomb-script, cuneiform of world war.

Up the river's stem:
Hebrew-tattooed headstones
torn from the soil like gold teeth from wasted jaws
seventy years they shored up the banks of
the once-drowning river.

Up came resurrected bodies, too:
returned, gap-toothed, goldless, into the depths,
foundations for roads and forecourts: we drive
our carts over the bones of the dead.

Up they come again:
those smashed-up tombstones, mislaid stelae
testimony of our amnesia
and of the slow death of our rivers.

'Resurrection', and its accompanying image (Figure 5.1), appeared in a COP27 publication.[1] In the extremely hot and dry European summer of 2015, when rivers were at their lowest levels in recorded history, drought revealed previously submerged graves. Near the site of a major 1939 battle, Poland's Bzura River receded to reveal the unofficial tomb of a Russian pilot, while on the dry banks of the Vistula River fragments of displaced Jewish tombstones appeared. These newly visible, provisional 'graveyards' present us with hard truths about the costs of conflict as well as provide

Figure 5.1 Corinna Wagner, *Resurrection* (2022). (Copyright © Corinna Wagner.)

visible evidence of climate change and environmental degradation. I take 'Resurrection', with its returns and resurrections, bodies and stones, relics and ruins, as a point of departure for this chapter.

We live in spectral times, an age of 'fearsome chiaroscuro', to borrow Jerry Hogle's phrase (2014: 5); so too did our nineteenth-century ancestors. Their partiality for Gothic literature, revivalist architecture, medievalist political and religious narrative attest to this, as does the Victorian fascination with both the myth of the 'Dark Ages' and the celebration of the chivalry and liberty of the Middle Ages. In a modernising age, the darkness of conflict, blackened industrial landscapes and shadowy slums threatened the 'light' of progress, order and advancement. At the same time, progress showed itself to be a destructive force. In the name of progress, Victorian 'improvers' co-opted, sanitised, knocked down and put up false ruins. The resulting disillusion and disenchantment fired *Ruinenlust*. The writers I look at here argued against progressive attempts to gentrify, to 'bury the past' by eradicating it or denying living history by preserving, sanitising or renovating it.

This chapter argues that Gothic graveyards, in particular, are anything but inert spaces filled with static markers – stone stelae – that characterise a benign relationship with the dead and the past. Rather, Gothic graveyards are and should be organic, living repositories, characterised, positively, by impermanence and slow ruin. Thus, efforts to preserve, conserve and renovate can, paradoxically, disrupt important individual and communal connections with the dead. To erase or destroy those spaces, with their ruins and relics, is to effectively erase or destroy important social and cultural bonds.

I began this chapter in the present day. I track back to the nineteenth century and forward to the twentieth. This comparative view reveals how *Ruinenlust* emerges as protest against a modernity that would deny or obscure the past by destroying the ruinous remnants of history. In recent decades, transformations of built and natural environments have roused what Patrick Wright terms a 'New Gothic sensibility', a new love of decay (in Seale, 2010). The Victorians had their destructive improvers; the late twentieth and early twenty-first century has commercial developers and a gentrifying heritage industry. Ruins are as endemic to the modern as Gothic. It therefore makes sense that both would inhabit a wide variety of texts, including the less conventionally Gothic genres of memoir and non-fiction. I explore these types of texts here. This chapter examines how, at specific historical moments, graveyard ruins and relics – official and unofficial, textual and visual, material and imaginative – facilitated certain kinds of vital encounters between the dead and the living.

Body as relic

According to Michel Foucault, when graveyards moved from 'the sacred and immortal heart of the city' to the 'other city' of the planned suburban cemetery in the nineteenth century, public attention focused on 'the dead body' (1986: 25). This is right – if Foucault's dead body is the polluting, risky body, as described by health officials and which resulted in mid-century graveyard clearances, sanitation movements and materialist views of the body that culminated in the 1832 Anatomy Act. But before this, much attention had focused on the *sacred* dead body. Through the ages, the living had a celebratory, mystical and tactile relationship with the dead. There were, for instance, the extravagantly bejewelled skeletons of the catacomb saints of Germany or Rome; the bodily relics held in little glass caskets in ancient churches; and tens of thousands of detailed, graphic paintings of the tortured bodies of Christ and the saints (now housed in museums and reproduced ad infinitum in the age of mechanical reproduction). Victorian lovers of Gothic ruins looked back to this long history of preserving, collecting and communing with the body as relic, which predates nineteenth-century graveyard clearances. They focussed attention on these dead bodies in order to resurrect a Gothic model of sustained devotion to the relics of the dead, in order to keep the past alive for a modern age.

Thomas Carlyle wrote forcefully and elegiacally about the enduring influence of the medieval relic as a way to rekindle the ritualistic, revered relationship the living once held with the dead. In *Past and Present* (1843), he recounts how, in the twelfth century, a fire at the monastery of Bury St Edmunds had damaged that saint's ancient shrine. Under the instruction of Abbot Samson, repairs were made and the wooden coffin that held St Edmund's body was carefully opened. According to Carlyle, Samson traced with his hands the lineaments of the uncorrupted body through a layer of linen, touching eyes, nose, chest, arms, fingers, feet and toes. To modern readers, this physical intimacy with the dead may appear foreign, primitive and perhaps even repulsive (2005: 121). Yet this story is about how powerfully affective rituals, relics and ruins can inspire the living to take stock of their lives, do great works, reach after ideals and act collectively to reform their society. In cultures as diverse as those of ancient Rome, medieval Northern Europe and the Dutch Golden Age, human remains were preserved as *memento mori* to remind the living of their materiality and eventuality. Carlyle's story about the ancient saint's body prompts readers to also live well in the face of soul-deadening industrialism, a capitalist system that turned bodies into labouring machines and a materialism that devalued human life.

Although a utilitarian advocate for the Anatomy Act, Jeremy Bentham shared with Carlyle a desire to devise rational and dignified ways of dealing with the material realities of death and of publicly commemorating them in ways that might stimulate social improvement. The public dissection and preservation of his own body was a posthumous demonstration of how new relics could best serve modern society (Bentham, 2002: 2). An 'auto-icon', Bentham's preserved body is a democratised, secular version of the holy relic or saint's body; it is Carlyle's uncorrupted and incorruptible Saint Edmund revisioned for nineteenth-century citizens. The auto-icon, surrounded, as Bentham suggests, by a small library, a modest archive of personal items, and a characterful monument, could become the destination of a modern form of medieval pilgrimage.

Personal relics and wooden crosses

In 1809, William Godwin had also suggested the idea of pilgrimage in his *Essay on Sepulchres*. Living generations might journey to the simply marked places of internment in order to properly 'speak' to the dead, whether departed friends or public figures like, Godwin fittingly suggests, Jeremy

Bentham, or even fictional characters such as Samuel Richardson's tragic heroine Clarissa Harlowe. Importantly, pilgrimage and communion provided the living with an opportunity to right the wrongs of history; so, for instance, moderns could visit the graves of women whose voices had been unheard, their accomplishments overlooked and desires thwarted in a male-dominated world.

By turns an elegy to friendship, a study of the psychological theory of associationism, a work of mourning and a meditation on how the dead might ameliorate present society, Godwin's *Essay on Sepulchres* is also 'necromantic'. It is, Paul Westover argues, part of the early nineteenth-century trend to 'route' modern anxieties through the relics and ruins of the dead (2012: 49). Godwin was anxious that moderns who no longer communed with the dead were suffering from an abject 'failure of cultural memory' (Westover, 2012: 1). The sacking of sacred burial sites and the deep religious upheaval of the Reformation had severed ties with the dead; now, nineteenth-century citizens were in danger of repeating history. Godwin's brand of necromanticism, or what David McAllister describes as a 'consequentialist ethics of burial' (2018: 92), sets a groundwork for thinking about the role of emotion in dealing with the dead in the face of modern political upheaval. Godwin identifies the kinds of objects, spaces, designs and buildings that would allow 'some spirit' to 'escape' from remains to 'whisper' to the living, inspiring in them 'things unfelt before' (1809: 77). Since affective responses are dependent 'upon the operations of sense', then we must be in the actual places where people lived and died (1809: 66). A person's virtues and actions are inseparable from their physical body, and our feelings for them are connected to their homes and possessions (a ring, watch or book, for instance). Since things have such a hold on our minds and emotions, they act as hearing aids through which we tune in to the voices of the departed.

As for monuments to the dead, Godwin is pulled between permanence and impermanence, between preservation and inevitable ruin. On the one hand, ancient ruins are, as he discovered, the means of understanding history and its values. 'The annals of chivalry', the cultural origins of courage and justice, were only revealed on a visit to the ruins of Kenilworth Castle, the living rooms of the Normans and Tudors, and the site of sieges and royal receptions (1809: 71). On the other hand, since neglect and vandalism, which turn monuments into 'a heap of ruins, even before they are fifty years old', seem to be 'characteristic of the human species', Godwin recommends as grave markers cheap wooden crosses that could easily be replaced or simply left to dwindle away (1809: 53, 90–103).

Today, people around the globe adopt rituals not so unlike those Godwin proposes. The simplicity and impermanence of wooden crosses suit them to memorials that mark the place of fatal roadside accidents or seaside suicides (Figures 5.2 and 5.3). For many (but not all), the cross as roadside

Figure 5.2 Corinna Wagner, *Roadside Memorial* (2021).
(Copyright © Corinna Wagner.)

marker is largely unmoored from its religious significance (as it may have been for the atheistic or at least agnostic Godwin). In countries where they are common and becoming more so – the Americas, Australia and some European nations – they are individualised with photographs, toys, sporting equipment and jerseys, poetry and personal messages. They are not without controversy. In Britain, for example, Surrey County Council describes them as hazardous clutter and a road safety risk; it insists that there is no 'deep

Figure 5.3 Corinna Wagner, *Seaside Memorial* (2020).
(Copyright © Corinna Wagner.)

cultural reason' to support a 'practice' that may also be seen as 'maudlin and unhealthy' (2015). But there are deep cultural reasons for their existence, very much concerned with health and well-being. Roadside memorials are place-specific familial and communal places of mourning and healing, sites of pilgrimage that share stories with passing motorists and walkers. Bereft families often make a concerted effort to care for the living by posting warnings about road safety or offering help for those contemplating suicide. The memorial in Figure 5.4, for example, has a handwritten note ('It won't feel like this forever') that offers contact details for mental health services. So, the simple, ephemeral wooden cross marks the spot of fellowship between living and dead, intimates and strangers.

In her study of a 600 km road in Australia, Donna Lee Brien characterises roadside memorials as Gothic commemorations that 'animate highways as Gothic landscapes' (2014). They could be said to embody what Dale Townshend describes as a 'dreadful sublimity' not unlike the feeling that Gothic architectural ruins inspired in antiquarian tourists in the eighteenth century (2019: 2). Today's uncanny, enigmatically spectral road- or seaside shrines are ephemeral and architectural, as well as textual. We could also classify them as one of Jodey Castricano's 'phantom' texts, which contain what they call, with reference to the work of psychoanalysts Nicolas Abraham and Maria Torok, 'the buried speech of another' (2003: 11). Or we

Figure 5.4 Corinna Wagner, *Shout* (2020). (Copyright © Corinna Wagner.)

could see them as one of Lorna Piatti-Farnell's 'encrypted passageway[s] through which the dead re-join the living in a responsive cycle of exchange and experience' (2013). Whatever terms we use to describe them, these impermanent memorials are responsive caches of ever-changing words and things. In a perpetual state of slow ruin, they are sun-scorched, wind-blown, coated with prairie dust and pelted with rain.

A century after Godwin's musings about wooden crosses, Thomas Hardy would also consider the simple, ephemeral cross. As an architect and, regrettably, a one-time church restorer and clearer of the Old St Pancras churchyard, Hardy was keenly aware of how the will for permanence came up against the reality of impermanence. He was also cognisant, as Godwin was, of a human compulsion to destroy, which is why satire so often rubs along with seriousness in his graveyard poems and commentaries.

Nearing his eighth decade in 1919, Hardy visited the Stinsford, Dorset, churchyard where his relatives and first wife Emma were buried. He and his friend Elliott Felkin looked at a pile of displaced stone tablets, victims of church renovation. Felkin recalled how, stopping in front of Emma's grave, Hardy had offered a somewhat confusing recommendation. If Felkin wanted 'to put up a tomb that ... won't be much cared for' in years to come, he should have a substantial one like Emma's (which was an elaborate coffin-shaped, body-length affair). By contrast, 'a cross, which falls over and has bad lettering,' Hardy continued, wryly, 'will last for hundreds of years' (quoted in Ray, 2007: 208). The then unmarried Elkin thought Hardy was somehow referring to his bachelorhood and lack of children. Subsequent readers have interpreted these types of comments as evidence of Hardy's advocacy of conservation against human neglect, vandalism and natural decay ('rain on a gravestone ... perturbs Hardy', as one critic puts it (Charlwood, 2017: 23)). I would offer that we should see Hardy as an advocate of 'slow ruin'. Without question, improvers, restorers and clearers of graveyards were destructive, rationalising, de-Gothicising. But, rain, natural decay and fallen crosses were part of organic relationships between the living and the dead, part of slow ruin in Gothic graveyards which were the centre of communities.

Hardy's poem 'The Obliterate Tomb' (c.1914) was likely written on the occasion of another graveyard visit, this time to Plymouth where Emma Gifford Hardy's family are buried. There he observed more mutilation of memorial stones and tombs in the name of restoration. The poem contrasts the slow ruin of tombstones, 'untouched, untended, crumbling, weather-stained', with the modern compulsion to improve (1987: 105). As Godwin observed, the living are indifferent: the poem is about descendants who intend to restore family tombs but never get around to it. But in a sense, that is fine, for half-effaced stones inspire visitors to use their imagination to fill in blanks, to wonder, to ask questions, to commune. Half-effaced inscriptions, faded photographs and broken stones are reparative fragments with a transformative power. This is impossible, however, when church restorers have 'scraped each wall / Pulled out the stately pews', and used stones for a broadened path (1987: 105).

A visit to the graveyard at Wimborne Minster, Dorset, in the 1880s prompted Hardy to write another graveyard poem. In 'The Levelled Churchyard' (1882), dead bodies are 'mixed to human jam' by renovators and their voices 'stifled' in a 'jumbled patch / Of wrenched memorial stones' repurposed as paving stones for 'some path or p---ing place' (1982: 196–7). In yet another poem, 'In the Cemetery' (1911), women fight over graves where their dead children were dumped 'at different times, like sprats in a tin'. Little do they know that the ground has been secretly cleared and their children's remains removed to make way for a drainpipe (1987: 143). Then, in the 1895 preface to his 1873 novel *A Pair of Blue Eyes*, Hardy offers a meditation on slow ruin and the interconnectedness of the built and natural environments. The novella was written in 'a time when the craze for indiscriminate church-restoration had just reached the remotest nooks' of Cornwall, a place 'where the wild and tragic features of the coast had long combined in perfect harmony with the crude Gothic Art of the ecclesiastical buildings' (Hardy, 1985: 3). Architectural ruins were as integral to place as the natural landscape. Attempts 'to restore the grey carcases [sic] of mediaevalism' were as destructive to land, society and cultural life as some sort of mad attempt to 'renovat[e] the adjoining crags themselves' (1985: 3).

For Hardy, modernity, capital and progress result in bodily and social dislocation. To sever headstones from burial sites and remains from their local soil is to sever citizens from their communities and their own history. Flattening ruins or conserving them meaninglessly damaged hearts and souls as much as forcing natural environments into unnatural forms. St Pancras's Hardy Tree – part nature, part culture – has stood for decades as testimony to the collateral damage of unsympathetic renovation in the name of progress (Figure 5.5). The legend holds that in the 1860s, when Hardy was a young architect clearing the Old St Pancras churchyard to make way for the Midland Railway Company, he hemmed the ash tree with a fan of dislodged headstones. It hardly matters whether the tree predated Hardy or came later as some people maintain. What matters is that for at least a century it has been an emblem of competing values in the nineteenth century and in our own. On the one side, progress, capital and the commodification of space; on the other, collective memory, national heritage and accumulated history. As I revise this chapter, however, the Hardy Tree has collapsed. No longer a living relic, it has become part of collective memory and the organic life of the Gothic graveyard. It is, by nature, an impermanent thing.

The Hardy Tree withstood World War II bombing, which made fast ruins of the buildings in surrounding neighbourhoods. Fast ruination is accelerated by environmental disaster, violence and conflict, by modern speed rather than neglect. An astute observer of ruin, Walter Benjamin identified nineteenth-century origins for some of the traumas – and the fast ruins – of the twentieth century. Under the banner of hygiene and health, renovation and modernisation, nineteenth-century Europeans had cast the dead from 'the perceptual world of the living' (2007: 94). For the first time in their long histories, they lived in rooms untouched by death. This was, effectively, to live without storytelling, since, at the moment of their death, loved ones transmitted a whole life of experiences – the very 'stuff that stories are made of' – to the living. In rooms where they had lived and now passed on, surrounded by their things, stories took on 'transmissible form' (2007: 94). Collective, connective stories passed from bodies via things and words through space. This intergenerational and collective wisdom would have contributed to prevent the kinds of unspeakable violence and tragic events of the 1940s. Like Hardy, Benjamin makes a case for another type of slow ruin.

Figure 5.5 Corinna Wagner, *Hardy Tree* (2022). (Copyright © Corinna Wagner.)

In recent years, a number of cultural geographers have extoled 'slow ruin' and urged us to reconsider our compulsion to renovate, conserve and halt decline at all costs. They have done so, like Bentham, Hardy and Benjamin, in response to sociocultural and environmental realities. Ruins can play an important cultural role in a future challenged by climate change and environmental disaster. Making a case against 'the ruination of the ruin', Caitlin DeSilvey argues that 'the disintegration of structural integrity does not necessarily lead to the evacuation of meaning; processes of decay and disintegration can be culturally (as well as ecologically) productive; and, in certain contexts, it is possible to look beyond loss to conceive other ways of understanding and acknowledging material change' (2017: 93, 5). Entangled materialities, unions of nature and culture, places of reflection, memory, imagination and reconsideration, ruins – along with their bodily counterparts, relics – are spurs to important conversations and actions.

Gothic graveyards are repositories of all these things. They are spaces of individual and collective histories that encourage us to consider – often deeply – how the past might be recruited to shape different futures. The transmission between the living and dead is so critical because the dead have the power to guide us, or as Hardy put it, to change our 'view of things' (1987: 287). The bodies of the dead speak of a lifetime of stories, tragic and joyous, mundane and heroic. The living may choose to follow in the footsteps of their precursors and honour tradition. Or they may alter their path and adopt new rituals, new ways of living. Either way, ruins and relics can only become part of life if they are allowed to … live. This means simply letting them be.

Photography as relic and ruin

From its invention in the mid nineteenth century, photography became and has remained intimately connected to death, grave sites and ruins. Photography has also been a tool of preservation and conservation, of documenting Gothic buildings and spaces. In 1875, the photographers who recorded the 'death' of medieval buildings due to urban redevelopment called themselves The Society for Photographing Relics of Old London. In 1859, the year photography was admitted to the Paris Salon, Louis Figuier observed that almost as soon as photographers understood 'the practical processes of photography on paper', they captured images of ruins across the globe (in Benjamin, 1999: 684). That same year, Baudelaire admitted that although photography could not replace arts like painting, it could 'rescue from oblivion those tumbling ruins' and 'precious things whose form is dissolving and which demand a place in the archives of our memory' (1999: 692).

Almost as quickly as photography became connected to architectural ruin, it became intimately connected to the body. For nineteenth-century mourners, photography was the new means of holding on to the dead, of keeping something of their body present. According to Deborah Lutz, the photograph replaced the relic in the mid nineteenth century (2011), but I would say rather that it *became* the new relic. Photographic paper supplanted biological material. Like bodily relics such as the preserved fingers of medieval saints, Bentham's auto-icon or Victorian hair jewellery, photographs are always at once real and symbolic, material and metaphysical.

And like bodily relics, photographs evoke presence; they comfort, spur memory and wound deeply – as Roland Barthes found when he looked in photographs for a 'living resurrection of the beloved face' of his dead mother (1980: 64).

It makes sense, then, that photographs would appear as portraits on gravestones. In nineteenth-century France, Italy, Eastern Europe, and Latin and North America, daguerreotypes, ambrotypes, tintypes and then ceramic or porcelain photographic portraits, round or oval, were embedded in marble or stone and sometimes covered with a metal lid. Much more often, they were entombed in glass, like the one pictured below (Figure 5.6). This one decorates the grave of the grandmother of the American poet Robert Pinsky. She was born Rose Schacter in Europe in 1896 or 1897 and died Rose Pinsky some twenty-seven years later at Long Branch, New Jersey.[2] In the 1920s, Rose's husband, a bootlegger, tavern owner and sometime gangster, had erected an elaborate tree-themed headstone ('a little vulgar' is how his grandson describes it) (Pinsky, 1996: 4). As a child, Robert Pinsky would visit the family plot in Long Branch, each time leaving a customary pebble on Rose's grave. Although he never knew her, he was drawn to the oval portrait of the fine-featured, 'animated', mischievous-looking face, which year on year remained 'clear and sharp' under its thick protective glass (1996: 4). The photograph made her tangible, so that Robert could imagine her personality and a lifetime of stories.

I will return to Pinsky and Rose in a moment, but first let me push the body-photograph-relic relationship further. Earlier I said that photographs did not *replace* relics in the nineteenth century but rather became the new relics – so intimate was the connection between photograph and body. We can see this conflation clearly in Hardy's poem 'The Photograph' (1917). In it, a man clears out the cupboards and finds an old photographic portrait of a long-lost lover. He decides to burn it, but finds he can hardly stand to watch the flames consume her body and face and hair. The fire does not so much consume the photograph as the woman's physical body. While she is put 'to death', all that remains is the 'ashen ghost' of the photographic card (1987: 207–8). The photographic portrait is the body's double, an uncanny copy of the real. The photograph is ghostly, a spectral presence that hovers about the subject and outlives her. Always 'latent', the photographic portrait is, to use French photographer Hervé Guibert's phrase, a 'ghost image' (2014: 56). And, like bodies, the photograph-as-relic maintains a materiality, a corporeality, which makes it prey to decay and ruin, sometimes fast, as in Hardy's poem, and sometimes slow.

If I can indulge this thinking further, let me bring Guibert's short autofictional essay 'The Cancerous Image' into the mix. From his collection *Ghost Image* (1981), Guibert/the narrator forms an intimate and fetishistic

Figure 5.6 Corinna Wagner, *Grave of Rose Pinsky* (2022). (Copyright © Corinna Wagner.)

relationship with a photograph. Guibert first spies the photograph of an unknown leather-jacketed teenage boy at the apartment of an unnamed older man. Profoundly attracted to something in the posture, clothing, appearance and expression of the subject, Guibert steals the photograph. He keeps it under his armpit for days. Eventually, it gets soiled, comes away from its backing, discolours and becomes pitted, so as to appear 'cancerous'. Guibert knows it could be repaired or re-photographed but prefers to let it/him decay, to watch how the surface grows scales and splits so that the youth's face appears syphilitic. This slow ruin of face and body is part of the fantasy of the photograph. Guibert considers speeding up the process by poking holes and applying acids to it (fast ruin), but decides instead to attach the photograph to his torso with bandage and tape. Life carries on. He sweats. He sleeps. And the photograph softens and sticks, so that when he finally removes it, the backing paper comes away, leaving the image stuck to his skin as a tattoo of 'chemical pigments' (Guibert, 2014: 158).

The hallmarks of Gothic are here. The photograph is a relic of a boy that is 'dead' because unmet, unknown, existing only as spectral image; yet, the photograph-boy is companion, brother, conjoined twin ('he was my heteradelphus'). The photographic paper is second skin; it quite literally inhabits the body, fuses with skin and psyche. The photograph dies, too, and becomes buried in Guibert's torso. But as with graveyard ruins, the slow ruin of the photograph is also redemptive. Guibert negotiates his own dis-ease, comes to know himself through its destruction. It 'saved him', he writes, from his own unspecified 'illness' – the ambiguous 'him' here referring at once to the boy, to the photograph and to himself-the-narrator (2014: 158). I may seem to have veered off from Victorian graveyards, but Guibert's is a pertinent meditation on the intense intimacy between body, death, ruin and the photograph-as-relic.[3]

Destructive ruin

To return to Robert Pinsky in the graveyard: there came a time when vandals struck the Jewish cemetery where grandmother Rose was buried. Soon after, Robert returned to Long Branch for a family funeral and he visited her grave to assess the damage. To his relief, it was minimal, though a blow from a tire-iron or hammer had left a small white streak across Rose's photograph. Pinsky imagines the perpetrators who, according to statistics, were likely a small pack of young males. In that moment of imagining, he thinks, too, of a seventeenth-century poem he knows by heart and which he often recites, particularly in anxious times: George Herbert's 'Church-monuments' (1633).

Herbert's spectre is meaningful enough that it becomes part of Pinsky's own poem about the vandalism. 'Desecration of the Gravestone of Rose P. (1897–1924)', subtitled 'Antiphony with "Church Monuments" by George Herbert', is not only a sandwiching of the two poets' words, past and present, but also the imagined words of the vandals. High on bravado, testosterone and beer, Pinsky's boys speak:

> ... We thought ourselves evil, and,
> To prove it in our own eyes we four striplings
> Ventured long off to the boneyard October night.
>
> Drives all at last with lights, brews, hammers, crowbars,
> Long-handled shovel, Exhalation, male
> Exhilaration, primate packing out
> Under clear autumn Zodiac with dead
>
> To desecrate.
>
> (Pinsky, 1996: 5)

And then, seamlessly, Herbert's words, which are the imagined words of the dead in a medieval churchyard, slide into 'Desecration of the Gravestone of Rose P.'. Herbert's censure of those who overlook gravestones and take no notice of the dead:

> These laugh at Jet and Marble put for signs,
> To sever the good fellowship of dust,
> And spoil the meetings.
>
> (2016: 42)

becomes:

> Into the space, team cursels and gigging, shoves,
> Shovelblade under a graven toppling. These laugh
> At jet and marble put for signs, To sever
> The good fellowship of dust, And spoil the meeting.
>
> (Pinsky, 1996: 5)

The severing of fellowship between living and dead is most acute when the boys turn to the photographs, to 'the striking of oval portraits' on the gravestones:

> Photographs from the nineteenteens and so on
> Well sealed in domes of thick defiant glass
> Banged with a hammer. Glancing off cheekbone and gaze,
> Cracked gaze, glance clouding white time's bleach. Crazed glass.
>
> (1996: 5)

Is this random mindless vandalism? Is it racially or religiously motivated? Why damage the photographs in particular? We might expect such questions and the expression of rage or sadness in Pinsky's poem.

But no. Instead of questions and condemnation, Pinsky offers an elegy to destructive ruin, which is as much a part of communing with the dead as seventeenth-century metaphysical poetry. This is youthful disaffection, rebellion that flies in the face of order, and rite-of-passage vandalism is as ritualistic and as meaningful here as the funeral, the burial, the headstone and the photograph. As the defaced ghost image of an unknown subject offers Guibert solace, so the damaged photograph of an unmet grandmother offers Pinsky a form of redemption. In the old graveyard, with its jumble of languages and narratives, the site/sight/insight of the 'ruined' image facilitates fellowship between a living twentieth-century American poet, a long-dead seventeenth-century Welsh poet, a more recently dead nineteenth-century emigrant grandmother *and* twentieth-century hooligans who we suppose are very much alive. None of these people will ever meet physically, but they do commune in Pinsky's imagination.

In a gloss to the poem, Pinsky describes his thrill at the idea that Rose could 'somehow' have known Herbert's poem and that they could somehow unite together in the 'conspiratorial laughter of the male pack' (1996: 4). Pinsky thrills, too, at joyfully joining in, via 'a spirit of anarchic truth', with all of them – the hooligans, Herbert and Rose. They would share 'in the insight that grief, though ineluctable, is foolish', whether that be 'grief for the body, or for the body's representation in a photograph' or in the 'symbolic stone tree' of the headstone (1996: 4–5). And, all of these people, dead and alive, known and unknown, were joined by language. Words, like photographs, are relics of a sort. Certainly, words inscribed on stone, but also stories passed down through the generations, as well as elegiac poetry, are textual relics. Poetry is ballast against foolish grief or anger. Poetry is part of 'art's babble' against a too great 'attachment to matter', Pinsky writes, though is quick to add that art's babble is necessarily 'accomplished in matter, in the human body that breathes these words' (1996: 5). All of this offers a remarkably joyful communion of image and body, ruin and relic, destruction and philosophy, intimates and strangers, language and action, and, most of all, dead and living. Communion needs the space of the graveyard.

I end with two historical bookends for the nineteenth century: the seventeenth and the late twentieth centuries. In this I take an example from the Victorians. They looked back to the Gothic Middle Ages and brought that past forward not only into the present but also the future, as in William Morris's *News from Nowhere* (1890). Pinsky has written of his love of Herbert's verb 'intomb', as in the lines: 'Here I intomb my flesh, that it betimes / May take acquaintance of this heap of dust' (2009). 'Intomb' is the act of going amongst old graves that are, like the body and all material things, in the process of decay. It could be said that this chapter has been about intombing; about fellowship that requires being in the space of the dead, and going among their material remains. Carlyle's medieval saint's body, Godwin's sepulchres, Hardy's old Cornish graveyards, Pinsky's New World Jewish cemetery and modern roadside memorial sites: all obviously different but Gothic spaces nonetheless. Repositories of memory and story, they are also places of meditation and learning. Hardy's Cornish graveyards encourage community and a respect for environment. Pinsky's damaged photograph of the 'nineteenteens' inspires tolerance and acceptance. And, in 2015, broken Jewish tombstones on dry riverbanks and revealed resting places of young pilots testify about prejudice and war. The mere fact that they surfaced, seventy years after their 'burial', bears witness to the devastation of climate change. They confront us; they prevail upon us to stand for peace, to agitate against authoritarianism and to act now on environmental degradation.

Notes

1 'COP27' was the acronym used to refer to the 2022 United Nations Climate Change Conference.
2 Rose's dates are a little vague here: the gravestone reads 1923, but Pinsky's poem on the subject dates her death as 1924.
3 Another essay in the collection is titled 'The Photograph, as Close to Death as Possible'.

References

Barthes, Roland (1980) *Camera Lucida*, trans. Richard Howard (New York: Vintage).
Benjamin, Walter (1999) [1982] *The Arcades Project*, trans. Howard Eiland and Kevin McLaughlin (Cambridge: Belknap Press of Harvard University Press).
Benjamin, Walter (2007) [1968] *Illuminations: Essays and Reflections*, trans. Harry Zohn (New York: Schocken).
Bentham, Jeremy (2002) [1832] *Bentham's Auto-Icon and Related Writings* (Bristol: Thoemmes Press).
Brien, Donna Lee (2014) 'Forging Continuing Bonds from the Dead to the Living: Gothic Commemorative Practices along Australia's Leichhardt Highway', *M/C Journal*, 17:4, https://doi.org/10.5204/mcj.858.
Carlyle, Thomas, *Past and Present* (2005) [1843], ed. Chris Vanden Bossche (Berkeley: University of California Press).
Castricano, Jodey (2003) *Cryptomimesis: The Gothic and Jacques Derrida's Ghost Writing* (Montreal: McGill-Queen's University Press).
Charlwood, Catherine (2017) 'What Profit?': The Morality of Mourning and Remembering in Hardy's Verse', The Thomas Hardy Journal, 33 (Winter), 14–32.
DeSilvey, Caitlin (2017) *Curated Decay: Heritage Beyond Saving* (Minneapolis: University of Minnesota Press).

Foucault, Michel (1986) [1967] 'Of Other Spaces', trans. Jay Miskowiec, *Diacritics* 16:1, 22–7.
Godwin, William (1809) *Essay on Sepulchres* (London: W. Miller).
Guibert, Hervé (2014) [1981] *Ghost Image*, trans. Robert Bononno (Chicago: University of Chicago Press).
Hardy, Thomas (1982) [1882] 'The Levelled Churchyard', in *The Complete Poetical Works of Thomas Hardy*, ed. Samuel Hynes, vol. 1 (Oxford: Oxford University Press), pp. 196–7.
Hardy, Thomas (1985) [1873] *A Pair of Blue Eyes*, ed. Alan Manford (Oxford: Oxford University Press).
Hardy, Thomas (1987) *The Complete Poetical Works of Thomas Hardy*, ed. Samuel Hynes, vol. 2 (Oxford: Oxford University Press).
Herbert, George (2016) [1633] 'Church-monuments', in *George Herbert: 100 Poems*, ed. H. Wilcox (Cambridge: Cambridge University Press), p. 42.
Hogle, Jerrold E. (2014) 'Introduction: Modernity and the Proliferation of the Gothic', in *The Cambridge Companion to Modern Gothic* (Cambridge: Cambridge University Press), pp. 3–19.
Lutz, Deborah (2011) 'The Dead Still Among Us: Victorian Secular Relics, Hair Jewelry, and Death Culture', *Victorian Literature and Culture* 39:1, 127–42.
McAllister, David (2018) *Imagining the Dead in British Literature and Culture, 1790–1848* (Basingstoke: Palgrave Macmillan).
Piatti-Farnell, Lorna (2013) 'Words from the Culinary Crypt: Reading the Cookbook as a Haunted/Haunting Text', *M/C Journal*, 16:3, https://doi.org/10.5204/mcj.640.
Pinsky, Robert (1996) 'Desecration of the Gravestone of Rose P. (1897–1924)', *The Three Penny Review* 64 (Winter), 4–5.
Pinsky, Robert (2009) 'Golden Grammar: The Unexpected Pleasures of George Herbert's Sentences', *Slate*, 1 September, www.slate.com/articles/arts/poem/2009/09/golden_grammar.html (accessed 18 April 2023).
Ray, Martin (2007) *Thomas Hardy Remembered* (Abingdon: Ashgate).
Seale, Kirsten (2010) 'Review of Patrick Wright, *A Journey Through Ruins: The Last Days of London*', *Literary London: Interdisciplinary Studies in the Representation of London*, 8:1, www.literarylondon.org/london-journal/march2010/seale.html (accessed 18 April 2023).
Surrey County Council (2015) 'Roadside Memorials', www.surreycc.gov.uk/roads-and-transport/policies-plans-consultations/policies-and-plans/traffic-policy-and-good-practice/roadside-memorials (accessed 8 November 2023).
Townshend, Dale (2019) *Gothic Antiquity: History, Romance, and the Architectural Imagination, 1760–1840* (Oxford: Oxford University Press).
Westover, Paul (2012) *Necromanticism: Traveling to Meet the Dead, 1750–1860* (Basingstoke: Palgrave).

6

The colonial Australian Gothic and the grave

Ken Gelder

This chapter looks at colonial grave sites and – to a degree – the question of memorialisation in Australia. The colonial grave sites of settlers and Aboriginal people have, of course, been memorialised in radically different ways. They might both be a consequence of the so-called frontier wars in the Australian colonies, but the way grave sites are recognised and commemorated is entirely to do with who was killed and under what circumstances, what was known about the event and the participants, and where their grave sites might actually be (which is not always clear or accurate). It is worth noting here that the contemporary recognition of Aboriginal grave sites on the frontier is increasing – slowly, perhaps – and the question of their memorialisation has lately been much considered. The relatively new digital archive *Colonial Frontier Massacres in Australia, 1788–1930*, produced by researchers at the University of Newcastle, chronicles sites across the country where significant numbers of Aboriginal people were killed by settlers from the earliest days of colonisation, giving us a sense of the enormity and persistence of the killings and raising the question of how these killings might be memorialised today.[1] When a massacre site becomes a memorial site, it can also become a place of repatriation and help towards reconciliation and a fuller, truer understanding of the sheer scale of colonial violence on the frontier. More inclusive forms of commemoration – if we think, for example, about recent calls to include the names of more Aboriginal soldiers killed abroad in the commemorative parts of Australia's war memorials – are also sometimes cast as forms of reconciliation in Australia today (see Torre, 2022). But most war memorials do not recognise the frontier wars and the often large-scale massacres of Aboriginal people during that time. These are, usually, people without names in graves (if they were buried at all) that have been long forgotten.

Settler graves and memorialisation

Let us begin, however, by looking at early settler grave sites in Australia. The historian Michael Cathcart was not thinking about Aboriginal people and the frontier wars when he suggested that Australia's sense of itself as a nation has been built around a perennial commemoration of the 'nameless dead'. He was instead thinking of events such as Gallipoli during the Great War. Looking only at non-Aboriginal settlers (and soldiers), Cathcart calls Australia's ongoing commemoration ('We shall remember them') of the otherwise forgotten nameless dead from these wartime events 'necronationalism' (2009: 163). Some dead settlers in colonial Australia, of course, might remain both nameless and *un*commemorated; they have this in common with the many Aboriginal people killed in settler massacres. But settler cemeteries with *named* grave sites were built early on in the first colony. St John's Cemetery in Parramatta opened in 1790, with graves that named and commemorated a significant number of settlers from the First Fleet, among others. Even so, settlers could themselves die violently or unexpectedly, and not only in the frontier wars. Violent settler deaths were an act of *unsettlement* in the midst of colonisation, not least when they happened close to what was soon regarded as home. The shock of recognition of a settler's corpse in the proximity of the colony is a reminder of just how easily and mercilessly death could intervene in colonial life, fracturing it rather than holding it together. In the earliest moments of colonisation, a dead settler might be someone who had in fact tried to leave the colony everyone else had worked so hard to establish. Here is an entry in the *Sydney Gazette* from June 1806:

> Last week a native informed Tarlington, a settler, that the skeleton of a white man, with a musket and tin kettle laying beside him, had been seen under the first ridge of the mountains. The settler accompanied the native, and found the skeleton, &c., as described; the bones of which being very long, leads to a more than probable conjecture, that the remains are those of James Hughes, who absconded from Castle Hill the 15th of February, 1803, in company with 15 others, most of whom had recently arrived in the Hercules, on the ridiculous pretext of finding a road to China, but in reality to commit the most unheard of depradations [sic]: the consequences of which were, that the whole except Hughes were shortly apprehended, and 13 capitally convicted before a Criminal Court, of whom two were executed, and 11 pardoned.
>
> ('Sydney', 1806: 1)

In this account, Hughes is already estranged from the colony whose laws he and others (many convicts attempted similar kinds of escapes) had long since rejected; his unburied corpse, when discovered, is more than three years old. David Carter has suggested that 'stories of dying in the bush and being buried in the earth' are a way of 'claiming possession' of the landscape: 'what better way to fuse identity and place?' (Carter, 2017: 3). But stories of death in the bush can often work in the opposite way, as a means, for example, of suggesting that dead settlers do not always belong where they lie.

A convict like Hughes is literally *out of place* here, a sort of anti-settler. Mary Grimstone's early poem 'On Visiting the Cemetery in Hobart Town' (1826) suggests that even a proper burial in the colonies is nothing more than an indication of just how wide the gap between settler identity and place might be:

> And here like England's exiles! – this wild spot,
> The sad conclusions of their mournful lot!
> Here a true type of all their griefs I find,
> This scene neglected, naked, and unkind.
> Here, as I wander through the weed-grown groves
> Of some, perchance, yet lov'd beyond the waves,
> The splashy waters rise at every tread
> As if the tears of the indignant dead,
> Reproaching with mute eloquence the race,
> That could assign them *such a resting place*.
>
> (Grimstone, 1826: 4, original emphasis)

In this poem, to be buried in the colonies is to be 'neglected' in one sense and identified (and eulogised, commemorated) in another. It is not quite an expression of necronationalism, not so much because these settlers are named but because they are thought to have ended up in a place where they should not be. They have, at best, an abject (or even, in the poem, reproachful, 'indignant') relation to colonisation itself.

To die in the colonies can also mean a body does not remain where it should. An article titled 'Terra Incognita', also published in 1827 (in *The Monthly Magazine* and then in *The Australian*), tells of a new settler who arrives at Sydney Cove and comes to occupy a house once owned by the colony's governor, John Hunter. One of the first things this new settler sees is a gibbet. Nevertheless, he praises the embryonic colony and affirms the value of both colonial development and Indigenous dispossession. But Hunter's house stands near another place of execution and seems to be haunted by the restless ghosts of some lawless marines; it is full of 'mysterious noises, as of skeletons tumbling and scampering about the floor' ('W-- --G', 1827: 256). This is a settlement already haunted by its own dead soldiers. Later, the new settler finds the partially covered grave of an old man on the outskirts of Sydney, 'a gardener, who had there been robbed and murdered, and whose murderer had fairly driven the scull [sic] half way into the ground' (1827: 260). Death seems to be everywhere in this account, which ends with a note on another execution. A murderer is hanged, and his body 'gibbetted'; shortly afterwards, his young son *went alone one night, took it down, and buried it!* (1827: 261, original italics).

This account gives us an early chronicle of a haunted settlement, full of unquiet, uncommemorated settler graves. Not long before – in June or

July 1826 – an ex-convict named Frederick Fisher was murdered. William Worrall was convicted of the murder, but Fisher's body was not found. Namut Gilbert was a Dharug man and an expert tracker; he went down to a creek in Campbelltown with some local police and smelled the water, shoving an iron rod into the ground: 'On drawing out the rod he smelled it also, and then exclaimed that the body of a dead man ... was buried underneath. The earth was removed, and the body of Fisher exposed to view. This evidence was given before the Coroner; and this way, strange as it is, was the way in which the body was discovered' ('Criminal Court', 1826: 3).

The case of Frederick Fisher made its way into early colonial ghost literature. 'The Sprite of the Creek' was a poem published in a short-lived newspaper, *Hill's Life in New South Wales*, in September 1832. The account of Fisher's murder is presented in a faux-Spanish manner, with the wounded ghost of Fisher – now 'Fredro', a bailiff – seen on a bridge by 'Falvonis' ('The Sprite of the Creek', 1832: 4). The 'chieftain' Gilbert finds evidence of the killing in a creek (''Tis fat of the white man') (1832: 4) and soon he uncovers the mangled body. The murderer, 'Wurlow', is arrested and hanged and the 'sprite of the creek' (1832: 4) is finally laid to rest. This is the first attempt to turn the robbery and murder of a law-abiding (or here, law-enforcing) settler into a ghost story. The narrative is then taken up by John Lang, who published his short story 'Fisher's Ghost: A Legend of Campbelltown' in *Tegg's Monthly Magazine* in March 1836. It was reprinted in *The Colonist* later in the same month and hailed as a compelling example of 'a literature of our own' ('Literature and Science', 1836: 86); later on, in 1853, it was published in Dickens's *Household Words* and anthologised as 'The Ghost upon the Rail' in Lang's collection of stories *Botany Bay, or, True Tales of Early Australia* (1859) – where a guilty verdict for Fisher's murderer divides the embryonic colony.

The afterlife of a settler's grave is a familiar trope in colonial Australian writing, and sometimes it works to cohere the colony rather than divide it. Ian Reid has written about 'epitaphic' colonial poetry, beginning with Barron Field's early sonnet in *The Kangaroo and Other Poems* (1823), 'On Visiting the Spot Where Captain Cook and Sir Joseph Banks First Landed in Botany Bay'. Here, the identification of the sailor Forby Sutherland's grave (he died of consumption on 30 April 1770) folds landfall and burial together, as if, under colonisation, the one cannot proceed without the other (Reid, 2002:15–17). This is a kind of prologue to settlement, a commemoration that retrospectively provides settlement with a point of origin in a sailor's grave. In Henry Kendall's poem 'Sutherland's Grave [*The first white man buried in Australia*] (1863), the sailor's burial site is now not only commemorated but sacralised, generating a 'Voice supernal' in the wind above. This is indeed a case of necronationalism that aims to provide both a supernatural and a quotidian foundational image for settler Australian identity (Kendall, 1869: 117). But Reid also discusses the 'remote burial' and the 'lonely grave' in colonial poetry, which often identified nameless, uncommemorated locations outside or beyond the realm of an emerging national consciousness. Kendall's 'A Death in the Bush', for example, eulogises a remote 'shepherd's grave', mourned only by a widow and a 'wild-dog ... howling through the gloom / At hopeless shadows flitting to and fro' (1869: 56). The colonial journalist and politician Thomas McCombie also wrote about forgotten bush graves in *Australian Sketches* (1861), where a cemetery set aside for 'old settlers' during the 1850s gold rush was mostly populated by 'those persons who died without friends or money, the "loafers" of the district', and 'where the unknown and unrecorded dead lie buried' (McCombie, 1861: 175). These are settlers who do not contribute to settlement. For necronationalism to flourish in early Australian writing, the deceased settler had to be much less peripheral to the project of colonial expansion and development.

A contrast to this, as Cathcart notes, are lost explorers (2009: 154). The exploration of Australia's interior was fundamental to the success of settlement; but what if those explorers never returned? In some cases, the bodies of lost explorers were also never found – like the German explorer Ludwig Leichhardt, who disappeared somewhere in the Queensland interior in 1848. George Grey led an expedition into north-west Western Australia in 1837; he went on to become governor of South Australia and, later on, a premier of New Zealand. In his journal of the expedition, he recounts an attack by Aboriginal people where he is speared. Hallucinating and barely conscious, he contemplates his own death and reflects on the deaths of other explorers on the frontier. 'A strange sun shines upon their lonely graves', he writes; 'the foot of the wild man yet roams over them: but let us hope when civilization has spread so far, that their graves will be sacred spots, that the future settlers will sometimes shed a tear over the remains of the first explorer, and tell their children how much they are indebted to the enthusiasm, perseverance, and courage of him who lies buried there' (Grey, 1841: 155). This is an expression of wishful thinking (and potential self-monumentalisation) that imagines dead explorers who are neglected now might be remembered, and memorialised (or sacralised), at some future stage in the ongoing colonial project.

The best-known – and most overwrought – colonial tribute to settler burial is Charles Harpur's 'The Creek of the Four Graves', serialised in the short-lived *Weekly Register of Politics, Facts and General Literature* in August 1845. A group of settlers at some earlier historical moment make their way into the interior looking for land to colonise: these are settler-explorers. One night they camp by a 'nameless creek'. For the poem, these settlers have travelled beyond the frontier and are in a sense already dead and buried, 'laid ... to rest': 'a grave mood ... reached into the night'. A group of local Aboriginal men suddenly spring out of the forest and attack them, chasing one of the would-be settlers, Egremont, into the creek, where he hides and survives. The chase scene owes much to Robert Burns's 'Tam o'Shanter' (1791), with Aboriginal people given a demonic force as they pursue Egremont, who flees for his life. The poem then projects the early settlers' graves into the present day and memorialises them by naming the creek as a settler massacre site, infusing it with a Gothic sensibility:

> Four grassy mounds, stretched lengthwise side by side,
> Startled the wanderer; – four grassy Mounds
> O'erstrown with skeleton boughs and bleaching leaves,
> Stript by each winter winged gale that roamed
> Those solitudes, from the old Trees that there
> Moaned the same leafy dirge that too the heed
> Of dying ages: these were all; and thence
> The place was called, passingly called, the Creek
> Of the Four Graves.
>
> (Harpur, 1845a)

Kenneth Slessor thought Harpur's poem about the violent end of settler life marked nothing less than the beginning of 'the history of Australian poetry' (Slessor, 1970: 71): as if (although Slessor never seemed to read the poem as an act of memorialisation) that history is somehow built upon settler deaths and their graves. But is this poem really about necronationalism? In fact, the name of the grave site is both invoked and already forgotten ('The place was called, passingly called'). The settlers go exploring beyond the frontier because they want to colonise and farm new land; but, as Ivor Indyk notes, the grave in this poem 'stands as a negation of the ideal of pastoral fulfilment' (Indyk, 1993: 842). It is difficult to agree with Elspeth Tilly's point that the poem makes 'a claim to naturalised white belonging through the enactment of white vanishing' (2012: 278). These settlers have not yet settled, and it seems there is little sense of colonial confidence in their undertaking. The only settler other than Egremont to be described in the poem is a man already without hope, a 'vagrant' ('I was never yet happy'). They are in any case either killed or driven out of this place by Aboriginal people who, at this early colonial moment, are still in possession of their land. The murdered settlers are buried in this spot, but the poem does not ever suggest they belong there.

Aboriginal massacre sites and memorialisation

In Henry Knapp's short story 'The Shepherd's Grave', published in the *Australian Journal* in April 1874, some gold prospectors arrive at a place called Murdering Flat, near Ballarat in Victoria. They hear an account from 1849 which tells of the discovery of the body of a shepherd found 'pierced through ... with spears'. The shepherd's brother Hugh rounds up some men and they go out into the night; later on, locals hear that a large number of Aboriginal people – 'twenty males and females' – have 'disappeared'. So Murdering Flat is both the site of a violent settler death and a massacre site that registers large-scale retaliatory killings of Aboriginal people. The story has much in common with Harpur's 'The Creek of the Four Graves' – both return to an earlier historical moment – except for the settler retaliation. Knapp's story ends with a description of two quite different kinds of graves:

> [T]he larger one is in a secluded spot which only a chance traveller passes by; he looks at it, wonders what it is, and how it came there; – that is the burial place of the natives killed by Hugh and his mates ... [T]he other, and smaller mound, is on the verge of some cultivation, and near to a main thoroughfare, on which coaches and carriages pass at every hour of the day, bearing their living freight; a telegraph wire runs along the road, on which sometimes messages flash through Europe. Round this smaller mound children prattle and play as they gather wild flowers, telling each other the story in whispers, and pointing to the grave of the murdered shepherd.
>
> (Knapp, 1874: 446)

In this fascinating passage, an Aboriginal massacre site is hidden away, unmemorialised; while the grave of a murdered settler could in this case hardly be more visible, right on the 'verge' of colonial development and with an afterlife that connects it, remarkably, to nothing less than global modernity ('telegraph ... messages flash through Europe'): as if it literally underpins, or signals, the success and achievements of the colonial project.

Murdering Flat is the name of an actual Aboriginal massacre site in Victoria, although it is a long way west of the location in Knapp's story. Ian Clark's register of Aboriginal massacre sites in the western part of that state – an important source for the University of Newcastle's *Colonial Frontier Massacre Map* – is an important reminder that colonialism was also an enactment of what Achille Mbembe has called 'necropower' (2019): where a government and its terroristic agents (squatters, shepherds, boundary riders and so on) authorise genocide and as a consequence turn the landscape into a spiralling series of deathscapes. There is certainly an unresolved relationship between necropower and necronationalism in Australia, partly to do with the still open question of how to commemorate, or even recognise, these deathscapes. A June 1838 editorial in the *Sydney Gazette*, on the 'cold-blooded massacres' of Aboriginal people in Victoria and elsewhere around this time, insightfully noted: 'Whenever Europeans have attempted to establish themselves, their pathway to colonisation has invariably been thickly strewed with the graves of the native population' ('The Route to Port Phillip', 1838: 2). But settlers rarely took the opportunity to bury the Aboriginal people they murdered. Murdering Flat – near Casterton in western Victoria – refers to an actual event four months later that involved the killing of a shepherd and subsequent settler retaliation that saw the murder of around forty Aboriginal people. Clark quotes an account that adds, 'As far as is known there was no grave; the bodies were put in the river' (Clark, 1995: 26). This is the opposite of memorialisation; here, bodies are contemptuously disposed of and uncommemorated. The starkly evocative English names for Aboriginal massacre sites in this area include Murdering Flat, Murderers Flat and Murdering Gully. The latter is the site of a massacre the following year, 1839, of around forty Tarnbeere Gundidj people of the Djargurd Wurrung in the Camberdown district of Victoria. In the aftermath of these killings, the squatter Frederick Taylor – owner of one of the largest sheep stations in the area – fled to India, most likely in response to the arrest, conviction and execution of seven settlers for their role in the Myall Creek Massacre the previous year. Myall Creek is in north-eastern New South Wales, inland from Coffs Harbour. Around May 1838, a number of Wirrayaraay people, already dispossessed and reduced in numbers, arranged to camp on the squatter Henry Dangar's land. A month or so later a group of settlers arrived armed at the camp and slaughtered around thirty men, women and children. The massacre saw the Supreme Court trial and execution by hanging of seven of the murderers, an exceptional outcome for the colony at the time. 'I counted twenty eight heads and forms of bodies', Dangar's superintendent William Hobbs had testified at the trial; 'a number of heads had been burned; some of the skulls were quite burned' (Hobbs, 1838: 2).

Charles Harpur published a poem about the Myall Creek Massacre, 'A Wail from the Bush', in the *Weekly Register*, July 1845, just a few weeks before that newspaper went on to serialise 'The Creek of the Four Graves'. 'It will be remembered', he wrote in a short preface, 'that, a few years back, a party of stockmen (several of whom were afterwards executed for the crime) made wholesale massacre of a small tribe of defenceless Blacks, to the number, it is believed, of more than a score, heaping their bodies as they slaughtered them, upon a large fire kindled for the purpose' (Harpur, 1845b). The poem presents the voice of an Aboriginal woman carrying her child as she flees the killings, singing a lament for her murdered partner:

> The streams have lost for ever
> The shadow of a chief;
> The fading track of his fleet foot
> May guide not as before;
> And the echo of the mountains
> Shall answer him no more.
>
> (Harpur, 1845b: 41)

'A Wail from the Bush' was reprinted as 'An Aboriginal Mother's Lament' in Harpur's *The Bushrangers, A Play in Five Acts, and Other Poems* (1853). Harpur's poem was not especially original, however; in fact, it reproduced much of the content of an earlier poem about the Myall Creek Massacre by Eliza Hamilton Dunlop, 'The Aboriginal Mother [From Myall's Creek]', published in *The Australian* in December 1838. The publication of Dunlop's poem was in fact contemporaneous with the execution of seven of the Myall Creek murderers. As Anna Johnston has noted, Dunlop closely followed the Supreme Court trial and the testimonies from Hobbs and others and also knew about 'the escape of one woman and one infant' from the massacre (Johnston, 2018: 70). The Aboriginal 'lament' was an available mode of address in colonial (and even some early twentieth century) Australian poetry. Perhaps the earliest example is the anonymous 'The Native's Lament' (1826), published during Tasmania's Black Wars and written in the voice of an Aboriginal man as a bitter complaint about the arrival of a 'stranger' in the colony who 'usurps the best lands of thy native domains, / And thy children must fly, or submit to his chains' (Anon., 1826: 4). These settler ventriloquisms of Aboriginal voices are certainly examples of what Patrick Brantlinger has called colonialism's 'extinction discourse', that is, an insistence on the inevitability of the disappearance of colonised peoples that also expresses itself as an act of mourning, an elegy for what colonisation has taken away (see Brantlinger, 2013). Tying the Aboriginal lament to a massacre, however, complicates this conventional view just a little. In the poems by Dunlop and Harpur, the Aboriginal mother and her child are, of course, massacre survivors. The mother's voice mourns the loss of a community and its leader (the 'chieftain'), but it also expresses a traumatic relationship to the massacre site and in doing so performs its own act of memorialisation. The question of how to memorialise Aboriginal massacres is a modern rather than colonial one these days, and ongoing. There are very few actual, physical memorials to massacres of Aboriginal people across Australia. The Myall Creek memorial site opened in June 2000, 'after years of advocacy by Sue Blacklock, a descendent of one of the survivors' (Dovey, 2017). It aimed not only to commemorate these particular 1838 killings but also to become representative, a meta-memorial that spoke to a meta-deathscape, a place of contemporary significance 'to all those who had been killed along the frontier of European settlement in what had always been Aboriginal land' (Lydon and Ryan, 2018: iii). To draw on Pierre Nora, it works by turning history, 'a representation of the past', into memory, 'a perpetually actual phenomenon, a bond tying us to the eternal present'. It is not a burial site; it is instead a 'site of memory' (Nora, 1989: 7–8).

Grave-robbing and the weird colonial grave

The Sydney journalist Robert Dudley Adams's 'Trucanini's Dirge' (1876) is another Aboriginal woman's lament, devoted to Trugernanner or Truganini, a survivor of the Tasmanian Black Wars and the last survivor of the Oyster

Cove group on that island. It was published just two weeks after her death. The poem's epigraph from Psalm 103 – 'And the place thereof shall know them no more' – certainly suggests an unfolding extinction discourse here, underscored by the view of Truganini as 'the last / of the tribes!' Yet the poem gives her a burial on Aboriginal land, a 'lonely grave' in 'my long last home'; 'Lay me to rest', she urges, 'in the silent breast / of the solemn mountain chain' (Adams, 1876: 24). The extinction discourse of the poem is thus also a burial fantasy, a literalisation of a footnote that quotes Truganini's final, dying words: 'Don't let them cut me up, but bury me behind one of the mountains' (1876: 24). She was thinking of the fate of her late partner, the Aboriginal man William Lanney, who had died in 1869. In a struggle over the scientific and institutional ownership of his body parts, William Crowther, an honorary medical officer at the General Hospital (and later on, premier of Tasmania), robbed Lanney's grave, peeled away the facial skin and removed his skull, replacing it with another. The resident surgeon of the hospital, George Stokell, discovered the theft the next day and, under instructions from the Royal Society, 'resurrected the body from its grave' and 'spent the next day in a back room at the hospital harvesting Lanney's bones' (McDonald, 2004: 49). As Helen McDonald notes, this case of colonial body-snatching by 'race scientists' – some forty years after the notorious 'resurrectionists' Burke and Hare in Edinburgh – quickly became a public scandal (see McDonald, 2003: 88–90). Truganini was right to be concerned about similar scientific claims on her own body after her death. She was buried inside the walls of the former Female Factory at Cascades 'so as to secure ... protection against body snatchers' ('Friday Morning', 1876: 2). The funeral was organised by the undertaker William Hamilton and presided over by the Reverend Canon Parsons who, as McDonald reports, read the Church of England burial sermon, 'I am the resurrection and the life' (McDonald, 2010: 147). But two years later, in December 1878, her body was exhumed by the Royal Society, which stripped away the remaining flesh and took possession of Truganini's bones 'on the condition that they were not placed on public display' (2010: 151). Much later on, in 1904, they were sent to Baldwin Spencer at the University of Melbourne, who assembled a skeleton which was then returned to Hobart and put on display, as Truganini knew it would, in the Tasmanian Museum. In Hobart, *The Mercury* commented on Truganini's burial at the time, noting the precariously protected location of her grave and, in doing so, soundly rejected Adams's poetic fantasy: 'Future generations will tell how, to defeat the contending interests that claimed on behalf of Science the right to preserve what can be preserved of the remains of the last aboriginal, her body had to be buried within high walls so as to secure that protection from body snatchers which is to be found in the watchful care that secures us from the escape of prisoners' ('Friday Morning', 1876: 2). Her burial was in effect another kind of incarceration. It was not until May 1976 that her remains were finally cremated and her ashes scattered in D'Entrecasteaux Channel, south of Hobart, close to her traditional lands.

The illegal exhumation, collection and sale of Aboriginal bones persisted well into the twentieth century. Alexandra Roginski has looked at the New South Wales phrenologist and grave-robber A. S. Hamilton; in 1889 his widow Agnes Hamilton-Grey (who wrote a biography of the poet Henry Kendall) donated his extensive collection of Aboriginal skulls to the University of Melbourne and the Museum of Victoria (Roginski, 2015: 57–63). A notorious late colonial case of grave-robbing involved Ramsay Smith, then Adelaide's city coroner, who prompted a public inquiry when it was discovered he had secretly dissected the body of a local Ngarrindjeri man, Poltpalingada Booboorowie or 'Tommy Walker', after his death in 1901, the year of Australia's Federation. Only Poltpalingada's 'soft remains' were placed in his coffin; Smith sent his skeleton on to Edinburgh University (Pickering, 2006: 46). Paul Daley notes that the public inquiry 'revealed sordid details about the illicit trade in body parts (skeletons £10 apiece) that flourished in Ramsay Smith's morgue. Aboriginal bodies were in particular demand ... At Ramsay's death in 1937, well over a hundred human skulls were found in his Adelaide home' (Daley, 2014).

Henry Lawson's 'The Bush Undertaker' (1892) is one of late colonial Australia's best known Gothic short stories. Its protagonist is an old shepherd who lives with his sheepdog in a small hut by a creek and, despite his advanced years, continues to manage the livestock on the property. He is still, in other words, an active agent in the project of colonisation. After dinner one evening, he goes out with his dog, looking for bones. He is especially 'curious' about a 'black fellow's grave' nearby: 'I'll take a pick an' shovel with me an' root up that old black fellow', he tells the sheepdog (Lawson, 1913: 230). The grave itself is 'a little mound of earth, barely defined in the grass and indented in the centre as all blackfellows' graves were'; the shepherd digs it up and 'in about half an hour he bottomed on payable dirt' (1913: 251). How did he know about the grave? Was he once involved (like so many shepherds before him) in a retaliatory killing? Robert Dingley is one of the only commentators on this story who has commented on this macabre scene and situated it in the context of the 'widespread and lucrative' colonial trade in Indigenous skulls and bones by collectors and grave-robbers such as Ramsay (1998: 156–9). The shepherd puts the bones in his bag and then stumbles across the burnt body of a settler, who he recognises as a local drunk, Brummy. He then digs a grave and buries Brummy, saying some familiar commemorative words: 'I am the rassaraction' (1998: 239). The shepherd is himself a kind of 'resurrectionist', although the story is never explicit about what he plans to do with the Aboriginal bones he collects.

Instead, it ties the exhumation of an Aboriginal grave to a series of spectral effects, beginning when the shepherd – heading for home with his 'bag of bones' – is startled by a 'great greasy black iguana' (1998: 231). Another black iguana appears soon afterwards; it suddenly seems as if there is a 'flock' of them. Inside his hut the sheepdog whimpers, and the shepherd feels 'the icy breath of fear at his heart' (1998: 236). Wondering if he is somehow under attack, he waits outside with his gun. 'After watching for about an hour, he saw a black object coming over the ridge-pole. He grabbed his gun and fired. The thing disappeared. He ran around to the other side of the hut, and there was a great black iguana in violent convulsions on the ground' (1913: 237). It is difficult not to read this as a displaced representation of an Aboriginal attack on the shepherd, who shoots and kills in retaliation. The story itself is not set on the frontier, so the displacement is both temporal and symbolic: a distant and imaginatively reconfigured echo of a violent frontier encounter. Aboriginal people are already dead here; what triggers that figurative attack on the shepherd is his exhumation of an Aboriginal grave (does it explain why he knew where it was?) and his removal of the bones from the burial site.

Lawson's 'The Bush Undertaker' ends by identifying the spectral events triggered by the desecration of an Aboriginal grave near the shepherd's hut as peculiar to (late) colonial Australia, 'the home of the weird' (239). The story shares its strange conflation of extinction discourse, grave-robbing and 'weird' spectral effects with other contemporaneous late colonial narratives: for example, William Sylvester Walker's 'The Evil of Yelcomorn Creek', from Walker's collection of stories *When the Mopoke Calls* (1898). Here, the narrator is an opal prospector. With his Aboriginal guide Bobbie, they go into remote Australia and find what looks like a 'paradise' beyond the frontier, where they begin to dig for opals. It seems the place is uninhabited, a *terra nullius* available to plunder for personal gain: 'No man's land, I call it' (Walker, 1898: 100). But it turns out to be an unmarked Aboriginal burial ground, perhaps even a massacre site: 'Oh Lord, what's this? A native grave! And another! ... Under the "mulgas" more graves, thousands of them' (1898: 98). The narrator, to his horror, stumbles across Bobbie's dead body and then sees 'the skeleton-painted wraiths, tall and weird, of those warriors who fought and fell in the dim long ago'. He fires his gun and kills 'a king, I think' (1898: 100): which puts him, too, in a genealogy of settler retaliation against Aboriginal people. The narrator then faints away but wakes the next morning and buries Bobbie, leaving the site empty-handed, too frightened to take any opals with him. This is another post-frontier story that imagines the spectral echo of an earlier frontier encounter, triggered by a disturbed Aboriginal burial site. It combines the colonial racism of *terra nullius* ('No man's land') with the belated recognition that this place is also what Ross Gibson has called a 'badland': 'a tract of country that would not succumb to colonial ambition' (Gibson, 2002: 14). The 'weird' vision of skeletal Aboriginal warriors recalls the bones collected by Lawson's grave-robbing bush undertaker and the shooting of the black iguana ('home of the weird'). It also reproduces Marcus Clarke's famous 1876 account of 'weird melancholy' in the colonies, an account that similarly triggers a spectral vision of 'natives painted like skeletons' in the bush (Clarke, 1911: x). Why is the *weird* so important here? For Mark Fisher, the *weird* is close to, but not quite the same as, Freud's sense of the uncanny: 'the weird', he writes, 'is that *which does not belong*. The weird brings to the familiar something which ordinarily lies beyond it, and which cannot be reconciled with the "homely" (even as its negation). The form that is perhaps most appropriate to the weird is montage – the conjoining of *two or more things which do not belong together*' (Fisher, 2016: 10–11, original emphasis). Colonial Australian grave literature works in precisely this way. Settled settlers come across the dead bodies of settlers who tried and failed to leave the colony; other settlers are buried precisely in places where they do not belong. Aboriginal people are massacred at the site of their own dispossession; different skulls are attached to different bodies; settlers desecrate the graves of Aboriginal people and remove their contents, sending them elsewhere and thus repeating the settler act of dispossession even after death. Violent encounters on the frontier are spectralised long afterwards in post-frontier narratives that reanimate or memorialise the dead; and 'no man's land' also turns out to be a badland. Nameless or otherwise, the colonial grave in these accounts never seems to be at rest; and, as we have seen, its afterlives can reach into modern Australia and in some cases demand acknowledgement and recognition.

Note

1 The *Colonial Frontier Massacres in Australia, 1788–1930* digital archive can be accessed at: https://c21ch.newcastle.edu.au/colonialmassacres/ (accessed 5 December 2023).

References

Adams, Robert Dudley ('R. A.') (1876) 'Trucanini's Dirge', *Australian Town and Country Journal*, 27 May, p. 24.
Anon. (1826) 'The Native's Lament', *Colonial Times and Tasmanian Advertiser*, 5 May, p. 4.
Brantlinger, Patrick (2013) *Dark Vanishings: Discourse on the Extinction of Primitive Races, 1800–1930* (Ithaca: Cornell University Press).

Carter, David (2017) 'Bush Legends and Pastoral Landscapes', in Nicholas Birns et al. (eds), *Teaching Australian and New Zealand Literature* (New York: Modern Language Association of America), pp. 42–54.

Cathcart, Michael (2009) *The Water Dreamers: The Remarkable History of Our Dry Continent* (Melbourne: Text Publishing).

Clark, Ian (1995) *Scars in the Landscape: A Register of Massacre Sites in Western Victoria, 1803–1859* (Canberra: Aboriginal Studies Press).

Clarke, Marcus (1911) 'Preface', in Adam Lindsay Gordon, *Poems* (Melbourne: A. H. Massina & Co.).

'Criminal Court' (1826) *The* Australian, 1 November, p. 3.

Daley, Paul (2014) 'Restless Indigenous Remains', *Meanjin*, 73:1, https://meanjin.com.au/essays/restless-indigenous-remains/ (accessed 10 November 2022).

Dingley, Robert (1998) '"Resurrecting" the Australian Past: Henry Lawson's "The Bush Undertaker"', in Leigh Dale and Simon Ryan (eds), *The Body in the Library* (Amsterdam: Rodopi), pp. 155–67.

Dovey, Ceridwen (2017) 'The Mapping of Massacres', *New Yorker*, 6 December, www.newyorker.com/culture/culture-desk/mapping-massacres (accessed 10 November 2022).

Fisher, Mark (2016) *The Weird and the Eerie* (London: Repeater Books).

'Friday Morning' (1876) *The* Mercury, 12 May, p. 2.

Gibson, Ross (2002) *Seven Versions of an Australian Badland* (St Lucia: University of Queensland Press).

Grey, George (1841) *Journals of Two Expeditions of Discovery in North-West and Western Australia, during the Years 1837, 38, and 39*, vol. 1 (London: T. and W. Boone).

Grimstone, Mary (1826) 'On Visiting the Cemetery in Hobart Town', *Colonial Times and Tasmanian Advertiser*, 15 September, p. 4.

Harpur, Charles (1845a) 'The Creek of the Four Graves', *Weekly Register of Politics, Facts and General Literature*, 23 August, p. 90.

Harpur, Charles (1845b) 'A Wail from the Bush', *Weekly Register of Politics, Facts and General Literature*, 26 July, p. 41.

Hobbs, William (1838) 'Supreme Court – Criminal Side', *The Australian*, 17 November, p. 2.

Indyk, Ivor (1993) 'Pastoral and Priority: The Aboriginal in Australian Pastoral', *New Literary History*, 24:4 (Autumn), 837–54.

Johnston, Anna (2018) '"The Aboriginal Mother": Poetry and Politics in Eliza Hamilton Dunlop's Response to the Myall Creek Massacre', in Jane Lydon and Lyndall Ryan (eds), *Remembering the Myall Creek Massacre* (Sydney: NewSouth Books), pp. 68–84.

Kendall, Henry (1869) *Leaves from Australian Forests* (Melbourne: George Robertson).

Knapp, Henry (1874) 'The Shepherd's Grave', *The Australian Journal*, 9:107 (April), 445–6.

Lawson, Henry (1913) *While the Billy Boils* (London: Angus and Robertson).

'Literature and Science' (1836) *The Colonist*, 17 March, p. 86, https://trove.nla.gov.au/newspaper/page/4246995 (accessed 23 November 2023).

Lydon, Jane and Ryan, Lyndall (eds) (2018) *Remembering the Myall Creek Massacre* (Sydney: NewSouth Books).

Mbembe, Achille (2019) *Necropolitics* (Durham: Duke University Press).

McCombie, Thomas (1861) *Australian Sketches: The Gold Discovery, Bush Graves, &c. &c.* (London: Sampson Low, Son, and Co.).

McDonald, Helen (2003) 'Reading the "Foreign Skull": An Episode in Nineteenth-Century Colonial Human Dissection', *Australian Historical Studies*, 37: 125, 81–96.
McDonald, Helen (2004) 'The Bone Collectors', *New Literatures Review*, 42 (October), 45–56.
McDonald, Helen (2010) *Possessing the Dead: The Artful Science of Anatomy* (Melbourne: Melbourne University Press).
Nora, Pierre (1989) 'Between Memory and History: *Les Lieux de Mémoire*', *Representations*, 26, 7–24.
Pickering, Michael (2006) 'Policy and Research Issues Affecting Human Remains in Australian Museum Collections', in Jack Lohman and Katherine Goodnow (eds), *Human Remains and Museum Practice* (London: UNESCO and the Museum of London), pp. 42–7.
Reid, Ian (2002) 'Marking the Unmarked: An Epitaphic Preoccupation in Nineteenth-Century Australian Poetry', *Victorian Poetry*, 40:1, 7–20.
Roginski, Alexandra (2015) *The Hanged Man and the Body Thief: Finding Lives in a Museum Mystery* (Clayton: Monash University Publishing).
Slessor, Kenneth (1970) 'Charles Harpur', *Bread and Wine: Selected Prose* (Sydney: Angus and Robertson).
'Sydney' (1806) *Sydney Gazette and New South Wales Advertiser*, 19 June, p. 1.
'The Route to Port Phillip' (1838) *Sydney Gazette and New South Wales Advertiser*, 7 June, p. 2.
'The Sprite of the Creek' (1832) *Hill's Life in New South Wales*, 21 September, p. 4.
Tilly, Elspeth (2012) *White Vanishing: Rethinking Australia's Lost-in-the-Bush Myth* (Leiden: Brill).
Torre, Giovanni (2022) 'Hidden story of Australia's first known Indigenous soldier to die fighting overseas uncovered', *National Indigenous Times*, 7 July, https://nit.com.au/07-07-2022/3410/noongar-man-honoured-as-first-aboriginal-soldier-to-die-in-service-with-australian-armed-forces (accessed 10 November 2022).
Walker, William S. (1898) *When the Mopoke Calls* (London: John Long).
'W-- --G' (1827) 'Terra Incognita', *The Monthly Magazine*, 3:15, March, pp. 233–61.

7

Weirding the Gothic graveyard

James Machin

H. P. Lovecraft is a Janus figure in the literature of the Gothic. His work looks back to the original Gothic novelists of the late eighteenth century, the Gothic literature of the nineteenth and Edgar Allan Poe's associated innovations in the short story and is steeped in the tradition they established. Lovecraft's fiction was also, however, coeval with modernism, and while he could be disparaging about the literary experimentation of T. S. Eliot and others, he also regularly used references to contemporaneous innovations in the plastic and visual arts as a descriptive shorthand to communicate the grotesque, 'non-Euclidean' geometry of incomprehensibly alien landscapes and architecture. Like other modernist writers and artists, Lovecraft's fiction was shaped by his knowledge of recent advances in physics, mathematics and astronomy. The critical term now used to discuss this shift away from the traditional Gothic idiom – in dialogue with other modernist responses to a troubling new understanding of the universe – is based on Lovecraft's own preferred designation of 'the weird tale', weird fiction or the Weird:

> The true weird tale has something more than secret murder, bloody bones, or a sheeted form clanking chains according to rule. A certain atmosphere of breathless and unexplainable dread of outer, unknown forces must be present; and there must be a hint, expressed with a seriousness and portentousness becoming its subject, of that most terrible conception of the human brain – a malign and particular suspension or defeat of those fixed laws of Nature which are our only safeguard against the assaults of chaos and the daemons of unplumbed space.
>
> (Lovecraft, [1933–5] 1985: 426)

Scholars such as China Miéville, Benjamin Noys and Leif Sorensen have explored various aspects of Lovecraft's weird fiction as 'pulp modernism' (Miéville, 2008; Noys and Murphy, 2016; Sorensen, 2010). In this chapter, I look specifically at how Lovecraft's pulp modernism 'weirds' the graveyard: that is, updates this most archetypal of Gothic spaces as a site of modernist uncertainty and cosmic fear.

This chapter focuses on how Lovecraft uses the graveyard in several of his earlier short stories in which the site is a principal component, discussing 'The Tomb' (1922), 'Herbert West – Reanimator' (1922) and others in this context. I argue that Lovecraft's treatment of the graveyard emerges from a Decadent Gothic sensibility, positioning the graveyard primarily as an aesthetic site of limit-experience and a catalyst for jouissance, using a definition of that Lacanian term broadly analogous to transgressive joy. The closing section of the chapter shows how Lovecraft's later fiction, including the famous short story 'The Call of Cthulhu' (1928), builds upon this jouissance and complicates the graveyard further by reshaping it through the prism of a very modernist artistic and scientific sensibility: what Benjamin Noys has designated 'the Lovecraft event' (2007: 1). I argue that while recent Lovecraft criticism has been productive in its treatment of his fiction as 'the horror of philosophy', his stories are also rooted in his specific aesthetic responses to the material world of things, one of those things being the graveyard.

The Gothic/Decadent graveyard

Lovecraft first read Edgar Allan Poe in 1898, at the age of seven or eight (Joshi, 2013: 50–1). Poe wrote about death, tombs, interment and the 'conqueror worm' to an almost monomaniacal degree – a preoccupation reflecting the wider 'cult of death and remembrance' of his age, which manifested in death being 'fetishised and memorialised as an event of ethereal beauty … making the funeral into an elaborate aesthetic spectacle' (Hutchisson, 2012: 23). The year of Lovecraft's first encounter with Poe's short stories was also the year of the death of Lovecraft's father, Winfield Scott Lovecraft, from late-stage syphilis, after five years of hospitalisation resulting from a psychotic episode in 1893. This occurred while Lovecraft's family had been emerging from a period of mourning after the death of his maternal grandmother in 1896, an event which 'plunged the household into a gloom from which it never fully recovered' (Joshi, 2013: 34). Given this morbid context, it is unsurprising that among surviving juvenilia is a story written c.1898–9 titled 'The Mystery of the Grave-yard', though, as S. T. Joshi notes, the tale is a histrionic 'action-thriller' that reveals a young boy's enthusiasm for the detective, espionage and cowboy antics of the dime novels rather than his reading of Poe (2013: 52–3). However, one of Lovecraft's earliest published short stories, 'The Tomb', is a Poesque narrative incorporating 'a number of autobiographical details … relating to HPL's childhood' (Joshi, 2002: 368). It is inspired by Lovecraft's encounter with a specific grave dating from 1711 while on a walk with his aunt in Swan Point Cemetery in his hometown of Providence, Rhode Island (2002: 368).

'The Tomb' is the first-person account of an inmate of a 'refuge for the demented', a self-described 'dreamer and … visionary' named Jervase Dudley

(Lovecraft, 2001: 1). During his boyhood he develops a morbid fascination with an abandoned family vault in a local wood, the tomb of the Hydes, to the extent of spending nights sleeping among the coffins (or so he thinks) and the ruins of the Hydes' mansion, which had been unoccupied for more than a century. Here he experiences visions of, or hauntings by, the Hydes and their boisterous eighteenth-century social milieu, with the mansion's fires lit and thronging with revellers. However, Dudley's visions tip over into insanity when he encounters what he believes to be his own grave. It is revealed at the end of the story that the young man had never had access to the tomb, which had always remained gated and locked. The story is predicated on a Poesque monomania with the dead, but it also makes a connection between the dead and revelry and the carnivalesque that Lovecraft further intensifies in subsequent writing. As we shall see in this chapter, Lovecraft moves away from what are arguably the dominant registers of Poe – aestheticised melancholy, yearning and mournfulness – to an emphasis on the aesthetics of the graveyard as the site of ecstatic limit-experience.

By 1922, this dynamic – the connection between the graveyard and the aesthetic limit-experience – is developed in Lovecraft's fiction into a position of prominence, and the graveyard's role as a locus of ecstatic aesthetic uplift becomes central to the affect of the stories. There are several theoretical terms available for discussion of Lovecraft's ecstatic aesthetics of the graveyard. 'Limit-experience' is one, a contested term with connotations of a dark mysticism achieved through transgression, or – considered more neutrally – 'an intuition of perfect correspondence between perceiving and thinking'; a revelatory, mystical synthesis of physiological and philosophical experience (Klemm, 2008: 66). Another relevant term is 'jouissance', in its broader sense of transgressive joy not solely or emphatically rooted in sexuality or eroticism. In the context of this chapter, I consider it a more capacious term than one strictly beholden to recondite Lacanian psychoanalysis, though one which (as Patricia MacCormack puts it, when discussing Lovecraft) shares with eroticism 'a state of both being within and beyond a frenzy of potential, and an excitation that is also a dread' (2016: 210). Offering a stricter account of jouissance's meaning is complicated by the apparent lack of any comprehensive definition, strict or otherwise, in Lacan's work and a recurrent circularity in critical explanations. In his commentary on Lacan's lectures, for example, Raul Moncayo suggests that jouissance 'points to the impossible experience of bearing the unbearable':

> In this sense jouissance is intrinsically related to suffering and not just to pleasure or enjoyment or even sexuality as the word commonly refers to in the French language. This conception of jouissance highlights the connection between jouissance and the death drive.
>
> (2017: 49–50)

In *Seminar VII*, Lacan specifies that 'jouissance implies precisely the acceptance of death' (Lacan, 1992: 189), suggesting a libidinal process nevertheless involving a philosophical dimension other than, and not reducible to, eroticism or necrophilia. For present purposes, I will be using the terms 'limit-experience' and jouissance' as indicative rather than specific, carrying the suggestion of 'the liminal point where states of ecstasy and anguish encounter each other at the limits of the human' (Baumgartner, 2020: 67).

This account gestures towards the aesthetic frisson which generates an ecstatic uplift: in Lovecraft's texts (as I have discussed elsewhere – see Machin, 2020); in the term 'dark mysticism'; and the more recent coinage 'weird mysticism' explicated by Brad Baumgartner in his monograph of the same name (Baumgartner, 2020). This weird jouissance also emerges from the Decadent tradition that Lovecraft both worked within and responded to, a movement characterised by its morbid obsessions with 'decline and decay' and frequent use of mycological imagery, such as grave mould, and the creeping fungus of rot. Decadents both symbolised the inexorability of death and revelled in the sustaining meaning generated by this aestheticising symbolism in an otherwise meaningless universe (Rodensky, 2006: xxiv).

Lovecraft's interest in this jouissance, and his engagement with a Decadent graveyard aesthetic, can be seen in numerous early stories. In 'The Statement of Randolph Carter' (1919) Lovecraft's narrator recounts the events leading up to the disappearance of Carter, a scholar whose 'weird studies' have led them both to an isolated swampland cemetery with the intention of performing some sort of excavation. Lovecraft provides an extravagantly detailed description of its setting: a lonely burial ground with 'a repellent array of antique slabs, urns, cenotaphs, and mausolean facades; all crumbling, moss-grown, and moisture-stained, and partly concealed by the gross luxuriance of the unhealthy vegetation' (Lovecraft, 1999: 8). The passage's Decadent aesthetic is achieved by Lovecraft's juxtaposition of the human-made, lifeless masonry memorialising the dead and the teeming plant life that seems to mock this anthropocentric reverence (hence, 'unhealthy'). This juxtaposition of the cemetery as the site of human physical termination and vegetal superabundance, or teeming biodiversity, establishes the graveyard as a liminal space confusing the life/death binary, a conflation I will return to when considering 'The Call of Cthulhu' below.

In 'Herbert West – Reanimator', a potboiler serial first published in 1922, the titular character is a doctor who indulges in clandestine experiments in the reanimation of recently dead corpses. The first-person narrator, a colleague of Dr West, initially collaborates in the experiments until he becomes increasingly squeamish about the associated ethical and other transgressions and appalled at the non-scientific nature of West's enthusiasm. In the first episode of the story, he remarks that the grave-robbing 'might have been gruesomely poetical if we had been artists instead of scientists' (Lovecraft, 1999: 53), but this observational aside about what for him is 'a repulsive task' necessary for their research develops into an entrenched moral repulsion at West's artistic appreciation of their activities:

> that was when it dawned on me that his once normal scientific zeal for prolonging life had subtly degenerated into a mere morbid and ghoulish curiosity and secret sense of charnel picturesqueness. His interest became a hellish and perverse addiction to the repellently and fiendishly abnormal; he gloated calmly over artificial monstrosities which would make most healthy men drop dead from fright and disgust; he became, behind his pallid intellectuality, a fastidious Baudelaire of physical experiment – a languid Elagabalus of the tombs.
> (1999: 72)

The problem with West's activities is that they are a source of ecstatic limit-experience, or transgressive joy; or in the pulpier register of the tale, 'the gruesome thrill which would attend the uncovering of centuried grave-secrets' (1999: 78). Pulp context aside, this is still the 'gruesome thrill' of the aesthete, or what Brian Stableford has called – in the context of Decadence – 'horror as a positive sensation':

> Baudelaire found his antidote to spleen [or ennui] in a paradoxical readjustment of his attitude. Rather than settling for the consolations of faith, as his spiritual brother Poe had done, he elected to re-evaluate horror as a positive sensation, to be welcomed for its preferability to the corrosive tedium of ennui.
> (2007: 75)

The experiments become unacceptable to the narrator when it becomes clear West is no longer undertaking them as a dispassionate man of science, but as a Decadent seeker of jouissance. West's transformation, or decline, through the course of the story is from a medical researcher with 'the zeal of the born scientist' to a dedicated aesthete who has dropped all pretence of a scientific rationale to justify his enthusiasms:

> West's last quarters were in a venerable house of much elegance, overlooking one of the oldest burying-grounds in Boston. He had chosen the place for purely symbolic and fantastically aesthetic reasons, since most of the interments were of the colonial period and therefore of little use to a scientist seeking very fresh bodies.
> (Lovecraft, 1999: 78)

'Herbert West – Reanimator' enables layers of fictive and meta-fictive reading of the graveyard aesthetic: if the first layer is the idea of the graveyard aesthetic as limit-experience, and the second the recognition of that aesthetic by the first-person narrator, often with reference to other literary or cultural analogues (Baudelaire, Elagabalus and so on), then the third and final layer is Lovecraft's own literary evocation of that aesthetic. In the fantastic, painterly, breathless detail of his descriptions Lovecraft evokes both the graveyard and contemplation thereon through his elaborate literary representation, and it seems impossible to read such scenes as exercises in pure fear or melancholy; the affect is clearly calibrated to produce an aesthetic frisson in the reader. Lovecraft's early graveyards thus support Stableford's claim that 'writers inspired by Baudelaire' (of whom Lovecraft was one) took up the 'notion that horror itself – or, at least, the ability to derive aesthetic satisfaction from horror – might constitute an antidote to cosmic pessimism' (2007: 75).

The outlines of this strategy are evident in another of Lovecraft's graveyard scenes, from his 1923 story 'The Lurking Fear':

> The scene of my excavations would alone have been enough to unnerve any ordinary man. Baleful primal trees of unholy size, age, and grotesqueness leered above me like the pillars of some hellish Druidic temple; muffling the thunder, hushing the clawing wind, and admitting but little rain. Beyond the scarred trunks in the background, illumined by faint flashes of filtered lightning, rose the damp ivied stones of the deserted mansion, while somewhat nearer was the abandoned Dutch garden whose walks and beds were polluted by a white, fungous, foetid, overnourished vegetation that never saw full daylight. And nearest of all was the graveyard, where deformed trees tossed insane branches as their roots displaced unhallowed slabs and sucked venom from what lay below. Now and then, beneath the brown pall of leaves that rotted and festered in the antediluvian forest darkness, I could trace the sinister outlines of some of those low mounds which characterised the lightning-pierced region.
>
> History had led me to this archaic grave.
>
> (Lovecraft, 2005: 72)

The painterly detail of the passage utilises horizontal and vertical planes and layer upon layer of visual and sensual information, shifting focus between widescreen atmospheric conditions and a microscopic, naturalistic consideration of fungal growth and rotting vegetation, each component framing the focal point of the graveyard. It invokes not only centuries of human history culminating in obscurity and disintegration, but also – in its evocation of the slow collapse of masonry in the 'antediluvian' forest – what Aaron Worth has called 'Deep Gothic', a response to a revolutionary and traumatising awareness of 'deep time' precipitated by nineteenth-century advances in geological and evolutionary science (2018: xxii–xxiii).

In 'Herbert West', the narrator uses the term 'charnel picturesqueness' (Lovecraft, 1999: 72), the latter word selected for its specific meaning in aesthetics; the late eighteenth-century Picturesque being the movement which, though calibrated towards a refinement of taste and harmonious compositional unity, also valorised the 'destruction of symmetry' and the 'splendid confusion and irregularity' of Gothic architecture and of the ruin, as well as taking pleasure in the 'veneration of high antiquity' (Price, 1796: 64, 66). The Picturesque sought to theorise the aesthetic affect of the total assemblage of myriad components in the landscape – both architectural and natural – and by the end of the eighteenth century was an established 'way of describing the relationship of interior mood to exterior stimulus, of understanding the effects of light and colour, in nature and in architecture, on human sensibility' (Hill, 2009: 18). Lovecraft also imbues this 'charnel picturesque' scene with an additional temporal depth (the Deep Gothic again), framing it in terms of both the Anthropocene (the deserted mansion, the abandoned 'Dutch garden', the displaced grave slabs) and within the vaster, non-anthropocentric context of scientific naturalism where the traces of human activity are extinguished by inexorable absorption into the teeming wilderness. The cumulative effect is one of sublime uplift, with awe or aesthetic rapture being the dominant register rather than immediate existential fear, supernatural horror or graveyard-poet melancholy.

Lovecraft's weird graveyard aesthetic is given a more explicit reflexive and meta-fictive treatment in a further tale from 1922, 'The Hound', in which the two protagonists (including the narrator) are specific in describing their grave-robbing as an artistic endeavour, arrived at after exhausting their pursuit of 'every aesthetic and intellectual movement which promised respite from [their] devastating ennui' and 'jaded sensibilities' (Lovecraft, 1999: 81–2). The narrator defends, or at least apologises for, their charnel transgressions on the grounds that they were responses to a 'frightful emotional need', suggesting that only an experience at the 'hideous extremity of human outrage' could provide the necessary jolt or frisson to relieve their existential despair:

> The predatory excursions on which we collected our unmentionable treasures were always artistically memorable events. We were no vulgar ghouls, but worked only under certain conditions of mood, landscape, environment, weather, season, and moonlight. These pastimes were to us the most exquisite form of aesthetic expression, and we gave their details a fastidious technical care. An inappropriate hour, a jarring lighting effect, or a clumsy manipulation of the damp sod, would almost totally destroy for us that *ecstatic titillation* which followed the exhumation of some ominous, grinning secret of the earth.
>
> (1999: 82–3, emphasis added)

S. T. Joshi argues convincingly that Lovecraft's tone here consciously mimics the Decadent movement and that the story is an 'obvious self-parody' (2013: 432), but once again Lovecraft explains the affective lode of his own writing style, or at least makes explicit his intention in that regard; the ecstatic graveyard aesthetic is being sought after both by the Decadent protagonists of the story and by Lovecraft as the story's author, with the further connotation that the reader may experience this same ecstatic affect. Moreover, the protagonists join the reader in experiencing pleasure in seeing themselves not only as subjects but as further objects among other objects in the graveyard:

> I remembered how we delved in this ghoul's grave with our spades, and *how we thrilled at the picture of ourselves*, the grave, the pale watching moon, the horrible shadows, the grotesque trees, the titanic bats, the antique church, the dancing death-fires, the sickening odours, the gently moaning night-wind, and the strange, half-heard, directionless baying, of whose objective existence we could scarcely be sure.
>
> (Lovecraft, 1999: 83, emphasis added)

In the short story 'Pickman's Model' (1927), the Bostonian artist Richard Upton Pickman uses such scenes as the basis for his paintings, which are additionally disturbing to the narrator precisely because they are freighted with ecstatic carnivalesque celebrations of their subjects: one 'shewed [*sic*] a *dance* on Copp's Hill [cemetery] among the tombs'; '*dances* in the modern cemeteries were freely pictured'; 'the fellow must be a relentless enemy of all mankind to take such *glee* in the torture of the brain and flesh and the degradation of the mortal tenement' (Lovecraft, 2001: 85–6, emphasis added). Pickman's subjects are bestial 'ghouls' and anthropophagus grave-robbers, resonating with specifically New World colonial fears: the displaced slabs intended to cover the entire grave sometimes mentioned by Lovecraft would be identifiable to his contemporary readership as 'wolf stones', which were 'placed over the graves to prevent the wolves from digging them up and dining on the corpses' (Lightfoot, 2019: 180). Besides their 'callous cruelty', the narrator states that the paintings 'terrified because of their very greatness' – their aesthetic achievement (Lovecraft, 2001: 86).

Inevitably, 'The Hound' concludes with the protagonists both punished for their pursuit of aesthetic jouissance beyond the symbolic and into transgressive charnel activity: one being mauled to death by the supernatural entity they unwittingly disinter, the other by suicide in response to the knowledge his own similar fate was inevitable. The specificities of their persecutor are left vague, however, though its presence is marked by the spectral baying of a hound – the author concludes that death is his 'only refuge from the unnamed and unnamable [*sic*]' (Lovecraft, 1999: 88). A possible reading is that their dark ecstatic, mystical encounter with some sort of noumenal 'world without us' – to use Eugene Thacker's term – is a terminal experience that is impossible to accommodate through retreat into the normal life. Thacker describes 'the world without us' as a 'spectral and speculative' conceit of the non-anthropocentric, and horror as an exercise in psychic confrontation with 'the world without us', straining the limits of thought in a 'negative philosophy': horror being 'about paradoxical thought of the unthinkable' (2011: 5–9).

My phrasing of this 'retreat into the normal life' intentionally echoes that of one of Lovecraft's major literary influences, Arthur Machen, a writer regarded by Lovecraft as unequalled in his ability to generate 'cosmic fear raised to its most artistic pitch' in his fiction (Lovecraft, 1985: 494). In Machen's 'The White People' (1904), a claim is made in the opening sentence that 'sorcery and sanctity ... are the only realities. Each is an ecstasy, a withdrawal from the common life' (2018: 261). In his 1902 monograph on literary theory, Machen argues that the presence or otherwise of 'ecstasy' in literature is the primary metric by which it must be judged, offering partial definitions of the term's application, including 'things that are symbols, proclaiming the presence of the unknown world' (Machen, 1923b: 49). Although, as a committed Christian, Machen saw a moral difference between 'sorcery and sanctity', he recognised the potential in both to achieve this ecstatic revelation of this unknown world, perhaps analogous to what Thacker calls 'the world without us'. Machen went so far as to suggest that what he regarded as his literary failures were also moral failures on some level: 'Here then was my real failure; I translated awe, at worst awfulness, into evil' (1923a: 127). As an atheist, Lovecraft was not subject to such crises of conscience over this specific binary, and in fact enthusiastically explored the potential of 'sorcery' or 'evil' to achieve this dark mysticism. Lovecraft develops a notion of the noumenal 'world without us' in 'The Unnamable' (1925), and has one of the characters situate it explicitly within aesthetic theory:

> Moreover, so far as aesthetic theory was involved, if the psychic emanations of human creatures be grotesque distortions, what coherent representation could express or portray so gibbous and infamous a nebulosity as the spectre of a malign, chaotic perversion, itself a morbid blasphemy against Nature? Moulded by the dead brain of a hybrid nightmare, would not such a vaporous terror constitute in all loathsome truth the exquisitely, the shriekingly *unnamable?*
>
> (2005: 86–7)

The appearance of the word 'exquisitely' in the final sentence also connotes the emphasis on an affect more aligned with the sublime than the horrific. As Roger Luckhurst has argued, this intersection of the sublime, the unnameable and the horrific is reinforced by Lovecraft as a stylist and his use of a language 'that continually stumbles against the trauma of the unpresentable Thing, the shards of the sublime falling back into the debris of his busted sentences' (2013: xx).

The modernist/weird graveyard

While the graveyard aesthetic (or Aesthetic graveyard) in Lovecraft's earlier fiction is rooted in the Gothic, the sublime and associated Decadent preoccupations – with death, decay, corruption, the worm, charnel mycology, the contemplation of human mortality and their symbolic proclamation of 'the presence of the unknown world' (to use Machen's term) – it also contains an ecstatic consideration of the 'world without us'. The graveyard is a symbolic and literal reminder that the world exists apart from and beyond the individual human subject. Lovecraft's later fiction, which was written in the decade or so leading up to his own death and established his posthumous reputation, develops the graveyard aesthetic to the extent that its roots in both the Gothic and Decadence are no longer as clearly apparent, reconceptualising it within a modernist framework. Perhaps the most well-known example of this modernist graveyard aesthetic appears in the short story 'The Call of Cthulhu'. 'The Call of Cthulhu' is presented as a sequence of connected fragments, presenting different anecdotal accounts of encounters – oblique and otherwise – with the baleful alien entity Cthulhu. The climax of the story is the statement of a Norwegian sea captain recounting a voyage during which he and his crewmates accidentally stumbled upon the 'the nightmare corpse-city' and tomb of Cthulhu, called R'lyeh, which, while usually isolated from humanity in the abyssal depths of the south Pacific, has been disgorged to the surface due to an 'earthquake-born tempest which ... heaved up from the sea-bottom the horrors that filled men's dreams' (Lovecraft, 1999: 164–5). While described as a 'city', with the breached portion referred to as a 'citadel', Lovecraft's descriptions of R'lyeh are replete with monoliths, 'slimy vaults', 'colossal statues and bas-reliefs', the entire necropolis representing the 'tomb' of Cthulhu (1999: 165). This is the posthuman graveyard aesthetic stripped of the human component entirely, with the focus entirely on the non-human 'world without us', or Machen's ecstatic 'unknown world'.

Lovecraft consolidates this conceit of the posthuman graveyard in one of his final published works, the novella *At the Mountains of Madness* (1936), in which an American research team discover the ossified remains of an alien civilisation in Antarctica that flourished and then declined eons before the human race evolved. Some 'Elder Things' are reanimated from their frozen immurement and undertake unfathomable funerary rites on those that did not survive. Lovecraft frequently uses variations of the terms 'madness' or 'insanity' to convey the otherness of their physiology and mortuary practices and distance them from human conception: the 'insanely buried biological specimens'; 'the row of insane graves with the five-pointed snow mounds'; 'it surely looked like madness to find six imperfect monstrosities carefully buried upright in nine-foot snow graves under five-pointed mounds' (Lovecraft, 2001: 276, 279, 273). In attempting to convey how 'utterly alien' the culture of the Elder Things is, the first-person narrator also uses contemporary modernist art and ultra-modern sciences as reference points (2001: 289): 'Those who see our photographs will probably find its closest analogue in certain grotesque conceptions of the most daring futurists'; 'yet such parts sometimes involved designs and diagrams so uncannily close to the latest findings of mathematics and astrophysics that I scarcely know what to think' (2001: 295, 298). As with R'lyeh in 'The Call of Cthulhu', Lovecraft's depiction of the subterranean necropolis of the Elder Things is distinguished by its preoccupation with liminal states between life and death, immurement and reanimation, in the context of deep time. This aspect of Lovecraft's weirding of the Gothic graveyard can be further understood by considering Thacker's discussion of the 'world without us' and Brad Baumgartner's study of 'weird mysticism', concepts which both draw upon Lovecraft's contemporary, the French philosopher Georges Bataille (Thacker, 2011; Baumgartner, 2020). Thacker locates Bataille's 'religious horror' or '*Angst*' as 'existential-phenomenological' and specifically reliant 'on a basic metaphysical dichotomy of life and death', with 'the horror elicited in the passage *between* them' (2015: 92, original emphasis). Thacker goes on to describe 'a transformation that is neither that of life into death nor death into life, but a kind of hypostasis of persisting, subsisting and abiding – the religious horror of passing time' (2015: 92). Although Thacker gives the example of 'the tomb' generally as the 'artificial symbol of this transformation' between human life 'above ground' and the 'life below ground' (the invertebrate life consuming the corpse), he also provides a conceptual link between Lovecraft's Gothic graveyards and his 'cosmic' graveyards, where the conceit is recast in deep time, as in his famous couplet:

> That is not dead which can eternal lie,
> And with strange aeons even death may die.
>
> (2005: 30)

While usually associated with 'The Call of Cthulhu', the couplet earlier appeared in 'The Nameless City' (1921). In 'The Nameless City', the unnamed protagonist travels to the eponymous shunned, ruinous antiquity hidden among the sands 'remote in the desert of Araby', described as far older than the pyramids, than Babylon, than Memphis (Lovecraft, 2005: 30). Penetrating its 'tomb-like' depths, he discovers alcoves populated with 'cases … ranged along each side of the passage at regular intervals' and which are 'oblong and horizontal, hideously like coffins in shape and size' (2005: 35). The crisis of the story occurs at the point at which he fears he has disturbed the occupants' hypostasis, the terror elicited from the understanding of the unfathomably deep time of their persistence. The site is associated with the 'mad poet' Abdul Alhazred, author of the *Necronomicon* (2005: 30).

The setting of this story suggests its provenance in Lovecraft's enduring devotion to the *Arabian Nights*, a 'seminal book in his aesthetic development' (Joshi, 2013: 31). In the story 'The City of Brass', travellers in a similar, eerie desert populated by 'ruined cities' and the traces of 'lost civilisations' encounter 'the living tomb' of the monstrous afrit (demon) Dahesh, a 'half-living, half-dead thing' who 'rages against his sentence of eternal petrification' for his 'rejection of the true God' (Warner, 2012: 54–5). Marina Warner comments that Dahesh, 'imprisoned in his pillar of basalt, corresponds to other disturbing figures in the *Nights*, a book which continually tests the limits of animate life' (2012: 59). Lovecraft's reiteration of this conceit in 'The Call of Cthulhu' ('In his house at R'lyeh, dead Cthulhu waits dreaming' (Lovecraft, 1999: 150)) is, as Noys has demonstrated, mediated 'through the avant-gardes of his time, in both art and science', including quantum physics, non-Euclidean mathematics and Futurist and 'cubist fragmentation' (2007: 3–5). When a Cthulhu cultist in the story explains his devotion to the baleful entity, he offers a vision of a radically posthuman world, or a world of becoming posthuman:

> The time would be easy to know, for then mankind would have become as the Great Old Ones; free and wild and beyond good and evil, with laws and morals thrown aside and all men shouting and killing and revelling in joy. Then the liberated Old Ones would teach them new ways to shout and kill and revel and enjoy themselves, and all the earth would flame with a holocaust of ecstasy and freedom.
>
> (Lovecraft, 1999: 155)

Here, Lovecraft presses the register of eschatological religious fervour to the service of a kind of Nietzschean materialist 'heaven' on earth. It is another vision of dark ecstasy in contemplation of the 'world without us'.

Graham Harman writes of Lovecraft that 'perhaps his major stylistic trait as a writer [is] the gap he produces between the ungraspable thing and the vaguely relevant descriptions that the narrator is able to attempt' (2012: 24). But when we turn our attention away from the various alien entities that Lovecraft is celebrated for to focus on the *mise en scène* of, in this instance, Lovecraft's graveyards, a very specific arrangement of material culture, biological matter and climatic conditions are not only graspable but precisely specific to the aesthetic affect that Lovecraft was trying to achieve, both for the reader and often his characters. Lovecraft's graveyard aesthetic emerged from and was continually in dialogue with a distinct Gothic tradition. However, because of his rejection of Judeo-Christian metaphysics, and his engagement with modernist art and contemporary science, the Gothic graveyard was transformed into the weird graveyard. In his later writing, the human aspect of the graveyard was jettisoned altogether, along with any reassuring anthropocentric conceptions of the universe: the crumbling, mould-covered gravestones of the Gothic are transmuted into the non-Euclidean modernist sepulchre of R'lyeh. Despite this, and as Stoekl writes of Bataille, Lovecraft was not able 'to separate entirely materialism from a "weird mysticism"' (Stoekl, 2007: 208). Moreover, he relied heavily upon a material *bricolage* to assemble the aesthetic tableau necessary to precipitate his dark ecstacies. Though this does nothing to undermine the consideration of Lovecraft's fiction as primarily conceptual or philosophical – undoubtedly an important, even primary, component of the ongoing critical interest it generates – Lovecraft himself was a dedicated aesthete, and his philosophies were rooted in the picturesque and the sublime in terms of landscape, architecture and materiality. In no other site is this more evident than in the graveyard, with its intersections of the aesthetic, the philosophical and the material.

References

Baumgartner, Brad (2020) *Weird Mysticism: Philosophical Horror and the Mystical Text* (Bethlehem: Lehigh University Press).
Harman, Graham (2012) *Weird Realism: Lovecraft and Philosophy* (Winchester: Zero Books).
Hill, Rosemary (2009) *God's Architect: Pugin and the Building of Romantic Britain* (New Haven: Yale University Press).
Hutchisson, James M. (2012) 'Introduction', in Edgar Allan Poe, *Selected Poetry and Tales*, ed. James M. Hutchisson (Peterborough: Broadview Press), pp. 11–34.
Joshi, S. T. (2002) 'Explanatory Notes', in H. P. Lovecraft, *The Thing on the Doorstep and Other Weird Stories*, ed. S. T. Joshi (London: Penguin), pp. 367–443.
Joshi, S. T. (2013) *I Am Providence: The Life and Times of H. P. Lovecraft*, 2 vols (New York: Hippocampus Press).
Klemm, David E. (2008) 'Philosophy and Kerygma: Ricoeur as Reader of the Bible', in David M. Kaplan (ed.) *Reading Ricoeur* (Albany: State University of New York Press), pp. 47–70.
Lacan, Jacques (1992) [1986] *The Ethics of Psychoanalysis 1959–1960: The Seminar of Jacques Lacan*, trans. Dennis Porter (Hove: Routledge).
Lightfoot, D. Tulla (2019) The *Culture and Art of Death in 19th Century America* (Jefferson: McFarland).
Lovecraft, H. P. (1985) [1927, rev. 1933–4] 'Supernatural Horror in Literature', in S. T. Joshi (ed.), *Dagon and Other Macabre Tales* (London: Panther), pp. 421–512.
Lovecraft, H. P. (1999) *The Call of Cthulhu and Other Weird Stories*, ed. S. T. Joshi (London: Penguin).
Lovecraft, H. P. (2001) *The Thing on the Doorstep and Other Weird Stories*, ed. S. T. Joshi (London: Penguin).
Lovecraft, H. P. (2005) *The Dreams in the Witch House and Other Weird Stories*, ed. S. T. Joshi (London: Penguin).

Luckhurst, Roger (2013) 'Introduction', in H. P. Lovecraft, *The Classic Horror Stories*, ed. Roger Luckhurst (Oxford: Oxford World's Classics), pp. vii–xxviii.

MacCormack, Patricia (2016) 'Lovecraft's Cosmic Ethics', in Carl H. Sederholm and Jeffrey Andrew Weinstock (eds), *The Age of Lovecraft* (Minneapolis: University of Minnesota Press), pp. 199–214.

Machen, Arthur (1923a) [1922] *Far Off Things* (London: Martin Secker).

Machen, Arthur (1923b) [1902] *Hieroglyphics* (London: Martin Secker).

Machen, Arthur (2018) [1904] 'The White People', in Aaron Worth (ed.), *The Great God Pan and Other Horror Stories* (Oxford: Oxford World's Classics), pp. 261–93.

Machin, James (2020) 'Lovecraft, Decadence, and Aestheticism', in Clive Bloom (ed.), *The Palgrave Handbook of Contemporary Gothic* (Basingstoke: Palgrave Macmillan), pp. 1223–37.

Miéville, China (2008) 'M. R. James and the Quantum Vampire', *COLLAPSE* 4 (May), 105–28.

Moncayo, Raul (2017) *Lalangue, Sinthome, Jouissance, and Nomination: A Reading Companion and Commentary on Lacan's Seminar XXIII on the Sinthome* (London: Karnac).

Noys, Benjamin (2007) 'The Lovecraft Event', www.academia.edu/548596/The_Lovecraft_Event (accessed 20 November 2021).

Noys, Benjamin and Timothy S. Murphy (2016) 'Introduction: Old and New Weird', *Genre*, 49:2, 117–34.

Price, Uvedale (1796) *An Essay on the Picturesque: As Compared with the Sublime and the Beautiful; and, on the Use of Studying Pictures, for the Purpose of Improving Real Landscape* (London: J. Robson).

Rodensky, Lisa (2006) 'Introduction', in Lisa Rodensky (ed.), *Decadent Poetry from Wilde to Naidu* (London: Penguin), pp. xxiii–xlviii.

Sorensen, Leif (2010) 'A Weird Modernist Archive: Pulp Fiction, Pseudobiblia, H. P. Lovecraft', *Modernism/Modernity*, 17:3, 501–22.

Stableford, Brian (2007) 'The Cosmic Horror', in S. T. Joshi (ed.), *Icons of Horror and the Supernatural* (Westport: Greenwood Press), pp. 65–96.

Stoekl, Allan (2007) *Bataille's Peak: Energy, Religion, and Postsustainability* (Minneapolis: University of Minnesota Press).

Thacker, Eugene (2011) *In the Dust of This Planet: Horror of Philosophy*, vol. 1 (Winchester: Zero Books).

Thacker, Eugene (2015) *Tentacles Longer Than Night: Horror of Philosophy*, vol. 3 (Winchester: Zero Books).

Warner, Marina (2012) *Stranger Magic* (London: Vintage).

Worth, Aaron (2018) 'Introduction', in Arthur Machen, *The Great God Pan and Other Horror Stories*, ed. Aaron Worth (Oxford: Oxford World's Classics), pp. ix–xxxvi.

8

Graveyards in Western Gothic cinema

Xavier Aldana Reyes

James Whale's *Frankenstein* (1931), one of the staples of horror cinema responsible for the crystallisation of the genre in the 1930s, opens in a graveyard.[1] The camera pans past a collection of mourners gathered to pay their last respects to a loved one, the only accompanying sounds a funeral toll and woeful crying. To the right of the party hide two ominous onlookers, Henry Frankenstein (Colin Clive) and assistant Fritz (Dwight Frye), who await impatiently the departure of the gravedigger. The contrast between the grievers and the body snatchers is important to the scene's foregrounding of Frankenstein's resurrectionist scheme as morally dubious. The lighting dramatically sharpens his and Fritz's features, as does the tight close-up over a tilted fence. The effect is calculated to generate an unambiguous first impression that the men are up to no good. Further, it prefigures a point that will be emphasised throughout the film: Henry's 'insane ambition' to advance medicine by bringing patchwork corpses to life is severely compromised by his lack of empathy.[2] His hubristic fall is partly propelled by an inability to care for the deceased, to observe the sacrosanct nature of religious burial rituals and to generally treat the dead as anything but instruments in his goal to know, in his own words, 'what it feels like to be God'. The opening scene serves to reify many of the character traits of the mad scientist, a recurring human monster in US horror cinema: self-absorption, obsession and untrustworthiness (Frayling, 2005: 116–7). However, the scene is interesting for an ancillary reason. The statue of a hooded skeleton, an anachronistic neo-medievalism, presides over the entirety of the procedure, from legitimate pining to illicit unearthing. Aside from being one of the main aesthetic indicators that events are taking place at a grave site, the figure speaks volumes about the role of graveyards in Gothic cinema.

The statue looks magnificent, regal and stoic, a reminder of the slower time of graveyards and of the commemorative function of tombs and mausolea, commonly made of hard-wearing materials. Covered in a monastic robe, hunched over the hilt of a sword and peering into a metaphysical world inaccessible to the living, the skeleton seems more contemplative than combative.[3] In its role as overseer of desecration, its stone-cold imperviousness expertly juxtaposes the neighbouring flurry of maniacal movement. A particular image stands out: Henry appears to hit the skeleton in the face with a shovelful of earth flung in haste and implicit disregard (Figure 8.1). Frankenstein's general irreverence for memorials and for the sorrow of the bereaved is thus contraposed with a *memento mori* that, in its immutable reserve and silence, mocks the scientist's delusional beliefs that he can conquer death. The statue is more than a cue pointing to the futility of humanity's striving to overcome the inevitable, though. Like graveyards more generally, mortuary monuments externalise and enhance the Gothic's interest in the blurring of boundaries between the living and the dead. The legions of monsters that populate the Gothic, from vampires to zombies, have been connected to graveyards because these have traditionally been the resting places for the dead, but also because they act as liminal spaces. As I show below, the graveyard is often pictured as a threshold or portal between worlds. The skeleton in *Frankenstein* is thus a broader intimation of the Gothic's interest in prodding the limits between the present and a potential afterlife, between what we know and what we imagine, between the factual and the magical. And since horror film is a genre marked by fear and suspense, the ruminative promise of graveyards usually transmutes into an atmospheric build-up of unexpected, whimsical encounters with dwellers from beyond.

Figure 8.1 Henry profanes a grave under the watchful eye of a *memento mori* in *Frankenstein* (1931).

Graveyards had been a significant part of the shorter narrative films that preceded Whale's *Frankenstein*, especially of *féeries* (films based on fairy tales and legends), where they served as the backdrop for supernatural manifestations both affable and mean-spirited. In Georges Méliès's *La Fée Carabosse ou le poignard fatal* (*The Witch*, 1906), Lothaire, a troubadour escaping from a witch he has cheated out of a magic charm, stumbles upon a haunted cemetery. As he kneels in front of a cross, coffin lids open up to liberate a fright of ghosts. The graveyard is another setting where magical phenomena may spontaneously occur, functioning much as the sacred Druid field earlier in the film or the grounds of the enchanted castle at the end. Films made during the first few years of cinema history were particularly invested in visual spectacle, so set pieces that allowed for displays of the medium's trademark optical illusions, from superimpositions to stop-motion photography, were popular. My point is not to suggest that graveyards had a purely aesthetic value, but rather that these tended to accentuate the fanciful elements of stories that naturally veered towards the extraordinary. In Segundo de Chomón's *La Légende du fantôme* (*The Black Pearl*, aka *Legend of a Ghost*, 1908), a young woman (Julienne Mathieu) passing by a churchyard becomes embroiled in a plot to aid its residing ghost. The apparition, surrounded by foreboding ruins, is the catalyst for an adventure that sees the protagonist descend into Satan's kingdom to retrieve a special life-giving elixir. The graveyard of the film's first few minutes, like hell in the second half, plays an atmospheric role that is nevertheless part and parcel of the story. Given their source material, *féeries* contained a roster of monsters that are now genre mainstays, such as witches, demons and ghosts. Similarly, graveyards became a crucial location in Gothic film among a number of sinister and mystical fixtures, such as alchemist workshops, medieval castles, derelict churches, inquisitorial chambers, dark caves and claustrophobic grottoes.[4]

By the late nineteenth century, graveyards were part of the iconography of Gothic visual arts and of pre-cinematic phantasmagoria shows (Jones, 2018: 21). Later, now canonical, films such as *The Bride of Frankenstein* (1935), *The Wolf Man* (1941), *The Ghost of Frankenstein* (1942), *The Mummy's Tomb* (1942) and *Frankenstein Meets the Wolf Man* (1943) cemented these aesthetic and affective connections at the level of genre.[5] Graveyards combined enchantment with anxiety, the normative with the exceptional. If, in the popular imagination, they have long been associated with solitude, tranquillity and reflection, in the Gothic mode they thrive with life. As bastions of memory guarding the remains of those who have passed away, it is only logical that they have come to articulate the permeability between life and death that is still such a significant trope in the Gothic. They can mediate complex religious explorations on the nature of consecrated ground or its role in resurrection, as well as serve more prosaic, oftentimes pragmatic, purposes.[6] They act as passageways for supernatural creatures or phenomena, generally real but sometimes imagined. There is hesitancy about the Gothic graveyard, where the dead are often restless and thirsty for blood and revenge, and a tension between the ponderous, the gleeful and the truculent aspects of its landscape. The remainder of this chapter seeks to position graveyards, which have received little attention in horror scholarship, at the heart of Gothic cinema's concerns. First, I turn to zombies as their most characteristic metonymic character and read them as incarnations of the metaphysical quandaries posed by Gothic horror. I then turn to the graveyard's other main role as hinge, not just between the here and the beyond, but between defined factions and communities, normative ones and those relegated to social ostracism. The filmic examples in this chapter are drawn primarily from US and European cinema, since their industries have been instrumental in the creation of a Gothic aesthetic in the history of horror film, and their cemeteries have been the most foundational to its associated penumbral iconography.

Sometimes they come back

Writing of the chilling effect of carved skulls and messages on gravestones that point to the fleetingness of life, poet Jean Sprackland suggests that the graveside imagery of twenty-first-century Britons is more likely to give prominence to scenes taken from life than that of their eighteenth-century predecessors, for whom death was a more present physical reality. The Victorian preference for angels, crowns and doves signals a shift in the perception of graveyards as 'a realm beyond death, a place of transcendence' (Sprackland, 2020: 35). By contrast, to mark graves with skulls today is hard to imagine; the choice would seem 'morbid, inappropriate, in bad taste' (2020: 35). Equally abject is to rest one's eyes on the spoils of life, on the 'fearful object of the corpse' (2020: 35). Drawing on Julia Kristeva, Sprackland explains that corpses are fearful because they are 'paradoxical: abandoned by life but still bearing its resemblance, neither person nor non-person, precious but requiring disposal because' they lose their 'wholesomeness so quickly' (2020: 35). Horror revels in repressed images and behaviours and celebrates the return of the dead in the form of nightmares. The same qualities that Sprackland ascribes to corpses apply to their supernaturally animated cousins, whose interstitial nature and active decay make them living reminders of the inescapable end we must all meet. Among all Gothic monsters, they are the most intimately associated with graveyards and their cultural meanings.

George A. Romero's zombie classic *Night of the Living Dead* (1968) begins in Evans City Cemetery in Butler County, Pennsylvania. Although an unremarkable and subdued location by today's horror standards or those of contemporary efforts like Hammer's *The Plague of the Zombies* (1966), *Taste the Blood of Dracula* (1970) and *Lust for a Vampire* (1971), its emptiness conveys a sense of isolation that is only amplified by the claw-like branches of the local trees and the film's ominous score. As Ben Hervey points out, the opening line announces the arrival of summer, yet the dreary landscape and coats worn by Barbra (Judith O'Dea) and Johnny (Russell Streiner) betray the fact that the scene was actually shot in November (2020: 31). The cemetery is also a hostile place: the siblings get lost in search of their father's tomb and are soon attacked by a marauding zombie. As tends to happen in horror, irreverence and selfishness are often paid for dearly, and *Night of the Living Dead* sets a clear distinction between the pious Barbra and her unscrupulous brother, who complains about the six-hour drive to the cemetery. While still in the car, he dismisses a cross-shaped wreath intended for their dad, chiding that he does not even 'remember what the man looks like' anymore. Johnny's thriftiness (he would like to be able to reuse the same ornament every year), derision (he mocks his infirm mother's wishes that they visit the tomb on her behalf) and lapsed faith (he no longer attends church) are all underscored before he falls prey to a zombie, a sign that Gothic horror leaves no room for disrespect of the dead or light-hearted stances towards memorialisation.

Two of the main emotions favoured by Gothic texts are fear and suspense, so graveyards in horror films can operate like jack-in-the-boxes, as shocking containers of secrets intended to surprise or influence the plot.[7] This more overt employment of the graveyard can be observed in the last sequence in Brian Yuzna's *Bride of Re-Animator* (1990), where Herbert West's (Jeffrey Combs) laboratory is revealed as sharing a wall with a cemetery crypt hosting discarded test subjects. This finale is a smorgasbord of reanimated prosthetic grotesqueries that may also be read as a cathartic release of the characters' barely contained sexual urges. The old dark house in Lucio Fulci's *Quella villa accanto al cimitero* (*The House by the Cemetery*, 1981) also hides a skeleton in the cupboard, or rather a series of them under its floorboards. When the Boyle family move from New York to New Whitby, Boston, little do they suspect the tendrils of their neighbouring cemetery reach as far as their property's foundations. When they eventually break into their cellar, they must face Dr Freudstein (Giovanni De Nava), an undead Victorian surgeon who has been using his victims to 'renew his [blood] cells'.[8] Monsters conceal themselves and come back in these examples; graveyards are put to the service of postponing the unmasking of their creatures' repugnant appearances and of the unethical principles behind their resuscitation or expanded lifespans. Other times, underground stowaways can play a more subtextual role, particularly because whatever is buried or killed in Gothic horror rarely stays quiet for long. Famously, Brian de Palma's *Carrie* (1976) closes with a nightmare scene in which the hand of the titular telekinetic teenager reaches out from the ground to grab the arm of a classmate – a reminder that monsters cannot be defeated. The lasting motif of the avenging ghost or waif has been exploited in numerous films, perhaps most conscientiously in *La maschera del demonio* (*Black Sunday*, 1960), *Amanti d'oltretomba* (*Nightmare Castle*, 1965) and other Italian Gothics of the 1950s and 1960s. The returning agent does not have to be a silenced benevolent voice and can be fundamentally evil, like the trio of 'greasers' in the Stephen King adaptation *Sometimes They Come Back* (1991). Yet the revenant is routinely imbued with metaphorical value as an expression of grief or of anachronistic beliefs and habits.

In Amando de Ossorio's cult classic *La noche del terror ciego* (*Tombs of the Blind Dead*, 1972), graveyards, like their undead inhabitants, are arbiters of the old ways. The Blind Dead of the title are a fictionalised version of the Knights Templar, a medieval chivalric order dissolved in the fourteenth century due to charges of heresy and occultist practices. Their remains, skeletons blinded by crows in the gallows, lie in the ruins of Berzano, an abandoned medieval village on the border between Spain and Portugal. The grey monastic robes that clothe the Blind Dead fit the arid and neglected surroundings of the abbey they protect and strongly contrast with the modern flares, miniskirts and bikinis of the human protagonists. The behaviour of these youths, who flirt freely with each other, enjoy busy holiday resorts and listen to jazz music, is presented as modern and liberated, even licentious. Much as the stalker does in slashers, the Blind Dead punish those who venture into their territory for their temerity, but also for their sins. The first victim, Virginia (María Elena Arpón), is shown reminiscing about a lesbian affair before she is killed. And in the climax of the film, sex is one of the catalysts for the second awakening of the Blind Dead. The knights may represent the suppression of repressed libidinal forces, but they also stand for an older authoritarian order, one that is out of sync with a materialist present dominated by 'progress' and 'science'.[9] It is no coincidence that *La noche del terror ciego* was made towards the tail-end of Francisco Franco's dictatorship, following the gradual 'aperturismo' of the 1960s.[10] Neither is it surprising that the attire and lodgings of the living dead connote the religious and military spheres if one considers the pivotal role the army and the church had in the success of Francoism. The Blind Dead, and their misty, forlorn tombs, can thus be interpreted as allegories for political persecution and despotism (Figure 8.2). In fact, many of the Gothic monsters created

Figure 8.2 Repressive ideologies rise from the tomb in
La noche del terror ciego (1972).

by Spanish filmmakers during this period exhibit tyrannical traits typically linked to fascism and authoritarian governments.

In Gothic horror, graveyards can stage the tensions between the conservative and reformist forces that have shaped countries like Spain. In its case, they may be considered metaphors for collective forgetting, for a country's decision to put aside painful moments in recent history. The 'Pacto del Olvido' (Pact of Forgetting), given legal basis two years after Franco's death, was drawn to avoid confronting his direct legacy and ensure a smooth transition to democracy. Yet trauma, as the Gothic mode which often gives it a voice, tends to surface. By the twenty-first century, a self-imposed pristine culture of silence had begun to show cracks, and many Spaniards took to digging up the civilian dead in a shared effort to recognise and mourn the victims of the war. Concurrently, the horror genre saw a resurgence as part of a wider 'memory boom', which often relied on Gothic tropes of hauntings and curses and whose plots took place during or directly after the Civil War (1936–9), as in *El espinazo del diablo* (*The Devil's Backbone*, 2001) and *Insensibles* (*Painless*, 2012). Even wholesale national efforts cannot definitely put the past to rest; the ghosts and revenants of war come out of their unmarked graves to demand admission in the popular imagination. At the end of Pedro Almodóvar's *Madres paralelas* (*Parallel Mothers*, 2021), a group of gravediggers looking to grant relatives proper burial assume the position of the bones they have recovered in a macabre and evocative substitution that draws a material line between past crime and present reparation.

Gothic cinema mobilises metaphysical ideas thanks to the imaginative, hallucinatory and transgressive language of the fantastic. Some films, like *Dellamorte Dellamore* (*Cemetery Man*, 1994), based on the 1991 novel by Italian writer Tiziano Sclavi, do this so decisively that they practically amount to philosophical treatises. The plot of *Dellamorte Dellamore* follows the adventures of loner Francesco (Rupert Everett), the caretaker (the 'watchman of the cemetery', as he is affectionately called) of Buffalora, a town where the dead have begun to rise on the seventh night after interment for no obvious reason. The film tracks Francesco's descent into insouciance and despondency, as various love affairs fail and the humdrum job of keeping the dead at bay grows tedious. These are not Romero's scary zombies, but, in the words of scriptwriter Gianni Romoli, the incarnation of 'routine, the boredom of life, the impossibility of recovery, and the impossibility to escape this pain'.[11] *Dellamorte Dellamore* is also peppered with downbeat and gloomy lines such as 'we all do what we can not to think about life'; 'time passes. Nothing seems the same. It just gets worse'; 'we are born to die'; and 'everything that's not shitty is sleep'. As the title suggests, Francesco's life, whose mother's maiden name happens to be Dellamore, is also structured by love, or the need to find an emotional partner. When he is not polishing off the mischievous dead, we see him failing to date three different women – all played by the same actress, Anna Falchi, in a triptych that represents archetypal female unattainability (McDonagh, 1996: 47). 'Through with love' and no longer able to 'tell who's dead or alive', Francesco decides to escape Buffalora in a bid to seek transcendence and fight 'provincial asphyxia' (Pinkerton, 2006). The trip is short-lived, for he soon discovers the motorway ends abruptly in an open chasm. As the credits roll, a match cut suggests Francesco may actually have been residing inside a snow globe.

Whether taken as a serious narrative invitation or an enigmatic associative image, the ending enhances the overall message that 'life is hard and then you die', that existence is made up of repetitive drudgery, disappointment and delusion rather than emancipatory pleasure. The only consolation is true friendship, which Francesco finds in assistant Gnaghi (François Hadji-Lazaro). A true companion can help us relativise injustices understand our irrational impulses and passions, and lighten up misfortune with laughter. A comparable catharsis may be found in the consumption of a more playful graveyard Gothic where zombies do not horrify but nudge towards the acceptance that, as *Dellamorte Dellamore* would put it, 'the living dead and the dying living are the same'. The graveyard in Buffalora, and in the broader Gothic mode, is a microcosm, an incongruent edgeland able to encompass everything from excitement to tongue-in-cheek gallows humour and sobering tragedy.

The underworld's other worlds

Barriers between the living and the dead are at their most porous in cemeteries, where the rules of urban bustle seem suspended. French director Jean Rollin, whose *fantastique* films usually blended Gothic settings (ruins, castles, grand manors, cemeteries) with erotica, explored these ideas in the dreamlike *La Rose de fer* (*The Iron Rose*, 1973). The film centres on two youngsters who visit a cemetery on their first date and get irremediably lost. The young woman (Françoise Pascal), initially reticent and frightened at the thought of being trapped in such a hostile environment, grows morbid and moody as the night advances, and eventually leaves her lover (Hugues Quester) to suffocate in the crypt where they previously made love. When the dawn arrives, she locks herself in too, uttering a quizzical 'all of them are dead; we are alive'.[12] The film's early dialogue frames this strange turn of events. The man is sceptical about the value of memorials and paints the cemetery as peaceful and green. By contrast, the woman asks questions about the possible connection between our bodies and souls and, once their nocturnal ordeal starts, addresses the dead personally. At a key point, she wonders: 'Why be obsessed by death when surrounded by this beautiful garden with trees above us and sand beneath, and small houses like homes for us? And statues to protect us?' This short speech is telling, for it speaks to her rethinking (and implicitly, the viewer's) of cemeteries as welcoming cities of the resting dead. The woman's donning of a skull over her own face, a macabre mask, hints at the slippage between worlds. Rollin is keen, as in all his other works, to both demystify and embellish funereal landscapes, to estrange them by indulging in their images. In *La Rose de fer*, to stay too long in a graveyard is to risk being infected by the logic of death. After all, little separates sepulchral visitors from perpetual residents. And yet, there is nothing supernatural about the film, only surreal moments, like the appearance of a mourner dressed as a clown and of another wearing what looks like a vampiric cape. As in much of Rollin's cinema, brooding shots and an apparently aimless narrative render events oneiric.

Other Gothic films make more decided leaps towards the exploration of graveyards as other worlds or as doors to them. Upon re-entering the cemetery in *La Rose de fer*, the young man paraphrases the famous line from *Inferno* (*Hell*) 'Lasciate ogne speranza, voi ch'intrate'. Commonly translated as 'abandon all hope, ye who enter here', the inscription frames the gates to hell in Dante Alighieri's epic poem. The man's remark is intended to humour his companion for her hesitation, but it takes on an eerier, much less comforting hue once the sun has set and the graveyard begins to resemble a confining limbo. The same sentence is uncovered deep in the Paris Catacombs by the protagonists of the found-footage horror *As Above, So*

Below (2014). The famous French underground ossuary, itself boasting the cautionary injunction 'Arrète! C'est ici l'empire de la mort' (Stop! This is the empire of death), stands as the world's largest mass grave, holding the remains of more than 6 million people. In graveyard Gothic, such a vast negative space – a chthonian city of the dead – is naturally injected with dark magic: the off-limits cave tunnels double as infernal ingress. As many other horror films do, *As Above, So Below* establishes a continuity between real locations that accommodate bones and spiritual ones that carry their souls.

Much as, in Greek mythology, the Styx (the river and threshold dividing the living from the dead) needs a psychopomp (Charon) to ferry the newly deceased, graveyard Gothic cinema requires its sentinels. From fictional 'bio-exorcists' of the netherworld like Betelgeuse in Tim Burton's *Beetlejuice* (1988) and horror hosts like the Crypt-Keeper (created by EC Comics, but making a jump to film in the 1970s and 1980s) to supernatural figures based on religious beliefs, such as Baron Samedi, one of the loa (spirits) of the dead in Haitian Vodou and who appears in films like Paul Maslansky's *Sugar Hill* (1974), gravesides in the Gothic tend to be well guarded. Nowhere is this concept better exploited than in Dan Coscarelli's *Phantasm* (1979), whose Tall Man (Angus Scrimm) has become a modern addition to horror's monster pantheon. In the film, the evil undertaker who looks after Morningside Cemetery is secretly turning the dead into dwarf zombies he then enslaves and takes to a planet accessible through a funeral parlour. The Tall Man's background is uncovered later in the series, in *Phantasm IV: Oblivion* (1998), but his origins as a nineteenth-century mortician who becomes a time-travelling, transdimensional alien are less interesting than the series' barely repressed anxieties about the mortuary handling of bodies. Evidently a symbol for death, the Tall Man also represents the perplexing nature of funeral practices to young Mike (A. Michael Baldwin), who grieves his dead young brother and parents. His defeat of evil plays out like a *Bildungsroman* of sorts, a coming-of-age story in which awareness of death and the pain that follows loss accelerate Mike's growing-up. Accordingly, the film's striking coda, in which the Tall Man appears reflected in the boy's bedroom mirror before a pair of arms pull the victim inside, spells another adult truth: there is no defeating death, only its temporary postponement. The portal here is not to hell, rather to another dimension that resembles it, but the conceit speaks to metaphysical speculations about what lies beyond. It is little wonder that open casket wakes, with their blurring of lines between the realms of the living and the dead, have been the source of many fictional supernatural happenings.[13]

In the Gothic, graveyard thresholds are not relegated to *tableaux vivants* of hell and loss. Their inherent seclusion and distance from the vagaries and protocols of society also make them interesting places for the celebration of difference and inclusivity. In Clive Barker's *Nightbreed* (1990), an adaptation of his own 1988 novel *Cabal*, Midian, a massive city beneath a picturesque graveyard (Figure 8.3), acts as refuge for the 'remains of races' that humanity has 'almost driven to extinction'.[14] There, juvenile delinquent turned messiah Aaron Boone (Craig Sheffer) is inducted into the worship of Baphomet, the baptiser, a deity representing the equilibrium of opposites and therefore also a balanced social order (Introvigne, 2016: 108–9).[15] Midian is an Elysium where 'all your sins are forgiven', a place to 'escape' to when 'there's no place else on Earth would take [you] in'.[16] Like the 'happy Gothic' (Spooner, 2017: 3) of Tim Burton's *Frankenweenie* (2012) and the *Hotel Transylvania* franchise (2012–22), where graveyards are full of lively and amusing monsters, *Nightbreed* puts forward a tolerant message about its creatures. It pits a psychotherapist, the police and a priest – stalwarts of (hetero)normativity, law and convention – as the unconscionable ones, thereby short-circuiting the ableist chain of associations that renders uniqueness a character flaw and paints the outsider as anomalous. As a film made by an openly gay writer and filmmaker, *Nightbreed* invites a queer reading of alterity that encourages a re-evaluation of the Other as misunderstood, sympathetic hero and a condemnation of nonconformity as homogenising, manipulative psychopathy.[17] The image of the graveyard is therefore renovated in a horror film with an openly 'anti-horr[ific]' agenda (Winter, 2001: 190).[18] Reconceived

Figure 8.3 In *Nightbreed* (1990), a necropolis is the gateway to Midian, a sanctuary for persecuted monsters.

as pagan fortresses of 'weird' anti-assimilationist resistance, Gothic graveyards may also provide solace.

Graveyards in Western Gothic cinema have become an intrinsic part of the aesthetic vocabulary of horror, bridging the gaps between effect-driven atmospherics and serious subject matter, and suturing specific cultural anxieties into canonical narrative conventions that speak to the mode's interest in the unearthing of the past – its unspeakable secrets, injustices and repressions. Their metonymic figuration of death, the greatest human fear, sometimes takes anthropomorphic shape in the Gothic's infinite revenants and crepuscular dwellers, who claw their way out of tombs and mausolea to force the living into earth-shattering moments of reckoning and acceptance of the inexorable progress of ageing and the finitude of life. Other times, graveyards act as literal passageways, as corridors to the great unknown, the numinous and imponderables that exist beyond the metric grasp of empiricism and the exacting test tubes of science. In the process, they make us question who gets pushed underneath, below the fabric of acceptable society, who is forced to inhabit subterranean spaces that defy majoritarian understandings of the traditional and the expected. Like the Cenobites in Clive Barker's *Hellraiser* (1986), graveyard creatures exist in the interstices between reality and the joys and risks of imagining life otherwise. Graveyards invite us to think about humanity's greatest obsession – what film critic André Bazin identified as the plastic arts' 'mummy complex', or the drive to find a defence against 'death' and 'the victory of time' (2005: 9) by embalming change. For Bazin, photography and cinema were a logical evolution of this basic psychological human need. Cinema's capacity to capture moving images allows the medium to etch ever closer to 'a total and complete representation of reality' (2005: 20).

If graveyards in Gothic cinema serve to channel concerns about the ephemerality of life, about the vulnerability of our bodies, about the fragility of memory and the unlikelihood of anything ever enduring in a constantly changing world where chaos rules, about the impossibility of accurately retrieving foregone events, cinema simultaneously acts as a Gothic repository of mortal fears. Sometimes, as in the case of recovered lost films like J. Searle Dawley's *Frankenstein* (1910) and F. W. Murnau's *Nosferatu, eine Symphonie des Grauens* (*Nosferatu: A Symphony of Horror*, 1922), this cinematic graveyard persists against the odds, for Gothic horror has not always been perceived as worthy of critical attention or preservation. Gothic cinema both conserves the influential work of countless directors, screenwriters, actors and cinematographers and allows us to observe the evolution of the anxieties bespoken by their dreadful scenarios. To study the history of Gothic horror is to examine distinct cross-sections of sociopolitical and economic concerns from the late nineteenth century to the present time. Gothic cinema is a memorial to its own artists, as well as a mass grave for our collective worries about dying, the burden of history, the irreversibility of time and the effects of trauma. It is this admonishing function, its warning against complacency and mindlessness, its demand that we take the past and history seriously, that makes it so attractive, even compulsive, to so many viewers and film critics.

Notes

1 The film has a pre-credits cautionary address to the audience, which I am not counting as a first scene.
2 The words are spoken by Dr Waldman (Edward Van Sloan), Frankenstein's former teacher.
3 This symbology is not limited to skeletons but is observable in the wider hauntological nature of funerary effigies (see Schnitt 1998).
4 Throughout, I use the term 'Gothic cinema' to designate an aesthetic mode that can be neatly separated from the wider horror genre, and may include melodrama and romance (see Aldana Reyes, 2020: 6–17). In practice, the textual examples in this chapter belong to the Gothic horror tradition, that is, to horror films with a marked Gothic aesthetic.
5 Some examples of horror-driven films that feature cemeteries, but which I do not have the space to cover here, include *I Bury the Living* (1958), *Planet 9 from Outer Space* (1959), *The City of the Dead* (1960), *The Omen* (1976), *Return of the Living Dead* (1985) and *Army of Darkness* (1992). I am also leaving aside films about ancient burial grounds, such as *Poltergeist* (1982) and *Pet Sematary* (1989), because these are the focus of Kevin Corstorphine's chapter in this collection. Vampire films' engagement with folkloric burial practices are similarly sidestepped due to their complexity and number, but interested readers should consult Paul Barber (2010).
6 Andrew Smith refers to the strained relationship between meaning and affect when he writes about the dead becoming embroiled in the 'rhetorical construction of emotion in [the] emerging Gothic aesthetic' (2016: 193) of the late eighteenth and early nineteenth centuries.
7 Inscriptions in tombstones usually provide additional clues to the characters' lives, as happens in *Great Expectations* (1946), *The Others* (2001) and *The Woman in Black* (2012).
8 The line is taken from the dubbed version of the film in the 2017 Arrow Video DVD release.
9 The words are spoken by Professor Cantell (Francisco Sanz) in the original Spanish, available in the 2005 Anchor Bay DVD release.
10 'Aperturismo' designates a number of progressive policies introduced in 1960s Spain by those politicians who felt the regime needed to become less authoritarian to continue in power in the context of a more liberated Europe.
11 The quote is taken from the English subtitle for the director and writer's Italian commentary in the 2012 *Shameless* DVD release. The dialogue cited elsewhere in the paragraph is also taken from this edition of the film.

12 The English subtitles cited in this paragraph are taken from the Redemption 2014 DVD release.
13 A good example of this trope is the hallucination induced on Herman (Anton Walbrook) by his encounter with the corpse of the deceased countess (Edith Evans) in Thorold Dickinson's *The Queen of Spades* (1949).
14 The line is spoken by Rachel (Catherine Chevalier), who also defines the Nightbreed as 'shapeshifters' and 'freaks', and suggests that the reason they are hated is because their abilities are secretly envied by humans.
15 The Satanic Temple have used Baphomet in this manner, as 'a symbol of man's inherent nature, representative of the eternal rebel, enlightened inquiry and personal freedom' (Morgan 2015).
16 These lines are spoken by Dr Decker (David Cronenberg), Boone (Craig Sheffer) and Narcisse (Hugh Ross), respectively. Midian is mentioned in the Bible, a passage of which is quoted later in the film by Father Ashbury (Malcolm Smith).
17 Indeed, the film has been read as a 'coming-out narrative' (Benshoff, 1997: 263) and the Nightbreed as a symbol of 'openly queer communit[ies]' (Adams, 2017: 140).
18 For Douglas E. Winter, 'anti-horror' is ambiguous and liberating, avoids Manichean constructions of good versus evil, and uses the genre's tropes not to horrify but 'to force the reader to imagine' (2001: 191).

References

Adams, Mark Richard (2017) 'Clive Barker's Queer Monsters: Exploring Transgression, Sexuality, and the Other', in Sorcha Ní Fhlainn (ed.), *Clive Barker: Dark Imaginer* (Manchester: Manchester University Press), pp. 129–47.
Aldana Reyes, Xavier (2020) *Gothic Cinema* (Abingdon: Routledge).
Barber, Paul (2010) *Vampires, Burial, and Death* (New Haven: Yale University Press).
Bazin, André (2005) [1967] *What Is Cinema?*, ed. and trans. Hugh Gray (Berkeley: University of California Press).
Benshoff, Harry M. (1997) *Monsters in the Closet: Homosexuality and the Horror Film* (Manchester: Manchester University Press).
Frayling, Christopher (2005) *Mad, Bad and Dangerous? The Scientist and the Cinema* (London: Reaktion Books).
Hervey, Ben (2020) [2008] *Night of the Living Dead* (London: Bloomsbury).
Introvigne, Massimo (2016) *Satanism: A Social History* (Leiden: Brill).
Jones, David Annwn (2018) *Gothic Effigy: A Guide to Dark Visibilities* (Manchester: Manchester University Press).
McDonagh, Maitland (1996) 'Vintage Soavi', *Film Comment*, 32:2, 47–50.
Morgan, James (2015) 'Decoding the Symbols on Satan's Statue', BBC News, www.bbc.co.uk/news/magazine-33682878 (accessed 7 February 2022).
Pinkerton, Nick (2006) '*Cemetery Man (Dellamorte Dellamore)* Review', *Reverse Shot: Museum of the Moving Image*, www.reverseshot.org/reviews/entry/1467/cemetery_man (accessed 7 February 2022).

Schnitt, Jean-Claude (1998) [1994] *Ghosts in the Medieval Ages: The Living and the Dead in Medieval Society*, trans. Teresa Lavender Fagan (Chicago: Chicago University Press).

Smith, Andrew (2016) *Gothic Death 1740–1914: A Literary History* (Manchester: Manchester University Press).

Spooner, Catherine (2017) *Post-Millennial Gothic: Comedy, Romance and the Rise of Happy Gothic* (London: Bloomsbury Academic).

Sprackland, Jean (2020) *These Silent Mansions: A Life in Graveyards* (London: Jonathan Cape).

Winter, Douglas E. (2001) *Clive Barker: The Dark Fantastic* (London: HarperCollins).

9

The ventriloquised corpse and the silent dead: Gothic of the British First and Second World Wars

Sara Wasson

In June 1940, the *Times* newspaper published a letter a British airman had written to be sent to his mother in the event of his death. Vivian Rosewarne wrote of his willingness to die in the combat, as a sacrifice to support 'the British Empire where there is a measure of peace, justice and freedom for all … I count myself lucky … to throw my full weight into the scale' (1991: 307–8). The letter was enormously popular, reprinted as a pamphlet and ultimately a film, Michael Powell's *An Airman's Letter to His Mother* (1941). Rosewarne's words offered comfort to many. The war dead might speak; more, they might say their sacrifice was willing.

This chapter, by contrast, is about the silence of the dead. Existing criticism within Gothic studies has considered the soldier revenant, who resents their sacrifice and bears malice towards the living (Soltysik Monnet and Hantke, 2016: xv). This present chapter, too, shows how Gothic representations may undercut national commemoration's narratives of willing, heroic death, but here I explore the issue with a different emphasis. This different emphasis stems from my taking, as my focus, war graves and the *interment* of the dead, both of which take on particular complexity during the First and Second World Wars. Rather than the speaking spectre, this chapter concerns the silent corpse – rotting and speechless, it cannot be readily recruited to narratives of national glory or resilience. As such, it disrupts those mythologies, while simultaneously bringing awareness of the grief, chaos and squalour of war.

This chapter draws on work in a range of forms, but most notably poetry and prose of first-person experience. Indeed, the very categories of 'memoir' and 'fiction' become blurred in multiple ways in many of these works. Combatants, for example, may draw on first-person experience to inform ostensibly fictional writing, or adopt highly hallucinatory and feverish narrative modes to describe equally hallucinatory and feverish lived experience. As such, many of these works invite us to consider how 'Gothic' has always also been a discursive mode that can break fictional confines. Gothic tropes, forms and intertextualities can be deployed outside of the pleasure-space of fiction and can be used, among other things, to represent historical suffering in an 'unofficial history', in David Punter's words (1996: 187). A wide range of scholarship has examined how Gothic discursivity may be deployed to articulate such lived suffering (e.g., Blake, 2008; Mulvey-Roberts, 2016; Wester, 2012; Wasson, 2010; Wasson, 2020). Such Gothic discursivity is not, however, predictable in its effects, and is as multivalent and ambiguous as the forms it takes in fiction. In *Transplantation Gothic* I propose the coinage of 'bodies dis(re)membered' to describe the need for cautious recognition of four contradictory ways that Gothic 'can conduct ambiguous cultural work within these discursive borderlands':

> First, in their preoccupations with dismemberment – with dissection and vivisection – these works may mark efforts to subversively remember ... Secondly, any such work is always a *dis*remembering in the sense that it is a failed effort to represent, since it can always only ever be incomplete ... Thirdly, Gothic representations can mediate a more conservative re-membering, more obedient to dominant trends ... Fourthly, the prefixes *dis-* and *re-* speak of collapse and assembly and capture something of ... a process involving human and nonhuman entities.
>
> (2020: 9)

Fraught, contrary and ambiguous, Gothic can be bent to multiple ends. With that caveat, what I will offer in this chapter is a consideration of the first of these movements: the work of re-membering suffering. Such work must also always, inevitably, acknowledge the second point: the simultaneous necessity and impossibility of such representation (Derrida, 1986; Derrida, 1989; Derrida, 1994; Wasson, 2010: 157–62).

The ventriloquised corpse and the work of the dead

As the fervour for Rosewarne's letter shows, wars can evoke popular and government appetite for the trope I call the 'ventriloquised corpse', 'in which, in the imagination of the living, the dead declare that their sacrifice was willing and worthwhile' (Wasson, 2010: 132). Such speech can be precious, not only for the bereaved but also for a nation. Benedict Anderson has shown how combatant death is sacred within national story, for such deaths become woven into a narrative which 'makes each death ... a foreshadowing of each succeeding death, in a long movement toward a resplendent living present' (1986: 659; cf. Anderson, 1991: 9). During both World Wars commemorative practices explicitly wove combatant death into stories of national identity and resilience. London's Cenotaph, for example, was described by Prime Minister Lloyd George as 'a national shrine, not only for the British Isles, but also for the whole Empire', and the Unknown Warrior was interred under a marble slab commemorating that his death had been 'for King and Country, for loved ones, home and Empire' (Hanson, 2007: 462).

In what follows, I in no way cast aspersions on the solace such commemorative practices can bring to those who grieve. I do, however, wish to acknowledge potential risks around commemorative practice, including the way that it may sometimes marginalise certain lives at the expense of others or, alternatively, make it harder to question national management of a conflict, including the way that soldiers – including living veterans – may be neglected or unheard. Faced with such problems, some critics articulate a range of non-normative forms of mourning which lack some of the closures of traditional commemoration. In lacking such closure, such practices can frame a space for ongoing questioning of dimensions of the war, inequalities and its human cost. Jahan Ramazani, for example, speaks of 'depathologised melancholia' (2007); Patricia Rae speaks of 'resistant mourning' (2007); Judith Butler suggests value in 'remaining exposed to its unbearability' (2004: 30); and Jacques Derrida articulates a complex ethical state in which a griever seeks to remain haunted by the lost (1986: xvii; 1989: 35; 1994: xix). In varying ways, such writers consider the need for death representation that unsettles a reader in the service of respecting the particularity of the dead, and confronts the reader with suffering. As I say elsewhere, '"resistant" mourning discerns political value in incomplete mourning and ongoing emotional pain, denying neither the painful loss nor the circumstances that caused it. Such grief arguably has political force' (Wasson, 2020: 158). Much Gothic writing offers exactly such unease.

From one perspective, the dead at this time were increasingly articulate thanks to the surge of interest in spiritualism (Winder, 1995: 54). This 'necromantic religion', as Owen Davies phrases it, purported to connect with the beloved dead via mediumistic intervention (2009: 132). Andrew Smith has shown the rich heterogeneity of fiction and spiritualist writing about World War soldier ghosts, who ranged from benevolent (especially in spiritualist periodicals) through to more disturbing fictions in which a soldier-spirit may wish revenge or become corrupted in the spirit world (2022: 110–56). Even more mainstream media publications could attempt such contact. One of the more startling representations of combatant ambivalence appeared in the *Sunday Pictorial*, when journalist H. Shirley Long hired a medium to investigate the question, 'Can our heroes who have given their lives ... come back to give a message of hope to the living?' (1940: 25). In an article titled 'To a Boy Who Was Killed Two Weeks Ago!', Long purportedly talks via a medium to a young sailor who died violently, but Long finds little hope, for his alleged spiritual interlocutor is disoriented, fearful and unaware of his own death. Indeed, part of the appeal of the safely ventriloquised corpse is that it can soothe anxieties about what *else* the war dead might want to say. Steffen Hantke and Agnieszka Soltysik Monnet point out, for example, a hint of menace even in the pastoral graveyard of John McCrae's famous poem 'In Flanders Fields', which includes the lines, 'If ye break faith with us who die / We shall not sleep, though poppies grow / In Flanders fields' (2006: 155). Soltysik Monnet and Hantke identify a long tradition of fiction and film in which soldier-revenants return for revenge (2016: xv); unlike Rosewarne, these war dead resent their sacrifice. Veteran Siegfried Sassoon imagines spectral resentment in his poem 'On Passing the New Menin Gate' (1927), occasioned by the inauguration of the war memorial at Ypres. He speaks scathingly of the Gateway's claim that 'Their name liveth for ever', and asks,

> Who will remember, passing through this Gate,
> the unheroic dead who fed the guns?
> ...
> Well might the Dead who struggled in the slime
> Rise and deride this sepulchre of crime.
>
> (1984: 188)

Avery Gordon has explored how ghost fictions can speak to suppressed horrors on a mass scale (1997), and at times, especially if conscription methods are unequal or the management of the war neglected combatant welfare, such fictional spectres may have ample cause for resentment.

In this chapter, however, I foreground the corpse rather than the ghost. This focus is markedly different from the lens that dominates national war commemoration in both Wars. The reality of dead bodies can pose challenges to national commemoration, as is borne out by the efforts made by government to minimise their visibility. Death has of course become increasingly less visible ever since the eighteenth century, with cemeteries being moved to the peripheries of towns, and changes occurring in the cultural processes of mourning, reducing sight of the dead (Ariès, 1976; Bauman, 1992: 134; Cannadine, 1981), but war saw even further urgency in concealment (Wasson, 2010: 135). Allyson Booth has coined the term 'corpselessness' (1996: 11) to describe the results of the British government's efforts to obscure public sight of corpses and coffins during both Wars. In World War I, the government decided not to repatriate the fallen, but to inter them near battlefields. On the World War II home front, photographers and war artists were forbidden to represent the dead, and censors checked photographs to ensure compliance. Sight of the dead posed significant challenges for public morale, as well as to national narratives of resilience and noble death in the service of the country.

If we focus on the corpse rather than the ghost, then two possible lacunae within national commemoration come into sharper relief. First, focusing on the corpses of the war dead arguably helps us reflect more on the embodied experience of those who died. Different in life, with radically varied experiences of conscription/voluntary, class, age, religion, ethnicity and more, their intersectionalities shaped not only their lives but their experience of the war and their death within it. Historians show that the anonymity of Tombs of Unknown Warriors can lend itself to a tendency to assume the figure within is a member of dominant majorities (Whalan, 2007). In the case of the British home front, for example, before the Unknown Warrior was interred at Westminster, the Dean of Westminster refused to consider making the church service less overtly Christian, rejecting the possibility that the Soldier might be Jewish (Hanson, 2007: 480). The Imperial War Graves Commission, in managing the military cemeteries of World War I, took care to respect non-Christian burial practices for soldiers of other faiths, and each such cemetery featured a secular 'Stone of Remembrance'. However, the other commemorative monument was the overtly Christian 'Cross of Sacrifice'.

Second, focusing on the corpses of the war dead helps us recognise the silence of the dead. After all, notwithstanding Rosewarne and the efforts of enterprising *Sunday Pictorial* journalists, most war dead did *not* speak or write from beyond the grave about their willingness to die. Offering neither consolation nor threat, the silent corpse confronts us with something more difficult to recuperate into a story of national resilience. Instead, it draws attention to the embodied suffering and passing of an individual person, the finality of death and the human cost of war.

Combatant graves in the First World War

Rupert Brooke's poem 'The Soldier' (1914) enshrines an idyllic vision of the war dead at peace: 'That there's some corner of a foreign field / That is for ever England' (1970: 23). In the dust of that earth lies 'a richer dust concealed; / A dust whom England bore, shaped, made aware' (1970: 23). The poem presents the ground as blessed and the war dead as at peace, consoled by a sense of national endurance. The poem quickly became enormously popular and was even woven into church services (Scutts, 2009: 392), and collections of Brooke's verse continued to significantly outsell the works of Wilfred Owen and many other war poets for decades (Hanna, 2013: 12–14). There was – and arguably still is – more willingness to hear of war death in terms of pastoral, peaceful endurance rather than the agonies of trench warfare. Though very different from the anonymous foreign grave of Brooke's poem, the majestic monuments of the Whitehall Cenotaph (built 1919–20) and Westminster Abbey's Tomb of the Unknown Warrior (1920) also invoke a sense of soldiers laid to peaceful rest in service of national story. As mentioned above, these structures were framed in terms of willing sacrifice for 'King', 'country' and 'Empire' (Hanson, 2007: 457, 431, 462, 474, 479; Ariès, 1976: 74–5). Thousands of smaller, local commemorative monuments and statues were also erected all around the country.

Actual war graves, however, were not easy to recuperate into forms that evoke peaceful death in the service of a nation. The sheer mass of death, as well as the violence of it, made such a story harder to tell. The Imperial War Graves Commission registered 1,081,952 as buried or missing in combat (Hanna, 2013: 8). Initially there was no centralised system for tracking the location of such graves, but in 1914 Fabian Ware began efforts to document them. His work laid the foundations for what ultimately became the Imperial War Graves Commission (IWGC) in 1917. The IWGC oversaw the creation of military cemeteries both during and after the War.

Initially, the army had worked on the assumption that only officers would receive individual grave markers (Carter and Jackson, 2000: 182), but it rapidly became clear that there was public expectation that each fallen soldier be so acknowledged (Wittman, 2011: 19). In reality, many of these sites conceal some shared graves (Fussell, 2013: 6). Furthermore, despite the individual markers, the war cemeteries were stark and lonely, and efforts were necessary to persuade the public of the appropriateness of these places of interment. One of the most important interventions in this regard was a reassuring article which Rudyard Kipling wrote for the *Times* newspaper, describing plans for the war cemeteries (1919). His article was so popular it was later printed as an illustrated booklet, *The Graves of the Fallen* (1919).

The IWGC sought to make the cemeteries visually and lexically part of the wider national narrative of combatants at peace and connected in their willing sacrifice for the nation. This cohesive narrative required '[p]ermanence and uniformity' (Scutts, 2009: 389), and the ensuing blueprint was used in the thousands of military cemeteries managed by the IWGC along the western front and in other theatres of war, including Greece, Italy, Palestine and Gallipoli. Each grave marker was carved in an identical shape from pale British Portland stone and used standardised lettering, symbols and layout (IWM, 2020). Joanna Scutts observes:

> Every aspect of the planning, creation and care of the British cemeteries was overseen by the independent Commission … Its single authorship ensured the cemeteries' legibility as symbolic spaces both in themselves and as part of an international network of remembrance. By its controversial decisions to limit the scope for personal messages and to ban any individual monuments, the Commission imposed a coherent memorial narrative across the wide diversity of sites where the graves were located.
>
> (2009: 389)

In his 1917 proposal for the cemeteries' design, Sir Frederic Kenyon recognised families might be dismayed that their loved one's death would be commemorated within tightly controlled ways:

> relatives have been looking forward to placing a memorial of their own choosing over the graves which mean so much to them ... Yet it is hoped that even these will realise that they are asked to join in an action of even higher significance ... the service of a common cause, the comradeship of arms ... the representatives of their country in the lands in which they served.
>
> (1917: 7)

Epitaph wording, too, was regulated in ways to not disrupt the uniformity of the site. Standardised wording was offered, mostly crafted by Kipling, who also wrote the inscriptions for the two main monuments which were built within each British war cemetery. For the 'Cross of Sacrifice', Kipling gave the inscription 'Lest we forget', and for the 'Stone of Remembrance', he chose a Biblical verse from Ecclesiastes: 'Their Name Liveth for Evermore'. Scutts comments on the tension between the two phrases, which 'turns visitors ... into active readers, challenging them to interpret and to reconcile the two poles of warning and reassurance' (2009: 397). In fairness, Kipling's short stories hold space for lacerating and ambiguous affects attendant on bereavement (Montefiore, 2007: 144), and he himself grieved his son who was killed at the Battle of Loos. This personal loss added poignancy to his decades of work with the Commission until his own death, and outside his work for the IWGC some of his writing was bitter with grief. Notably, on his son's death, he wrote the poem 'Epitaphs of the War' (1919), which includes the heartbroken and guilt-ridden couplet, 'If any question why we died, / Tell them, because our fathers lied' (Kipling, 2000: 172). Yet most of the epitaphs Kipling and others crafted for the IWGC cemeteries tended to reinforce the sense of combatant peace within a framework of soldierly fellowship and national sacrifice.

The Commission was initially hesitant to allow families to choose their own commemorative wording, but permission was eventually given, within constraints. Families had to pay a fee to personalise the epitaph, so not everybody who wished to could afford to. Further, the inscription had to be within 'three lines and "of the nature of a text or prayer"', and the IWGC had to approve each one. Ware warned the IWGC should prevent 'the effusions of the mortuary mason, the sentimental versifier, or the crank' (IWM, 2022). The headstones nonetheless encompass a range of tones. The veteran and historian Paul Fussell notes, 'some read as if refusing to play the game of memorial language at all', and he cites 'A sorrow too deep for words' as an example (2013: 77). Grief can be too vast to be encompassed by a national story of war.

These war cemeteries also remind us of the cultural processes involved in constructing a 'place of memory' according to Pierre Nora's definition: 'any significant entity, whether material or non-material in nature, which by dint of human will or the work of time has become a symbolic element of the memorial heritage of any community' (1996: xvii). Nora sees such cultural practices as fundamentally illusory and a marker of an evacuation of a more vivid relationship with memory operating in earlier times. Other scholarship foregrounds how such memory work also involves forgetting (Renan, 1882: 251). Guy Beiner analyses subtle ways in which 'social forgetfulness' works alongside memory in the cultural work of nations (2018). He draws on the work of Nancy Wood, who speaks of *lieux d'oubli*, 'places of forgetfulness', 'sites that public memory has expressly avoided because of the disturbing affect that their invocation is still capable of arousing' (Wood, 1999: 10; quoted in Beiner, 2018: 5). This chapter acknowledges both kinds of sites: on the one hand, national war cemeteries where the 'grave' is a carefully crafted marker created to reinforce a national story of shared resilience; and, on the other hand, other sites of *interment*, which take on uneasy qualities of a grave – specifically, trenches and ruined homes. I suggest these places offer *lieux de corps oubliés,* sites of *bodies forgotten*, insofar as they relentlessly bring attention back to the specific detail of the decay of particular bodies. In the process, the texts refuse to elide the material impact of war.

A graveyard is, of course, usually different from a place where dying occurred. A graveyard is often represented as a place of peace, as Serena Trowbridge says, an 'unchanging and tranquil setting' (2017: 38). Central to that peace is that the graveyard is a site where the dead are laid to rest, people gathering to dignify them by placing them in the ground among other dead in a necro-sociality. Nonetheless, during and after the World Wars, literature often represents trenches and bombed homes in terms evocative of a grave, in the sense that these became sites where the dead were taken into the earth, literally covered by mud, stone or brick.

Interment is the conceptual fulcrum on which, in the writing of the time, trench and bombed street edge towards 'grave'. The Oxford English Dictionary defines interment as 'The action of interring or burying in the earth; burial' (2023); crucially, the agent of the action is not specified. These other interments were not performed by grieving loved ones but by bombs, gunfire, rain-sodden soil, barbed wire. Though usually (but not always) temporary, the trenches and bombed streets were sites of a form of burial, and as such these sites troubled the boundary between spaces for the dead and the living.

Trenches as graves

A grim icon of World War I, trenches had been used in earlier combats but reached a hitherto unimaginable scale on the First World War European Front. Fortifications stretched for hundreds of miles and could even be mapped. Their durability earned them nicknames harking back to streets back home: '*Piccadilly* was a favorite; popular also were *Regent Street* and *Strand*; junctions were *Hyde Park Corner* and *Marble Arch*' (Fussell, 2013: 46). Yet while a trench was a dwelling place – a place to sleep, eat and live – it was also always a place of death. They were not only places to die during shelling, gas attack or infantry onslaught, but also places to *remain* dead. Corpses decayed not only in the adjacent no man's land but within the trench walls themselves. Fussell recalls, 'Dead horses and dead men – and parts of both – were sometimes not buried for months and often simply became an element of parapets and trench walls' (2013: 52), and Edmund Blunden's memoir *Undertones of War* (1928) describes corpses becoming building material: 'the deep dugouts ... were cancerous with torn bodies, and to pass an entrance was to gulp poison; in one place a corpse had apparently been thrust in to stop up a doorway's dangerous displacement, and an arm swung stupidly' (2010: 98).

Cemeteries are designed to manage decay in such a way that the dead do not overwhelm the living, but these places of corpses in earth lacked such order and a key marker of that lack was olfactory. Robert Graves recalls, 'The trenches stank with a gas-blood-lyddite-latrine smell' (1960: 164); J. L. Jack describes 'the stench from the older corpses in our parapets' (1964: 164); and Fussell remembers, 'The stench of rotten flesh was over everything, hardly suppressed by the chloride of lime ... You could smell the front line miles before you could see it' (2013: 52). In David Jones's epic poem *In Parenthesis* (1937), the protagonist Private John Ball is disgusted by the futile efforts to extricate dead tissue from the trenches: 'From this muck-raking are singular stenches, long decay leavened; compounding this clay ... chemical-corrupted once-bodies', a 'sepulchre' 'white-brighten[ed] ... with powdered chloride of lime' (Jones, 1937: 43). More than a bleak objective correlative or pathetic fallacy, this terrain was literally corpse-infused. In a grotesque intimacy, combatants breathed the decay of fellow soldiers.

Trench memoirs and fictions emphasise the mud as pervasive, horrifying and relentless. Frederic Manning's novel *Her Privates We* (1930) describes soldiers enervated by the overwhelming mud: 'All the fire died out of them as they dragged themselves laboriously through', until eventually, 'They became almost indistinguishable from the mud in which they lived' (1993: 183). Blunden recalls, 'Men of the next battalion were found in mud up to the armpits, and their fate was not spoken of; those who found them could not get them out. The whole zone was a corpse, and the mud itself mortified' (2010: 98). The menace of mud was very literal. Fussell notes, 'Thousands literally drowned in the mud', particularly in the disastrous conflict of Passchendaele (2013: 17). Given these realities, it is not surprising that mud itself takes on Gothic overtones as itself monstrous and malevolent. Blunden describes 'grey chalky mud ... crawl[ing] down the dugout entrances' (2010: 101), and in Manning's novel the protagonist Bourne dreams about the mud:

> He became aware of himself walking through a fog, only less thick than the mud underneath; it became almost impossible to breathe in it; and then he felt the mud sucking him down ... terrible dead hands came out of that living mud and fastened on to him, dragging him down inexorably, and the mud seemed full of rusty cruel wire.
>
> (1999: 224)

Infused with repulsive Gothic animism and rapacity, the mud became a grave: the mud of the front was earth that killed, as well as earth that interred the dead. The graveyard quality of the trenches is further underscored in Wilfred Owen's poem 'Anthem for Doomed Youth' (1920), in which battle is itself a funeral:

> What passing-bells for these who die as cattle?
> – Only the monstrous anger of the guns.
> Only the stuttering rifles' rapid rattle
> Can patter out their hasty orisons.
>
> (1983: 99)

Owen underscores the obscenity of these abject deaths by using savage irony to parody the sacred ceremonies which accompany burial.

Ultimately, even living soldiers could feel that they were living in a grave. Fussell admits, 'It was the sight of the sky, almost alone, that had the power to persuade a man that he was not already lost in a common grave' (2013: 55). In Jones's *In Parenthesis,* Private John Ball sees fellow soldiers move like 'Lazarus figures, where water gleamed between dilapidated breastworks, blue slime coated' (1937: 43). Blunden recalls being compelled, alongside others in his unit, by the sight of a shelled French graveyard near the front, where 'Greenish water stood in some of these pits: bones and skulls and decayed cerements'; he describes the soldiers' fascination as stemming from the fact that they were 'nearly corpses ourselves' (2010: 37). Interment and the grave become structuring tropes for some veterans' experience of the front. Contrasting with the peace of the IWGC cemeteries, such literature offers a counter-tale of two forms of grave, one literal and one metaphorical: dead bodies becoming part of earthwork structures, and the living rendered deathly while struggling on the front.

'Rubble that is rotting': the Second World War home front

In the same way that the trenches of the First World War became disturbing sites of interment, so too did bombed homes of the Second World War. Again, technological innovations changed the form of war, aerial bombing raids becoming key to both Axis and Allied practice. The ensuing war deaths were woven into national rhetorics and commemoration. As civilian deaths mounted, Winston Churchill declared in 1940 that 'This is a war of the Unknown Warriors ... The whole of the warring nations are engaged, not only soldiers, but the entire population' (1951: 233).

As in World War I, huge efforts were made to obscure corpses as much as possible, including in art and photography. However, while government policy ensured that no dead were visible in photographs and artwork of ruin, that wreckage increasingly became metonymic for the dead often literally buried within those sites. The rubble of brick and stone, entangled with the fabrics and scraps and detritus of human life, were also entangled with the bodies of the once-inhabitants. The significance of the bombed house as evocative of death also partly explains the pains to which the British government went to not only censor the photographs to ensure that no dead were visible, but also to obscure location cues within images. Winston Ramsey notes, 'The Censorship Bureau went to extreme lengths to avoid particular places being identified. Ostensibly to deny German Intelligence the opportunity to establish the accuracy of their bombing, it additionally served to "anaesthetise" the public from particularly severe incidents' (1987: 107).

Yet even if photographs could be controlled or censored, the reality of the dead was often acutely present to inhabitants' senses. London, for example, had 41,987 casualties during the raids of 1940–1. Workers clearing rubble had to unstick body fragments from brick (Haslewood, 1940: 5; S. Jones, 1995: 19), and the cleared rubble still held the tissue of the dead. As in the trenches, the smell was penetrating and hard to bear (Greene, 1981: 83, 88; Leslie, 1942: 8). In Cyril Connolly's non-fiction work *The Unquiet Grave* (1944), one survivor laments, 'the smell down in them craters is somethink [sic] awful. They can't get them out sometimes for days. There's been a child under 'ere for the last week' (1944: 8). The dead could also be visible: corpses could heap up at some street corners (Warner, 1943: 85) and bombing could yield 'bits of bodies ... in puddles of water, blood and filth' (Haslewood, 1940: 4). Swimming pools were commandeered for temporary mass graves (Hanson, 2007: 185–6). Live burial also occurred: in one case, for example, a woman was buried under rubble for over a hundred hours with a dead child in her arms (Calder,1969: 202). Living and dead again blurred, with places of dwelling becoming places of interment.

As such deaths from bombing raids increased, those who sought to write of ruin increasingly adopted a powerful technique to convey the metonymic link between ruined structure and broken body: bombed buildings could be personified, but in order to show them *as dead*. Connolly's *Unquiet Grave*, for example, describes a terraced street after bombing, with houses 'upright ... bomb-shattered but unbowed' (1944: 8), but closer scrutiny shows something terrible:

> a nearer and more intimate survey would disclose a nightmare vision, unreal and unbelievable; insane. A mound of fallen masonry and plaster, a rubbish heap harbouring entities that had astoundingly survived extermination. A ragged edge of wall, gaily distempered; a porcelain enamel bath upon its side; a velvet cushion, suppurating a grey matter of down.
>
> (1944: 8)

The 'nightmare' of this sight accrues from the parallel of bombed home and rotting body. The wreckage of disintegrating plaster and walls becomes somehow organic, 'suppurating ... grey matter'. The ruins are emblems of the decaying bodies hidden within them. Similarly, Mervyn Peake's poem 'London, 1941' describes buildings as 'Half masonry, half pain' (2008: 89), and his poem 'The Shapes (London)' (1940) describes ruins as though they are corpses: 'The winds can circle now where blood ran warm, / And where the heart once stood the cold mist hovers', 'rubble that is rotting in the rain', and these dismembered houses stand in '*silent* profile' (2008: 84, emphasis added). Here is no reassuring ventriloquism of the war dead.

Fine art and art criticism also sought to communicate the death-saturated ruins of the (un)built environment. Artist John Piper wrote in 1941 that war pictures should not be about 'camouflage nor uniforms, nor the clean lines of a gun, nor even heroic profiles', but should instead take as their focus 'death and destruction, and the agony that stays about the rubbish pile and the grave ... [A] wall falling like a short man; the broken carcase of a lift-shaft; machinery dangling its severed limbs in the bare well of a mantle-factory' (2000: 50). More wreckage than resilience, these ruins not only house the dead but confront the living with mortal disintegration.

This chapter opened with a confident voice from beyond the grave mediated through Rosewarne's letter to his mother. I will end with a very different kind of letter. Rose Macaulay's story 'Miss Anstruther's Letters' (1942) describes a woman whose home has been destroyed in an air raid, but that loss is not what devastates her. Her lover has died, and all that was left were letters from him accumulated over decades. Those letters were burned in the raid. Now, all that remains is 'a drift of grey ashes that once were fire' (1988: 47). She, too, drifts, spectral and hollowed out by grief: 'like a revenant, Miss Anstruther still haunted her ruins, where now the demolition men were at work' (1988: 42). Here, no letter mediates a voice from beyond the grave, and haunting becomes a trope for understanding the conditions of the bereaved living. All that remains is decay, burnt fragments and the end of things.

As vividly as the graves of any fiction, the graves in these works of witness draw on a Gothic discursivity to convey anguish that is hard to recruit into other kinds of national story. Indeed, the work of representing these real graves arguably requires such a discourse of boundary violation and transgression, for graveyards become oddly located in these wars. Bodies are 'interred' in trenches, poppy fields and the rubble of homes. Each case sees a blurring of burial place and a place of dwelling. The smell, chaos and squalor of these sites of interment trouble any elisions of the corpse in the service of national commemoration. Silent and rotting, these dead confront readers with the human price of war. These works ask us to notice the bodies of the dead.

References

Anderson, Benedict (1986) 'Narrating the Nation', *Times Literary Supplement*, 13 June, p. 659.
Anderson, Benedict (1991) *Imagined Communities*, 2nd edn (London: Verso).
Ariès, Philippe (1976) [1974] *Western Attitudes towards Death from the Middle Ages to the Present*, trans. Patricia Ranum (London: Marion Boyars).
Bauman, Zygmunt (1992) *Mortality, Immortality and Other Life Strategies* (New York: Polity).
Beiner, Guy (2018) *Forgetful Remembrance* (Oxford: Oxford University Press).
Blake, Linnie (2008) *The Wounds of Nations* (Manchester: Manchester University Press).
Blunden, Edmund (2010) [1928] *Undertones of War* (London: Penguin).
Booth, Allyson (1996) *Postcards from the Trenches* (Oxford: Oxford University Press).
Brooke, Rupert (1970) *The Poetical Works*, ed. Geoffrey Keynes (London: Faber).
Butler, Judith (2004) *Precarious Life* (London: Verso).
Calder, Angus (1969) *The People's War* (London: Jonathan Cape).
Cannadine, David (1981) 'War and Death, Grief and Mourning in Modern Britain', in Joachim Whaley (ed.), *Mirrors of Mortality* (London: Europa), pp. 187–242.
Carter, Pippa and Norman Jackson (2000) 'An-aesthetics', in Stephen Linstead and Heather Höpfl (eds), *The Aesthetics of Organisations* (London: Sage), pp. 180–97.
Churchill, Winston (1951) *War Speeches*, vol. 1, ed. Charles Eade (London: Cassell).
Connolly, Cyril (1944) *The Unquiet Grave* (London: Curwen Press).
Davies, Owen (2009) [2007] *The Haunted* (Basingstoke: Palgrave).
Derrida, Jacques (1986) 'Fors', trans. Barbara Johnson, in Nicolas Abraham and Maria Torok (eds), *The Wolf Man's Magic Word* (Minneapolis: University of Minnesota Press), pp. xi–xlviii.
Derrida, Jacques (1989) [1986] *Mémoires*, trans. Jonathan Culler, Cecile Lindsey and Eduardo Cadava (New York: Columbia University Press).
Derrida, Jacques (1994) [1993] *Specters of Marx*, trans. Peggy Kamuf (New York: Routledge).
Fussell, Paul (2013) [1975] *The Great War and Modern Memory* (Oxford: Oxford University Press).
Gordon, Avery (1997) *Ghostly Matters* (Minneapolis: University of Minnesota Press).
Graves, Robert (1960) [1929] *Goodbye to All That* (London: Penguin).

Greene, Graham (1981) [1980] *Ways of Escape* (London: Penguin).
Hanna, Emma (2013) *The Great War on the Small Screen* (Edinburgh: Edinburgh University Press).
Hanson, Neil (2007) [2005] *The Unknown Soldier* (London: Corgi).
Haslewood, I. S. (1940) 'The Blitz on London', Ts. 04/40/1, Imperial War Museum Archives (London: Department of Documents).
IWM (2020) 'Their Name Liveth for Evermore', Imperial War Museum, www.iwm.org.uk/history/their-name-liveth-for-evermore (accessed 5 October 2022).
Jack, J. L. (1964) *General Jack's Diary, 1914–1918*, ed. John Terraine (London: Eyre and Spottiswoode).
Jones, David (1937) *In Parenthesis* (London: Faber).
Jones, Steve (1995) *When the Lights Went Down* (Bulwell: Wicked).
Kenyon, Frederic (1917) *War Graves: How the Cemeteries Abroad Will Be Designed*. Report for the Imperial War Graves Commission.
Kipling, Rudyard (1919) 'War Graves: Work of Imperial Commission', *The Times*, 17 February, p. 4.
Kipling, Rudyard (2000) *Selected Poems*, ed. Peter King (London: Penguin).
Leslie, Doris (1969) [1942] *House in the Dust* (London: Heinemann).
Long, H. Shirley (1940) 'To a Boy Who Was Killed Two Weeks Ago!' *Sunday Pictorial*, 17 March, p. 25.
Macaulay, Rose (1988) [1942] 'Miss Anstruther's Letters', in Anne Boston (ed.), *Wave Me Goodbye* (New York: Viking Penguin), pp. 40–7.
Manning, Frederic (1999) [1930] *Her Privates We* (London: Serpent's Tail).
McCrae, John (2006) [1915] 'In Flanders Fields', in Matthew Walter (ed.), *The Penguin Book of First World War Poetry* (London: Penguin), p. 155.
Montefiore, Jan (2007) *Rudyard Kipling* (London: Tavistock).
Mulvey-Roberts, M. (2016) *Dangerous Bodies: Historicising the Gothic Corporeal* (Manchester: Manchester University Press, 2016).
Nora, Pierre (1996) 'From *Lieux de Mémoire* to Realms of Memory', in Pierre Nora and Lawrence Kritzman (eds), *Realms of Memory*, vol. 1 (New York: Columbia University Press), pp. xv–xxiv.
Owen, Wilfred (1983) *The Complete Poems and Fragments*, ed. Jon Stallworthy, vol. 1 (London: Oxford University Press).
Oxford English Dictionary (2023) 'interment (n.)', www.oed.com/search/dictionary/?scope=Entries&q=interment (accessed 14 November 2023).
Peake, Mervyn (2008) *Collected Poems*, ed. Rob Maslen (Manchester: Carcanet).
Piper, John (2000) [1941] 'New War Pictures', *John Piper*, ed. David Jenkins (London: Philip Wilson).
Punter, David (1996) *Literature of Terror*, vol. 2 (Edinburgh: Pearson Education).
Rae, Patricia (2007) 'Introduction', in Patricia Rae (ed.), *Modernism and Mourning* (Lewisburg: Bucknell University Press), pp. 13–49.
Ramazani, Jahan (2007) 'Afterword', in Patricia Rae (ed.), *Modernism and Mourning* (Lewisburg: Bucknell University Press), pp. 286–95.
Ramsey, Winston (ed.) (1987) *The Blitz Then and Now*, vol. 1 (London: Battle of Britain Prints).
Renan, Ernest (2018) [1882] 'What Is a Nation?: (Qu'est-ce qu'une nation?, 1882)', in Dick Giglioli (ed.), *What Is a Nation? And Other Political Writings* (New York: Columbia University Press), pp. 246–63.
Rosewarne, Vivian (1991) 'Letter from an Unknown Airman', in Ronald Blythe (ed.), *Private Words, Letters and Diaries from the Second World War* (London: Viking), pp. 306–8.

Sassoon, Siegfried (1984) *Collected Poems* (London: Faber).
Scutts, Joanna (2009) 'Battlefield Cemeteries, Pilgrimage and Literature after the First World War', *English Literature in Transition*, 52:4, 387–416.
Smith, Andrew (2022) *Gothic Fiction and the Writing of Trauma, 1914–1918* (Edinburgh: Edinburgh University Press).
Soltysik Monnet, Agnieszka and Steffen Hantke (2016) 'Ghosts from the Battlefields: A Short Historical Introduction to the War Gothic', in Agnieszka Soltysik Monnet and Steffen Hantke (eds), *War Gothic in Literature and Culture* (New York: Routledge), pp. xi–xxv.
Townsend Warner, Sylvia (1943) *A Garland of Straw and Other Stories* (London: Chatto and Windus).
Trowbridge, Serena (2017) 'Past, Present, and Future in the Gothic Graveyard', in Carol Margaret Davison (ed.), *The Gothic and Death* (Manchester: Manchester University Press), pp. 21–33.
Wasson, Sara (2010) *Urban Gothic of the Second World War* (Basingstoke: Palgrave).
Wasson, Sara (2020) *Transplantation Gothic: Tissue Transfer in Literature, Film and Medicine* (Manchester: Manchester University Press).
Wester, Maisha (2012) *African-American Gothic* (Basingstoke: Palgrave)
Whalan, Mark (2007) '"How did they pick John Doe": Race, Memorialization, and Modernism in US Interwar Literature', in Patricia Rae (ed.), *Modernism and Mourning* (Lewisburg, PA: Bucknell University Press), pp. 85–101.
Winter, Jay (1995) *Sites of Memory, Sites of Mourning* (Cambridge: Cambridge University Press).
Wittman, Laura (2011) *The Tomb of the Unknown Soldier* (Toronto: University of Toronto Press).
Wood, Nancy (1999) *Vectors of Memory* (Oxford: Berg).

10

Home among the headstones: graveyards in Western Gothic television

Stacey Abbott

Graveyards are a prominent space in Western Gothic television, whether as an address for the Addams Mansion located at 1 Cemetery Lane (1964–6); as the place where Count Dracula hides among the dead and seduces the living; or where the protagonist of Nigel Kneale's *The Woman in Black* (1989) first catches sight of the eponymous spectre who will seal his doom. Buffy Summers patrolled the cemeteries of Sunnydale on a weekly basis for seven years in *Buffy the Vampire Slayer* (1997–2003); the vampires and witches in *The Originals* (2013–18) regularly used the cemeteries of New Orleans to commemorate and communicate with their ancestors; and, arguably, the entire French Mountain village of *Les Revenants* (2012–15) was a graveyard, partially buried beneath a flooded reservoir. All these programmes, and many more, use the graveyard to confront the audience with images of death, decay and mourning. In Gothic television, graveyards are loaded locations, holding a myriad of meanings and associations drawn from Gothic literature and film, as well as sociocultural conceptions of death and grief.

Graveyards also offer television writers, directors and producers a rich setting in which to locate their narratives – a setting that is both familiar and unfamiliar, uncanny and mundane. The episodic and serial nature of television asks the audience to invite the graveyard into their homes and return to it on a regular basis. This, arguably, risks rendering the graveyard familiar and homely through the media's association with, and location in, the domestic space. This comfort is, however, often thrown into relief through the intrusion of the Gothic, which can unsettle our perception of the home both on- and off-screen. As Helen Wheatley argues, the 'relationship between the imagined and the real, or the strange and the familiar, highlighted by Freud in relation to the uncanny, is significant in understanding the structures of feeling within Gothic television. This closeness accounts for Gothic television's simultaneous reference to its domestic reception context, in order to produce its lucid sense of the uncanny' (2006: 7). The root of Gothic television's uncanniness, as Wheatley argues, is that it is often about the home and is viewed within a domestic space. This mirroring renders the viewing experience itself uncanny.

Associating the Gothic graveyard with the domestic through television does not, therefore, necessarily domesticate the space but rather often accentuates its own uncanny nature. This is readily apparent in the first segment of the pilot episode of *Rod Serling's Night Gallery* (1969–73), titled 'The Cemetery', in which the painting of a cemetery is presented as a portal between the family home and the grave ('Pilot' 1.1). The palpable connection between an actual cemetery and the house is established in the opening long shot of a large Southern mansion, which pans over to the family graveyard before dissolving to a close-up of a Gothic painting of the same cemetery. The proximity of the graveyard to the house in this opening shot, as well as the central presence of the painting in the mansion's main reception, signals the looming presence of death in this home, which becomes increasingly transparent as the episode progresses. The opening, however, also highlights the presence of the domestic in the graveyard. This is a painting of a family crypt after all, representing the weight of family inheritance that so often underpins Gothic texts.

The connection between the painting, the home and the cemetery is further developed when Jeremy, the ne'er-do-well nephew of the wealthy painter, appears to be haunted by the painting as a form of retribution for murdering his uncle in order to inherit the house. At regular intervals, the painting changes, charting the uncle's burial and eventual return from the grave to punish the nephew for his crimes and transgressions. This causes Jeremy to descend into further hysteria with each alteration. The final painting shows the uncle standing at the door as footsteps are heard from the veranda and there is a knock at the door. The graveyard has literally come home to displace Jeremy from the house he has usurped. Through this episode, television, like the painting, is a portal through which the audience is confronted by the grave and all that it represents. Instead of television rendering the graveyard safe and comfortable, the graveyard opens Gothic television to explorations of the legacy of death and grief, alongside other traumas.

This chapter therefore seeks to demonstrate how the utilisation of the graveyard in Gothic TV serves as a shorthand to create an unsettling atmosphere but also a location that facilitates a renegotiation of the Gothic for television. I demonstrate how graveyards in Gothic TV weave together the familiar and the unfamiliar, inspiring chills, unease, horror and existential confrontations with mortality, while also evoking loss, grief and mourning – feelings that are all too familiar, if often repressed. These locations are populated by two groups, equally abject: decomposing corpses and grief-stricken mourners. While this abjection is traditionally contained by the boundaries of the grave and the cemetery, as well as traditional funereal rituals, this chapter will examine how Gothic television uses the cemetery, and its recognisably melancholic *mise en scène* projected into the domestic environment, as a liminal space in which the barriers between the living and the dead are ruptured. This makes way for a series of uncanny encounters where that which is traditionally repressed – decay and grief – is released.

Graveyard as uncanny *mise en scène*

As Roger Luckhurst notes, 'it used to be easy to define the Gothic. A castle on a precipice, silhouetted against a gibbous moon. Next door, a ruined church with arched windows, the gravestones at crazy angles. Something unholy and transgressive stirring in the shadows under the twisted yew tree. The mist would be optional, but the bats and screech-owl compulsory' (2021: 8). Television in its early days, however, did not have the budget or production time to build large Gothic sets as used in classic examples of cinematic horror. Furthermore, the relocation of the Gothic from Europe to contemporary USA in many classic American television series, from *Dark Shadows* (1966–71) to *Buffy the Vampire Slayer*, also meant a dearth of local ancient ruins in which to set their narratives or to use as a location. As a result, the established tropes described by Luckhurst are often infused into more commonplace settings associated with the domestic nature of television. Classic examples of these are the two family sitcoms *The Munsters* and *The Addams Family* (both 1964–6). Both are based upon pre-existing Gothic texts, with *The Munsters* reimagining the Universal monsters as a suburban family, while *The Addams Family* was a televisual adaptation of the popular Charles Addams comic strip for *The New Yorker* (1938–64) about a rather strange Gothic family. Both series are a hybrid of horror and sitcom, often labelled 'magicom', in which the home is the main setting, but the domestic space is reimagined through the lens of the supernatural (Marc, 1989: 29). The Addams family's address – 1 Cemetery Lane – is significant in this regard, for although there are no cemeteries in either series, supernatural sitcoms tend to overlay a graveyard *mise en scène* upon domestic environments (Figure 10.1). American family homes, positioned on recognisable suburban streets, are remodelled as a form of ancient, dilapidated ruin, replete with the cobwebs, skeletons, crypts and other *memento mori* often associated with the grave. Establishing shots of the houses, repeatedly emphasise not only their looming stature – an overwhelming presence on these suburban streets – but the large, bare, twisted trees and spear-topped wrought-iron fences that surround their properties, along with an often-clanging gate. The Munsters' property, in particular, is crowded with overgrown hedges, blowing leaves and tumbleweeds that call to mind the neglect

Figure 10.1 Family home overlain with graveyard *mise en scène* in *The Addams Family* (1964).

of an abandoned graveyard. The cemetery is, after all, the home of the dead, as is the Munsters' house. Grandpa sleeps on his coffin in the crypt; the creaking sound of a coffin lid being closed is heard through the door after son Eddie is told to go to sleep; and Herman and Lily's four-poster bed is covered in the cobwebs and decaying tapestries associated with an ageing mausoleum. In *The Addams Family*, the house is filled with Gothic statues, exotic plants and nocturnal animals suited to the grave, while son Pugsley informs his parents that he is going out to play in the cemetery, presenting it as an extension of the family home – a Gothic backyard ('The Addams Family Goes to School', 1.1 – the cemetery is unseen on-screen). Both series use this graveyard *mise en scène* as a type of catalyst for the eruption of the Gothic past into the present through the domestic language of television.

Bernice M. Murphy has argued that these 'supernatural sit-coms' undermine the conventions of the Gothic by stripping 'classic horror icons and paranormal beings ... of any threatening qualities they might otherwise have possessed and relocat[ing them] within decidedly conventional, domestic settings' (2009: 50). In contrast, Lorna Jowett and I have argued that these Gothic sitcoms 'seek to subvert suburban conformity', challenging notions of 'normality' and celebrating the 'grotesque' and 'non-normative' (2013: 23–4). I would further add that the imposition of this graveyard *mise en scène* upon the suburban neighbourhood is utilised not to render the monsters unthreatening but instead to disrupt the conformity of the more conventional suburban landscape. Both series showcase the intolerance of the Addams' and the Munsters' neighbours. Delivery people hesitate to enter onto their properties; the local truant officer runs away from the Addams family's house and refuses to return ('The Addams Family Goes to School', 1.1). In *The Munsters*, the next-door neighbour Mrs Cribbins repeatedly refers to her neighbours as 'they' or 'them', telling the postman Mr Bloom 'since *they* moved in one has to be prepared for anything … This was such a nice neighbourhood until *they* moved in … I don't want *them* wandering over here.' To this, Bloom responds that they should 'keep *them* in *their* place' ('My Fair Munster', 1.2). In so doing, the series equates Cribbons and Bloom's discomfort with racial prejudice. The graveyard *mise en scène* in the home allows for the Gothic to serve as a disruptive presence within the heart of suburbia, challenging notions of conformity and segregation through the deliberate integration of the Gothic with other televisual genres. It weaves together an association between the Gothic and the domestic to construct a visual language that infuses modern television with the iconography of ancient architecture, monuments and ruins.

While *The Munsters* and *The Addams Family* do not feature cemeteries, the graveyard does feature in many other examples of Gothic TV. In part, this type of graveyard *mise en scène* is economical as the sets are easy to construct in the studio or commonplace locations on which to shoot. For instance, scenes from *Buffy* were often shot on location in the Angelus-Rosedale cemetery in Los Angeles but the producers also erected a makeshift cemetery in the parking lot of the Santa Monica studio. Cemeteries are also in keeping with the modern register of much Gothic TV as most communities have a cemetery, whereas they are less likely to have a Gothic mansion or castle. As a result, the graveyard often becomes a stand-in for more traditional locations. For instance, each episode of the Gothic soap opera *Dark Shadows*, set in modern-day New England, begins with a stock establishing shot of Collinwood, the mansion of the Collins family, and is accompanied by the voice-over of the governess Victoria Winters, deliberately evoking the narrations of *Rebecca* (1940) and *Jane Eyre* (1943) as well as their Gothic mansions, Manderley and Thornfield Hall. The interior design of Collinwood, however, is far more mundane, reduced to a stately living room and reception area, in keeping with the houses of the wealthy that are so often the settings for American soap operas. Instead, it is within the *mise en scène* of the graveyard that the show's most infamous character, the vampire Barnabas Collins, is introduced, thus exposing the Gothic roots of the Collins family.

While the show had begun to experiment with the supernatural through stories of ghostly visitations and monstrous mothers, it was through Barnabas's narrative (and the vampire's emergence in a cemetery setting) that the series reached its peak popularity and introduced its first central protagonist/antagonist. In episode 210, the familiar image of Collinwood that begins the episode dissolves to a close-up of a gravestone, which then tracks through the overgrown cemetery, establishing both locations as inherently connected: the contemporary family haunted by its ancestral past. The cemetery is overgrown, surrounded by overhanging leaves and vines, and enclosed by an iron fence, while the headstones are positioned at odd angles, appearing aged and unsteady. Through this *mise en scène*, the graveyard suggests neglect and decay but also a sense of deliberate isolation. This is further conveyed through Victoria's portentous voice-over as she describes the 'desecrat[ion of] sacred ground and violat[ion of] that which should remain sealed forever', a necessary prelude to the attempted grave-robbing that will conclude the episode. In the next episode (211), the cemetery caretaker, realising that the Collins family mausoleum has been broken into, similarly speaks of sacrilege and the violation of the resting place of the dead, but also warns that evil has been unleashed. The function of the cemetery to protect and contain the spirits and bodies of the dead has been disrupted. It is in these scenes in the graveyard that the Gothic horror erupts into the soap opera world that has largely been preoccupied with blackmail, extortion and robbery. It is in the cemetery that conman Willie Loomis – attempting to rob one of the graves of the Collins family jewels – discovers a hidden room within the mausoleum, containing a mysterious coffin wrapped in chains. Episode 210 ends on the cliffhanger as Loomis eagerly opens the coffin and is overcome with abject horror as a hand reaches out and grabs him by the throat. While Barnabas is not actually presented on screen until the end of episode 211, when he arrives at Collinwood and introduces himself as a cousin from England, this moment in the cemetery mausoleum is central to the series' narrative. Collins is the family secret, so monstrous that he is literally buried away, and it is through the *mise en scène* of the graveyard that this monster erupts from the past to the present, from the pages of Gothic fiction to Gothic television.

As Barnabas Collins's introduction attests, graveyards hold a particularly significant place in vampire television, serving as both a hiding place and a home, while also lending the series a touch of authentic Gothic heritage. The BBC *Count Dracula* (1977) was shot in Whitby and includes numerous scenes in the graveyard outside St Mary's Church and Whitby Abbey, while Granada television's *Dracula* (2006) staged Lucy's burial and resurrection in Highgate Cemetery. Both British series use the genuine Gothic architecture of these locations to add a layer of atmosphere and literary authenticity to the televisual *mise en scène*. In *Buffy*, by contrast, Spike's underground crypt is presented as homely, replete with a comfortable armchair, lamp and a television on which he watches his favourite soap opera, overtly linking the crypt to the domestic. As Agent Mulder explains in 'Bad Blood' (5.12), vampires are often drawn to cemeteries. As such, *American Horror Story* features a dazzling use of a cemetery in the opening episode ('Checking In', 5.1) of its vampire-themed series *Hotel* (2015–16). In this episode, the vampire, known as The Countess and played by Lady Gaga, is first introduced in a montage sequence of images of her preparing for an evening out, before leaving her suite and sweeping down the corridors of the Hotel Cortez, dressed in scarlet and accessorised with diamonds, sequined gloves and a black widow's veil. Her consort Donovan is equally elegant, dressed in black silk. The sequence then cuts to the couple emerging from the shadows of Hollywood Forever Cemetery, walking towards the mausoleum where F. W. Murnau's vampire film *Nosferatu* (1922) is being projected. This cemetery is an iconic location in Los Angeles, the resting place of old Hollywood, featuring the graves of such legends as Douglas Fairbanks, Faye Wray, Janet Gaynor and Cecil B. DeMille alongside more contemporary Goth and Gothic legends such as Maila Nurmi (aka Vampira), Darren McGavin of television's *Kolchak: The Night Stalker* fame and Johnnie Ramone of the punk rock band The Ramones (whose grave is a site of pilgrimage for his followers). The cemetery, therefore, exudes rich Hollywood and Gothic histories and fuses the glamour and horror that underpin the series.

Furthermore, Hollywood Forever is renowned for its regular outdoor film screenings, inviting audiences to sit among the graves and immerse themselves in often Gothic horror films. As the glittering vampires settle down on the grass, they make eye contact with another couple who they seduce through an exchange of glances intercut with images of Count Orlok stalking his prey. The vampires lure the couple back to the hotel to engage in group sex before tearing their throats open and drinking their blood in an orgasmic display of decadence and bloodlust. The sequence is cut to the driving rhythms of She Wants Revenge's song 'Tear You Apart' (2006) and the entire sequence is a callback to the opening of Tony Scott's *The Hunger* (1983). The sequence constructs a pastiche of vampire Gothic through its integration of exaggerated colour, extravagant fashion and Goth music alongside classic images from *Nosferatu*. Setting part of this heavily stylised scene within the iconic cemetery is designed as a contrast to the decaying art-deco design of the Hotel Cortez. The *mise en scène* of the cemetery therefore functions as a self-conscious nod to the legacy of association between vampires, coffins and graveyards, as well as a reminder that cemeteries represent the traditional resting place of the undead, a convention that the series will upend through its imaging of the Hotel Cortez as a modern graveyard and repository of lost souls.

Four months after the airing of this episode on *AHS: Hotel*, the revival season of *The X-Files* (1993–2002; 2016–18) also made notable use of a cemetery as Gothic backdrop in the episode 'Mulder and Scully Meet the

Were-Monster' (10.3). The episode is equally replete with intertextual references, but in contrast to *Hotel,* the utilisation of the graveyard is not in service of pastiche but used as a means of acknowledging shared loss. In this episode, Mulder is hunting a were-monster, whom he finally meets in a cemetery. This were-monster, played by New Zealand actor Rhys Darby, is, in a twist of convention, a lizard-man who turns into a human after being bitten by a man. In his human form, he sports a seersucker suit and straw hat worn in homage to Darren McGavin's iconic costume in *Kolchak: The Night Stalker* (1974–5). Significantly, when Mulder quietly approaches the monster standing at a grave, Mulder puts down flowers and lovingly touches a gravestone featuring the name Kim Manners, a director-producer of *The X-Files* between 1995 and 2002. This gravestone was erected as a tribute to the much-loved director who died in 2009, featuring the epigraph 'Let's Kick It in the Ass', a favourite expression of Manners' on set. The grave next to Manners is named for Jack Hardy, an assistant director on two *X-Files* spin-off shows, *The Lone Gunmen* (2001) and *Millennium* (1996–9), as well as being first assistant director on the film *The X-Files: I Want to Believe* (2008). The inclusion of these graves is a self-conscious memorial to those beloved members of the crew who had been lost in the intervening years between the series' end in 2002 and its 2016 revival. While *American Horror Story* uses a real cemetery as a form of pastiche to acknowledge the artifice of the vampire genre through the evocation of its legacy, *The X-Files* uses an artificial cemetery and gravestone to acknowledge shared grief and mourning, highlighting that graveyards are spaces that invite a very different encounter between the living and the dead.

Graveyards, grief and mourning

HBO's *Six Feet Under* (2001–5) is a taboo-breaking series focusing on a family-run funeral home and the industry surrounding death and mourning. Each episode begins with a death and, as Kim Akass and Janet McCabe explain, the series takes as its subject the 'liminal space between death and burial' (2005: 9). Mark W. Bundy further notes how the series 'plies the many visual and emotive conceits of death, dying and mourning while urging its audience to turn themselves inside out to have a look, if only for a short while' (2005: 38). Described as 'magic realism' and walking 'a fine line between comedy and tragedy', the series' focus on this liminality has much in common with the Gothic (Lavery, 2005: 20; Akass and McCabe, 2005: 2). The journey between life and death is conveyed in microcosm by the show's title sequence (Figure 10.2), highlighting how the role of the funeral home is to transition the body from life to death and decay. This is conveyed

Graveyards in Western Gothic television

Figure 10.2 Concealing the horrors of death and loss beneath a carefully manicured lawn in the credit sequence for *Six Feet Under* (2001–5).

through the transition from the medical *mise en scène* of the morgue to the Gothic *mise en scène* of the graveyard. While the visual language around the funeral home emphasises sterility and cleanliness conveyed through images of white tiles and sheets against stainless steel gurneys, the sequence ends in the graveyard with Gothic images of decaying flowers, coffins, granite headstones and crows. The smooth metallic texture of the morgue gurney is contrasted with the close-up of the headstone as the crow's talons scratch at the rock. The cemetery is here presented as the repository for the Gothic – the space in which, once the burial has taken place and the rituals of mourning completed, the dead are left to decay. The final image, however, of a grass-covered hill and a lone tree also signal the secure containment of that decay beneath a carefully manicured lawn.

The image of the covered grave is commonly repeated throughout much Gothic television and often stands in contrast to the graveyard *mise en scène* of *Dark Shadows* or *The Munsters*. These graves are generally tended and cared for, with the layer of grass serving as a barrier from the harsh realities of what is beneath the earth. They are more in keeping with the imagery of *Six Feet Under*: Gothic but seemingly contained. As Serena Trowbridge explains, 'ways of memorialising the dead have changed over the centuries; yet reflection on death has been a consistent preoccupation. Often, this takes place at a graveside where the memorial stone and the proximity of the corpse, juxtaposed with the unchanging and tranquil setting, elevate the mind to consider the eternal and the sublime' (2017: 21). Yet miniseries and TV films such *The Secret of Crickley Hall* (2012) and *The Woman in Black* present graves not as a source of comfort or memorial but clues to the shocking stories of the death of children. While it is the spectral hauntings that reveal the truth behind these violent deaths and signal the inability of the grave to contain the horror of death, the row of tiny, tidy tombstones, with heart-wrenching epigraphs such as 'Never Forgotten' and 'Always in Our Hearts', speaks to the Gothic by tapping into the trauma and horror surrounding loss. Furthermore, in supernatural series such as *The Vampire Diaries* (2009–17), *Buffy the Vampire Slayer*, *Angel* (1999–2004) and *Supernatural* (2005–20), where death occurs quite regularly, characters are often depicted standing over graves, expressing their grief, but these moments rarely serve to elevate the mind to consider 'the eternal and the sublime'. Characters from these series are far too exposed to the realities of the eternal to be overwhelmed by the sublime. Instead, in Gothic fashion, they focus on the pain and alienation of loss. For instance, in *Buffy the Vampire Slayer* Buffy spends a great deal of time looking down at fresh graves, usually awaiting the rising of a new vampire. But on three occasions she is there to mourn loss. In 'Lie to Me' (2.7) and 'Passion' (2.17), she stands with her watcher and mentor Giles, processing the death of her friend Ford and Giles's girlfriend Jenny Calendar, respectively. Both individuals were guilty of betrayal but also represent powerful bonds of friendship and love. These are contradictions that confound Buffy, who looks to Giles for comfort and adult reassurance, which comes in the form of a deliberate lie: 'it's terribly simple. The good guys are always stalwart and true. The bad guys are easily distinguished by their pointy horns or black hats. We always defeat them and save the day. No one ever dies and everybody lives happily ever after' ('Lie to Me'). These moments of contemplation at the grave speak to the pain of loss and the moral confusion of growing up. In the third example, 'Forever' (5.17), Buffy is at the cemetery to mark the death of her mother, where she confronts her feelings of fear and insecurity facing a life on her own. After the funeral, Buffy remains in the cemetery staring down at the grave transfixed, as everyone else slowly walks away, symbolically signalling their need to move on. When the sun eventually sets, her vampire ex-boyfriend Angel arrives to comfort her. As they sit on the grass of the cemetery, she is able to confront her uncertainties about what comes next now that the funeral rituals are done. The processes may have taken place, and Joyce's body is safely stowed beneath the earth, but it is the 'stuff of everyday living' that frightens Buffy now. Rather than invite the character or the audience to reflect on the eternal, these Gothic graveyard scenes expose the numbing pain that is the reality of life in the wake of death.

    Gothic television often undermines the presumed comfort of the manicured lawn as depicted in the *Six Feet Under* credits through the repeated disruption, rupture and eruption of the grave. For instance, some examples of Gothic television opt to present the grave uncovered like an open wound. Through the excesses of Gothic television, this image of the open grave often undermines funereal rituals as well as, in the case of *Twin Peaks* (1990–1;2017), the ritualised performance of mourning in favour of abject expressions of grief. In *Twin Peaks* ('Rest in Pain', 1.4), Laura Palmer's burial proceedings are disrupted first when her bad-boy boyfriend Bobby Briggs lets out a primal scream before pushing through the crowd and accusing everyone in attendance of hypocrisy as they all knew she was troubled but did nothing to help her. The ferocity of his expression of anger turns to hysteria as Laura's father, Leland, cries out and leaps on top of the casket, causing the mechanism to break and the coffin to repeatedly lower and rise up with Leland still on top. Laura's mother falls to the ground, telling Leland not to 'ruin this too', before weeping in abject grief as the deeply melancholic Laura's theme builds to a crescendo. The physicality of these actions and performances defies the restraint that usually characterises funeral scenes on television. This is an extreme moment, in which the secure containment of the dead and the proper rituals of mourning are disrupted by the Gothic and melodramatic tone of the series. This undermines the accepted processes of grief management by signalling how grief defies repression. Instead, in abject form, it comes pouring out.

Significantly, in Gothic television the graveyard is often a space in which the line between life and death is repeatedly ruptured, undermining any notion of finality. In the Gothic-inflected series *Sherlock* (2010–17), Watson stands over Sherlock Holmes's grave and confesses his faith in his friend and his sense of loss. Rather than treat this moment as a healing moment, allowing him to move on, Watson makes one last request: 'Don't – be – dead. Just for me – just stop this.' As if in response to his request or incantation, as Watson walks away from the grave the camera pulls back to reveal Holmes standing beneath the trees; death is not final, and closure for the audience and for Watson is withheld ('The Reichenbach Fall', 2.3). In *Buffy*, following her meeting with Angel after Joyce's funeral in 'Forever', Buffy returns home to find that her sister Dawn has enacted a ritual of resurrection. As Buffy tries to convince Dawn that their mom might come back 'wrong', the sequence cuts to a close-up of Joyce's feet walking slowly along the tidy cemetery lawn, flouting any suggestion of containment. Her slow movement, coupled with the loud banging on the door when she arrives back at Buffy's house, suggests that she is a zombie, a monster that represents the decay of the grave. The zombie confronts us with what is hidden beneath the grassy surface of the grave and which funereal processes attempt to conceal and deny.

This physical horror of death is reinforced in episode three, 'The Dark Compass', of BBC's *Dracula* (2020), where Dracula lures Lucy to a cemetery with a text, inviting her for a late night 'bite'. They sit on the grass and engage in flirtatious seduction as Lucy asks why they always meet in a cemetery, to which he glibly responds 'I like to spend time with people my own age', a reminder that vampires are the embodiment of death. This sequence also calls to mind the horror of decay and decomposition, a subject that has an established relationship with the vampire. Folklorist Paul Barber argues that many beliefs in vampirism have stemmed from the hidden reality of what happens to the body beneath the grave as it expands, shrinks and decomposes (2010: 124). Dracula tells Lucy that some of the dead remain sentient as they rot. As Dracula and Lucy place their hands on the ground, they gradually become aware of the disturbing sound of someone knocking on their coffin lid. As they continue to listen, the sounds of knocking and the murmuring of voices escalate. Eventually they even spot an undead child, who has managed to 'wriggle their way to the surface' of a, presumably, shallow grave, once again an evocation of the horror of death. While Lucy initially thinks it is cute, the horrific reality of this decaying child sinks in when the child follows her home and attempts to climb onto her bed. Like 'Cemetery' in *Night Gallery,* the dead from the grave defy containment and attempt to infiltrate the domestic.

This disruption of the grave turns to eruption in tales of zombies and vampires digging their way out of the earth to new life, the ultimate return of the repressed. On television, this moment is more commonly associated with vampires, but twice in *Buffy* it is the Slayer herself who crawls out of a grave. The first time is in 'Nightmares' (1.10), when Buffy's dream of being killed and transformed into a vampire is made real. This nightmare serves as a reminder that most slayers are doomed to die, but it also embodies Giles's fear that he will fail his charge and will be unable to protect her from this eventuality. The second is in season six when, after her death in the previous season, Buffy is resurrected by her friends and wakes up alone in her coffin. While 'Nightmares' presents her rising from the perspective of her mourner, Giles, kneeling by her grave, in 'Bargaining Parts 1 & 2' (6.1/2) Buffy's resurrection is presented from within the coffin. Her decaying body is shown quickly reconstituting as she awakens, after which she is forced to claw her way out (Figure 10.3). This horror of the grave from the perspective of the dead is articulated in *In the Flesh* (2013–14), which works as a strong companion piece to Buffy's resurrection. In *Buffy* we see the resurrection from inside the coffin, while in *In the Flesh* recovering zombie Kieren Walker is capable of describing the feelings and sensations of the 'rising' (2.4). By reframing the zombie narrative as a post-post-zombie apocalypse, where a treatment has been found and zombies are being reintegrated in their communities, the narrative of the series is built around the point of view of the zombie. As such, the show is able to offer a truly disturbing and honest evocation of the eruption of the grave from within. Kieren describes the

Figure 10.3 The horror of the cemetery from the perspective of the dead in *Buffy the Vampire Slayer* (2001).

experience in detail, emphasising the loneliness and isolation of waking up in pure darkness with the fear of being buried alive, the panic of smashing through the earth and terror of clawing one's way up. Once out in the graveyard, the image turns from terror to peace. The teenager explains:

> Then suddenly something's different. You feel the wind on the tips of your fingers and the rain. Because before that you're not really sure where you are. But now you know. And you're pushing through. And then all this stuff at once. The moon and this incredible storm blowing and the clock chiming midnight. And you're just standing there. Nobody else around ... That feeling is like what being born must be like except you've got context. Because honestly dead, everything up until then was fear. Everything. Even when I was alive, just different levels of fear. Then it's gone.

Kieren expresses the claustrophobic horror and panic from within the grave, visualised through Buffy's escape. He also captures the uncanny calm of the empty cemetery at this moment, which is a testament to the most abject breakdown of barriers between the living and the dead conveyed through the image of the fingers poking through the surface of the grave. This moment is an unsettling reminder of the loved ones beneath the earth and destabilises the intended comfort of the grave. Significantly, the serialised narratives of *Buffy* and *In the Flesh* enable both shows to depict characters – Buffy and Kieren – who embody both the corpse and the mourner. Both seasons of *In the Flesh* end with a funeral – Kieren first loses his love, Rick, and second his best friend, Amy. Through the uncanniness of Gothic television storytelling,

Buffy and Kieren have experienced the grave from either side of the earth and thus serve as unsettling reminders that everyone will eventually share this dual perspective.

The graveyard is an uncanny location that acts as a liminal partition between the living and the dead, designed to provide closure and comfort by safely stowing the dead away from the living. Gothic television repeatedly disrupts this separation through the rupture and eruption of the grave and presents the graveyard as a type of conduit between them. Significantly, Gothic TV achieves this by inviting the graveyard, and with it the dead, into our living rooms. The recurring confrontation with death within the domestic space signals the value of revisiting and discussing the popular usage of the graveyard in Gothic television. These texts use the graveyard to break down the barriers between the living and the dead, the seen and unseen, the said and the unsaid. Audiences are, as a result, invited to look beneath the surface of the grave – literally and metaphorically – and confront the abject realities of mortality and grief that are so often denied. Rather than domesticate the Gothic graveyard, rendering it safe and contained, television encourages the audience to face the horrors of death and make themselves at home among the headstones.

References

Akass, Kim and Janet McCabe (2005) 'Introduction: "Why Do People Have to Die?" "To Make Contemporary Television Drama Important, I Guess"', in Kim Akass and Janet McCabe (eds), *Reading* Six Feet Under: *TV to Die For* (London: I. B. Tauris), pp. 1–15.
Barber, Paul (2010) *Vampires, Burial and Death* (New Haven: Yale University Press).
Bunday, Mark W. (2005) 'Exquisite Corpse: Death as an Odalisque and the New American Gothic in *Six Feet Under*', in Kim Akass and Janet McCabe (eds), *Reading* Six Feet Under: *TV to Die For* (London: I. B. Tauris), pp. 34–8.
Jowett, Lorna and Stacey Abbott (2013) *TV Horror: Investigating the Dark Side of the Small Screen* (London: I. B. Tauris).
Lavery, David (2005) ' "It's Not Television: It's Magic Realism": The Mundane, the Grotesque and the Fantastic in *Six Feet Under*', in Kim Akass and Janet McCabe (eds), *Reading* Six Feet Under: *TV to Die For* (London: I. B. Tauris), pp. 19–33.
Luckhurst, Roger (2021) *Gothic: An Illustrated History* (London: Thames and Hudson).
Marc, David (1989) *Comic Visions: Television Comedy and American Culture* (Boston: Unwin Hyman).
Murphy, Bernice M. (2009) *The Suburban Gothic in American Popular Culture* (Basingstoke: Palgrave Macmillan).
Trowbridge, Serena (2017) 'Past, Present, and Future in the Gothic Graveyard', in Carol Margaret Davison (ed.), *The Gothic and Death* (Manchester: Manchester University Press), pp. 21–33.
Wheatley, Helen (2006) *Gothic Television* (Manchester: Manchester University Press).

11

The graveyard in neo-Edwardian fiction: refashioning the Victorian death space

Emma Liggins

The poet Jean Sprackland writes of the graveyard as an 'otherworldly', liminal place, 'dismantled gradually by the passing years, always in a state of becoming' (2020: 1). Its otherworldliness and liminality and its proud display of decay make it a quintessential Gothic space. Historians addressing mourning and 'the Victorian celebration of death' (Curl, 2004; Laqueur, 2015: 261) have dwelt on the Gothic excesses of nineteenth-century cemetery architecture and its archival and aesthetic functions. The angels, urns and mausoleums tell a story of the reification of death in all its religiously inflected splendour, a story which changes when writers of fiction look back on the nineteenth century and its aftermath. Andrew Smith has emphasised the importance of 'exploring how death and dying complicate our view of the Gothic [in the long nineteenth century]' (2016: 9). In nineteenth-century writing, he argues, the graveyard operates as a site 'where the family reconvenes (is resurrected) after death' (2016: 8) as well as stimulating narratives about burial practices and scientific scrutiny of the dead body. As if to symbolise the crumbling of religious faith and the rethinking of sacred space, Victorian burial grounds are often depicted in neo-Edwardian fiction as decaying, neglected, bare of visitors, their tombstones unreadable. Yet they also appear as everyday spaces of sexual desire and ritualised behaviours in which the buried secrets of female transgression can be brought to light.

Drawing on recent work on neo-Victorianism and the reimagining of the Victorian deathscape, this chapter begins by considering Foucauldian notions of the burial ground as an 'other place' which resonates death. Contemporary historical novelists Susan Hill and Tracy Chevalier refashion the Victorian burial ground in novels set in the early twentieth century. *The Woman in Black* (1983) and *Falling Angels* (2001) use the otherworldly graveyard as a key setting for the burial and discovery of family secrets. Operating as an 'other' site for mourning and excessive display, the neo-Edwardian burial ground also symbolises the breakdown of the family and the fracturing of Victorian belief systems. I explore the ways in which the memorialisation of the deaths of women and children, like a half-obscured epitaph, might prove inadequate in preserving their lost stories, and I argue that the ghostly and prematurely buried mothers and children of neo-Edwardian fiction symbolise the weight of the Victorian past and outdated models of mourning.

The neo-Edwardian burial ground: other space/otherworldliness?

In his meditation on counter-sites, 'Of Other Spaces' (1967), Michel Foucault singles out the nineteenth-century cemetery as a useful example of a heterotopia, an 'other place' or 'elsewhere' existing in relation to more common sites such as the home or the city (1986: 25). The cemetery breaks the rules of space, becoming 'a place unlike ordinary cultural spaces', yet one intimately connected with other sites through family ties (1986: 25). With their narratives of loss and lineage, headstones and inscriptions fulfil a significant archival function, yet also resist full disclosure. Sepulchral imagery was a key aspect of the nineteenth-century macabre used in phantasmagoria, according to David Annwn Jones, who notes that as a visual setting the graveyard, with its effigies, skulls, subterranean recesses and ruins, evokes the artificiality of the 'stage set' (2018: 21, 20). The Victorian architect John Loudon reiterated the dangers of burial grounds to the public, writing that if they were aware of the 'dangerous nature of the gases' emanating from the decomposition of dead bodies in crowded churchyards, 'they would not live in houses bordering on churchyards, which, though already full, are still used as burying-grounds' (1843: 5). The Victorian trend towards garden cemeteries, with landscaped flower-beds and park-like promenades, partially eclipsed the church graveyard as a final resting place and ushered in new forms of burial such as cremation. Thomas Laqueur writes, 'whether new or old, the churchyard was meant to be ancient, to belong in its place. Cemeteries were meant to be radically novel: spaces that broke with the historical past' (2015: 272). Although less of a sacred space in the later nineteenth century, where it came to be 'located at the outside border of cities' to minimise contagion, the desired liminality of the graveyard, argues Foucault, could not allay fears about 'the presence and proximity of the dead' (1986: 25).

Graveyard scenes are significant sites of terror in Victorian Gothic novels and their neo-Victorian counterparts. From Charles Dickens's *Bleak House* (1853) and Mary Elizabeth Braddon's *Lady Audley's Secret* (1862) to vampire narratives of the *fin de siècle* such as Bram Stoker's *Dracula* (1897), Victorian Gothic narratives have been used to explore notions of contamination and decay, the faking of death and the threat of the undead female vampire who cannot be contained in her tomb. For Loudon, the consolatory function of such 'places of meditation' was marred by the 'black unearthly-looking surface' (1843: 8) often found in urban graveyards where frequent disinterments meant that no grass would grow. The poetics of graveyard clearance in the later nineteenth century, argues Haewon Hwang, created 'supernatural fissures in the urban imagination', 'an "unnatural" break and displacement of corporeal identity in the new commodification of the spaces of the dead' that made the literary Victorian cemetery a spectral 'space of "unrest"' (2018: 116, 117, 123). Deathscapes and their environs have received limited attention from scholars of the neo-Victorian city, who have focused on these threats of contagion and dirt, as well as the relocation of bodies and burial reform. Susan Martin has argued that neo-Victorian 'cemetery fictions' 'double back' in their recreations of the Victorian world, reproducing the cemetery as a replication of the city with its hierarchies and class divisions (2015: 210). Hester Fox's dark romance *The Orphan of Cemetery Hill* (2020), set in 1850s Boston, brings together the caretaker's adopted lower-class daughter with her 'strange powers' of mediumship (Fox, 2020: 79) and the more respectable grieving Caleb Bishop, who investigate the grave-robberies for medical research taking place in the half-derelict cemetery. Indeed, as Barbara Braid has argued, the hauntological aspects of heterotopic spaces 'invite us to view the cemetery as a befitting metaphor of neo-Victorianism as a textualized space … haunted by spectres and phantoms' (2022: 2). Neo-Victorian texts certainly parade their obsession with death and contagion, with the strange politics of the haunted realm of the graveyard which both reveals and conceals its secrets.

Neo-Edwardian fiction is not often explored as a separate genre, yet there is a growing number of historical novels set in this transitional period, a time when attitudes to death and burial were shifting alongside rapid urbanisation and greater social mobility. According to Gina Wisker, neo-Victorian texts 'Gothicise' the nineteenth century by 'reread[ing] scenarios of gender and power, exposing hidden histories' (2016: 14). The transition into the 1900s, with its alternative mourning rituals and practices, can also be Gothicised. Thomas Laqueur identifies the advent of the nineteenth-century garden cemetery as a new necrogeography which would welcome both mass tourism and cremation by the century's end:

> [A] new kind of space had come into being that appropriated pieces of the past to make a future; as a museum of sculpture and architecture; as an arboretum; as a tourist attraction; as a pilgrimage site; as national, regional, communal, or familial place of memory.
>
> (2015: 288)

As a space governed by 'social expectation concerning mourning behaviour', a burial ground was an index of its era, and by the late nineteenth century the cultural ideal of the family grave, argues Julie-Marie Strange, was 'rather precarious' (2005: 164, 192). These shifting expectations are addressed in the neo-Edwardian texts discussed here, which present Victorian models of mourning as archaic, excessive or difficult to understand. The historian Helen Frisby has written of the abandonment of funeral customs and traditions, such as singing along the processional route, which accompany secularisation in the twentieth century (2019: 57). Writing at a time when cremation accounted for around 75 per cent of English funerals (Frisby, 2019: 66), neo-Edwardian writers of the late twentieth and early-twenty-first centuries explore alternative burial practices or present mourning as traumatic, offering some of the taboo or unexplored aspects of the earlier texts they reimagine. Figuring the graveyard as a contradictory shrine displaying family traumas and secrets, neo-Edwardian novelists revisit the border between Victorian and Edwardian worlds and worldviews, dwelling on the transition from the graveyard as sacred space to a site of decay, ruin, emptiness and loss of certainty.

The Woman in Black: the woman as headstone

When asked about the characteristics for a good ghost story, Susan Hill noted that the contemporary writer would not use all the trappings of eighteenth-century Gothic, such as 'monastic ruins at dusk', but that 'some of the traditional ingredients rarely fail – the old, isolated house, the churchyard' (2012). The eeriness of *The Woman in Black* lies in a refashioning of these Gothic spaces, with the churchyard's closeness to the remote Eel Marsh House, home of the recently deceased Alice Drablow, adding tension and fear. In this well-known novella, the modern solicitor Arthur Kipps attends Alice's funeral and spends the night in the eerie house on the marshes going through the family papers. The papers, the gravestones and several spectral encounters with the revengeful woman in black gradually reveal the hidden narrative of Alice's disgraced sister Jennet Humfrye, whose illegitimate son Nathaniel, brought up by Alice, died in a carriage accident on the foggy marshes years earlier. In the opening chapter, when Kipps's stepchildren are telling ghost stories around the fire on Christmas Eve, 'overgrown graveyards' feature in the litany of Gothic conventions alongside dank charnel houses, hooded monks and vanished corpses. Such details evoke a 'mounting unease' for the listening Kipps, whose 'discomfiture' is at odds with the 'choking laughter' of the others (Hill, 1983: 15). His traumatic memories of 'a story of haunting and evil, fear and confusion' (1983: 16) are repressed traces of the death of his own young son, claimed by the malevolent ghost. Although the time frame remains obscure, the Christmas scene and the death of Kipps's son seem to take place in the Edwardian period, with the solicitor looking back to the past – 'about sixty years before' (1983: 138) – to the time of Jennet's pregnancy and Victorian attitudes to maternal mourning and illegitimacy associated with the Drablow family. Significantly, Hill's novel was written in a decade when popular horror films such as *Poltergeist* (1982) and *The Entity* (1983) presented malevolent ghosts who would not let family secrets stay dormant.

The graveyard scenes in *The Woman in Black*, outside the church in the remote village of Crythin Gifford and in the disused burial ground adjoining Eel Marsh House, foreground the fragility of family ties and lost stories in an eerie deathscape. 'Most attachments to burial grounds were genealogical', argues Julie-Marie Strange, as family members accessed 'individual stories of love and loss ... made public via the headstone, the floral tribute and the visit to the grave' (2005: 168, 173). Often symbolically associated with headstones and their obscure inscriptions, the spectral woman in black, first glimpsed in the church during Alice's funeral service, struggles for her story to be made similarly legible. Entered through a wrought-iron gate from a 'deserted lane' (Hill, 1983: 58) down a path between two overhanging yew trees, the rural graveyard with its headstones overgrown by moss seems remote and picturesque. Yet it is positioned next to the school, so the melancholy children's faces looking through the railings hint at the threatening maternal violence of the woman in black. Visually out of place in 'rusty-looking' garments and Victorian bonnet at the Edwardian funeral, 'dressed in deepest black, in the style of full mourning that had rather gone out of fashion' (1983: 53), the ghost figures nineteenth-century excess and distress, here linked to a powerful malevolence. Likening Hill's dangerous dead woman to other black-clothed spectres such as Henry James's doomed Miss Jessel in *The Turn of the Screw* (1898), Catherine Belsey ponders, 'Is the black dress penitential, provocative, or simply funereal?' (2019: 162). But the fetishised funeral garb has an important symbolic function in Hill's novel, resonating the oddity of Jennet's half-forgotten Victorian story. Concealed 'in the shadows of the church', leaning on a headstone, then looking down into her sister's 'waiting, open grave' (Hill, 1983: 54), the bereaved ghost embodies both the secrecy and the archaic mourning etiquette of a time gone by. Arthur ponders 'what odd story might lie behind her surreptitious visit, and what extremes of sad feeling she was now suffering' (1983: 58), suggesting the archival function of the graveyard as a place for odd stories, as well as the display of loss.

In contrast to Eel Marsh House's function as a 'shrine to the memory of a past time' (1983: 80), the cryptic burial ground beside it refuses to tell the story of the dead mother and her lost child. This recalls Victorian sensation texts that locate the secrets of female transgression in the graveyard, buried from public view (Haewon, 2018: 125). The 'isolated' house is flanked by 'the fragmentary ruins of some old church or chapel' (Hill, 1983: 69) in a spot both 'rare and beautiful' yet inducing loneliness. Using his key to unlock cupboards containing Alice's lost letters and papers, Kipps is unable to unlock the secrets of the graveyard. The approach to the 'unwelcoming' Eel Marsh House fits in with notions of the rural eerie, associated with 'landscapes partially emptied of the human', places of both strangeness and serenity (Fisher, 2016: 11, 12). Initially captivated by 'the sheer and startling beauty, the wide, bare openness … the sense of space' (Hill, 1983: 67), Arthur then experiences the uneasiness of the abandoned house and elusive burial ground, where 'all was emptiness' (1983: 67). When the tide comes in or the sea fret descends, the path to the house disappears and becomes 'untraceable' (1983: 68), like the family secrets. The leaning headstones and the arch that dominate the front and back covers of the first edition are perhaps modelled on country churchyards, half-ruined and sometimes lacking a conscious design. With its fallen stones, a ruined burial ground can operate as a disturbing sight. Dylan Trigg has theorised 'the aesthetics of decay', in which the ruin functions as a dangerous, contradictory site, where the present-day onlooker senses the 'indelible mark' of those who have 'passed through the place' in the past (2006: 249). Decay ensures that the graveyard slips from decipherability, as suggested in Hill's description:

> There were perhaps fifty old gravestones, most of them leaning over or completely fallen, covered in patches of greenish-yellow lichen and moss, scoured pale by the salt wind, and stained by years of driven rain. The mounds were grassy, and weed-covered, or else they had disappeared altogether, sunken and slipped down. No names or dates were now decipherable, and the whole place had a decayed and abandoned air.
>
> (1983: 73)

At the mercy of the weather, stained by time and subject to disappearance and indecipherability, the headstones here conceal the family history, in the same way that the phantom pony and trap Arthur hears after dark conceal the story of the lost child. Writing in 1843, Loudon observes that 'in the country, the churchyard is commonly covered with rank grass abounding in tall weeds, and neglected grave-stones', making it a place to be 'shunned and avoided' (1843: 8). The ruined space is 'disused' and therefore uncannily 'altered', marked by 'erasure' but governed by the ideas which lie 'dormant in that space' (Trigg, 2006: 131, 97). Both the Eel Marsh headstones and the lost sister have been neglected by the family, disrupting lineage and leaving mourning unresolved, dormant in the altered space.

Haunted by vulture-like birds and indistinct in the fading November light, the graveyard symbolises the burial of female stories, the 'desolation' of the site figuring fallen femininity. Significantly, the adjectives, 'fallen', 'stained' and 'sunken' recall Victorian conceptualisations of the fallen woman, often represented visually as in a state of collapse mirroring her disgraced fall from virtue, as in Dante Gabriel Rossetti's unfinished painting *Found* (1853). In the remote burial ground, the ghost's 'desperate, yearning malevolence' (Hill, 1983: 75) is finally unveiled to Kipps: 'the combination of the peculiar, isolated place and the sudden appearance of the woman and the dreadfulness of her expression' (1983: 75) fill him with fear almost to the point of paralysis. The woman slips behind a gravestone into the shadows, then disappears through one of the 'broken gaps' (1983: 76) in the wall. Once examined, the gap leads to nowhere except a view of the estuary, where one could 'see for miles' (1983: 77). Wisker reads this haunting as a response to 'the Otherising, silencing and early deaths of thousands of women … [who] didn't fit society's formulae and norms', like the powerless working-class mothers of Thatcherite Britain (2016: 217). Jennet's disappearing acts symbolise her lack of the 'hidden dwelling place' (Hill, 1983: 77) imagined by the solicitor as a possible place beyond the wall. Alternatively (un)named as 'the woman in the graveyards' (1983: 79), a 'still, silent presence, in each case by a grave' (1983: 79), the unreadable body of the shadowy woman in black who cannot rest in peace doubles with the decaying and indecipherable headstones.

In an important discussion of the recurrent tropes of haunting and spectrality in neo-Victorian fiction, Rosario Arias and Patricia Pulham argue that 'contemporary revisions of the Victorian past offer productive and nuanced ways of unlocking occluded secrets, silences and mysteries which return and reappear in a series of spectral/textual traces' (2010: xx). Jennet's spectre draws attention to her headstone and the cruelty she suffered; in fitting with the gradual revelation of her lost history, the inscription becomes more decipherable as the narrative progresses:

In L…g Mem…
…net Drablow
…190…
…nd of He…
…iel …low
Bor…

(Hill, 1983: 127)

The name Drablow repeated in the second and fifth line (the names of Jennet and her son Nathaniel) is only preserved in its entirety as part of the mother's name though her actual surname Humfrye remains ambiguously unrecorded. Family ties and secrets, including dates of birth and death, are obscured; there is no record of the removal of the son's body from the fatal marsh, an erasure manifested later in the spectral 'scream of terror' (1983: 142) at the site of his death. Crumbling headstones, according to Sprackland, offer 'a few fragments of story waiting to be pieced together' (2020: 4). This unnerving fragmentation hints at past evils:

> Mr Jerome had hinted at some Drablow family graves, no longer used, in a place other than the churchyard and [I] supposed that this was the resting place of ancestors from years back. But it was quite certain that there was nothing and no one except old bones here now and I felt quite unafraid and tranquil as I stood there, contemplating the scene and the place which had previously struck me as eerie, sinister, evil, but which now I saw, was merely something melancholy because it was so tumbledown and unfrequented. It was the sort of spot where, a hundred years or more earlier, romantically minded poets would have lingered and been inspired to compose some cloyingly sad verse.
>
> (Hill, 1983: 128)

The 'tumbledown', 'melancholy', isolated spot, with its forgotten ancestors, is evocative of the sentimentalised sadness of eighteenth-century graveyard poetry. Yet the tranquillity experienced here is short-lived, as the 'old bones' of the graveyard are threatening to notions of the family; significantly, the idea of the family grave is here 'no longer used'. Cultural geographers have conceptualised the deathscape as productive of 'new performances, rituals, emotional geographies and affective atmospheres' (Young and Light, 2016: 61). The partially decipherable headstone hints at the less than loving memories troubling Jennet's unquiet spirit and the emotional response demanded by contemplation of the dead.

Neo-Victorian reimaginings of illegitimacy often generate more sympathy for the spurned mother by allowing her to voice her own stigmatisation. Here, maternal loss is filtered through male narrators, who may approve the cruel actions of the previous generation. In Mr Daily's final recounting of Jennet's story, he explains that 'whenever she has been seen ... in the graveyard, on the marsh, in the streets of the town', a child dies in some 'violent or dreadful circumstance' (Hill, 1983: 186). Her spirit becomes a harbinger of death, as her excessive mourning for her lost child transforms into evil intent against all children. Infant mortality from accidents and disease remained high throughout the Victorian period, a point reiterated by Kipps; the fear generated by the appearance of 'the woman of the graveyards' suggests that she visibly threatens family ties and will in turn take the solicitor's own son. The 'desperate, clinging affection' (1983: 139) detected by Kipps in Jennet's brief letters discovered at Eel Marsh House may appear a sign of maternal excess, which then changes from 'passionate outrage and protest' to 'quiet, resigned bitterness' in the face of her son's adoption: 'I am quite helpless ... [H]e is mine, mine, he can never be yours' (1983: 139). But this is the only time Jennet's voice is heard. Kipps in his delusive nightmares feels haunted by the letters and the death certificates, as well as the woman in black's face. It is significant that the male narrator identifies himself as one who had 'never truly mourned and suffered the extremes of grief' (1983: 157), yet when he enters the haunted nursery, he experiences 'not fear, not horror, but an overwhelming grief and sadness, a sense of loss and bereavement, a distress mingled with utter despair' (1983: 157). Once outside the nursery, the feelings 'dropped away from me like a garment that had been put over my shoulders for a short time and then removed again' (1983: 158), like the mourning dress usually worn only temporarily. The 'extremes of grief' manifest themselves in the woman in black, who symbolises not only unresolved maternal mourning but also the stigma of illegitimacy and family shame. Although Arthur's initial instincts are to 'flee from the graveyard' (1983: 77) and the unknown fears it generates, the fatal accident killing his wife and son activates a despairing grief that still surfaces as a memory trace in the Christmas family scenes with his second wife and stepchildren in the new century. Haunting the graveyard threatens notions of the Edwardian family with death's uncontrollable proximity, the trauma of loss, showing the dangers of burying rather than memorialising the secrets of female transgression.

Falling Angels: 'Desperate to get to the cemetery'

Inspired by Highgate Cemetery, Tracy Chevalier's *Falling Angels* plays on the idea of the burial ground as a contested space of disposal, decay and emotional excess in the transitional years after Queen Victoria's death. One of the 'Magnificent 7' cemeteries on the borders of London, Highgate boasted a steam-powered lift and the first macadam surface in England on its famous neo-Egyptian avenue, leading to the grand Cedar of Lebanon (Laqueur, 2015: 276). An early guidebook promoted its 'holy loveliness … as though kind angels hovered about it'; it is now famed for its ostentatious tombs, fulfilling its architect's aim for the place of death to be 'deeply theatrical' (Ross, 2020: 108, 106). For Loudon, the new Victorian cemetery should have encouraged 'moral sentiment' (1843: 1), an ideal called into question amid concerns about illicit uses of the burial ground as 'pleasure-ground', where death sat uneasily with recreation (Laqueur, 2015: 276–7). It became both a 'landscape for grief' and a place of regulation, though, 'unlike other public spaces … transgression of cemetery rules carried extra meaning in relation to the sanctity of the dead and the melancholy of remembrance' (Strange, 2005: 177, 163). Chevalier notes the influences of historical research on the Victorian celebration of death on her Highgate narrative but, more importantly, adds that 'the cemetery in this book is made up of a lot of fact and a fair bit of fiction – concrete details and flights of fancy interwoven, with no need to untangle them' (2001: 410). Set between 1901 and 1910, *Falling Angels* tells the story of three families, the middle-class Colemans, the aspiring Waterhouses and the grave-digging Fields, with the three children Maude, Lavinia and Simon first meeting by the Coleman and Waterhouse family graves. Such spaces of mourning were meant to foster what Smith has called 'the importance of family togetherness' (2016: 122), yet the reimagining of the Edwardian period dwells on the disintegration of familial ties and values.

Architectural features of Highgate, such as its Egyptian obelisks, columbarium and the Lebanon Cedar at the top of the hill, add authenticity, but the Gothic graveyard is also a fanciful site of transgression and darkness. Braid reads Chevalier's depiction in terms of Highgate's carefully curated decline and its heterotopic spatial dynamics, as well as an obscured 'vantage point' into a hard-to-grasp Victorian past (2022: 2). However, its transgressive possibilities demand more attention. The liminality of the deathscape might suggest it is 'alternative' and 'Other', yet its morbidity should not detract from the importance of its everyday uses (Young and Light, 2016: 64). The modern suffragette-to-be Kitty Coleman sees its architecture as over-sentimentalised, 'the excess of it all … is too much' (Chevalier, 2001: 17), whilst Lavinia finds it both 'delicious' (2001: 22) and ghostly, a realm of shadows. One chapter opens with the two girls Lavinia and Maude 'desperate to get to the cemetery' (2001: 53) so they can 'rush about and explore' rather than being 'quiet and solemn' with their families (2001: 54). In cemetery fictions, Martin argues, 'lack of surveillance means that transgressions and irregularities … can occur' (2015: 211) in relation both to sexual contact and the rules and rituals of the dead. The cemetery becomes a place of secrets, desire and danger, where the gravedigger's son Simon can spend a cold January night frozen and forgotten in an open grave, his father can be almost buried alive and women can enjoy dangerous liaisons in its hidden corners.

Chevalier maps 'enjoyment' of the Gothic architecture against the rejection of the 'falling angels' of traditional femininities. The symbolic figure of Ivy May, Lavinia's younger and often silent sister who 'sees everything' (2001: 205) but will be abducted and killed in a suffragette march at the end of the narrative, accompanies the girls on their cemetery visits. Like the ivy that threateningly entwines itself around the Coleman family grave, she is an otherworldly and unpredictable presence whose affinity with the cemetery foreshadows her own death. In one scene she looks down silently into an open grave and throws in a clod of clay, mimicking the rituals of burial. Her unnerving silence, aligning her with the Victorian funeral mute, is broken in the two sentences she narrates shortly before her death after the suffrage demonstration in London: 'Over his shoulder I saw a star fall. It was me'

(2001: 329). Described as 'angelic' and pure, yet also a 'thing like a sack of spuds', Ivy May's corpse, abandoned in a dark alley, appears as if 'she ain't there' (2001: 330). Her broken straw hat, 'the flowers crushed' (2001: 331), hints at sexual violation and the vulnerability of young women to defilement. The outdated mourning rituals and costly crape trimmings Lavinia indulges in for her dead sister discordantly echo the mass wearing of black for the Queen in 1901, contrasting with the more shocking colourful dresses worn by Kitty, who rejects such customs. According to Martin, Chevalier's novel 'caresses Victorian mourning culture, as it celebrates its passing' (2015: 212–13); certainly, this potential fetishisation of death is critiqued by the novel's close. Contrasted with the 'ridiculous' urn on the Coleman family grave, the 'sentimental' angel chosen by the Waterhouses becomes one of the falling angels of the narrative. Evoking the decay of Victorian traditions, the angels become chipped, 'vapid', weather-blasted. The gravedigger's son draws skulls and crossbones on the headstones as a visual reminder that 'it's all bones down there' (Chevalier, 2001: 12), whatever the ornamentation.

As in *The Woman in Black*, it is the female characters whose stories are buried in the Edwardian death-space. Yet Chevalier's novel is more typical of twenty-first-century neo-Edwardian Gothic fictions, such as Rosie Garland's *The Night Brother* (2017), which reimagine the oppressive past in terms of the suffragette's vulnerability in the dangerous urban space. The distaste of the modern woman for 'that blasted cemetery', despite its 'lugubrious charm' (Chevalier, 2001: 16) is punished by Kitty's violent death. The desperation to get to the cemetery takes on ominous overtones, as women are much more at risk by occupying the death-space, whether for recreation or cementing family ties; Chevalier dwells on the unplanned pregnancies suffered by both Kitty and her maid Jenny after cemetery trysts, which take place by the Dissenters' graves in a zone set aside for religious dissent. After a risky back-street abortion, the sight of the burial ground makes Kitty tremble. Lavinia conceives of Kitty's dissenting behaviour in terms of 'contamination' and 'Moral Repulsion' (2001: 210–11), as if it is the older woman, not herself, who has 'caught a chill down in the grave' (2001: 210). Maude reflects that 'Mummy's dead … [S]he's not going to design her grave' (2001: 342), believing that she would prefer 'Votes for Women' as her epitaph, unlike Mr Jackson, who imagines Kitty's choice would be 'no monument or words at all' but 'a bed of wildflowers' (2001: 342). Martin reads the ending as a 'symbolic shift from a figuring of the late Victorian city as one of the decaying dead to a concentration on the rebellious suffragette … ostensibly freed from both rigid urban structures, and the erotics of mourning' (2015: 223), yet this downplays the lingering questions about women's rights to 'design' their graves and to be commemorated. Women's limited control over their burial and commemoration is revisited in Chevalier's text.

Poised between tradition and modernity, the cemetery stages confrontations between advocates of burial and cremation, with its superintendent Mr Jackson championing ashes rather than decaying bodies. The time span of the novel encompasses the Cremation Act of 1902, which officially recognised the importance of the crematorium as a place of death to be regulated alongside other graveyards by the authorities. This new form of disposal had been legalised in 1885, with crematoria appearing in Manchester and London by 1892; 604 cremations took place in 1905, growing steadily to 1,279 in 1914 (Frisby, 2019: 51–2). Gothic appropriations of burial space in Victorian fiction have been read in terms of the transition towards cremation and the commercialisation of death (Haewon, 2018: 126). Kitty's Edwardian modernity is reinforced by her preference for cremation (balanced against her typically Victorian fear of being buried alive); her cremation is performed in secret, so as not to openly endorse what her conservative mother-in-law calls 'the attitude of this new age which doesn't respect the dead' (Chevalier, 2001: 101). In the final scenes, Lavinia's occupation of cemetery space to leave a posy on her sister's grave before ritualistically 'tour[ing] the angels' (2001: 402) is interrupted by her shocking discovery of the prying open of the Coleman grave. Mimicking the actions of grave-robbers with their 'unnatural violations ... [of] the sanctity of the grave' (Hwang, 2018: 125), Simon and Mr Jackson perform new ways of honouring the dead. Despite an erroneous belief that their 'gruesome task' is 'illegal and immoral' (Chevalier, 2001: 404, 403), Lavinia agrees to keep the secrets of female sexual and funerary transgression. The symbolic bonfire glimpsed by Maude among the 'dancing branches' of the cemetery ritualises the death of King Edward but feels almost as if 'it had been lit for [her mother] as well' (2001: 406). As the final narrator, Simon describes the burning of bones and the scattering of ashes in the wildflower meadow, 'a change from all them flowerbeds and raked paths' (2001: 407). Fertilising his grandfather's rosebush with the remainder, 'where some of her is, if ever Maude wants to know' (2001: 407), the forward-looking gravedigger creates an alternative family monument and ushers in new mourning practices.

If the heterotopian cemetery is a contradictory 'other city, where each family possesses its dark resting place' (Foucault, 1986: 25), it can be seen to function as an elsewhere of loss, a liminal space that challenges ways of thinking about death and spectrality. Neo-Edwardian fiction embraces the excesses of the Victorian death space, yet also sets out to desacralise and destabilise outdated notions of family, loss and female sexuality. The ruined burial ground in Hill's novel doubles with the indecipherable gravestones and lost story of the bereaved spectral mother, whereas in *Falling Angels* the conflict between tradition and modernity is played out in the cemetery as a place of both transgression and darkness. Chevalier's representation of the unsettling novelty of cremation practices after the Cremation Act does not have a parallel in most Edwardian fiction, which tends to replicate the Victorian way of death. Critical of the affectations of those who 'make a show of mourning' (Chevalier, 2001: 16) for their lost Queen, or of those who relish the intricacies of mourning etiquette, both *Falling Angels* and *The Woman in Black* dwell on the paraphernalia of death and the fallen female body as a symbol of mortality. In the gloom of modernity, the dead women who occupy the graveyard never fully reveal their buried secrets.

References

Arias, Rosario and Patricia Pulham (eds) (2010) *Haunting and Spectrality in Neo-Victorian Fiction* (Basingstoke: Palgrave).
Belsey, Catherine (2019) *Tales of the Troubled Dead: Ghost Stories in Cultural History* (Edinburgh: Edinburgh University Press).
Braid, Barbara (2022) 'Neo-Victorianism as a Cemetery: Heterotopia and Heterochronia in Tracy Chevalier's *Falling Angels* and Audrey Niffenegger's *Her Fearful Symmetry*', *Humanities*, 11:11, 1–16.
Chevalier, Tracy (2001) *Falling Angels* (London: Vintage).
Curl, James Stephen (2004) *The Victorian Celebration of Death* (Stroud: Sutton Publishing).
Fisher, Mark (2016) *The Weird and the Eerie* (London: Repeater Books).
Foucault, Michel (1986) [1967] 'Of Other Spaces', trans. Jay Miskowiec, *Diacritics*, 16:1, 22–7.
Fox, Hester (2020) *The Orphan of Cemetery Hill* (Ontario: Graydon House).
Frisby, Helen (2019) *Traditions of Death and Burial* (Oxford: Shire/Bloomsbury).
Hill, Susan (1983) *The Woman in Black* (London: Vintage).
Hill, Susan (2012) 'The Secret of Writing a Good Ghost Story: Susan Hill Launches Our Prize', *The Times*, 13 October, www.thetimes.co.uk/article/the-secret-of-writing-a-good-ghost-story-susan-hill-launches-our-prize-zvvf3t92hsf (accessed 20 November 2021).
Hwang, Haewon (2018) 'Exhuming the City: The Politics and Poetics of Graveyard Clearance', in Grace Moore and Michelle J. Smith (eds), *Victorian Environments: Acclimatizing to Change in British Domestic and Colonial Culture* (Basingstoke: Palgrave), pp. 115–34.
Jones, David Annwn (2018) *Gothic Effigy: A Guide to Dark Visibilities* (Manchester: Manchester University Press).
Laqueur, Thomas W. (2015) *The Work of the Dead: A Cultural History of Mortal Remains* (Princeton: Princeton University Press).
Loudon, John (1843) *On the Laying Out, Planting and Managing of Cemeteries* (London: Longman Brown).
Martin, Susan K. (2015) 'Neo-Victorian Cities of the Dead: Contemporary Fictions of the Victorian Cemetery', in Marie-Luise Kohlke and Christian Gutleben (eds), *Neo-Victorian Cities: Reassessing Urban Politics and Poetics* (Leiden: Brill), pp. 201–26.
Ross, Peter (2020) *A Tomb with a View: The Stories and Glories of Graveyards* (London: Headline).

Smith, Andrew (2016) *Gothic Death, 1740–1914: A Literary History* (Manchester: Manchester University Press).
Sprackland, Jean (2020) *These Silent Mansions: A Life in Graveyards* (London: Jonathan Cape).
Strange, Julie-Marie (2005) *Death, Grief and Poverty in Britain, 1870–1914* (Cambridge: Cambridge University Press).
Trigg, Dylan (2006) *The Aesthetics of Decay: Nothingness, Nostalgia and the Absence of Reason* (New York: Peter Lang).
Wisker, Gina (2016) *Contemporary Women's Gothic Fiction* (Basingstoke: Palgrave).
Young, Craig and Duncan Light (2016) 'Interrogating Spaces of and for the Dead as "Alternative Space": Cemeteries, Corpses and Sites of Dark Tourism', *International Review of Social Research*, 6:2, 61–72.

12

Unstable coordinates: textures, *tehkhana* and the Gothic in the horror films of the Ramsay brothers

Vibhushan Subba

The 1980s saw the rise of cassette culture in India when the government eased the import policy because of the Asian Games (Asiad) that were held in Delhi in 1982. Asiad 82 was a specific moment in Indian media history which, according to Ravi Sundaram, was a prelude to the globalisation that unrolled a media culture, one that looked towards a new visual regime, encouraged advertisements and consumption, softened 'old-style nationalist policies' (2010: 84) and explored computerisation and new networks. To meet the demand for live broadcast of the games, the government eased the import policy, which had the effect of fuelling import of TV sets and VCRs, fostering an equally robust audio and video cassette culture (2010: 85). The opening-up of new sites caused an upheaval in the media environment, which changed from a controlled and regulated space to one that operated out of the purview of government regulation and facilitated the growth of 'new parasitic media geographies' (2010: 115). As Sundaram points out, '[d]rawing from a growing infrastructure of small enterprises and an emerging class of entrepreneurs, cassette culture of both audio and video let loose a series of conflicts around piracy, between large and small companies, between pirates and copyright enforcement detectives and between large and small pirates' (2010: 115). It was in this transitional moment of new-found video audiences, piracy and evasion of censorship that the particular horror of the Ramsay brothers came into its own.

The Ramsays arrived on the Bombay Hindi horror scene in the early 1970s and set up their artisanal world of horror in the shadows of mainstream cinema. A family workshop of sorts, the Ramsays worked together as a film unit: Tulsi and Shyam directed most of the productions; Kiran focused on sound; Kumar wrote the screenplays; Gangu and Keshu handled camera and lighting; and Arjun was in charge of post-production (Nair, 2012: 125). Set in remote locations, their narratives unfold in the shadows of ruinous buildings haunted by the ghosts of past transgressors and their victims. Here, monsters lurking in dark subterranean basements come unstuck in time, acting as reminders – to inquisitive people from the present day – of medieval crimes, property feuds, feudal excesses, lust, greed and deceit. For the Ramsays, the Gothic operates as both a mode and a process, and their films become at once an aesthetic mode and a performance of signification and translation. Their films exemplify what Katarzyna Ancuta and Deimantas Valančiūnas consider the fluid category of South Asian Gothic, a 'distinctive aesthetic, a narrative practice, or a process of signification, where conventional Gothic tropes and imagery are assessed anew and where global forms get consumed, appropriated, translated, transformed, and even resisted' (2021: 4).

In this chapter, through an examination of the 1980s horror cinema of the Ramsay brothers, and especially *Dak Bangla* (*Guest House*, 1987), I argue that the *tehkhana* (an underground dwelling, cellar or dungeon used at times as a burial place) is a site marked by contradictions, one where multiple and often competing histories – feudal, colonial, postcolonial – reside. Whereas the aestheticised space of the graveyard identifiable in Western horror makes appearances as a shorthand for gloom in the Bombay horror films of the 1980s and in an earlier cycle of Gothic thrillers from the 1960s, it has also been a setting for parodic and playful encounters. Rather than being a mere extension of the graveyard, the space of the *tehkhana* emerges as a specific site of signification, as a distinct space and Gothic site rendered monstrous with the arrival of a particular kind of cinema and haunting. This haunting is symptomatic of a larger transformation of the Indian public sphere and media geography following the cassette and piratic networks of the 1980s and a response to the political climate of the 1970s. As a space that is frequently overlooked in Indian horror scholarship, the *tehkhana* not only complicates any imagining and representation of the Gothic in the context of South Asia but also acts as an entry point to explore the many overlapping flows and circuitous nature of histories – of power and territorialisation, of media geographies and of genres and tastes – in the context of Bombay horror.

Tehkhana: space, architecture, imagination

The *tehkhana* in Mughal architecture was an underground structure of palatial residencies (the *haveli*) that served several purposes: some were built to escape the summer heat; others were adapted into burial chambers; and some were dungeons and cellars. The *haveli* is a reminder of an abstracted past, an ambivalent cultural symbol that circulates as the central architectural icon of the feudal era in Hindi commercial cinema (Jaikumar, 2019). While the *haveli* languishes in a state of decay in the modern Indian landscape, having outlived its function as an efficient domicile, its affective topography in Hindi commercial cinema enjoys a different destiny. Through her exploration of the affective history of the *haveli*, which takes her into a narrative of asynchronicities in modern India, Priya Jaikumar argues that the *haveli* and its affective topography complicates the narrative of India's transition into a modern nation-state. Jyoti Pandey Sharma, in her study on cultural hybridity and sociability in eighteenth-century colonial India, finds the presence of *tehkhanas* even in the residences of European mercenaries. Drawing examples from the floor plans of the residences of Major General Claude Martin and others, who built large residencies in the cities and mofussil towns, Sharma offers a spatial investigation of the eighteenth century 'nabobian' *kothis*, which drew inspiration from both Mughal and European architectural styles: mainly the Mughal *haveli* and the European Palladian villa. She adds: 'The *haveli* archetype, with its quintessential Mughal spatial ensemble of chauk-bagh-tehkhana-zenana-hammam [courtyard-garden-seraglio-basement-bath] was used both to enable the nabobian lifestyle and mitigate the impact of climate' (2019: 16, original emphasis).

Relying on the postcolonial theory of 'cultural hybridity', Sharma asserts that, despite the oppression, the period of colonialism engendered 'cultural contacts' that manifested themselves in hybrid built forms, combining East and West spatiality, like the *kothi* (2019: 8). In these nabobian *kothis*, the *tehkhana* was a network of subterranean rooms used by the families during the summer and which often extended to several underground levels. They were also used to entertain guests; they sometimes served as a burial place; and, in the case of Claude Martin, the *tehkhanas* were 'two caves or recesses within the banks of the river' lived in during the hot season (2019: 21). Sharma observes that the 'Kothi, together with the *Haveli* and the Bungalow, represented the subcontinent's domestic architecture during the colonial period' (2019: 64). However, while the *kothi* fell out of fashion in the nineteenth century, 'the bungalow emerged as the epitome of British colonial domesticity' (2019: 21). Colonial India had a *dak* (post) system that extended across the country – a postal and transport system that moved a volume of mail carried on foot and on horseback. Since the post had to be delivered across vast distances, *dak* bungalows were set up to relay the post in stages. '*Dak* bungalows, for instance, were located in many districts of British India. Later, they became rest centres for traveling British colonial administrators and legal teams … Many *dak* bungalows survived Independence and still function as government bungalows' (Desai et al., 2016: 74–5). Rajika Bhandari tracks the story of the *dak* bungalow – the architectural style, the cuisine, the residents, the ghosts and its transition from a post house to a guest house – in her book *The Raj on the Move* (2012). 'From the time of the British Raj to this day there are stories of strange happenings in dak bungalows scattered across the Indian subcontinent, in large cities and in remote and rural locations', she writes (2012: 56). Was it the location of these large buildings in remote hilltops and deep forests, their isolation from civilisation, their proximity to wild animals and the sonic texture of nature that inspired ghostly folklores? Or perhaps it was that many British travellers and soldiers lost their lives in these bungalows, and in those cases the premises served as a burial place, a resting place for those who succumbed to diseases like malaria and cholera (2012: 56). Bhandari ascribes no particular reason but reminds us that these buildings retain a special place in folklore, literary fiction, architectural history and bureaucracy, inspiring a mysterious amalgam of eeriness and nostalgia.

Breaking with convention, rather than solely focusing on the symbol and the architectural space of the *haveli*, the Ramsays' *Dak Bangla* highlights the textural arrangement of the *tehkhana*. As a subterranean space, a cavernous labyrinth that stows away secrets and desires, the *tehkhana* emerges as a distinct space within the Ramsay horror films of the 1980s more broadly. The *tehkhana*, as a stand-in for a grave as well as a crypt and basement, becomes not only a site of contestation (as part of the larger structure of the *haveli* and in association with its legacies, histories and pasts), but more so a hidden, repressed and subterranean body and text, which implicitly connect the colonial past with feudal vestiges that modernity renders ghostly in the space of the film and beyond. In *Dak Bangla*, the Ramsays deploy their own hybrid architectonics by giving a textural arrangement to a building that shares some features with the earlier Mughal *havelis* and palaces while retaining the name and idea of the colonial *dak* bungalow, thus lending the *tehkhana* a palimpsest-like quality that collapses different worlds, histories and pasts together to produce an assemblage of meanings and associations.

The monster, the mode and the site in *Dak Bangla*

A sense of mystery pervades the *tehkhana* that is at the centre of *Dak Bangla*. It wrestles with its own past and a well-hidden secret. The house, we are told, once belonged to Thakur Mansingh (Narendra Nath), the powerful king of Chandan Nagar. His house courts danger when an incident at the edge of the forest sets off the events in the film's recounted past. While passing through some hostile territory, the princess (Mansingh's daughter, played by Swapna) stops the caravan, charmed by the beauty of the land. Kunal, her husband (Dilip Dhawan), who is travelling with her, warns her that the area is inhabited by a cult of satanic worshippers, but she ignores his warnings. As the caravan settles down, she slips into a quiet corner of the forest, where she is enchanted by the lush meadows and the wild sunflowers. When she drifts deeper into the woods, she is attacked by a man (Praveen Kumar Sobti) who is aroused by her beauty. However, she is rescued by her husband and the royal guards. The man receives a thorough whipping, and the royal retinue returns to the palace. The perpetrator, it turns out, is no ordinary man but Ozo, the son of a powerful cult leader and tantric, well versed in the dark arts. The tantric (Imtiaz Khan) is not pleased that Ozo has been flogged like a common thief, so he sends him to Chandan Nagar to remedy this ghastly humiliation. Emboldened by his father's encouragement, Ozo storms the mansion, makes short work of the royal guards, stabs the husband and kills the princess before he is overpowered. Distraught and enraged, Thakur Mansingh stops the guards from killing Ozo in an attempt to dispense a rather painful and drawn-out punishment. He orders his guards to lock Ozo in the *tehkhana*. In a particularly telling voice-over, we are told that even as Ozo is being led to the *tehkhana*, Thakur Mansingh fears that the man's beastly implacable appetite for sex and lust has not been satiated and worries about his escape. The Thakur then returns to the *tehkhana* to slowly dismember Ozo limb from limb, before finally beheading him for his crimes. He then sends his envoys to summon the tantric so that he can witness the fate of his son. Upon seeing the mutilated corpse, the tantric is emotionally overwrought and his grief travels as a powerful tremor that is felt across the mansion. Meanwhile, the Thakur asks his guards to seal the criminals in the *tehkhana*. He urges them to 'turn the *tehkhana* into their crypt, seal its doors forever and mark the walls with [the sun god] Suraj Devta's medallion so that they are never able to emerge'. Later, in the depths of the *tehkhana*, the tantric diligently sews Ozo's body together, stitching the limbs and wrapping it up with bandages. He summons all his powers and using his skills of dark magic transfers his life force drop by drop into the lifeless body. When the ritual is over, he collapses to the floor and the monster awakens. At the heart of the Ramsay horror film is a crime, a secret that needs to be hidden and buried.

This inextricable association of the crime and the burial appears in the filmography of the Ramsay brothers. In *Purana Mandir* (*Old Temple*, 1984), Samri, a dreaded monster played by Anirudh Agarwal, kills the princess, is apprehended, tried by a court, beheaded and buried in the *tehkhana*. In *Tahkhana* (*Dungeon*, 1986), one brother kills the other for the family treasure and is incarcerated in a dungeon for life. In *Hotel* (1981), a group of conniving building developers acquire a cemetery from a priest under false pretences, murder the commissioning partner's brother and hide the body and the uprooted gravestones in a shed behind the new hotel. In *Saamri* (1985), the eponymous character is murdered by his acquaintances and relatives for his wealth, but the body is stowed away by Saamri's loyal servant in the cavernous space below the sprawling house. In *Purani Haveli* (*Old Mansion*, 1989), a father buries his newborn in a *tehkhana*, fearing that it is the devil incarnate.

In *Dak Bangla*, the pervasive and malignant legacy of this crime and burial is signalled aesthetically, in keeping with Xavier Aldana Reyes's claim that the cinematic Gothic is primarily an aesthetic mode. As Aldana Reyes argues, 'its main recognisable traits' are visual or iconographic, a mode identified by its *mise en scène*, lighting, setting and tropes, and 'not by our reading of its social work as filtered through given national or psychological lenses, a process which is nevertheless manifest and of relevance' (2020: 17). During an interview with the author of the present chapter in September 2017, Iqbal Dhansey – electrician, spot operator, light man, and a constant on the Ramsay sets – imparted how such snapshots of fear were created in their films: 'Fog, coffins and storm fans were a must. Whether the fog came from a machine or by any other means, these were things that were brought to every set, whether they were required or not.' Hussain, who also worked alongside Dhansey in the Ramsay films in many capacities, added, again during a personal interview in September 2017, 'there was this bungalow in Juhu Tara road and if there was smoke coming out of it, it was understood that the Ramsays had arrived for a shoot' – an indication that the directors' films had become synonymous with the aesthetics of the Gothic and the mechanics of the horror genre.

In *Dak Bangla* itself, when the protagonist Ajay (Marc Zuber) is appointed as the new manager of the *dak* bungalow (henceforth *bangla*), the owner leaves him with a cryptic warning that this particular house is consumed by rumours and strange incidents, adding as an aside that the previous manager took his own life. On their way to the remotely located *dak bangla* of Chandan Nagar, Ajay and his wife Vaishali (Aaloka) stop several villagers to ask them for directions, but no one responds. In fact, they treat their presence and the reference to the *bangla* as a bad omen. The Ramsays assemble an atmosphere of gloom right from the outset. The couple finally arrive as night falls, when the austere building bathed in mists and nightly blue presents a grim picture. A sign that reads 'Dak Bangla' dangles from the imposing iron gate, which opens at the slightest nudge. The bungalow's lower floor disappears in generous doses of fog, which occasionally rolls in from the left. As the couple move towards the door, the camera tracks right and settles on a dead body lying on the veranda. With a vertical movement, the camera reveals the hammer-wielding killer, Shakaal (Ranjeet), a fugitive waiting for his posse to arrive, who has been posing as the caretaker Khurshid Khan. When Ajay knocks at the door, their luggage mysteriously disappears and the door opens with a wisp of fog that ushers them into the building.

The *tehkhana* beneath the *bangla*, and the secrets it keeps, seems to reach out to the new inhabitants in various spectral hauntings, as if to lure them below. On their first night at the guest house, Vaishali catches a glimpse of the golden medallion of Suraj Devta. She watches Ajay as he slowly descends the staircase, caresses the medallion and rests his ears on the wall that it hangs on, and as a monstrous hand breaks through the wall and grabs him – only to realise that this is a false awakening. She has recurrent visions of the medallion, the barricaded door in the basement, a secret chamber, flashes of Ozo slashing her sister Sapna with a sword, Sapna's lifeless body on the cold floor and snatches of Sapna's blood-streaked portrait. When Vaishali's visions become unbearable, she asks Ajay to take her down to the room that remains barricaded. From a low angle we see the couple approaching the door. While Vaishali disappears into the shadows, Ajay is partially lit in shades of blue. Ajay removes the wooden boards that fasten the door and, as they enter, we see them framed in a two-shot with a giant cobweb in the foreground. As we follow their gaze, we are introduced to a bed chamber awash with an orange tint, half lit and half in the shadows, again with a thick, knotty cobweb in the foreground. The camera returns to the two-shot and pulls out, giving us a wider glimpse of this chamber. As Vaishali describes her vivid dreams, Ajay moves forward into the bed chamber where, to his surprise, he finds Sapna's blood-streaked portrait on the wall. Before they can investigate any further, they are interrupted by the arrival of Sapna (Vaishali's sister) and her friends. As she spends time in the bungalow, Sapna has similar visions, visitations from the past as she calls them. Her uncanny resemblance with the woman in her dreams leads her to believe that she has a deeper connection with the place, perhaps a past life. Sapna is also beckoned by the bedchamber – as part of her oneiric fixation – where she and her lover Raj (Rajan Sippy) stumble upon an ancient journal that recounts the story of Sapna's past life. This is when we are introduced to the *tehkhana* in the present day, which up until now has appeared in visions, dreams and flashbacks. After reading the journal, Raj feels that beneath the bedchamber there is a *tehkhana*, where he can hear someone or something moving. This leads them to the medallion. As Raj tears off the medallion from the wall, the camera reveals the body of the monster. Everything is luridly lit in shades of red, yellow and orange, while the soundtrack wails like a distant siren. Raj breaks down the wall and leads us down to the *tehkhana* through reams of thick webs as his flashlight uncovers rat-infested corners. The cold stony walls of the *tehkhana*, now lit in blue and red, support pendulous snakes. Herein lies the monster, wrapped from head to toe, a putrid gelatinous matter from another world.

In the Ramsay films, the monsters' locales and malevolent environments are lit using red, blue, yellow and sometimes green gels all in the same frame. When there is a need to create hostile atmospheres, these colours are used to tinge the drifting smoke and mists, splash colour on the walls and mark fear on faces. Oversaturated blues, reds, yellows and greens are used to accentuate malevolence, often illuminating the monsters' gelatinous faces or settling deep into the interiors of the *haveli* or cavernous spaces of evil. These colours, accompanied by low-key lighting, create harsh angular shadows and high-contrast frames that nibble in and out of the edges of the dark night. Reams of thick and free-floating smoke, fog or mist underscore this dramatic chiaroscuro, generating lurid silhouettes of horror.

Meheli Sen notes that in the Ramsay films of the 1980s, the Gothic 'mutate[d] into an outlandishly overblown avatar':

> The most notorious components of the genre include[d] flimsy, often utterly inchoate plots punctuated by oddly placed song sequences and bizarre comic routines, horror set pieces involving burly monsters in old mansions, tacky prosthetic makeup, gratuitous exploitation of young female bodies, sexual violence and violence against women, patently fake blood and gore, and rudimentary special effects.
>
> (2017: 49)

The addition of the figure of the monster in these horror films of the 1980s is partly responsible for this mutation. Far from the elusive apparitions in the earlier cycle of supernatural thrillers, psychological tricks of the imagination, sleights of hand and gloomy locales, the low-budget horror film offers the palpable terror and anxieties of the body: the monstrous body, bodily transformations and defamiliarised bodies. This is not to suggest that all Ramsay horror of the 1980s are only body horror, but the anxieties around transformation, mutation and defamiliarisation of the body are abundantly available. In a coruscating scene from *Dahshat* (*Fear*, 1981), Dr Vishal (Om Shivpuri) claims that the human body is incomplete and that his experiments on corpses and animals allow him to challenge anatomical boundaries. Operating from his basement menagerie of monkeys, snakes, lizards and corpses, he seeks to complete the human body by uniting it with the animal frame, and in a twist of fate, when his wife injects his own experimental serum into him, Dr Vishal mutates into an unrecognisable monster: part human, part animal. The monster's body in the Gothic mode, as Jack Halberstam argues, represents all kinds of fears, anxieties and desires; it becomes a vessel that is able to hold and 'condense as many fear-producing traits as possible', making monsters effective 'meaning machines' (1995: 21–2). In other words, 'monster narratives … offer a space where society can safely represent and address anxieties of its time' (Levina and Bui, 2013: 1).

Several scholars have signalled how Hindi horror of the 1980s registered the collective pain and trauma of the 1970s in India's post-emergency period. Both Nair (2013) and Sen (2017) acknowledge the spectral traces of forced sterilisation in family-planning camps and state-sponsored violence in those films. Meraj Ahmed Mubarki detects the surge of 'traditional culturalism' in the Hindi horror genre and understands it alongside post-emergency disillusionment, Nehruvian secularism and scientific rationalism. In fact, he sees traditional culturalism circulating as a 'a repressed narrative, which has been sealed off in favour of adopting modernity and modernism', where the 'tralatitious order operates subterraneously and surreptitiously within the realm of the secular scientific order and the discursive practices of modern science and technology without being subjected to it' (2016: 77). With the arrival of the monster in Hindi horror, the *tehkhana* transforms into a distinct space that at once encapsulates, buries and releases these latent energies in equal atmospheric measures.

The *tehkhana* and the monster are inextricably linked and, 'through successive locales, the monsters carry with them their own violent environment' (J. D. Denne, quoted in Spadoni, 2014: 156). In these damp, cavernous, decaying and abandoned spaces, films such as *Dak Bangla*, *Purana Mandir*, *Purani Haveli*, *Saamri* and *Tahkhana* come to life. In *Purana Mandir*, after the monster Samri is captured, the king orders its decapitation. While the body is buried in a temple, the head is secured in a box with a holy trident and locked in the *tehkhana* of the Raja's *haveli*. The decapitated monster haunts the inhabitants of the *haveli* from the depths of this *tehkhana*. In *Purani Haveli*, the monster that is locked in the *tehkhana* uses inanimate objects in the *haveli* to deal death and destruction. The monstrous body in the process becomes a site that is written over constantly by the regimes of power – colonial, feudal – a body that in becoming the monstrous and subterranean confounds narratives of time, place and history. In the process, the *tehkhana* is rendered monstrous, a polyphonic space where subterranean histories, asynchronous temporalities and ghostly bodies reside. As a distinct form of the remote locations, crumbling houses, caverns and basements, the *tehkhana* is a space shot through with a sense of ruin and fear characteristic of the Ramsays' operational mode.

In this (forensic) light, the *tehkhana* functions analogously to a crime scene photograph. The crime scene photograph – even those without bodies in them – suspends the space, the victims and the familiars in an eternal present that lies somewhere between 'extinction and decay' (Sante, 1992: 131). Unlike photographs that preserve a particular moment in life, a fragment of memory or a capsule of time, the crime scene photograph, as Lucy Sante suggests, records the aftermath of that moment, something that has already passed. In doing so, these photographs, Sante reminds us, do not strive towards a finality or commemoration but rather activate a 'stage, an active moment of inactivity' (1992: 132). Similarly, the *tehkhana* does not spell a finality or prompt commemorative acts, as graveyards and tombstones do, but functions as an interregnum.

Activated by exchanges and encounters, the space of the *tehkhana* becomes a site of transition, a boundary crossing, an unruly hubbub of polyphonic voices where divergent temporalities of multilayered pasts and present collide and the continuity of time is questioned. *Dak Bangla* finds its impetus in the monster's trying to break out of its prison and sends forth early signals in the form of a disturbance. The film opens with an interruption. Two lovers are disturbed by a noise that seems to resonate upwards from the floor. As the couple curiously inquire, the monster breaks through the basement into the world of the living, thereby interrupting the lovers' lives. This rude incursion from another realm is also a warning of the doom and destruction that is yet to arrive. The *tehkhana* of *Dak Bangla* is a repository of past transgressions, a transitional space that is always caught in the act of performing this pastness. It is a frightening reminder of the ruins of history, the pasts that resist erasure and form a calligraphy of loss bringing to life the multiplicitous flows of time and disparate discourses that remain as a trace, a spectre that refuses to be forgotten. The monstrous body and the crypt of the *tehkhana* become the unrepresentable, a reflection of the incoherence that bleeds through the dark spaces, hidden crypts, dismembered bodies, disturbing secrets and violent desires.

Ultimately, the film's protagonists finally detect the weakness of the monster: light. In the final scene of the film, the monster is launched through the roof, where it bursts into flames and finally melts into dust. It is the *tehkhana* (and by association the *haveli*) that houses the monstrous as a reminder of the fractured history of Indian modernity and its relationship with the feudal and colonial past. This history though, like the monster, cannot endure the light. The colonial past appears rarely in Ramsay horror and when it does, it is caught in furtive references to architectural structures like the *dak bangla* of the film. It escapes through casual allusions to the English language. For example, earlier in the film, when Ajay is looking for a position, he comes across a newspaper advert which calls for a manager with good spoken English, to which Vaishali's terse rejoinder is that after the British it is Ajay that is left behind. The colonial past also manifests in the palpable muteness of the monster, which speaks to the untranslatability of the colonial experience. The monster and the space of the *tehkhana* are suspended between the excesses of the past, the incompatibility of the present and the uncertainty of the future, a historical blind spot where trauma, injustice, crime, passion, lust, wrath and vengeance all endure in an incoherent gelatinous loop, much like the monster in the film. However, the darkness and the shadow represent not just a void or an absence but a latent energy that surfaces when disturbed by modernity.

Conclusion

The impetus received from the Asian Games soon saw the emergence of what Ravi Sundaram calls a 'media urbanism' (2010: 84). The Games appeared 'as a caesura, a sign of a significant transition, which saw construction projects, mass migration of construction workers to the city, new squatter camps, and the emergence of media urbanism, color television, VCRs, electronics in general, and the acceleration of consumption' (2010: 84). This new media environment also facilitated the passage of a variety of films from Hollywood and beyond.

The films from the Ramsay brothers bear the marks of these disparate inspirations, ranging from the Hammer horror films to Sam Raimi's *Evil Dead* (1981) (Nair, 2009: 75), from the Italian *giallo* to popular music videos. For example, Michael Jackson's *Thriller* (1983) makes multiple appearances in song and dance sequences of Ramsay horror as comic relief. *Thriller's* 'categorization as horror music', Jeffrey Andrew Weinstock reminds us, is due to its 'lyrical content' and 'the allusions it makes to the horror genre through instrumentation and particularly the monologue delivered by horror screen legend Vincent Price, as well as the visuals that accompany the song when the video is viewed' (2019: 67). John Landis's video for *Thriller* draws on Gothic and horror iconography; it is replete with a haunted house, a mist-laden cemetery, creatures crawling out of tombs and zombies afoot. Interestingly, the cemetery/graveyard, unlike the *tehkhana*, becomes a ludic space where such popular cultural allusions can be thrown in for good measure. In *Saamri*, the chef of the house, Changez Khan (a play on Gengis Khan) played by comedian Jagdeep (Syed Ishtiaq Ahmed Jafri) has a song and dance sequence at the cemetery, which is a direct tribute to *Thriller*. Another cemetery dance also features in Mohan Bhakri's *Kabrastan* (*Cemetery*, 1988), this time with Jagdeep as Hitler, the timid son of Napoleon. Elsewhere, in the Ramsay universe, the spirited character played by Johnny Lever in *Mahakaal* (*Lord of Death/Time*, 1993) animates a number of Jackson-inspired moves. The allusions to *Thriller* were not limited to Bombay Hindi horror. Recently, a one-minute video clip from Chiranjeevi's film *Donga* (*Thief*, 1985) surfaced on the internet, where it was uploaded by an account called Hollywood Horror Museum on Twitter and swiftly gathered over a million views and thousands of likes. Wearing the iconic outfit, Chiranjeevi, like Jagdeep, dances with zombies, but this time in a Telugu film (Indian Express, 2022).[1] Perhaps this gestures towards the animated informal media geography of the 1980s. On a contributor platform at HuffPost, Vamsee Juluria, Professor of Media Studies at the University of San Francisco, recalls the days when bootleg VHS copies of *Thriller* travelled from home to home in India (Juluri, 2009). Thus, while the cemetery becomes a space of 'play' where the banal and the trivial can coexist alongside the monstrous, it is the *tehkhana* that becomes the truly monstrous as metaphor and as decayed space, as buried history and the ghostly, as an atmosphere of dread and darkness.

The space of the *tehkhana* is a site of both death and discovery, fear and curiosity. Dariusz Gafijczuk approaches ruins as an actively charged space of material and creative encounters that he calls 'inhabited ruins'; a space that 'allows several dimensions of reality to partially collapse, one falling into the other, disarticulating their previously sharply drawn lines of demarcation' (2013: 151). Placing them at the threshold of fragmentation, he approaches ruins as a trans-dimensional presence that challenges boundaries between absence and presence, past and present, materiality and abstraction. The subterranean space of the *tehkhana* not only reflects on the buried histories of India's relationship with its multifarious pasts but also resonates with the horror genre in India which emerged on the margins of the film industry in the B-grade circuit. The B-grade, when considered in relation to the mainstream Bombay film industry, occupies the space of the underbelly; it is the ignored object with a fragmented aesthetic that has an ambiguous relationship with censorship and can be understood as a fluid, informal economy hidden in plain sight. Like a palimpsest of histories, the space of the *tehkhana* leaves a material trace of diverse connections from feudal conquests to colonial correspondences, from regal heritage to subterranean networks, where it captures conflicting contexts in its vastly variegated vat of history.

Note

1 Telugu cinema is dedicated to the production of films in the Telugu language, spoken in the states of Andhra Pradesh and Telangana.

References

Aldana Reyes, Xavier (2020) *Gothic Cinema* (Abingdon: Routledge).
Ancuta, Katarzyna and Deimantas Valančiūnas (eds) (2021) *South Asian Gothic: Haunted Cultures, Histories and Media* (Cardiff: University of Wales Press).
Bhandari, Rajika (2012) *The Raj on the Move: Story of the Dak Bungalow* (New Delhi: Roli Books).
Desai, Madhavi, Miki Desai and Jon Lang (2016) *The Bungalow in Twentieth-Century India: The Cultural Expression of Changing Ways of Life and Aspirations in the Domestic Architecture of Colonial and Post-Colonial Society* (Abingdon: Routledge).

Gafijczuk, Dariusz (2013) 'Dwelling Within: The Inhabited Ruins of History', *History and Theory*, 52:2, 149–70.

Halberstam, J. Jack (1995) *Skin Shows: Gothic Horror and the Technology of Monsters* (Durham: Duke University Press).

Indian Express (2022) 'Watch: Chiranjeevi's 1985 Rip-Off of Michael Jackson's "Thriller" Is the most Entertaining Thing on the Internet Today', *Indian Express*, https://indianexpress.com/article/trending/trending-in-india/chiranjeevis-1985-rip-off-of-michael-jacksons-thriller-8216198 (accessed 15 March 2023).

Jaikumar, Priya (2019) *Where History Resides: India as Filmed Space* (Durham: Duke University Press).

Juluri, Vamsee (2009) 'Michael Jackson and the Dawn of Global India', HuffPost, www.huffpost.com/entry/michael-jackson-and-the-d_b_221853 (accessed 15 March 2023).

Levina, Marina and Diem-My T. Bui (eds) (2013) *Monster Culture in the 21st Century: A Reader* (New York: Bloomsbury).

Mubarki, Meraj Ahmed (2016) *Filming Horror: Hindi Cinema, Ghosts and Ideologies* (New Delhi: SAGE Publications).

Nair, Kartik (2009) 'Run for Your Lives: Remembering the Ramsay Brothers', in Leanne Franklin and Ravenel Richardson (eds), *The Many Forms of Fear, Horror and Terror* (Oxford: Inter-Disciplinary Press), pp. 71–80.

Nair, Kartik (2012) 'Taste, Taboo, Trash: The Story of the Ramsay Brothers', *Bioscope: South Asian Screen Studies*, 3:2, 123–45.

Nair, Kartik (2013) 'Temple of Womb', *The New Inquiry*, 12 July, http://thenewinquiry.com/essays/temple-of-womb (accessed 10 January 2023).

Pandey, Jyoti Sharma (2019) 'Sociability in Eighteenth-Century Colonial India', *Traditional Dwellings and Settlements Review*, 31:2, 7–24.

Sante, Lucy (1992) *Evidence* (New York: Farrar, Straus and Giroux).

Sen, Meheli (2017) *Haunting Bollywood: Gender, Genre and the Supernatural in Hindi Commercial Cinema* (Austin: University of Texas Press).

Spadoni, Robert (2014) 'Carl Dreyer's Corpse: Horror Film Atmosphere and Narrative,' in Harry M. Benshoff (ed.), *A Companion to the Horror Film* (Oxford: Wiley Blackwell), pp. 151–67.

Sundaram, Ravi (2010) *Pirate Modernity: Delhi's Media Urbanism* (Abingdon: Routledge).

Weinstock, Jeffrey Andrew (2019) 'Michael Jackson's "Thriller" (1982) and Stanley Kubrick's *The Shining* (1980)', in Simon Bacon (ed.), *Horror: A Companion* (Oxford: Peter Lang), pp. 67–74.

13

Conversations with spectres: Mexican graveyards and Gothic returns

Enrique Ajuria Ibarra

Throughout most of Western culture, the graveyard is the location for the rites of death. Cemeteries, tombs and burial ceremonies involve needed actions and spaces where the dead can find a place to rest and even get reprieve from the living. Graveyards function as places for departure, of finalising processes of mourning and as memorials to those who have lived before us. The graveyard as symbol grounds specific discourses surrounding what to do with the death of the other and the anticipatory expectation of one's own end. For Jacques Derrida, the experience of death 'is very much that which nobody else can undergo or confront in my place' (1992: 41), a suggestion that death itself frames one's identity, a singular experience that is driven by 'the being-towards-death that promises me to it' (1992: 45). Derrida claims that the death of the other cannot be replaced or avoided. Based on this, the graveyard gives meaning to this unavoidable expectation, setting into place a symbolic finalisation of the life-death of the other and a rem(a)inder of one's finitude. Graveyards represent this by laying down a location in which death can be mourned and remembered. For the Gothic, graveyards are ritual locations that generate anxiety, 'uniting the rational and the sublime in contemplating the terrible and unknowable' (Trowbridge, 2017: 24) in an encounter of religious belief systems regarding what to do with the dead and the possibility of an afterlife (2017: 22). Thus, British graveyard poetry of the mid to late eighteenth century may have influenced the rise of Gothic fiction when it comes to matters and interests of the living and the haunted resting places of the dead – what Vincent Quinn claims is a shift in writing that 'moves beyond iconographic similarities and becomes structural, even foundational' (2016: 52). The graveyard setting connects and cements an ambivalence towards the experience of death: something that cannot be taken from the other, yet inevitably returns to the self with a desire for anything beyond life that just does not end. What haunts at the graveyard is the return, whether as ghosts or living corpses, of our own inevitable and irreplaceable death. If this is so, what happens when the graveyard becomes the location for celebration and, most notably, a potential space for dialogue between the living and the dead?

When compared with this cultural and literary tradition, the Mexican celebrations of the Day of the Dead may seem a bit perplexing. The international success of the Pixar film *Coco* (2017), directed by Lee Unkrich, brought to worldwide attention a representation of social rituals that establish different meaningful connections with the dead in the afterlife. The film pays particular attention to the reunion of living families in cemeteries with rich, vibrant and colourful altars and other assorted decorations. *Coco* emulates this festive holiday that brings all family members together, alive and dead, praising the annual act of remembrance that is seemingly void of those anxieties towards death and the end of life. It also hints at a different understanding of haunting, one in which the spirits of the dead do not come to torment individual beings but where families engage in active communication with their deceased to maintain valuable social connections in everyday lived experiences.

Although this film could be considered a groundbreaking representation of the rituals of mourning and the social and cultural value of the graveyard, particularly in the Mexican context, it is important to take into account that this is not a novelty. In Mexican culture, the relationship with death and the process of mourning has been determined by a complex shaping of customs and traditions that hark back to pre-Hispanic times, have mingled with the Roman Catholic doctrine and been given a particular focus with the political ideologies of the modern Mexican State in terms of national identity. In this sense, the Day of the Dead celebrations should not be seen as a centuries-old tradition. Instead, they are a sociocultural construction that has been defined in the late nineteenth and throughout the twentieth centuries. *Coco* is just one of the ongoing visual and cultural processes that have recently helped validate this Mexican approach to death and mourning, but there is evidence of this cultural representation in literature and film throughout the second half of the twentieth century as well.[1]

Graveyards in Mexican literature and film

In his study of mourning practices and material culture at Panteón San Rafael in Mexico City, Marcel Reyes-Cortez acknowledges that the classic Mexican novel *Pedro Páramo* (1955), by Juan Rulfo, engages actively with the encounter between the living and the dead. In this novel, 'the dead and their essence are manifested in the narratives and practices of the living. The essence of the living is transferred and left behind engraved and fused to the material world and to places inhabited and now shared with the living' (Reyes-Cortez, 2013: 30). In this sense, Rulfo's novel becomes a prime example of active interaction and communication between living characters and the ghosts and shadows that still can be seen and felt in the town of

Comala, the novel's setting. The essences of those who have passed away continue to live in the town and engage in active conversation with the protagonist, Juan Preciado, who has come in search of his father, Pedro Páramo. In particular Gothic fashion, the essences of the inhabitants of the once thriving, living town still populate streets, houses and huts. Comala functions as a grand graveyard, and as Juan Preciado searches for people and his father, he not only becomes a participant in the memorisation of the town's past but soon becomes another ghost himself. The novel's plot twist reveals that Preciado had always been speaking with ghosts and that the retelling of his demise has been another conversation with the dead inside his grave. He finds himself entombed and embracing another dead one, Dorotea, and he tells her that 'the whispers killed me' (2004: 118). His demise was due to immaterial voices that were clearly heard in the air around him. The dead bury Juan Preciado and now he can 'feel as if someone is walking above us' (2004: 120). His body may be underground, but his essence, whatever is left behind, becomes bound to the community of Comala, perennially yearning for the father he never knew in life.[2]

Likewise, Mexican cinema has also explored the cemetery as setting in a few selected films. These films display a more nuanced experience of the graveyard, suggesting that the Mexican view of death is perceived as having a more active and engaging social role between the living and the dead. Salient among these films is *Cien gritos de terror* (*100 Cries of Terror*, 1965), directed by Ramón Obón. Presented in episodic format, the feature-length movie offers two tales of horror involving death by murder in one and the return of the dead in the next. This second instalment, titled 'Miedo supremo' (Supreme Fear), tells the story of a young physician who finds out upon his return from an internship in New York City that his fiancée has passed away. He decides to visit the mausoleum late in the evening to pay his respects. Whilst he prays by the niche, he overlooks the fact that a coffin has been walled in and that the mourners and bricklayers have left. He realises too late that he has been locked inside the mausoleum and that he will have to spend the whole night amongst the dead.

This narrative is influenced by Edgar Allan Poe's 'The Premature Burial' (1844), in which a young man who suffers from catalepsy fears that he will one day be buried alive. His fears come true after he wakes up from a cataleptic episode and finds he is lying in a narrow, enclosed space, very similar to a tomb or coffin. The initial horror upon waking suddenly diffuses when he realises he had been lying in a berth inside a ship. Unlike Poe's tale, the protagonist in 'Miedo supremo' is well aware of the fact that he has been locked inside the mausoleum, but the experience of terror is further instilled when he hears moans and cries coming from the recently lapidated coffin. He attempts to save the woman that has been buried alive, yet, as he opens the casket, he notices another woman shrouded in white standing up in terror from an open coffin that had been laid at the mausoleum's chapel. This is where the film takes a different turn in relation to the latent uncanny fear of being buried prematurely. The protagonist approaches his experience scientifically, calming down the frightened young woman and engaging in an active conversation that he believes will allow them both to keep their wits throughout the night. He tries to reassure the woman: 'When terror haunts reason, our instinct rules our mind and turns us instantly into beasts. This is called panic ... The antidote is calm and reason. We must reason everything, and give it its right proportion' (my translation). The protagonist clings to reason as his beacon inside the mausoleum, a place where the dead rest and are also apparently restless. Both he and the young woman spend the night hearing strange noises and whispers, for which the physician finds reasonable explanations. Finally, in a panic attack, the woman in white attempts to kill the physician. The man passes out and he is woken up the following day by two men who tend to the graveyard. The woman is nowhere to be found. The end of this film narrative puts the idea of reason at odds with the experience inside the mausoleum throughout the night. It is never certain if the woman was actually alive or if it was just the physician's hallucination, his coping mechanism to survive inside the place of the dead. This ambiguous ending points to a view of shared experiences between the living and the (possibly) dead that prompts metaphysical questions about the distance between the two. Unlike the narrator in Poe's tale, who experiences horror alone and in silence, the protagonist in 'Miedo supremo' uses his voice as a point of connection that allows him to recognise and value the space of the mausoleum and the graveyard and to express his sentiments towards death and the supernatural. That the spectator never knows for certain if she was really alive or was in fact a ghost reinforces this experience as an active engagement with the dead, rather than an outright abjection (Figure 13.1).

Whilst *Cien gritos de terror* evidently provides a nuanced exploration about our relationship with the dead, few other Mexican films do the same. Instead of seeing the graveyard as a setting that encourages such timely cultural engagement, other selected films use cemeteries as an excuse to borrow narrative tropes from the American and European horror film traditions. One such film, *Profanadores de tumbas* (*Santo vs The Grave Robbers*, 1966), featuring the famous Mexican wrestler El Santo, is about a group of grave-robbers exhuming bodies in a cemetery to sell them off to a mad scientist intent on creating the perfect human body, with nods to James Whale's *Frankenstein* (1931).[3] In the 1980s, director Rubén Galindo Jr offered a couple of films set in cemeteries: *Cementerio de terror* (1985) and *Ladrones de tumbas* (1989). The former's plot is similar to the Italian *giallo*, with a

Figure 13.1 The protagonist and the mysterious woman locked inside the mausoleum in *Cien gritos de terror* (1965).

few nods to American horror films such as *Halloween* (1978) and *The Evil Dead* (1981). The supernatural element that elicits the return of the dead is a book of black magic with invocations that are read aloud by some of the characters. The latter film focuses more on the theme of profanation, completely disregarding any cultural convention of the value of the graveyard in Mexican society.

Perhaps the most significant film where the cemetery is a space for social interaction completely disassociated from horror and the Gothic is *Día de difuntos* (1988), directed by Luis Alcoriza. This film focuses primarily on a realistic representation of the people who visit the graves on the Day of the Dead, paying close attention to their personal daily grievances. Alcoriza examines the social dimension of the cemetery. The first shots in the film offer panoramic views of the graves being prepared for the holiday and people buying flowers to decorate them. Middle-class men and women not only reunite with their deceased ones but engage in acts of celebration and conversation as they sit by the tombs. What brings them together is the public site of the dead. Here, they voice their concerns and their daily struggles, reflecting on how the harsh economic crisis has affected them. Alcoriza's film recognises the value of social reunion and engagement in the cemetery: a space enlivened by the conversations of the living where the dead are not forgotten. As one character claims, 'Also, we like to remember our dead as they were when they were alive, and we come to share with them the few things we have. That's why we decorate their graves, we pour them some tequila, we offer them food' (my translation). The dead are an active part of a social dynamic that refuses to acknowledge their absence. The offerings of food and drinks recognise the deceased as still being part of these engagements.

The conversational graveyard

The representation of the Day of the Dead in *Coco* brings attention to the conversational aspect between the living and the dead in Mexican culture. That living family relatives establish meaningful connections with their deceased is visually confirmed by the lavish altar at Miguel's house and the night visit to the cemetery. The film points to these locations as prime connections that incorporate into everyday living existence the memory of those who have passed away. Although loss and mourning are still important social processes, the Day of the Dead encourages living memory by means of the objects – such as photographs and food dear to those who have passed away – that are present in the altars. This holiday, as is represented in *Coco*, is indeed more celebratory in its approach to death. One of the elements that stands out about this view is that it shifts away from an individual experience and focuses more on a family and communal one. As was hinted before in relation to *Cien gritos de terror*, death and the graveyard carry strong communal connotations that are further reinforced in the social drama represented in *Día de difuntos*. Even though *Coco* is not a Mexican film, it still partakes of a social and cultural assumption that is evidenced in these earlier films. What we see in *Coco* is not just a stunning visual representation of a festive holiday but also the social dynamics that drive these celebrations.

In his exploration of death in Victorian literature, Andrew Smith notices concepts and concerns that have been carried on from the late eighteenth- and early nineteenth-century Gothic romances, particularly the presence of ghosts as forms that project views on death. In this sense, Smith claims that 'ghostliness becomes an aspect of introspection which is defined by its introjection of a new anxiety about death and dying' (2012: 156). According to this, the perception of death in Victorian literature and culture is tied to the individual self. Encounters with the return of the dead, such as ghosts or vampires, help frame bodily perceptions and awareness of life. Any attempt to break this bond assumes a confrontation with death itself. What these Victorian fictions reveal, Smith suggests, is that they 'explore how death shapes the subject's sense of what it means to be a person' (2012: 168). The emphasis on the self and on the awareness of the body and conscience dictates a Victorian cultural dynamic of how the single subject views itself in the social and ideological spheres.

Conversely, *Coco* emphasises community and shared social actions related with death and remembrance. What is represented is the dynamics of the social sphere, rather than that of a single individual. The graveyard becomes the key location for familial remembrance and interaction with souls and spirits in a conversational setting that reinforces collective memory. What elicits the conflict in the narrative is the fact that Miguel rejects tradition to pursue his own individual interests, putting himself before the rest of his family. The film depicts the tension between individual choices and community preservation in relation to death. The graveyard is the setting where this issue develops. Miguel decides to go to the mausoleum of musician Ernesto de la Cruz to request permission from the deceased to play at the town's music contest. He passes on to the realm of the dead within the mausoleum inside the graveyard, which allows him to encounter and interact with his past relatives. Thus, the graveyard in *Coco* suggests that a spiritual connection enhances communication. It grants, by means of the symbolic nature of its material location, the possibility to live beyond the world of the living and actually be able to speak with the dead in spirit.

The film features plenty of ghosts, but also prominently displays Day of the Dead altars inside family homes and a plethora of offerings on each family gravestone and mausoleum. Families bring their offerings to the cemetery as a form of direct and intimate connection with the ones who, although passed away, are able to come back in spirit every year. The graveyard acquires more than a sense of rest for the deceased and becomes enlivened by a visual manifestation of spiritual encounters that is activated by memory and materiality. *Coco* suggests that the dead are very much living, and that their families and friends materialise this idea with specific cultural rituals that are significantly cohesive.

At the centre of this cohesiveness are the locations specifically dedicated to remembering those who have passed away. These sites can be temporal, such as the altars that each family prepares during the Day of the Dead celebrations. At Miguel's house, the floor to ceiling offering is mostly adorned with colourful, decorative tissue paper (known as 'papel picado'), fragrant 'cempasúchil' flowers (or marigolds), votive candles, photographs of the deceased, and the things they enjoyed in life, such as food, drinks and cherished objects. This offering is testimony to the family members commemorated during the holiday, cementing the notion of family and home with the living and the dead. Likewise, the visit to the cemetery on the eve of the holiday involves another process of material embellishment. The tombs are adorned in the same way as the house offerings, thus establishing a link between the home and the symbolic place of eternal rest. Social spaces – both the intimate, domestic one and the public, sacred one – recognise those who have lived before and who still form part of the networks that coalesce community and family. In this sense, the ghosts do not return to haunt the living; rather, they are returned, or brought back, to enliven society and the spaces they inhabit.

This is similar to what Michael Mayerfield Bell proposes as 'the ghosts of place'; that is, '[g]hosts are much of what makes a space a place' (1997: 815), in the sense that their felt presence helps provide locations with a highly social auratic value. For Bell, these ghosts of place give 'a sense of social aliveness to a place' (1997: 815), and are caught up in the dynamics of the uncanny in their most ambiguous form. He suggests that '[g]hosts in this broader sense may be unsettled and scary, but they can also be rooted, friendly, and affirming – and they are never dead, although they may be of the dead, as well as of the living' (1997: 815–16). Thus, the idea of ghostliness is simultaneously rooted as a form of unsettling and as a form of comfort and spatial presence. Once again, it is the social weight that marks the difference: a ghost haunts an individual, but it may cement a sense of community through its enlivenment via materiality and place.

The cultural connection between location and objects in relation to the dead in Mexico suggests a politics of remembrance that projects ghostly presence by means of images and memories. Photographs make present, as does what the living remember the dead used to enjoy in life. The awareness of a vacuity is filled through the social assignation of objects that do not replace but represent and signify as projections of memory, enlivening the felt presence of those who have passed away. Mexicans display this particular relation with the dead in the social space that signifies a place of rest. Reyes-Cortez claims that 'mourners treat the cemetery space not as a reversal but as an extension of the intimacy of the domestic', and notes that the sense of community can be well perceived in the practices of the living in the graveyard (2013: 28). He points out that the prominence of objects associated with the deceased works as a link serving valuable social cohesiveness. The lack of a corporal presence does not mean that a person is forgotten. On the contrary, the objects chosen as offerings demonstrate respect through enlivened remembrance:

> Mourners who go to the cemeteries of Mexico City do not visit corpses, they visit and communicate with their loved ones as living social agents. Many mourners indicated that the person and its flesh might die but the social person or its social *ánima* does not. The social person and social *ánima* are also not immortal in the world of the living, they also need continuity or they too, just as memory, would cease to exist in the world of the living. The traces that are left and the material-visual aids created to prolong and preserve memory are embraced by mourners.
>
> (2013: 45)

It is clear then that, more than a departure, the Mexican graveyard represents a point of significant connection that extends familial conviviality. The pillar of social exchange is not limited to the body; instead, it extends to the spirit. Material objects attached to the locations of the Day of the Dead offerings channel communicative possibilities. Felt presence becomes essential in a social dynamic that not just commemorates through respect but remembers and still attaches social relevance to those who have (not quite) departed.

Coco visually displays this connection between the living and the dead during the graveyard sequences. The celebration is an open invitation for the souls of the deceased to be able to return to the land of the living. This return is validated in the land of the dead through materiality: if the photograph of the deceased is set in the offering, the soul can cross the bridge between these two worlds. Orquidea Morales notices that *Coco* establishes a clear division between the land of the living and the dead and that 'the plot is punctuated by the creation and breakdown of physical and metaphysical borders – particularly that between the living and the dead, which is controlled by border-patrol replicas' (2020: 41). For her, this amounts to a subtle, yet alarming, representation of 'the class-based and racialized structures of border communities' through 'the policing of the dead in terms of remembrance and forgetting' (2020: 45). In this sense, the policing of this connection and crossing amounts to a control of communication between the living and the dead that jeopardises the perception of family and community in *Coco*. Likewise, one of the major driving forces of the film's plot is the social incidence of the deceased in the matters of the living. Tired of his grandmother's ban on music in the family, Miguel communicates his desire to become a musician to his deceased elders.

The film itself proposes a thread connecting the dead, memory and family identity and history with the home and the cemetery. The opening sequence displays a colourful montage, with Miguel narrating the story of his family and how they chose to ban music and focus on shoemaking. As the film begins, a tracking shot moves smoothly towards a gravestone while an unknown woman places a candle on the tomb. Even though the film does not initially provide a panoramic shot, an association between the tombstone, the idea of death and the notion of memory and respect is already hinted at. The camera tilts up towards the evening sky and finally focuses on a series of hanging 'papel picado'. It is through this decorative tissue paper, as it has been cut up into intricate geometric figures, that the audience can get a glance of Miguel's family history. Each sheet fashions itself in such a way as to represent specific moments to which Miguel is referring. The last 'papel picado' brings the camera back down, but this time it tilts down to the huge Day of the Dead altar at the Rivera's family house. This opening montage sets up the tone of connectivity between cemetery and home.

Moreover, the Rivera's family saga is represented with a craft material that is typically used to adorn this holiday. Likewise, it works as a thread, linking past heritage in the graveyard with the liveliness of the home. This connectivity speaks of the importance of preserving memory, as well as the relevance that the actions and choices of ancestors have on the family living in the present. The thread that holds the decorative tissue paper reinforces the conversational and communal connection between graveyard and home and between different generations. The past continues to speak to the present as it reinforces a sense of origin, identity and family dedication.

That the cemetery is perceived as a space of social interaction between the living and the dead is better represented on the eve of the Day of the Dead. After his 'abuelita' has destroyed the guitar he kept hidden from the rest of the family, Miguel decides to steal acclaimed singer Ernesto de la Cruz's guitar from his mausoleum after he sees that the instrument on the family photograph of Mamá Imelda, her estranged husband (whose face was cut off from the picture) and her daughter Coco is the same as de la Cruz's. Once again, the narrative sets up a connection between the living and the dead when Miguel strums the celebrity's guitar inside the mausoleum. A flurry of marigold petals lifts off from the floor, enveloping the boy. Suddenly, he realises that someone has heard him. In his attempt to leave the mausoleum, he notices with horror that living people cannot see him. He has passed on to another plane of existence where he can see, interact and speak with the souls of the deceased who have come to visit their tombstones. What Miguel witnesses at the cemetery is even more alive now: souls pass by looking for their graves and admiring their living relatives. The sweeping shot reveals a more colourful cemetery. It is not just populated by the bodies of the ones who are alive, but it has also become filled with the souls of the deceased in skeleton forms that take traits of the flesh they used to inhabit. Hair, moustaches and dresses, they all point to a trace recuperation of the past living self, emboldened and connected by the process of memory that is materially represented through the offerings on each grave. Miguel notices one tomb where a mother and small girl look lovingly at the photograph of their deceased, whilst the spirits of an elderly couple comment approvingly on how much their granddaughter has grown. The sequence shows, then, an enlivening of the space dedicated for mourning, where the living and the dead can connect and actively communicate. It is through the graveyard that Miguel can pass on to the land of the dead and be able to ask for the blessing of de la Cruz in his attempt to become a musician. The graveyard habilitates the encounter between Miguel and his deceased ancestors and makes it possible for him to speak with the dead (Figure 13.2).

The return of the dead in *Coco* manifests a celebratory connection with the deceased that recognises an active social engagement in Mexican culture.

Figure 13.2 The spirits of the deceased visit the graveyard in *Coco* (2017).

More than places for uncanny Gothic hauntings, graveyards in Mexico are enhanced by community and ritual practices that link everyday living practices with the remembrance of the dead. Social experiences are shared in the graveyard, enlivening a conversational culture with the deceased as they are still valuable entities for the living. The success of the Pixar film has brought to worldwide attention this communication dynamic that was already hinted at in previous, selected Mexican films. Graveyards as sites for conversation help us think through the idea of haunting, not just exclusively as a return to amend past wrongs. On the contrary, the possibility to socially engage with the spirits of the deceased reconsiders the 'sociality of living with ghosts' (Gordon, 2008: 201). The conversational graveyard enhances the validity of a haunting return that is accepted as an essential part of family life. Rather than focusing on an individual experience of death, it also manifests an active social dimension. In *Coco*, Miguel's desire to play music is finally resolved through family conversation, reinstating the validity of community in which the living and the dead can happily be together with the help of memory and ritual.

Notes

1 Before *Coco*, 20th Century Fox released *The Book of Life* (2014), directed by Jorge R. Gutiérrez and co-produced by Guillermo del Toro. The plot of this animated film is similar to Pixar's, with a protagonist who wants to become a singer, defies his family's tradition of bullfighting, descends to the land of the dead, tricked by the deities La muerte and Xibalba, and then attempts to return

to the land of the living to save his family. A Mexican animated film titled *Día de muertos* (2019) was released after *Coco*'s success, featuring an orphaned young woman who descends to the land of the dead to discover her real identity.

2 Quotes from Rulfo's novel are my translations.
3 El Santo was a popular Mexican wrestler, who also became famous for featuring in several low-budget fantasy horror films during the 1960s and 1970s. The films mix Gothic and horror elements, and most antagonists are supernatural monsters such as vampires, zombies or aliens. El Santo was ideally pitched as a wrestler hero characterised by his sense of justice, but also for being a very attractive man to women because of his prowess.

References

Derrida, Jacques (1992) *The Gift of Death*, trans. David Wills (Chicago: University of Chicago Press).

Gordon, Avery F. (2008) *Ghostly Matters: Haunting and the Sociological Imagination*, 2nd edn (Minneapolis: University of Minnesota Press).

Mayerfield Bell, Michael (1997) 'The Ghosts of Place', *Theory and Society*, 26:6, 813–16.

Morales, Orquidea (2020) 'Horror and Death: Rethinking *Coco*'s Border Politics,' *Film Quarterly*, 73:4, 41–9.

Quinn, Vincent (2016) 'Graveyard Writing and the Rise of the Gothic', in Angela Wright and Dale Townshend (eds), *Romantic Gothic: An Edinburgh Companion* (Edinburgh: Edinburgh University Press), pp. 37–54.

Reyes-Cortez, Marcel (2013) 'Maintaining the Dead in the Lives of the Living: Material Culture and Photography in the Cemeteries of Mexico City', in Michele Aaron (ed.), *Envisaging Death: Visual Culture and Dying* (Newcastle upon Tyne: Cambridge Scholars Publishing), pp. 26–49.

Rulfo, Juan (2004) *Pedro Páramo*, 18th edn (Madrid: Cátedra).

Smith, Andrew (2012) 'Victorian Gothic Death', in Andrew Smith and William Hughes (eds), *The Victorian Gothic: An Edinburgh Companion* (Edinburgh: Edinburgh University Press), pp. 156–69.

Trowbridge, Serena (2017) 'Past, Present, and Future in the Gothic Graveyard', in Carol Margaret Davison (ed.), *The Gothic and Death* (Manchester: Manchester University Press), pp. 21–33.

14

Monsters of history: a tour of the cinematic Slavic cemetery

Agnieszka Jezyk and Lev Nikulin

In a recent 2020 adaptation of Nikolai Gogol's *Dead Souls* (1842) set in the present day, the trickster protagonist Chichikov has a new scheme to turn death into money. Whereas his nineteenth-century predecessor sought to buy up 'dead souls' – the deeds of dead serfs still listed as alive until the next census – modern-day Chichikov has another plan: hawking spots in the prestigious Novodevichie Cemetery in Moscow next to celebrities. His rich but naive provincial targets warm to the idea, conceptualising a prominent post-mortem placement as a way of fulfilling worldly ambitions such as wealth, fame and artistic acclaim. The situation is absurd, of course, and the enthusiasm with which the characters vie to secure a good spot after death is a dead end of personal and historical meaning. In an era when human lives are devalued, bargaining with bodies and square feet of earth has become viable business practice. Another aspect is that graveyards, especially such as Novodevichie, where prominent figures such as Anton Chekhov, Dmitri Shostakovich, Boris Yeltsin, Nikita Khrushchev and indeed Gogol himself found their rest, hold stories related to their dwellers. Consequently, this storytelling value points to a central concern in the use of cemeteries within the Slavic Gothic: the relationship between graveyards and personal stories as well as collective histories.

For late Soviet and post-Soviet Russian filmmakers, the Gothic was an exciting new possibility: after decades in which films had to adhere to a Soviet aesthetic as well as ideological messaging, the Perestroika brought a loosening of restrictions and the potential of creating dark, unpleasant and even horrifying films. Preceded by *Viy* (*Spirit of Evil*, 1967), this trend started building in the late 1970s – the first properly Gothic Soviet film in several decades was Belarusian-Soviet *The Wild Hunt of King Stakh* (1980) – and accelerated in the mid 1980s, when film became one of the key carriers of Perestroika narratives. This trend persisted through the 1990s, as the film industry all but fell apart and was rebuilt in the wake of the Soviet collapse. Aesthetic directions split, however. Some filmmakers turned toward aestheticised Gothic stories, often ones based on pre-Revolutionary plots;

for example, some films were shot based on the work of nineteenth-century Gothic writer Aleksei Tolstoy: *The Family of the Vourdalak* (1990) and Yevgeny Tatarsky's *The Vampire* (1991). Others adapted an anti-aesthetic stance that embraced the ugliness and chaos of social problems as well as material difficulties in creating traditional high-quality films. Focusing more on the family as a source of dread, the aforementioned late-Soviet productions recall the graveyard only in passing. In the context of the vampire figure, the cemetery's meaningful absence speaks of the endurance of class exploitation, which, paradoxically, has never really been put to rest and openly resurfaces after the fall of the Soviet bloc. Meanwhile, in *The Wild Hunt of King Stakh* (1980), a film that discusses, among other things, the question of modern disenchantment, the gesture to substitute a graveyard with a swamp that buries Nadzieja's father may signify removing the irrational element of Slavic beliefs to make room for materialist rationality.

In Polish cinematography, the representations of necropolises were often detached from Gothic aesthetics but preserved the symbolic connection to history and the persistent endurance of the past in the present. The motif was frequently and creatively used, for example, by Andrzej Wajda from the depiction of sewer systems under Warsaw as a mass grave of thousands of insurgents in *Canal* (1957), and the famous spirit scene in *Ashes and Diamonds* (1958) as commemoration of the dead, to intimate depictions of tombs of loved ones in *Maidens of Wilko* (1979). As Polish cinema of the 1990s extensively made popular gangster films – now probably the best cultural representations of radical social changes in the aftermath of the collapse of communism – graveyards and graves remained an important trope in small-scaled arthouse productions. Among these films, Ryszard Ber's *Stone Upon a Stone* (1995), Jan Jakub Kolski's *The Commander's Sword* (1996) and Robert Gliński's *The Call of the Toad* (2005) emphasise the importance of the burial site and its connection to history and memory, simultaneously linking it to the present. Ewa Mazierska points out that while Gothic-inspired cinema was practically absent in the early post-Communist era, films utilising tropes such as tombs and cemeteries were primarily concerned with social critique of the newly independent post-1989 Poland: 'To an extent, the lack of horror or fantasy films and the prevalence of realistic genres suggests that, contrary to the widespread accusations of critics, Polish directors do not escape from what is widely regarded as their principal obligation, namely depicting the present' (2007: 16–17).

With the growth of Gothic and horror studies more broadly, the graveyard has been studied in the context of nineteenth-century Gothic-Romantic elegiac poetry (see, for example, Yamaji (2016)). The use of the graveyard in the late Soviet and post-Soviet period, especially in cinematography, remains marginalised. In this chapter, we focus on the trope of the cemetery in Russian and Polish horror films of this transitional time: Marek Piestrak's *She-Wolf* (1983) and *The Return of the She-Wolf* (1990), Oleg Teptsov's *Master Designer* (1988), Andrzej Żuławski's *She-Shaman* (1996) and Aleksandr Itygilov's *The Humble Cemetery* (1989). In an attempt to address this underexplored theme, we look at the function of the graveyard in the period, during which it became a holding and processing mechanism for historical memories and traumas as well as a conceptual bridge between irreconcilable eras. In our case studies two directors use cemeteries to deal with the past (Marek Piestrak and Oleg Teptsov) and two use them to look ahead to an uncertain future (Andrzej Żuławski and Aleksandr Itygilov). These films utilise the imagery of graves and graveyards to bring expressions of cultural anxiety and elements of social critique into Gothic narratives. Despite radically different geopolitical positions, historical legacies and idiosyncratic cinematic styles, these East European directors all present cemeteries and tombs as places and objects that transform history from experience into discourse.

Given the heavy lifting around memory and history that the cemetery is tasked with performing, a conceptual tool that can bring together considerations of time and place is both useful and appropriate. For this, we turn to Mikhail Bakhtin's concept of the chronotope, or the interconnected relationship between time and space in literary worlds, which varies by genre. Bakhtin writes, 'In the literary artistic chronotope, spatial and temporal indicators are fused into one carefully thought-out, concrete whole' (1975a: 84, author's translation). Bakhtin's case study for the chronotope is the Gothic castle, chosen due to its marked and specific relationship with temporality. As Bakhtin proposed, it 'is saturated with time ... [and] this creates the meaningfulness [*siuzhetnost*] of the castle which unfolds in Gothic novels' (1975b: 394, authors' translation). The castle is anchored spatially, but not temporally; it keeps its history alive and allows the past to act upon human characters through revelations, which are often triggered by interacting with the building itself (exploring sealed-off passageways or speaking with ghosts, for example). The chronotope of the Gothic castle was further emphasised by Vadim Vatsuro, a scholar of the Russian Gothic, who considered it to be a fundamental feature of the Gothic as a genre (2002: 86). By acting as a bridge for informational transmission between otherwise distant time periods – the imagined 'ancient' and the modern – the castle becomes a key support and anchor for the structure of the text. A secret revealed in an old journal may, for example, reveal a forgotten heir or the truth of a maligned young woman's story, setting further events in motion.

According to this logic, what is the function of the Slavic Gothic graveyard? What histories does it keep alive and what skeletons does it hide? To answer these questions, we first consider the structure and import of the

Gothic cemetery as a chronotope and then move to a textual walking tour through Slavic cinematic graveyards as seen by directors Marek Piestrak, Oleg Teptsov, Andrzej Żuławski and Aleksandr Itygilov.

Marek Piestrak's *She-Wolves*: graveyards of the Romantic paradigm

Against the background of the overall disinterest in genre film typical of pre-1989 cinematography in Poland, the curious work of Marek Piestrak stands out as an exception. Sometimes spitefully compared to Ed Wood by critics, Piestrak is remembered in the history of Polish culture as the creator of science fiction films (*Inquest of Pilot Pirx* (1979), *Fly Vacation* (1999)), historical costume dramas (*Visors and Hoodies* (1985)), adventure films (*The Curse of Snake Valley* (1987)) and classic horror B-films such as *She-Wolf*, *The Return of the She-Wolf* and *The Tear of the Prince of Darkness* (1992). Nowadays, Piestrak's *She-Wolf* films provide a camp aesthetic experience and, through historical costume, reveal critical insights into the Polish reality of the late Communist period. According to scholars Kamińska and Mikołajczyk, the emphasis on formal elements and historical settings inscribes the films in 'classic' aesthetics: 'horror disguised as a fairy tale, horror disguised as science fiction, horror in a classical costume, and arthouse horror' (2021: 50). Using well-established Gothic tropes such as haunted space, black magic, cursed objects and werewolves, *She-Wolf* and *The Return of the She-Wolf* use the graveyard as a starting point for the plot and as a metaphorical carrier for a social critique of late-Communist and post-Communist society.

Set in 1848 during the Austrian partition of Poland, the first part of the diptych focuses on the story of Kacper, a war veteran, who comes back home to witness his wife Maryna's (Iwona Bielska) death from an unsuccessful abortion. Details such as the lack of a crucifix on the wall and a hare's paw implicate the woman in witchcraft. Since Maryna's corpse is cursed, the priest refuses to bury her, and Kacper's brother decides to pierce her heart with a stake to prevent the evil spirit from coming back. However, an Austrian cannon destroys the woman's unconsecrated grave and misplaces the stake, allowing Maryna to awake as a demon and pursue her husband. Kacper tries to find refuge at his friend's estate but soon finds out that the wife of the residence's owner, Julia (also played by Bielska), oddly resembles his late spouse. The two women act as each other's double (another Gothic trope) and constitute incarnations of a vital force (Rodan-Jóźwiak, 2020: 71–3). They stand on the side of life, while men engaged in fighting (and dying) for Poland are inherently linked to death. The film juxtaposes the collective and ideologically driven actions born from the Romantic paradigm with an individualistic, pleasure-oriented approach. Shot at the dawn of the Solidarity movement, *She-Wolf* questions Romantic models of patriotism that privilege dying for one's homeland.

In this context, the destroyed grave symbolically detaches Maryna from the past and positions her, the undead non-human, as a permanent presence. Set in the *fin de siècle*, *The Return of the She-Wolf* actualises this character as crucial for the plot and solidifies the cursed estate as a Bakhtinian chronotope. At the neighbouring cemetery, two servants accidentally dig up a suspicious artifact, a canine-looking skull that 'sexualises' those in its vicinity. It encourages Kamil, a young painter about to get married, to flirt with all women at the residence by exposing them to his erotic drawings and poetry and encourages the heiress Stefania's lust for the artist. Eventually, the skull turns one of her daughters, Ania, into a bloodthirsty she-wolf. Since it bewitches women and men equally, *The Return of the She-Wolf* breaks the gendered pattern of overly sexualised femininity and spiritually sublime masculinity by embroiling all available targets in hedonistic pleasure. Like turn-of-the-century Polish nobility, post-Communist society engages in fantasies about endless consumption, and Piestrak seems to suggest that the provenance of this desire is devilish. The act of digging out the skull from the burial site marks the end of stagnation and signifies a moment of radical change. In this way, it represents the collapse of the old order. However, since the werewolf's presence has a crucial impact on the plot, *The Return of the She-Wolf* claims that the past can never be simply obliterated. Regardless of burial and repression, it does not take much to wake the dead.

Oleg Teptsov and the problems of mimesis in spectral St Petersburg

Oleg Teptsov's Gothic throwback *Master Designer* was released in 1988, shortly before the collapse of the USSR; its action, meanwhile, is set in another era preceding cataclysmic change – the Russian pre-revolutionary period. The film takes place in two time periods, 1908 and 1914, placing its action squarely between the failed revolution of 1905 and the successful one to come in 1917. The protagonist, Platon Andreevich Gastman (Viktor Avilov), is a surviving Silver Age aesthete who finds himself staring down an increasingly hostile century. Formerly successful but now broke and nursing a nasty drug habit, Platon Andreevich moves further and further from his artistic vision of improving upon that which is made by nature or God (to whom he refers derisively as 'that one, with the halo').

Lushly shot and minimal in dialogue, Teptsov's film lingers on melancholy, beautiful images of St Petersburg and Platon Andreevich's artistic surroundings, including many shots lingering over Symbolist visual art. The film is brooding and melancholy, returning time and again to the topic of death with shots like a pale woman coughing into a bloody handkerchief; a mannequin that looks like a mummified human body and another smeared with red paint that looks like blood; a body covered in black cloth; and several locations of death, including a morgue, an oratory/mortuary, a coffin and a cemetery. The plot, too, is set into motion by an encounter with a ghost from the past. In 1908, Platon Andreevich creates a luxury storefront mannequin based on the likeness of a model, a young woman named Anna Beletskaia (Anna Demianenko); she apparently dies from tuberculosis, but he is unable to find her body in the morgue. In 1914, he meets a woman, the wife of a cash cow client, who looks just like Anna. However, she introduces herself as Maria and disavows any knowledge of the artist. He pursues her with increasing obsession, wanting her to reveal herself as Anna and casting about for anything that could act as evidence of her identity and their former connection. However, proof is hard to come by and ineffective.

Platon Andreevich shows Maria a printed book of his own works with a date of 1910 and a portrait of Anna/Maria, linking her image to a temporal stamp. But she simply repeats her denial, and without the confession he had hoped to draw out of her, Platon Andreevich does not fully trust his own portrait either. For reliable, fundamental proof he goes to the repository of historical knowledge: the cemetery, in this case an empty, idyllic green space where he indeed eventually finds a cheap, already half-rotten cross bearing the name of Anna Grigorievna Beletskaia and a death year of 1908. Platon Andreevich's final confrontation with Maria occurs in an oratory turned mortuary covered with gilded icons and holding a coffin with the body of Maria's recently deceased husband. Maria is now overtly supernatural – apparently (as he asserts and the narrative hints), she is the mannequin made from Anna's likeness come to life.

Master Designer revolves around a mimetic problem: Maria looks just like Anna, and to a visual artist like Platon Andreevich, that should be enough – but he finds that it is not. Only the cemetery can provide the 'proof' he needs, linking him to the past and to Maria's origin. His obsession is in part driven by the quest for perfection that characterises him as an artist, complaining about the limitations of things as they are in nature: '[God] creates. And I? I finish it … For example, he'll create a person. Lustrous skin, an antique beauty, a creation. And what then? This Antinous dies in an hour from some fever'. By 1914, it seems like he will not achieve this goal – and in this way Maria's appearance and her exact similarity to Anna allows him to experience the fulfilment of his artistic ambitions: to create something better than what nature and God intended, granting him a consummate Romantic-Gothic death.

The Gothic chronotope brings the past effectively – often forcibly – into the present, and supernatural antagonists are associated with the mythic-historical past, while modernity acts as a potential refuge. Tepstov flips this on its head: the supernatural antagonist is, despite her origin as Platon Andreevich's creation, a creature of twentieth-century aesthetics and artifice and is keen on moving forward while leaving her past – namely him, as well as pre-revolutionary Russia – behind. The mechanism of the cemetery, although bearing truth, has no ability to save Platon Andreevich from the onslaught of modernity. Fittingly, his death arrives in the form of an automobile which runs over him and speeds away towards the revolution and its attendant and invariable social upheaval.

Andrzej Żuławski's *She-Shaman*: Poland as capitalism's landfill

Andrzej Żuławski (1940–2016) is a unique director in Polish cinematography, not only due to his visionary films' ability to grapple with Poland's historical traumas or his method of establishing a relationship with the viewer through displays of shocking images such as rape, incest, orgies, childbirth and murder. With his idiosyncratic style, Żuławski was one of the very few cinematographers who used genre cinema, including the Gothic and horror, to speak to Poland's past and the universal dread of the human condition. Thus, it is hardly surprising that graveyards function as a significant element of his symbology, marking decay and fulfilled apocalypse. For example, in Żuławski's debut *The Devil* (1972), after an unsuccessful attempt to kill the king, Jakub travels back to his family estate amidst the upheaval of the Prussian invasion of 1793 to find the corpse of his father, which has been rotting in bed for weeks. As the protagonist buries him, the viewer is struck by the disturbing bareness of the final resting place and the lack of other tombstones or monuments at this noble ancestral home. Meanwhile, in the unfinished science fiction/horror film *On the Silver Globe* (1976/1988) two intriguing graveyard scenes are juxtaposed: the image of a modern cemetery, deprived of its meaning after the fall of Earth's civilisation, and the sky burial ritual, a funeral practice in Tibet where the corpse is placed on a mountain top and left to decompose. Practised on the dead astronauts by the moon dwellers in the film, the ceremony projects primeval performances of spirituality into the future.

A similarly intriguing graveyard trope appears in Żuławski's 1996 erotic thriller *She-Shaman*. Upon its release, the film was mercilessly condemned by critics, who called it 'pseudointellectual garbage' and even 'fecal matter disguised as philosophy' (Romaniak, 2015). The controversial themes pictured in the production (explicit sex scenes, cannibalism, suicide) and the critical attacks on the Catholic Church may have actually contributed to the film's popularity with the audience. It has had a lasting critical impact as well; for example, cinema studies scholar Kaja Klimek considers it an allegory of the brutal system transition of 1989 and names *She-Shaman* one of the most undervalued Polish films after the fall of Communism (Klimek, 2020). The film follows 'The Italian' (Iwona Petry), a rebellious girl from a dysfunctional family, as she moves into an apartment formerly occupied by Michał's (Bogusław Linda) brother, a cleric who decides to leave the priesthood and eventually commits suicide. The Italian and Michał immediately engage in sex, and as the plot moves forward, professional and private matters become entangled.

In one of the first scenes of the film, Michał, an anthropologist, digs up the well-preserved corpse of a mysterious shaman from twenty-five centuries ago. This 'young old man', as Michał calls him, died in the swamps and was found with arrows without spearheads, indicating a compliance with this tragic fate. The figure of the improperly buried becomes central to the film, and the anthropologist becomes gradually obsessed with or bewitched by the mystery of the body. Michał's fixation on the shaman is reinforced by the corpse's ambivalent ontological status: he was buried improperly and, though dead, acts on Michał as a narrative force. In a desperate quest to reveal the mystery, the anthropologist wants to change his field of expertise to psychology and starts seeing a reflection of the shaman's demise in his own fate. In one scene, an intoxicated Michał converses with the suddenly animated corpse. The conversation also reflects many themes so frequently utilised by Żuławski: the femme fatale figure, madness, transgression through excess and the desire to achieve the sublime through bodily experience.

As social commentary, the presence of the undead shaman brings in other intriguing associations. In this context, the place of his burial is symbolic. The shaman is discovered at a construction site, marking the fundamental rupture between Poland's history and its capitalistic, consumer-oriented present. A similar chasm is visible in Michał's life: he is constantly torn between the desire to satisfy the materialistic drive of an average insatiable Pole (a fancy house, a future wife from an upper-class family, the prestige of his academic career) and the urge to search for spiritual fulfilment with The Italian. Żuławski seems to conclude that in post-1989 Poland spirituality and religion have been replaced with radical consumer materialism.

In *She-Shaman*, we witness the reversal of a burial, in which the shaman is extracted from the ground and moved into a lab. This movement from the sacred sphere of resting to the scientific space also signifies the transition from body to medical subject. The contrast between spirituality and technology also resonates in some of Michał's statements. In his lecture, he takes a clear stand: 'An astronaut lives only in a physical world, a shaman in the psychic one. Shamanism was the first religion of mankind; this is why I pick the shaman over the astronaut.' In this way, Żuławski diagnoses the political transition of 1989 as another upheaval in Polish history, emphasising the removal of a metaphysical experience substituted by empty consumption.

Sergio Naitza emphasises the role of cannibalism in the last scenes of the film as a metaphysical gesture of losing oneself to reject death (Naitza, 2004: 56). In this way, Żuławski demonstrates only a superficial rejection of materiality. The body, much as in Georges Bataille's conception of inner experience, may be used as a vehicle to achieve spiritual awakening, because 'in human consciousness eroticism is that within man which calls his being in question' (1986: 29). In *She-Shaman*, bodily boundaries are transgressed not only in Michał and The Italian's sexual encounters. Their demise mirrors the tragic fate of the shaman. In the previously recalled scene, when the (un)dead (symbolically played by the same actor as the cleric) speaks to the anthropologist, the shaman claims he was sexually violated by his beloved, who wanted to deprive him of energy. It is then through the figure of a femme fatale that Michał starts to perceive The Italian.

Aleksei Itygilov's trash cemetery and the encroachment of modernity

The late Soviet period was marked by the slow re-emergence of the Gothic, which (along with supernatural horror more broadly) was banned from Soviet screens throughout most of the Soviet period, with few exceptions. While some films like *Master Designer* pursued glitzy throwback aesthetics, others embraced the grime, revelling in the ability to tell unsanitised stories. Our final case study is the 1989 film *The Humble Cemetery*, directed by Aleksandr Itygilov, a hyperrealistic, endlessly bleak film about the workers and hangers-on at a cemetery in Moscow in the 1990s. In this hostile landscape, the cemetery becomes a temporary and unreliable refuge for the 'trash' of society – the people who have been discarded and left to suffer. Most of them, including protagonist Vorobei ('Sparrow'), are disabled middle-aged or old men facing grim prospects. In this film, historical memory assumes a new form and draws a new meaning out of the chronotope of the cemetery: the cemetery is also the trash pile of history, where epochs come to die and slowly rot.

In her book *The Literature of Waste: Material Ecopoetics and Ethical Matter* (2015), Susan Signe Morrison looks at Western cultural production through the lens of waste. Following Polish philosopher Zygmunt Bauman, she argues for the importance of garbage in conceptualising history: 'History not only contains trash, but also history is trash. History can be read not as a collection of fragments, but "as an unclassifiable scrapbook" that constructs the past "as a ruin"' (2015: 57). She analyses waste and death from various angles, examining Hamlet's graveyard as an illustration of the 'garbaging of the body' (2015: 152) and the rhetorical use of waste as a propagandistic tool in the Third Reich in portraying Jews as 'their own graveyards' (2015: 115). The death/garbage dialectic is strongly present in *The Humble Cemetery*, in which the graveyard appears as a garbage heap rather than a beautiful mausoleum. The characters who inhabit the space of the cemetery in Itygilov's film are classed as 'trash' themselves – they are the discarded members of society who have no home or place in the mundane world.

The liminality of graveyards often attracts characters who are themselves somehow liminal and exist outside many, if not all, societal institutions – often, old men, like the companion of Reb Arye-Leib in Isaac Babel's short story 'How It Was Done in Odessa', in the collection *Odessa Stories* (2018, published in Russian in 1931), who sit on the cemetery wall 'with glasses on [their] nose[s] and autumn in [their] heart[s]' as semi-ascetic witness-narrators (Babel, 2018: 20). Of course, they live on the cemetery wall not because they are mystically liminal but because they are poor beggars; this aspect of the graveyard – its association with poverty and disability – is central to Itygilov's film. Released soon after *Master Designer*, this film could not be more distinct in tone: while Teptsov's story is aesthetic, Itygilov's is anti-aesthetic, revelling in the ugliness of its setting as well as its cinematography. Filmmakers in the early post-Soviet period had very limited access to high-quality film stock and equipment, which resulted in a bevy of barely watchable and semi-audible films. Yet, while low quality is a detriment to most films in this category, Itygilov uses it as a strength.

The Humble Cemetery is proximal to *chernukha*, 'dark stuff' or 'black film' (Isakava, 2018), a direction in late Soviet and post-Soviet film that called on filmmakers to express the darkest impulses of society. A reaction to the shock of the Soviet collapse, it also represented possibilities that had been absent for many decades: films no longer had to align either with Soviet ideas or Soviet moods, so filmmakers were free to show violence, sexual content, bleak narratives and irredeemable characters. *Chernukha* is associated, on the one hand, with scandalous, attention-grabbing films emphasising sex and violence; for example, the seminal *Little Vera* (1985), which portrayed sex work, or many *boeviki* – action films with an emphasis on gangsters – such as vampire hunter/gangbuster film *Upyr* (1997). On the other hand, it is associated with underground and independent filmmakers in the post-Soviet period, who produced extremely grim and sometimes barely watchable experimental films that relished in violence, such as the phantasmagoric, Lynchean *Daddy, Father Frost is Dead* (1992) or the experimental supernatural horror film *Gongofer* (1992). *The Humble Cemetery* is solidly in this latter category, presenting the viewer with squalid, grimy interiors and frank-to-voyeuristic depictions of abject human misery and despair.

There is no future for graveyard worker Vorobei ('Sparrow') (Vladimir Gostiukhin), who is suffering from a Dostoevskian injury: he recently got hit in the head with an axe by his own brother, leaving him with a healing wound and a gap in his skull. He is like an open nerve, metaphorically as well as physically, because the after-effects of the hit (which seem to include hearing loss, mood swings and cognitive issues) render him unable to drink and, thus, unable to cope. He is subjected to the evil of the grimy, corrupt, downtrodden world he inhabits and is unable to look away or numb himself to it, which makes its cruelty impossible to ignore. The fundamental, existential despair inherent in every element of Vorobei's world comes through in the closely shot, cramped, grimy interior spaces of the cemetery, in which its residents hide from the cold and where they drink, fight and care for each other. The interior scenes are shot with deep background shadows and single overhead lamps casting dramatic noir-interrogation-room beams of light; in conjunction with the poor film stock and audio quality, this creates a feeling of claustrophobia and confusion. Every surface is either dark or overly lit; conversations are either barely audible or painfully loud; and the film leaves the viewer, and its own characters, little room to breathe. The uniformly grimy, hyperreal interiors are reminiscent of those seen in the opening scenes of Andrei Tarkovsky's *Stalker* (1979), and there is a similar paradoxically dreamlike quality here too. Another potential parallel is found in the cemetery dogs, liminal and precarious creatures for whom the cemetery is also a rare refuge and who later find themselves threatened by the encroachment of the cruel outside world in the form of a city dog catcher.

There is some chance for hope and human connection in the underground, however; the interactions between the variously downtrodden and disenfranchised inhabitants of the graveyard and their surly but well-meaning boss – who uses his meagre position of power to employ people who would otherwise be cast out on account of age and disability – carry real warmth and hint at the found family trope. These 'underground' people have indeed forged a degree of community; they are aware of and mostly deferential to each other's suffering and make efforts to accommodate each other – for example, the director uses sign language with one of his deaf employees. It is quickly obvious that the director is seen through a lens of bemused affection rather than fear; sometimes he is even in on the joke, as when, after ineffectually scolding his employees for drinking after work, he quips, 'I'll fire you all', provoking more laughter.

In a key sequence of hope and heartbreak, Vorobei receives permission, on account of his fortieth birthday – and seemingly for the first time in his life – to climb to the top of the belltower, which he wants to do because 'I'm always down here with the corpses'. The belltower is set apart as its own forbidden sanctuary within the cemetery; it is the only structure that extends upward and thus the only refuge from the pull of the grave. None of the downtrodden characters who inhabit the cemetery are allowed into this sanctuary, including Vorobei, and thus are shut off from experiencing any of the lofty emotions and experiences of the Gothic-Romantic graveyard. In this film, the cemetery is beautiful when seen from an elevated removal and hideously ugly otherwise. Thus, in addition to bridging past and present, the cemetery also contains distinct and opposing topographies. Vorobei's ascent of the tower towards the beaming bright light coming down from above is accompanied by non-diegetic choral singing, which swells as he reaches the top platform and looks out over Moscow as though for the first time in his life. The film cuts to a sequence of beautiful, spacious shots of the treetops of the cemetery and the city vista and ends on Vorobei's contemplative and quietly despairing face as the uplifting experience of visiting the belltower is soured by the knowledge that he will not be allowed to live at this elevation but must go down below, where he is doomed. His birthday celebration that night, for which he ventures back down to the surface and into the underground of a dank basement, sets off a chain of problems and tragedies that leave Vorobei completely devastated; self-destructing completely, he begins to drink again, knowing it will kill him, and his death puts him back in the cemetery in which he had previously worked. The camera pans up from his fresh grave with a cheap, hand-painted plaque reading 'Vorobiev A. S.' and then upward, back to the rarefied air Vorobei could only briefly enjoy before he was returned to the squalid ground.

As for historical memory, that, too, is subordinate to the whims of the new and incoming power structures shaping the late Soviet landscape. The cemetery comes under fire after the director conspires with Vorobei to dig up and sell off valuable relics from a grave belonging to the Decembrists – even the buried histories of storied epochs are not safe from the encroachment of post-Soviet reality. *The Humble Cemetery* uses the cemetery to interrogate the conditions and possibilities of the late Soviet period, concluding that this period is hostile to life and corrosive of history itself.

Dead in good company: cemeteries and historical narratives

In his influential essay 'Theses on the Philosophy of History', Walter Benjamin describes an angel looking back on the ever-accumulating cataclysm of history: 'one single catastrophe which keeps piling wreckage upon wreckage ... [t]he pile of debris before him grow[ing] skyward' (1968: 257–8).

The model of the cemetery portrays history similarly. Graveyards are a great equalising mechanism, awaiting their due through every cataclysmic conflict and ideological shift; the burial ground is happy to welcome monarchs, Bolsheviks and lumpenproles, absorbing their stories into its own but also discursively drawing the past closer to a model of the trash pile, where history accumulates, settles and slowly decomposes. While within Gothic aesthetics the castle functions as a chronotope linked to the privileged elites whose lifestyle is sustained by the work of invisible serfs, the graveyard is, for one, a more democratic Gothic location than the castle – even beggars are buried there. Gothic castles are populated by one or a small number of ghosts, whose individual stories weave through the fabric of the castle itself. Cemeteries, however, are crowded, collecting masses of the dead drawn from different classes and different cultural, political and ethnic groups. Instead of solitary, individual narratives, the stories held by a cemetery are composed of a multitude of voices. This brings the cemetery closer to a repository of historical memory, without guaranteeing anything like objective truth – graves may be exhumed, tombs raided and, as in *The Humble Cemetery,* cemeteries can be rased. The wholesale destruction of cemeteries and burial grounds has been used as a particularly pernicious form of cultural erasure; for example, many Jewish cemeteries in Slavic regions have faced the threat of destruction.

Unlike castles, graveyards are also inherently linked to the supernatural, acting as they do as thresholds between life and death. According to Christopher Putney, thresholds are key to the threat of the undead in Slavic folk tradition, because they are apertures: openings through which the undead may come into the mundane world. These may be physical (gates, rivers), conceptual (borders) or temporal (dusk, dawn); people are especially vulnerable when passing from one state of existence into another during birth and death (Putney, 1999: 137–43). In Piestrak's *She-Wolf* series, for example, the eponymous beast wakes from the grave when her tomb is desecrated or her remains misplaced. Acts of transgression also expose necropolises as strongly regulated and tabooed spaces where supernatural forces can intervene. This occurs because cemeteries exist outside of the mundane human world and are rich with death. At the same time, their existence on the threshold renders them sanctuaries – not from the undead but from the intrusion of the mundane world outside. They are 'timeless' while holding individual and collective histories, and their keepers and dwellers often take on some of these characteristics – in particular, those of old age and removal from societal institutions. They also facilitate transitions through grief and can thus paradoxically act as places of healing.

In the East European context, Slavic cemeteries become liminal spaces encapsulating past traumatic violence, fear of social change and political uncertainty. As the late Soviet and post-Soviet Polish and Russian films reveal, graveyards store history and represent a crucial mechanism for mediating contradictions and disjunctions between past and present. By existing outside time, they can bridge the temporal gap while providing a stable spatial stage that can absorb the multitude of the stories and histories of its many dead. In the films by Marek Piestrak, Oleg Teptsov, Andrzej Żuławski and Aleksandr Itygilov, the layers of time form a kind of Möbius strip through the images of graves and graveyards. The past constantly displays itself in the present. This phenomenon causes the late Julia to keep returning as a she-wolf in Piestrak's series, and is what replicates Anna in Maria in Teptsov's *Master Designer*. The impossibility of abandoning the past is also represented in Michał's obsession with the corpse of the shaman in Żuławski's *She-Shaman* and Vorobei's imperative to return to the cemetery despite his physical condition in *The Humble Graveyard*. The idiosyncratic connection between present struggles of post-Soviet reality and the inability to dig out of the accumulating debris of history so intensely present in Russian and Polish cultural production makes East/Central Europe, to rephrase Norman Davis, not God's but the dead's playground.[1]

Note

1 British historian Norman Davies famously called Poland's complex history 'a God's playground', which served as a title for his comprehensive Polish history book.

References

Babel, Isaac (2016) *Odessa Stories*, trans. Boris Dralyuk (London: Pushkin Press).
Bakhtin, Mikhail (1975a) *Formy vremeni i khronotopa v romane: Ocherki po istoricheskoi poetike* (Moscow: Khudozhestvennaia literature).
Bakhtin, Mikhail (1975b) *Formy literatury i estetiki* (Moscow: Khudozhestvennaia literature).
Bataille, Georges (1986) [1957] *Erotism: Death and Sensuality*, trans. Mary Dalwood (San Francisco: City Lights).
Benjamin, Walter (1968) *Illuminations*, trans. Harry Zohn (New York: Shocken Books).
Isakava, Volha (2018) 'Reality Excess: Chernukha Cinema in the Late 1980s', in Birgit Beumers and Eugénie Zvonkine (eds), *Ruptures and Continuities in Soviet/Russian Cinema: Styles, Characters and Genres before and after the Collapse of the USSR* (Abingdon: Routledge), pp. 147–65.
Jóźwiak-Rodan, Paweł (2020) *Polski horror: o filmie grozy słów kilka* (Łódź: Unsin Studio).

Kamińska, Magdalena and Maja Mikołajczyk (2021) 'Wampir z realsocu: O horrorach w kinematografii krajów socjalistycznych', in Piotr Kletowski (ed.), *Europejskie kino gatunków*, vol. 3 (Kraków: Wydawnictwo Uniwersytetu Jagiellońskiego), pp. 47–63.

Klimek, Kaja (2020) 'O blokowiskach w polskim kinie', *Słowo i film* (e-lecture), www.youtube.com/watch?v=Od0MvKC63Ps&t=3799s (accessed 29 March 2023).

Mazierska, Ewa (2007) *Polish Postcommunist Cinema: From Pavement Level* (Bern: Peter Lang).

Morrison, Susan Signe (2015) *The Literature of Waste: Material Ecopoetics and Ethical Matter* (New York: Palgrave Macmillan).

Naitza, Sergio (2004) 'Kino ciągłego ruchu', in Sergio Naitza (ed.), *Opętanie: Ekstremalne kino i pisarstwo Andrzeja Żuławskiego* (Warsaw: Wydawnictwo Książkowe Twój Styl), pp. 47–57.

Putney, Christopher (1999) *Russian Devils and Diabolic Conditionality in Nikolai Gogol's* Evenings on a Farm Near Dikanka (New York: Peter Lang).

Romaniak, Damian (2015) 'Trans i ekstaza: "Szamanka Andrzeja Żuławskiego po latach"', 29 December 2015, https://kultura.onet.pl/film/recenzje/trans-i-ekstaza-szamanka-andrzeja-zulawskiego-po-latach-recenzja/lb73wp (accessed 29 March 2023).

Vatsuro, Vadim (2002) *Goticheskii roman v Rossii* (Moscow: Novoe literaturnoe obozrenie).

Yamaji, Asuta (2016) 'Russian Poets on Death and the Dead', *Quaestio Rossica* 4:4, 162–76.

15

Indian burial grounds in American fiction and film

Kevin Corstorphine

The return of the native

The 'Indian burial ground' is a staple of the American cultural imagination and a well-worn trope in fiction and film, evoking guilt, or simply fear, over the possibility of revenge enacted by the wronged Native American dead. This lends itself easily to the assumptions of Gothic criticism, centring on notions of cultural anxiety that are always lurking in the background of society but brought to the fore by horror narratives such as the haunted-house story. There is still much, though, that the prevalence of the Indian burial ground can reveal. By tracing the theme to its earliest and most influential fictional iterations in Philip Freneau and Washington Irving, as well as a popular trend in horror fiction in the late twentieth century, this chapter goes beyond accepted truisms by combining historical analysis, postcolonial criticism and Gothic genre studies to place the Indian burial ground in a wider chain of cultural connections. The aim is to thus contextualise as well as signal how the theme is evolving in the light of changing cultural expectations and the wider possibilities of decolonisation, as well as what this means for horror fiction.

It is crucial to establish the principle that the Indian burial ground is not a genuine facet of Native culture, but a malleable trope that appears in American Gothic fiction for the specific purpose of playing on colonial anxieties. The typical narrative is about a (usually white) family who move into a new home, are subject to a set of disturbing supernatural events and eventually uncover the fact that the house has been built on an old Indian burial ground. The desecration of this holy land triggers vengeance in the form of hauntings by spirits, possession of individuals and even the possession of the house itself. Whichever it may be, what drives the narrative is the torment inflicted on characters who are personally innocent of wrongdoing or at least well intentioned. As Hawthorne writes in the preface to *The House of the Seven Gables* (1851), 'the wrong-doing of one generation lives into the successive ones' (1851: iv).[1] It is important to remember Leslie

Fiedler's influential claim that 'the slaughter of the Indians, who would not yield their lands to the carriers of utopia' (1966: 143), provides a Gothic sensibility to American literature, which cannot help but return obsessively to the notion that the sins of the nation's past will be avenged, even by supernatural means.

The version of the Indian burial ground story that has become crystallised in popular culture stems from a limited flourishing in horror from the late 1970s to the early 1990s. Grady Hendrix traces the beginnings of a 'horror gold rush' (Hendrix, 2017: 176) towards Native American-themed monsters back to the success of Scottish author Graham Masterton's *The Manitou* in 1975. Perhaps a perspective from outside the United States was needed to clearly pick out the inherent power in the idea of bloody revenge in the present day for the brutalising of Native people over the centuries. *The Manitou* is about a young woman called Karen Tandy who is admitted to hospital with a large tumour on her neck. After the doctors X-ray the tumour and find a foetus, it transpires a Native American shaman called Misquamacus has performed a magical rite whereby he dies and is reborn into the body of a person in the future. He has apparently performed this ritual in an attempt to escape Dutch soldiers in the seventeenth century and to get his revenge on them later. It is perhaps Masterton's perspective as outsider that allows him to write explicitly what is the implicit concern of much American fiction of the time. Karen's doctor (speaking to Harry Erskine, the narrator) explicitly sums up the main essence of the novel:

> 'Look at it this way,' he said. 'The fascinating thing about America is that it was always supposed to be a brand new nation, free of oppression and guilt. But from the moment the white man settled here, there was a built-in time bomb of guilt ... Gradually the guilt of what we did to the Indians has eroded our sense of owning and belonging to our own country. This isn't *our* land, Harry. This is the land we *stole*.
>
> (Masterton, 1975: 79–80)

Masterton's thesis on American guilt directly echoes Fiedler's academic perspective and sets the tone for a slew of horror novels to come. If these novels acknowledge the injustices perpetrated upon Native Americans, they also clearly demonise these same people as monsters. In an attempt to evade accusations of pure exploitation, such fictions often 'take great pains to point out that [the Native villain] is not from any tribe we know but from a far older tribe, far more ancient than any that exist today' (Hendrix, 2017, 176–7). What this narrative sleight of hand achieves is to appeal to both an old American tradition of casting the 'Indian' as the enemy and to a modern liberal sensibility that is more attuned to a sense of guilt and the insecurity of living on the product of a colonial land grab.

The impact of this Native craze in horror writing led to subsequent parodies in television shows like *The Simpsons* ('Treehouse of Horror', 2.3, 1990) and *Family Guy* ('Petergeist', 4.26, 2006), and an entry on the website TV Tropes, which considers it now hackneyed enough to qualify as a 'dead horse trope' (TVTropes, 2022). The target of these parodies is usually one of a limited number of famous texts from the late 1970s and early 1980s, including Jay Anson's *The Amityville Horror* (1977) and its subsequent 1979 film adaptation; Stanley Kubrick's film version of *The Shining* (1980); and Stephen King's novel *Pet Sematary* (1983), as well as its own later film version (1989). Colin Dickey's reading of these narratives echoes Fiedler's idea of colonial guilt:

> The narrative of the haunted Indian burial ground hides a certain anxiety about the land on which Americans – specifically white, middle-class Americans – live. Embedded deep in the idea of home ownership – the Holy Grail of American middle-class life – is the idea that we don't, in fact, own the land we've just bought. Time and time again in these stories, perfectly average, innocent American families are confronted by ghosts who have persevered for centuries, who remain vengeful for the damage done. Facing these ghosts and expelling them, in many of these horror stories, becomes a means of re-fighting the Indian Wars of past centuries.
>
> (Dickey, 2016: 45)

This spectral return of the past occurs within a set of specific sociopolitical circumstances that drove the creation and reception of these highly influential Indian burial ground stories. Following decades of activism by Native Americans, the Indian Self-Determination and Assistance Act was passed in 1975, ushering in greater Native sovereignty. This was seized on by individual tribes and nations, who used copies of old treaties as the basis for restitution, winning significant settlements in states such as Alaska, Massachusetts and Maine (Tindall and Shi, 1984: 1084–5). Maine, of course, is a setting for much of Stephen King's fiction, including *Pet Sematary*, in which the author tackles the Native American land debate. When Louis Creed and his family move into their idyllic new home, one of the most striking things about it lies beyond the house itself: 'I know it sounds funny to say your nice little house there on the main road, with its phone and electric lights and cable TV and all, is on the edge of a wilderness', neighbour Jud Crandall tells the family, 'but it is' (King, 1989: 30). This 'wilderness' is specifically undeveloped due to restitution claims:

> Beyond the house was a large field for the children to play in, and beyond the field were woods that went on damn near for ever. The property abutted state lands, the realtor had explained, and there would be no development in the foreseeable future. The remains of the Micmac Indian tribe had laid claim to

nearly 8,000 acres in Ludlow, and the complicated litigation, involving the Federal government as well as that of the state, might stretch into the next century.

(1989: 4)

Events similar to this were contemporary with the publication of King's novel in 1983. Some Mi'kmaq peoples do indeed live in Northern Maine, in Aroostook County on the Canada–United States border, where the real town of Ludlow is situated, although issues over contested treaties stretched much further. As Joy Porter points out, 'when King wrote his novel, the state was embroiled in a legal fight over sixty percent of its territory with the Maliseet, Penobscot, and Passamaquoddy bands of the Wabanaki Confederacy' (Porter, 2018: 53). Despite large payments and land concessions, the state 'continues to fight Indian peoples over clean water, potential gaming revenue, and the treaty obligations inherent in its 1820 constitution' (2018: 53). The wilderness has been long synonymous in the American imagination with the threatening figure of the Indian, stretching at least as far back as the 'captivity narratives' of the seventeenth and early eighteenth centuries, such as Cotton Mather's account of Hannah Duston's capture and subsequent bloody revenge (1702) or Mary Rowlandson's autobiographical account of her own capture and ransom (1682).

In *Pet Sematary*, it is not the house itself that is built on an Indian burial ground but a patch of ground in the wilderness beyond (Figure 15.1). Moving past a pet cemetery (which a previous generation of children have misspelled on a sign) into this deeper territory, Louis Creed discovers that

Figure 15.1 The supernatural burial ground in *Pet Sematary* (1989).

the ground has the power to resurrect first his cat, killed on a busy road, and then, with horrific inevitability, his young son, who likewise falls victim to a speeding truck. Both come back from the dead fundamentally changed. Although the physical bodies are more or less restored, both pet and son become evil, tainted by the process of their return. Old Jud Crandall relates the story that the Micmacs had stopped using the place because 'the ground had gone sour' (2018: 36). King's chilling description works well to create atmosphere but bears little relation to any real Native burial practices – nor does it claim to. What is often missed in a reading of the novel is that King uses a device derivative of the themes of H. P. Lovecraft (and also identified by Hendrix in 1970s horror novels) of an ancient evil that goes further back than even indigenous history. The Micmacs have no memory of how and why their ancestors used the land, and this is clearly connected to an ancient and malign force that may be older than the human race itself. Jud suggests that the Micmacs had resorted to cannibalism during harsh winters, invoking the evil spirit of the Wendigo, but it is highly possible that this is hearsay and projection. As Porter notes, 'Indian ghosts, like other ghosts, increasingly became inhabitants and products of the mind rather than exterior entities' (2018: 51); a repository of sorts for settler fears and justification of violence enacted by the colonisers rather than against them. It is interesting to note that, in King's earlier novel *The Shining*, it is European pioneers who are associated with cannibalism with reference to the historically documented case of the snowbound Donner Party in the Sierra Nevada in the winter of 1846–7. Although it is inevitable that some Native American groups did resort to such measures at some point in history, it was early pioneers who were more likely to find themselves starving to death in an unfamiliar and unforgiving land. This projection of anxieties onto another group is embodied in the figure of the Wendigo.

Rooted in the folklore of the native Algonquian peoples of the northern United States and Canada, the Wendigo is a spirit associated with starvation and cannibalism, but also greed and destruction in the broader sense. This symbolic aspect is more important than the notion of the Wendigo as a literal monster akin to a European werewolf. It is little wonder, then, that stories of the Wendigo abound in colonial encounters and that Europeans would become so fascinated by a creature that so closely reflects their own rapacious plundering of the American continent. The Wendigo is mentioned in *Pet Sematary* but is never explicitly seen. King's handling of the concept echoes Algernon Blackwood's novella 'The Wendigo' (1910), where a group of colonial settlers are menaced in the backwoods of Northwestern Ontario. Jo Nazare points out that the way Blackwood describes the creature in the context of Native people 'transforms the Wendigo from a native myth into a descriptive template for the Indian Savage' (Nazare, 2000: 40).

This is played out in King's narrative, which features no Native American characters but only the monstrous presence of the Wendigo, wrenched out of context but continuing to serve as a haunting reminder of the violence of colonialism.[2]

The Indian burial ground as haunted territory

The power of the association of ancient vengeance and Indian burial grounds is such that one of the most popular horror films of the 1980s, *Poltergeist* (appearing a year before *Pet Sematary*), is frequently cited as the prime example of the theme when in fact there is no mention of an Indian burial ground in the film (Figure 15.2). Set in a planned community in California, a family home has been built over a cemetery, but the developers have failed to move the bodies – only the gravestones. The two key strands of the Indian burial ground discussed here (the disturbance of the dead and ancient evil) both have a long history in Gothic novels and ghost stories that have no reliance on an appeal to Native American traditions. Horace Walpole's *The Castle of Otranto* (1764), generally considered to be the first Gothic novel, even specifically prefigures the anxieties of the Indian burial ground narrative. Manfred, the owner of Otranto, is forced to flee his castle when the original owner (murdered by Manfred's grandfather) returns in giant ghostly form to take his revenge, killing Manfred's son. The sins of the fathers, as in Hawthorne, are visited on the children. In the

Figure 15.2 Not an old Indian burial ground! The cemetery in *Poltergeist* (1982).

American context, it is the 'original sin' of colonial theft and violence that poisons the well and leads to an uncertainty about ownership that is easily exploited in horror. In the case of *Poltergeist*, the expectation is so strong that it overrides the actual content in the popular imagination. In fact, the film is very much a ghost story in the vein of nineteenth-century spiritualist belief, where the restless dead simply need to be appeased through recognition and treatment with respect. This is a theme mercilessly skewered by Shirley Jackson in *The Haunting of Hill House* (1959), where the idealistic Mrs Montague insists that 'empathy' and 'pure love' (Jackson, 1999: 217) are what is needed to resolve the supernatural occurrences. In the case of Hill House, such naïveté does not account for the possibility that the house itself has become a force of pure malevolent evil and that humans can only ever become victim to its insane whims.

The tone of the American haunted house story is, generally speaking, one of deep pessimism. In *The Haunting of Hill House* this pessimism is played out through the narrative trajectory of the protagonist, Eleanor Vance. Invited to take part in a scientific investigation into hauntings, she puts all her hopes and dreams for the future in the invitation to stay at the house, where independence, adventure and even romance seem to be possible. Instead, her deep investment in this prospect results in madness and death. The message is clear, and it is also one that applies to the prosaic business of buying a home: if it seems too good to be true, it probably is. Haunted house stories reflect the socio-economic conditions of their production, and global recessions in the 1970s and 1980s no doubt contributed to the appeal of owning a dream home, no matter what the catch might be. This partly explains the *Amityville Horror* cultural phenomenon. Jay Anson's original book was published in 1977 and details the events that drove George and Cathy Lutz, together with their three children, to flee their home two years earlier. Presented as a true story, rather than fiction, its success quickly translated into a franchise which has spawned at least five further books and more than a dozen films, although many of these texts stray very far from the potential plausibility of the original. Early US editions went so far as to print the title as *The Amityville Horror: A True Story*, and the 1978 UK edition uses the following tagline: 'More hideously frightening than *The Exorcist* because it actually happened!' (Anson 1978). *The Amityville Horror* is constructed along the lines of a factual account, even containing floor-plans of the interior of the property. Anson's book reads like a true crime novel, except the crimes committed are largely supernatural in nature. It is here where supernatural and human horrors become entangled, as 112 Ocean Avenue had actually seen traumatic violence at the time of the purchase. In 1974 Ronald 'Butch' DeFeo Junior was convicted of killing his parents and four siblings with a high-powered rifle in their sleep. He claimed to have heard voices, but as he testified, 'whenever I looked around, there was no one there, so it must have been God talking to me' (Anson, 1978: 17–18). This seems unlikely, but something, Jay Anson's book suggests, was in fact whispering in his ear.

Having moved to the house, ironically named 'High Hopes', George becomes more and more irritable with his family. It becomes clear that he is taking on the aspect of DeFeo, or perhaps something older that is coming into being through him, just as it did with the earlier inhabitant of the house. Number 112 Ocean Avenue becomes the archetype of the 'Bad Place', to use Stephen King's terminology. As he writes in his non-fiction *Danse Macabre* (1981), 'the good horror story about the Bad Place whispers that we are not locking the world out; we are locking ourselves in ... with *them*' (King, 1993: 299, original emphasis). King's dramatic use of the term 'them' is indicative of the othering that occurs within such narratives. In the case of Indian burial ground stories, the image is a dual one: on one level the Indian has returned to carry out revenge, but as this is an imaginative construction of the Indian, the horror is already within and, further to this, becomes intertwined with colonial anxiety and guilt. The forces of historical violence are so powerful as to become cosmic. In the case of *The Amityville Horror*, it is here that the narrative turns towards this source of horror. The ancient evil that is brought into being through George, and Ronnie DeFeo before him, is explicitly associated with Native history, albeit not strictly a burial ground:

> It seems the Shinnecock Indians used land on the Amityville River as an enclosure for the sick, mad and dying. These unfortunates were penned up until they died of exposure. However, the record noted that the Shinnecocks did not use this tract as a consecrated burial mound because they believed it to be infested by demons ... In the late 1600s, white settlers eased the first Americans out of the area ... One of the more notorious settlers who came to the newly-named Amityville in those days was a John Catchum or Ketcham who had been forced out of Salem, Massachusetts, for practising witchcraft. John set up residence within 500 feet of where George now lived, continuing his alleged devil worship.
>
> (Anson, 1978: 80)

None of this holds up to scrutiny: the Shinnecocks did not inhabit this area; none of these practices are genuine; and Native beliefs (in a long tradition of American Gothic fiction) are conflated with Christian mythology around demons. The euphemism that the first Americans were 'eased' out is also dubious. John Catchum is similarly invented. Despite this, the ideas play powerfully into the received narrative around Native Americans and mysterious ancient evil that constitutes the Indian burial ground story, with the 1979 film stating that Indians are actually buried in the ground. A similar tweak occurs in Stanley Kubrick's film version of *The Shining*: the Overlook Hotel, which in King's novel is imbued with an ambiguous evil compounded throughout history, is given a more straightforward origin as having been built over an Indian burial ground. Perhaps in a self-conscious nod to colonial history, Jack Torrance quotes Kipling to the bartender conjured up by the hotel's malicious consciousness, declaring '[w]hite man's burden, Lloyd my man, white man's burden'. The 2005 remake of *The Amityville Horror* adds a postcolonial twist: rather than being a devil worshipper, Ketchum is now portrayed as a puritan minister who tortured and killed Natives in a demented religious quest of conversion. In a process beginning with Native American activism in the late twentieth century, and continuing in the twenty-first with increased calls for decolonisation, political awareness of the hypocrisy and misdeeds of Christian colonists have become so fully integrated into mainstream American culture that this itself has become the source of horror, signalling the death of the straightforward Indian burial ground motif.

Structurally, haunted house stories are at least as old as Pliny the Younger's Letter to Sura in the first century CE, and probably older. Pliny's tale stands out due to having all the key elements of a text like *The Amityville Horror*. Athenodorus, the philosopher, buys a house that seems too cheap, but he cannot resist the bargain. He is then haunted by a spectre that disturbs him with clanking noises and generally frightening behaviour. It is discovered that a corpse, weighed down with chains, has been improperly buried under the courtyard. When it is reburied with the proper respect and ceremony, the haunting no longer occurs. Perhaps even more notable than the familiar plot elements is the way that the tale purports to be a true story. This trick would be repeated when the Gothic novelists revisited ancient superstition for their material and sometimes claimed (as Walpole did with *Otranto*) that these were 'found' manuscripts rather than fictional inventions of the author. Crystal B. Lake notes that *Otranto* is 'encoded with political allusions' (2013: 511), and certainly each version of this story speaks to its own socio-historical moment, sometimes purposefully, sometimes unconsciously reflecting the concerns and mood of its day. In the United States the treatment of Native Americans was always going to rise to the surface in Gothic narratives, specifically in the politically charged era under discussion. The 1970s, in particular, had seen highly public protests from groups such as the American Indian Movement (AIM), including the occupation of Alcatraz (1969–71), the Trail of Broken Treaties (1972) and the Wounded Knee Occupation (1973). The events at Wounded Knee were given huge public attention following Sacheen Littlefeather's appearance at the Oscars, where she talked about Wounded Knee alongside the poor representation of Native Americans in Hollywood and rejected the Oscar for best actor on behalf of Marlon

Brando, who supported AIM. Running parallel to these wider movements was a specific focus on burial grounds. As James Riding In notes, 'throughout the 1970s and 1980s, AIAD [American Indian Against Desecration] challenged the human remains collections and curatorial policies of government agencies, museums, and universities', with AIM forcibly reclaiming artefacts and burning field notes at a Minnesota dig site in 1972 (1996: 242). Riding In comments that in Pawnee spiritual belief 'wandering spirits often beset the living with psychological and health problems' (1996: 240) and that to bring this about through disturbance of graves 'constitutes abominable acts of sacrilege, desecration, and depravity' (1996: 240–1). Thus, there is a conflict between the rights of living Native Americans to maintain the sanctity of their own dead and the colonial scientific ideology that places European systems of knowledge above these rights.[3]

A seam of anxiety over these unresolved historical and continuing injustices has run through American cultural productions for a long time. Fiedler's argument, taken up by countless critics since, suggests that there is a foundational trauma that authors and filmmakers cannot help returning to. Likewise, Teresa Goddu casts the situation in the language of psychoanalysis:

> The nation's narratives – its foundational fictions and self-mythologizations – are created through a process of displacement: their coherence depends on exclusion. By resurrecting what these narratives repress, the gothic disrupts the dream world of national myth with the nightmares of history.
>
> (1997: 10)

'History' is a crucial word here: the popular notion that the United States lacks history rests on the erasure of Native cultures, or to be more precise the mythologising of Native Americans into a timeless, stereotyped projection of otherness. It is telling that in so many of these narratives the most fearful spectre that can be conjured is the idea that something is incredibly *old*. In *Pet Sematary*, Jud Crandall notes how the Micmacs sanded off the top of a hill to make the flat area for the supernatural burial ground, claiming that 'no one knows how, no more than anyone knows how the Mayans built their pyramids. And the Micmacs have forgot themselves, just like the Mayans have' (1997: 130). The ground, as noted earlier, has 'gone sour'. Similarly, in *The Amityville Horror* it is not necessarily the house itself that causes problems but the ground it is built on. A reporter after the events allegedly discovers that 'tragedy had struck nearly every family inhabiting the place, as well as an earlier house built on the same site' (1997: 12). There is a sense that this Bad Place is literally timeless, yet danger is always possible in the moment. This projected eternal immanence is summed up by a character in a slightly earlier (explicitly fictional) novel with a similar theme: Robert Marasco's *Burnt Offerings* (1973). Here, a sinister old woman tries to rent out her grand old family home for the summer, claiming that '[t]here's centuries in these rooms, Mrs. Rolfe. This house – why it's been on this land longer than anyone can remember … It's practically immortal. I sincerely believe that' (Marasco, 1974: 54).

History, myth and reality

The Indian burial ground narrative conflates this sense of a sublimely terrifying past with a version of Native American history filtered through the lens of European settlers. Colonial systems of knowledge were cast as superior and a justification for taking land. The idea that indigenous people might know more about this land, and might have access to power through this knowledge, is one that leads inevitably to the demonisation of the Native. The association of Native Americans with the Devil runs deep in Puritan settler culture and continues until relatively recently. In *The Amityville Horror* there is a logical chain from Native cultural practices to the mention of demons and the devil-worshipping Catchum. The association is a staple of American Gothic: Hawthorne's 'Young Goodman Brown' (1835), for example, sees its protagonist embark on a journey where he fears the 'devilish Indian behind every tree' (Hawthorne, 1863: 88). Hawthorne's short story, however, exposes this idea of the devilish Indian as a projection. It is in fact Brown who meets with the Devil in the forest, and his pious Puritan friends and family who congregate in a ritual black mass. Alfred A. Cave makes the distinction between actual Native American religious practices and how this was interpreted in the colonial period, arguing that 'Puritan accounts of shamanic practice relied upon a false analogy with English witchcraft that reinforced long-standing prejudices and misconceptions' (1992: 15). Going further back to the first encounters with America, Cave notes that, 'those 16th century Englishmen who gave any thought to the New World generally believed that its inhabitants were cruel, degenerate Devil worshippers' (1992: 15). For example, the famous Captain John Smith, reporting from Virginia, was 'convinced that the Powhatan Indians were ruled by Satan himself' (1992: 16).

The first notable literary work on the theme of the Indian burial ground is Philip Freneau's poem 'The Indian Burying Ground' (1787). The speaker suggests that the spirits of the Native dead do not rest easy but continue to hunt and feast as they did while alive. It warns, 'Thou, stranger, that shalt come this way / No fraud upon the dead commit' (Freneau, 1948: 9), but does not specify any particular consequences. Instead, the atmosphere is one of supernatural frisson, suggesting 'And Reason's self shall bow the knee / To shadows and delusions here' (1948: 10). Through this Romantic version of the 'Indian' (as opposed to any real Native American individual or culture) cemented in the popular imagination, cemeteries become a flexible tool to add plausibility to supernatural narratives. Washington Irving's 'The Devil and Tom Walker' (1824) exemplifies the swirling mixture of Indians, violence, revenge and the Devil that characterise the Indian burial ground narrative. Set near Boston, it describes the events triggered when Tom Walker takes a shortcut past an old Indian fort, 'used as a place of refuge for their squaws and children' (Irving, 1897: 96) but now destroyed and scattered with rusted weapons and bones. The blame for the traumas of the past might be put firmly on white colonialism but, predictably, the Indian is seen as culpable: 'the common people had a bad opinion of it ... [I]t was asserted that the savages held incantations here, and made sacrifices to the evil spirit' (1897: 97). Walker finds a skull, cracked open with a tomahawk, and on picking it up is confronted by a 'black man' who is specifically 'neither negro nor Indian' (1897: 97). He is in fact the Devil, or 'Old Scratch', as he is known. Notably, Old Scratch reinforces the stereotype of the savage, devil-worshipping Indian, but at the same time turns the table on the Puritans who have supplanted them:

> I am he to whom the red men devoted this spot, and now and then roasted a white man by way of sweet-smelling sacrifice. Since the red men have been exterminated by you white savages, I amuse myself by presiding at the persecutions of Quakers and Anabaptists; I am the great patron and prompter of slave dealers, and the grand master of the Salem witches.
>
> (1897: 99–100)

Old Scratch's declaration makes clear the way that land becomes tainted by violence, hypocrisy and injustice. As with Goddu's argument, this resurrects what has been buried in order to exclude it from the national narrative of what Fiedler refers to as 'a dream of innocence' opposed to 'the compounded evil of the past from which no one in Europe could ever feel himself free' (1966: 143). The Indian burial ground, far from being reflective of Native American culture, is rather a repository of the compounded evil of the American past. Walker sells his soul to Old Scratch in exchange for buried pirate treasure, but when he is eventually claimed as a result of this Faustian pact, his money turns to ash and dust and he is forever damned to haunt the fort. There are clear parallels between Irving's supernatural tale and later American horror narratives such as *The Amityville Horror*, where the spirit of Ronnie DeFeo becomes attached to the house, having been affected by some ill-defined historical events involving Native Americans and the Devil.[4]

Critics have long identified a shift in American writing that moves away from British archetypes of castles, abbeys and the specifically European forest landscapes of the early Gothic towards the expansive wilderness of the North American continent and the dangers found therein. Goddu, for example, has proposed that the American Gothic creates its own sites of the Gothic imagination that 'not only replace but exceed their British types' (1997: 56). The Indian burial ground has captured the American (and global) imagination in its ability to articulate an unease over colonial history that has been buried, but not deeply enough. The cultural currency of such sites continues to extend beyond horror genre fiction into 'real-life' ghost stories and documentaries. A good example is Lake Shawnee Amusement Park in Mercer County, West Virginia, which featured in a 2009 episode of the Travel Channel's *Most Terrifying Places in America*. The park was shut down in 1966 after a series of tragic accidents, and a 1988 archaeological dig uncovered Native American bodies buried on the site. An early settler, Mitchell Clay, supposedly killed several Shawnee Natives after his son was kidnapped and burned alive. Despite this, the Mercer County Convention and Visitors Bureau advertises tours, and calls the place 'a true Mercer County highlight' (Visit Mercer County website). Stories such as this have some historical truth but blend together the familiar elements of Native/settler conflict, death and tainted land that characters the Indian burial ground story. Importantly, Native people themselves rarely feature in the texts but exist only as a symbol of past violence and to infer the supernatural. This Romantic transformation of the Indian into a mythical being continues to erase awareness of Native cultures as they exist today. Shea Vassar, a citizen of the Cherokee Nation of Oklahoma, scathingly drives the point home:

> We are not all buried in some unmarked grave, driving a stepfather to murder like in *The Amityville Horror*, or turning your dead cat into some sort of demonic being like in *Pet Sematary*. For the most part, we are working to fill the gaps where the American educational system has failed to teach about our existence and are attempting to reverse the harm from underdeveloped plot devices like the IBG [Indian Burial Ground].
>
> (Vassar, 2020)

Although Native Americans across the United States continue to suffer the legacy of colonialism, cultural erasure and injustice, the cultural conversation and expectations of a media-savvy audience have moved on from the possibility of using the device of the Indian burial ground in the way that it was exploited in the handful of novels and films that made it famous.

The likely future path in horror fiction is one that has already begun to flourish: the transformation of the device by Native creators. Most contemporary fiction avoids the motif of the Indian burial ground in favour of what Porter describes as the use of 'horror to introduce American Indian perspectives on the past, counter-memories that challenge ideas on ownership and sovereignty of material, psychological, and spiritual space (2018: 55).[5] *The Only Good Indians* (2020), by Blackfoot Native author Steven Graham Jones, is a notable example of a horror genre novel that moves past the Indian burial ground as a motif but keeps the thematic element of supernatural revenge for past injustices. Here, the spirit of a slaughtered Elk, Po'noka, carries out revenge on a group of Blackfeet men who killed her and her foetal calf in a section of the reservation they lacked the right to hunt in. Although they had attempted to distribute the meat in the community to be used properly, they do not escape the consequences of their actions. In this novel, realistic Native characters are foregrounded, rather than appear as a narrative device or refracted by the distorted lens of a colonial perspective. What is more, they do not line up with stereotypes of either pagans or noble savages, but are human, flawed and just as terrified as the reader. The Indian burial ground in horror fiction worked within a framework established by ghost stories over a long historical period and exhibited a specifically American aesthetic of Puritan hellfire and stereotyped Natives. It may have had only a tangential relationship with reality but drew energy from powerful cultural anxieties. It is to be hoped that laying it to a final rest will clear space for a more nuanced exploration of America's colonial history in horror.

Notes

1 *The House of the Seven Gables* is not itself an 'Indian burial ground' novel.
2 The Wendigo has now joined the canon of horror monsters, making a notable appearance, for example, in the 2015 videogame *Until Dawn*. As Grady Hendrix notes of *The Manitou*, it has become one of 'our homegrown monsters ripe for exploitation' (2017: 176).
3 For more on this wide-ranging issue, see Roger C. Echo-Hawk and Walter R. Echo-Hawk (1994).
4 *The Amityville Horror* is a curious 'possession' narrative, as DeFeo was still alive at the time of the reported events.
5 See Porter (2018) for a full list of examples.

References

Anson, Jay (1978) The Amityville Horror: A True Story (New York: Bantam).
Cave, Alfred A. (1992) 'New England Puritan Misperceptions of Native American Shamanism', *International Social Science Review*, 67:1 (Winter), 15–27.
Dickey, Colin (2016) *Ghostland: An American History in Haunted Places* (New York: Penguin).
Echo-Hawk, Roger and Walter R. Echo-Hawk (1994) *Battlefields and Burial Grounds: The Indian Struggle to Protect Ancestral Graves in the United States* (Minneapolis: Lerner Publications Company).

Fiedler, Leslie (1966) *Love and Death in the American Novel* (New York: Stein and Day).
Freneau, Philip (1948) 'The Indian Burying Ground', in Louis Untermeyer (ed.), *The Pocket Book of American Poems, from the Colonial Period to the Present Day* (New York: Pocket Books), pp. 8–10.
Goddu, Teresa (1997) *Gothic America: Narrative, History and Nation* (New York: Columbia University Press).
Hawthorne, Nathaniel (1851) *The House of the Seven Gables* (Boston: Ticknor, Reed and Fields).
Hawthorne, Nathaniel (1863) 'Young Goodman Brown', in *Mosses from an Old Manse* (Boston: Ticknor and Fields), pp. 87–105.
Hendrix, Grady (2017) *Paperbacks from Hell: The Twisted History of '70s and '80s Horror Fiction* (Philadelphia: Quirk Books).
Irving, Washington (1897) 'The Devil and Tom Walker', in Bliss Perry (ed.), *Little Masterpieces* (New York: Doubleday and McClure), pp. 91–113.
Jackson, Shirley (1999) [1959] *The Haunting of Hill House* (London: Robinson).
King, Stephen (1989) [1983] *Pet Sematary* (London: New English Library).
King, Stephen (1993) *Danse Macabre* (London: Warner Books).
Lake, Crystal B. (2013) 'Bloody Records: Manuscripts and Politics in *The Castle of Otranto*', *Modern Philology*, 110:4, 489–512.
Marasco, Robert (1974) *Burnt Offerings* (London: Coronet).
Masterton, Graham (1975) The Manitou (London: Neville Spearman).
Nazare, Joe (2000) 'The Horror! The Horror? The Appropriation, and Reclamation, of Native American Mythology', *Journal of the Fantastic in the Arts*, 11:1, 24–51.
Porter, Joy (2018) 'The Horror Genre and Aspects of Native American Literature', in Kevin Corstorphine and Laura Kremmel (eds), *The Palgrave Handbook to Horror Literature* (New York: Palgrave), pp. 45–60.
Riding In, James (1996) 'Repatriation: A Pawnee's Perspective', *American Indian Quarterly*, 20:2 (Spring), 238–50.
Tindall, George Brown and David Emory Shi (1984) *America: A Narrative History*, 4th edn (New York: W. W. Norton).
Vassar, Shea (2020) 'Digging Up the Indian Burial Ground Trope', *Film School Rejects*, 15 October, https://filmschoolrejects.com/indian-burial-ground-trope/ (accessed 16 March 2022).

16

Adolescent existence and resistance: graveyards as a Gothic chronotope in twenty-first-century fiction for young people

Debra Dudek

As the twentieth century ended and the twenty-first began, young adult (YA) television series such as *Buffy the Vampire Slayer* (1997–2003) and *The Vampire Diaries* (2009–17) featured graveyards as a space for temporary contemplation. For example, Buffy spends an inordinate amount of time in graveyards waiting for vampires to dig themselves out of their human graves; while the killing usually happens fairly quickly, the waiting may be for hours. Similarly, in the first season of *The Vampire Diaries* Elena goes to the cemetery to write in her diary at the grave site of her parents. In both series, graveyards represent a pause, a space of self-reflection. With the publication of Neil Gaiman's *The Graveyard Book* (2008), the graveyard came to the foreground as a place of safety and belonging for young people. For instance, Michelle J. Smith sees the graveyard in Gaiman's novel as a historical site that naturalises the ghosts who live there and illuminates humans – and especially adult humans – as evil and dangerous (Smith, 2017: 194). Anne K. Burke Erickson (2022) analyses the graveyard, its inhabitants and *The Graveyard Book* itself as liminal beings and spaces that challenge categorisation.

Since *The Graveyard Book*, graveyards have become agential sites. Young people live in graveyards (Gaiman's *The Graveyard Book* (2008); Aiden Thomas's *Cemetery Boys* (2020)) or adjacent to them (J. W. Ocker's *Death and Douglas* (2017); Martin Matthews's *The Graveyard Girl and the Boneyard Boy* (2017); Netflix's *Chilling Adventures of Sabrina* (2018–20); Lisa Thompson's *The Graveyard Riddle* (2021)), pets are resurrected (Tim Burton's *Frankenweenie* (2012); Sigi Cohen's *My Dead Bunny* (2015)) and humans work together with the undead to seek justice for wrongdoings (Laura Terry's *Graveyard Shakes* (2017), Amy McCaw's *Mina and the Undead* (2021)). In each case, graveyards are a chronotope for adolescent liminality, that space and time between childhood and adulthood. Although graveyards appear in many texts for young people, their significance has not been the focus of much academic scholarship beyond attention to Gaiman's novel. In this chapter I focus my analysis on a selection of texts published between 2017 and 2021 in which graveyards are implicit sites of being: Terry's *Graveyard Shakes*, Thompson's *The Graveyard Riddle*, Ocker's *Death and Douglas*, Matthews's *The Graveyard Girl and the Boneyard Boy* and Thomas's *Cemetery Boys*. Each text features a graveyard or cemetery as a Gothic chronotope, a space the young protagonists occupy to negotiate and fortify their sense of self. These graveyard narratives represent graveyards and adolescence as liminal locale and, as I contend, a space and time for young people to express and develop their being in an ontological exchange with an Other.

I employ Mikhail Bakhtin's notion of the chronotope to analyse the space and time of a graveyard. In his essay 'Forms of Time and of the Chronotope in the Novel: Notes toward a Historical Poetics', Bakhtin theorises the artistic chronotope as an intertwining of time and space, which may be applied to the graveyard, a space that contains the past in the present. Bakhtin writes:

> In the literary artistic chronotope, spatial and temporal indicators are fused into one carefully thought-out, concrete whole. Time, as it were, thickens, takes on flesh, becomes artistically visible; likewise, space becomes charged and responsive to the movements of time, plot and history. The intersection of axes and fusion of indicators characterizes the artistic chronotope.
>
> (Bakhtin, 1990: 84)

The graveyard space embodies the time between past, present and future, and allows the adolescent protagonists to contemplate their sense of self in this liminal space between life and death.

To say adolescence is a liminal space may be redundant because adolescence is commonly understood as the state between childhood and adulthood. Deborah Wills and Amy Bright elaborate on this seeming redundancy to argue:

> Adolescence is a threshold state, poised between categories, discourses, and definitions. It exists primarily between other conditions: between childhood and adulthood, dependence and autonomy, inexperience and maturity. The ontology of adolescence is often contradictory ... [I]t may be represented both as residually partaking of the purity of early childhood ... and as contaminated by imminent adulthood ... North American social, cultural, and developmental narratives frequently suggest that the successful conclusion of adolescence lies primarily in moving through and past it ... Adolescence is thus represented as both transitional and transitory, a briefly liminal state meant to be resolved by a conclusive departure. The maturing adolescent must

> exchange his or her threshold status, defined chiefly by being simultaneously 'no longer' and 'not yet,' for the more settled, singular category of adulthood.
>
> (Wills and Bright, 2011: 100)

To this list of in-between categories, I add life and death, for the adolescent exists also in the precarious space between birth and death, leaning closer to newly born life than to the life fully lived of death. The death of a young person invokes greater tragedy than the death of an adult who has lived a full life. As Feaster in *Death and Douglas* says, '"ain't nothing sadder than a kid in a cemetery" – "Unless that kid is alive,"' responds Moss (Ocker, 2017: 9). This exchange points to normative ideas about the tragedy of a child's death but also to adult conceptions of the graveyard as a space unfit for children.

The adolescent protagonists in YA Gothic resist adult ideologies, even as most of them are on the cusp of adulthood themselves. The liminal space of the graveyard is well suited to foster contemplation about the self, and twenty-first-century Gothic texts for young people often focus on such themes of liminality. As Kristine Moruzi and Michelle J. Smith argue:

> The traditions of the genre are repurposed and reconfigured in contemporary fiction for young adults to reflect on the importance of young adults for their future possibilities, as well as their present modes of existence and possible resistance … [C]hanging conceptions of young adults as liminal figures operating between the modes of child and adult can be mobilised when combined with Gothic spaces and concepts in texts for young people.
>
> (Moruzi and Smith, 2021: 1–2)

This essay builds upon these ideas by focusing on how the graveyard as a Gothic chronotope functions as a liminal place where young people shape their existence through resistance. These adolescent protagonists resist normative ideologies often articulated by adult authority figures. Although this resistance shapes the adolescent's sense of self, it is often initiated by love for someone else.

This blending of love and horror validates Catherine Spooner's observation that '[c]ontemporary Gothic can increasingly be described as comic, romantic, celebratory, gleeful, whimsical or even joyous', leading her to coin the phrase 'happy Gothic' (Spooner, 2017: 3). In this context, 'happy' becomes 'a mobile, oppositional term that groups together a range of positively inclined emotions or moods that are unexpected in conventional Gothic critical discourse' (2017: 3). Spooner's framework applies well here: the 'happy Gothic' helps to foreground how the positively inclined emotions, such as love – whether familial, filial or romantic – guide young people's ontology in its relation to an Other, an ontological exchange that takes place in a graveyard.

The significance of relationality announces itself even before the narrative in each novel begins. Each of the texts I analyse features at least two young people on the front cover, and this paratextual information aligns with the narratives themselves. In each case, two adolescents engage in what Lisa Sainsbury terms an 'ontological exchange', which she argues 'is an ontic meeting of self and other during which being is tested and made aware of its status as being ... whereby being asserts or defends itself, against a threat from the other' (Sainsbury, 2021: 16–17). The cover of Terry's graphic novel *Graveyard Shakes*, for instance, features three people triangulated around a gravestone. Two of them – sisters Katia and Victoria – are depicted on the ground and one – a ghost – dances joyously in the sky. The two adolescents on the ground, however, react to the ghostly presence very differently: one faces the ghost, dancing and jumping gleefully; the other holds her arms tight against her chest, her mouth agape in fear while staring at the ghost, her legs outstretched as though mid-stride fleeing from the scene. This cover encapsulates the initial relationship between the two sisters and Little Ghost and serves as a snapshot of each character's personality.

In *Graveyard Shakes*, the representation of an ontological exchange is doubled as two sets of young people – the living sisters, Victoria and Katia, and the undead friends, Little Ghost and Modie – assert their sense of being against a threat from the Other, to use Sainsbury's terminology. The narrative features Victoria and Katia, two sisters newly arrived at Bexley Academy, which is adjacent to the cemetery where Little Ghost and Modie live. The story begins with Little Ghost flying into the open grave in front of the headstone depicted on the front cover. Once underground, he emerges into a catacomb filled with dancing ghosts. Little Ghost joins them on the edges of the celebration, but he escapes when the other ghosts gang up on him to scare him for being different from them, for being more aligned with the daylight than the darkness. This opening scene immediately represents an ontological exchange in which Little Ghost's being is tested against the threat from the other ghosts.

As Little Ghost escapes to a different part of the graveyard, he encounters another threatening Other in the form of an adult human: Modie's father, Nikola. This fraught dynamic between adult and child is foregrounded by Michelle J. Smith in her essay 'Dead and Ghostly Children in Contemporary Literature', in which Smith argues:

> Gothic fictions for young people mobilise ghostly children to critique or remedy adult actions, often expressing distrust in adults as authority figures. The dead or ghostly children in these works do not unsettle other characters or the reader as they do in many ghost stories, but instead expose the serious harms posed to children by selfish or evil adults.
>
> (Smith, 2017: 192)

In *Graveyard Shakes*, Nikola is the biggest threat to childhood well-being; he seeks eternal life for his son, which he can only achieve by taking the life of another human child every thirteen years. Modie tries to convince his father that his actions are wrong, but his father refuses to listen and rationalises that the life of one child every thirteen years is a sacrifice worth making if it keeps Modie alive.

Nearly thirteen years – and one page turn – later, the narrative introduces the second set of adolescents: Katia and her older sister, Victoria. Their story begins on their first day of school at Bexley Academy, which is next to the graveyard. The sisters are depicted as opposites: Katia embraces her nonconformity in the way she dresses, moves and plays, and Victoria does her best to fit in, aligning her appearance and demeanour with the other students at school. When Victoria wants to escape the scrutiny of the school's mean girls, Katia leads her to the cemetery next door. As Katia lounges against a gravestone and ruminates on how 'this place reminds me of home' (Terry, 2017: 40), Victoria stares longingly over the stone fence that separates the graveyard from the schoolyard, replying to Katia that she thought they 'came to boarding school to get away from home' (2017: 40). While the sisters have different ways of being, they both see the graveyard as a place where they can escape the authority of school and the threat of bullies.

Although the graveyard offers the sisters a safe space from school, it also puts them in danger of Modie's father, who seeks a new child to sacrifice for Modie's life. When Nikola sends his henchmen to capture Victoria and then Katia, Modie and Little Ghost help them escape. Little Ghost is ultimately vaporised by the other ghosts, and Modie smashes the scarab that Nikola requires to keep Modie alive. In the end, Nikola apologises to Victoria and Katia and leaves the graveyard to atone for his wrongdoings; Modie takes Little Ghost's place as Victoria's 'favourite fully dead boy'; and Little Ghost is memorialised with his own headstone in the cemetery (Terry, 2017: 194–208). The young people take over the graveyard and transform it into a celebratory place for the living and the dead, therein resisting and remedying wrongful adult actions.

The final page of the text features a parallel illustration to the front cover that has been altered to represent the sisters' development. In this final full-page bleed panel, Katia and two friends play musical instruments in a clearing in the graveyard, while Victoria dances joyously with Modie. Victoria's interaction with her sister and with the spectral Little Ghost and now ghostly Modie has transformed her from a fearful young woman, who runs from ghosts, to 'a little more ferocious like [Katia]' (Terry, 2017: 183), while Katia shifts from being a lone wolf to playing in a band called Katia and the Wolf Pack. The graveyard, represented on the cover of the book in dark purple hues and as a space from which Victoria flees, is now situated in undulating green hills as a liminal place of suspended time in which Modie's body drifts vertically into the sky parallel to the lines of music emanating from the band's musical instruments. The graveyard chronotope thickens time through this joyous musical moment that implies an assertion of being in the process of perpetual becoming.

In Lisa Thompson's junior fiction novel *The Graveyard Riddle* (2021), the graveyard features as a place of escape and peace for thirteen-year-old Melody Bird. As she narrates:

> Some people thought I was weird because I liked going to the graveyard. To them, a graveyard is creepy. It makes them think of spooky things like rotten corpses and wailing ghosts. I don't feel like that at all. To me it's full of colour and light and wildlife. In fact, it's probably my favourite place in the world ... When Dad lived with us I used to go to the graveyard when he and Mum started arguing. There was no shouting here. It was always peaceful.
> (Thompson, 2021: 7–8)

Melody's phenomenological interaction with the graveyard addresses Gothic tropes of terror and replaces them with sources of beauty and peace. The graveyard itself speaks softly to her with the 'trees making a soft *shhh* sound' (Thompson, 2021: 7) that soothes her when her home is no longer a place of safety and comfort. Melody's unusual relation to this space is a source of self-reflection about her own being as 'weird', a word repeated throughout the novel and a source of Melody's self-consciousness.

Although there is a lightness to this novel, the main adolescent characters – Melody, Matthew, Jake and Hal – all suffer emotionally and sometimes physically and often in relation to adult authority figures. Through most of the novel, Melody is angry at her mother for putting their home up for sale without consulting her. Melody suffers from severe distrust because her father led a double life, living between two families without their knowledge. When he is finally forced to choose between the families, he leaves Melody and her mother. Matthew, Melody's best friend, who struggles with obsessive compulsive disorder, hurts her by spending more time with Jake than with her; Jake, although sometimes nasty to Melody, is severely bullied by Mr Jenkins, the school's physical education teacher; and Hal, whom Melody finds in a graveyard, has been abandoned by his mother due to her mental health issues. These four young people support each other and develop resilience together when adults in their lives fail them.

Melody's home is under siege for most of the novel, so she often seeks refuge in the graveyard and ultimately finds Hal, whose home has ceased to be safe. Melody refutes the idea that graveyards are places of sadness and death, which her mother articulates early in the novel: '"it'll do you good to have a break from that place for a while. It's not healthy, Melody, being surrounded by all that death … all that sadness." It baffled me how anyone could find the graveyard a sad place. To me, it was full of history and beauty and, now, a boy who claimed to be a *spy*' (Thompson, 2021: 49, original emphasis). Melody replaces her mother's idea of death with history and sadness with beauty, aligning with Bakhtin's definition of the space of the chronotope being charged with history. In this space, Melody's beliefs are tested against her mother's ideologies and asserted alongside Hal, whom she befriends and supports.

The novel's denouement pairs Melody and Hal – both of whom are shaped by the actions of their mothers. Melody's mother accepts financial help from Melody's father, so they do not have to sell their house, and Hal's mother is put into a psychiatric hospital where she can receive the medical attention she requires. The novel ends in the graveyard, where Melody, Jake and Matthew are reading a letter from Hal, updating them on his foster parents. Melody reflects, 'I took a long deep breath as I looked around at the beautiful graveyard. I was so incredibly grateful that I didn't have to move away from the place I loved. I was also grateful for the two friends sitting beside me and for my other friend, Hal, living just a letter away' (Thompson, 2021: 202). This conclusion situates Melody's happiness within the graveyard and alongside her friends. Although their future is unknown, their joy is infused with gratitude for existing in this space and with these people.

Unlike Melody's mother in *The Graveyard Riddle*, the parents of the protagonist in J. W. Ocker's *Death and Douglas* (2017) accept death and graveyards as aspects of everyday life. Douglas's parents are third-generation morticians, whose house is only a few streets away from the cemetery. The first chapter establishes Douglas's connection to the cemetery, which he visits 'almost every day' (Ocker, 2017: 9). As in *The Graveyard Riddle*, the cemetery is described as a peaceful place in which to play, a place where:

> Large mausoleums sprang from gentle hills, life-sized statues writhed in grief, tombstones sprouted in hundreds of different shapes, their eloquent epitaphs discussing eternity together. A cold stream cut a thin Styx through the back of the cemetery, where it was more forest than cemetery. Over that stream was a covered bridge where Douglas would play.

(2017: 10)

The personification of the cemetery – of mausoleums springing from gentle hills, of statues writhing in grief and of tombstones whose epitaphs discuss eternity together – suggests it is a place of life, a place that facilitates Douglas's personality through play.

The cemetery shapes Douglas's character, for Douglas's love for the cemetery is second only to his connection to his family and to his friends Lowell and Audrey. This feeling is made explicit early in the novel: 'Douglas loved Cowlmouth Cemetery. It was his park, his backyard, his playground. It was a foundation for his imagination and a forum for all his big questions' (2017: 27). Although the nature of Douglas's 'big questions' is never explicitly stated, the novel's title and the serial-killer plot line imply that Douglas's big questions relate to the nature of evil. As a twelve-year-old who grows up in a funeral home, Douglas sees death as something natural. The serial killer, however, renders death unnatural, and the killer himself shifts from being a man to a monster.

The cemetery offers sanctuary to Douglas and Lowell, who work together and rely upon each other to thrive in the unsafe space of the town outside the cemetery. When Douglas and Lowell learn about the serial killer, they decide to meet in the cemetery to discuss how they might catch him. Focalised through Douglas, the narrative constructs the cemetery as a place of safety, and Douglas's connection to it shapes his emotions:

> Once they entered the towering gothic gates of Cowlmouth Cemetery, Douglas felt safe again. He always did … Cowlmouth Cemetery at night was a particularly special place. This late, he could believe all the stories of monsters that Moss and Feaster fed him as they buried the dead … Sometimes, the stories of monsters scared Douglas a little, not that he'd ever admitted that to anybody, and not so much that it ever stopped him from visiting the cemetery at night.
>
> (2017: 75)

Douglas's sense of safety and fear arises from his relationships with Moss and Feaster – and the stories they tell him – and with Lowell, and the cemetery provides the space and time for these relationships to flourish. The cemetery is a place of protection, despite the stories he has heard about monsters who live there. The monsters that populate Douglas's imagination, however, are not contained in the cemetery. Rather, a human monster roams the town killing people seemingly at random.

Douglas's knowledge of, and relationship with, the cemetery ultimately stops this human monster. When the serial killer chases Douglas and Lowell, they lead him to the cemetery: 'Soon, the large, familiar black gates loomed in front of them. The murderer had made almost the entire town of Cowlmouth seem alien to Douglas and Lowell, but the cemetery – Cowlmouth Cemetery – was their park, their backyard, their playground, their haven' (2017: 188). This description of the cemetery echoes the earlier characterisation (2017: 27), but instead of the cemetery being *his* park, backyard, playground, now it is *their* park, backyard, playground and, in addition, haven. In Douglas's characterisation of the graveyard, he moves from focusing on his singular subjectivity to a sense of self shaped alongside and in relation to Lowell.

In the end, the cemetery frees Douglas, Lowell and the town from danger by providing Douglas the space in which to kill the human monster.

As he hides in the graveyard from the murderer, Douglas ruminates on his understanding of being: 'there, crouched in the snow ... his only company a cemetery full of the dead and a pursuer that wanted him to end up the same way, Douglas did finally think he understood death. ... In that strange calm that only cemeteries have, Douglas realized how much he wanted to live' (2017: 197–8). The cemetery, in its unique calmness, provides Douglas with the space to answer the big questions he has about the relationship between life and death. To Douglas, though, living ultimately means sharing experiences with 'Lowell, his best friend in the whole world, at his side' (2017: 198). To have that life, that ontological exchange with Lowell which defines his being, he must rid his town of the human monster haunting it. To do so, he beckons the man away from Lowell and towards himself. In his pursuit of Douglas, the murderer falls into an open grave and dies, the cemetery thus ending the danger that threatens the lives of Douglas, Lowell and the rest of the town.

As in *Death and Douglas*, in *The Graveyard Girl and the Boneyard Boy* the main character, Drake, and his family are connected to a graveyard when Drake's dad takes a position managing Centralia Cemetery, 'the largest and oldest cement city in the state' (Matthews, 2017: 8). Sixteen-year-old Drake, an outsider in the new high school he attends, is rendered even more of an outsider by his type-one oculocutaneous albinism. As a person with albinism, his skin is 'really *really* pale. Like ghost-status pale' (2017: 9). His ghostly appearance, however, also aligns him with the titular graveyard girl, Scarlet, who actually *is* a ghost, or at least is represented as such until the novel's denouement, which reveals that the grave she has been visiting is that of her twin sister, Hara, while the body of Scarlet herself is on life support. Without going into the details of the rather complicated backstory, the central mystery circulates around uncovering the secret of the car accident that killed Hara and put Scarlet in a coma. This mystery, Drake's love for Scarlet and the expansion of his sense of self to include new-found friends, propel the narrative against the backdrop of the cemetery.

The first time Drake sees Centralia Cemetery he personifies it as a mouth, even while he himself gapes in its presence, each thus being aligned with the other. In this first encounter with the other, Drake sees the cemetery as a part of his being:

I gasped.

Even with my weak eyes I saw, moonlit and white against the deepening indigo of night, the largest cemetery in the state rolling away in every direction before me ... Not so much a graveyard, but a grave-*city*, complete with paved roads and signs naming the streets; ornate Victorian lampposts casting hexagonal pools of warm amber light; towers of marble and stone jutting skyward, dotting the spaces between giant willow trees like ghostly sentinels. And the endless ranks of headstones, row upon row of grey and white and black and brown teeth set in the dark gums of the earth, yawning into the quiet night seemingly forever.

'Wow,' I breathed.

(2017: 26–7, original emphasis)

In this description of the headstones as teeth in the gums of the earth yawning forever, we can see time take on flesh and space charged with time and history, to recall Bakhtin's chronotope. In Drake's gasp and breath, he, too, opens his mouth to the night.

This cemetery is where Drake encounters Scarlet and where their love develops, but it is also a place that shapes his friendship with Sasha, a girl from school who was also Hara's best friend. The first time Sasha comes to Drake's house, they sit on the porch swing overlooking the cemetery: 'The waning moon was doing its thing above Willow's Peak, the headstones so many pale teeth in a black maw. It was anything but bucolic, really. A garden of dead, a forest of buried dreams. Each stone a life lived and lost' (2017: 111). The mouth and teeth in Sasha's presence seem more foreboding, but when Sasha asks if it is ever spooky living by the cemetery, Drake responds, 'People scare me way more than the dead' (2017: 112). This response flags the central conflict in the novel, as Drake admits to his insular nature: he exists mostly alone, without friends and within a family where his parents are always fighting and in which his sister Brie tries to kill him on a regular basis.

Drake's personality changes and develops through his relationship with Scarlet and Sasha and in resistance to the threat from another schoolmate, Calvin. As the novel unfolds, the secret about who was responsible for Hara's death is revealed. Calvin, one of the school's popular students and son of the town's mayor, tried to kill Drake, raped Brie, shot Chase and was responsible for the car crash. In a rather overtly didactic and slightly cringeworthy exchange when Sasha's spirit is reunited with her body so she can finally die in peace, Sasha says to Drake, '"*Live*, Drake Stevenson" ... "Live for your friends, your family. They need you so much. Now more than ever"' (2017: 359). Putting its didacticism aside, the exchange parallels Douglas's revelation, in *Death and Douglas*, that living means doing so in relationships with others, and Drake makes this realisation overt in the epilogue, which takes place in the cemetery. The final scene features Drake sitting next to Scarlet's headstone, taking out a notebook and beginning to write. The narrative thus concludes with Drake's being defined through the Gothic chronotope of the cemetery, informed by the presence of Scarlet and ultimately asserted through his own writing.

I conclude this chapter with an analysis of Aiden Thomas's *Cemetery Boys* (2020), a young adult novel in which the graveyard chronotope intersects with ontological liminality in the most overt assertion of intersectional being as existence and resistance. The main character, sixteen-year-old Yadriel, is a transgender gay man, whose best friend Maritza is the only vegan in their 'brujx' community. As friends who are both labelled as 'black sheep' (Thomas, 2020: 13) within their communities, Yadriel and Maritza develop together and in resistance against the adult authorities who pressure them to conform to the ideologies of their community. Because Yadriel was born a girl, he is not allowed to go through the brujo ritual or to partake in brujo responsibilities because these rituals and responsibilities are traditionally reserved for men only (2020: 16).

The novel begins with Yadriel defining his relationship to the cemetery and asserting his resistant being. The first paragraph reads in full, 'Yadriel wasn't technically trespassing because he'd lived in the cemetery his whole life. But breaking into the church was definitely crossing the moral-ambiguity line' (2020: 1). Yadriel and Maritza break into the church, so Yadriel can perform his 'quinces ceremony' – a Latinx ritual to celebrate a girl's fifteenth birthday and her transition from girlhood into womanhood – which his family postponed indefinitely because of his trans identity. For Yadriel to prove himself a brujo, he must perform a ceremony in which Lady Death gives him her blessing and 'ties their magic to their chosen conduit, their portaje' (2020: 9). For men, the portaje is often a dagger, which they require to cut the thread that binds a spirit to their body. Yadriel and Maritza successfully perform the ceremony, in which Yadriel receives Lady Death's blessing and learns he has magic, but during the process he learns that Miguel, a brujo in their community, has died and his body has gone missing.

Yadriel decides to find Miguel's body to prove himself a brujo, but instead comes upon the tether of another spirit. Using his magic, Yadriel summons the spirit, hoping to thus find Miguel's. Instead, he summons Julian Diaz, a boy who goes to the same high school as Yadriel but has seemingly been murdered. Solving the mystery of Julian's and Miguel's deaths and the developing romance between Yadriel and Julian drive the rest of the narrative. Together, Yadriel, Julian and Maritza discover that Yadriel's uncle, Catriz, has been performing an ancient human sacrifice ceremony to provide him with powers unseen in their community for thousands of years. When they stop the ceremony and reunite Julian's spirit and body and therein bring him back to life, Yadriel's father and the community finally accept and honour Yadriel as a great brujo.

Since Yadriel has lived his whole life in a cemetery, his entire being has been overtly shaped by it. As with Thompson's Melody and Matthews's Drake, Yadriel's ontological connection to the graveyard has often been labelled as 'weird'. In opposition to this categorisation, the bond between Yadriel and Julian first becomes overt when Julian learns that Yadriel lives in a graveyard:

> 'Yo, you live in a graveyard?' Julian asked in bewilderment.
>
> Yadriel shifted the weight of his backpack. He was used to the strange looks and laughs that came when people at school found out he was the weird kid who lived in a cemetery. Throw in being openly trans, and he was very used to stares and jokes. 'Yeah,' he said, anticipating a similar reaction.
>
> Instead, a wicked grin curled Julian's lips. 'Sick,' he said, nodding his approval.
>
> (2020: 69)

In this exchange, the graveyard initiates a conversation that strengthens the connection between Yadriel and Julian, with Julian's approval reasserting Yadriel's sense of self. This scene becomes especially important when Yadriel later repeats almost the exact wording to Julian about an earlier incident at school, in which he is 'the weird kid who was talking to himself, who *also* lived in a cemetery *and* had no friends!' (2020: 94, original emphasis). Julian's expression of admiration towards Yadriel for living in a cemetery thus recasts, but does not eliminate, Yadriel's subjectivity, which he characterises as being weird and alone.

In the novel's epilogue, however, Yadriel's being is transformed, so he is no longer the weird kid who lives in the cemetery and has no friends. Instead, he is a celebrated brujo who runs through the cemetery, holding the hand of his beloved:

> Yadriel raced through the cemetery, pulling Julian along after him. Julian's hand was warm, his grip strong, his palm calloused. As they ran for the church, Julian easily kept up as they wove between headstones. Yadriel looked over at him. Julian flashed him a cheek-aching smile and squeezed his hand. Laughter bubbled past Yadriel's lips as he squeezed it back. He was there – he was real – and Yadriel would take any chance to grab him that he could.
>
> (2020: 333)

The first paragraph of the novel places Yadriel in the cemetery engaging in a morally ambiguous act, but this first paragraph of the epilogue shows Yadriel in full flight, celebratory and joyous, accepted by his community and openly expressing his desire and connection to Julian. Yadriel asserts his agency through his relationship with Julian, and the cemetery provides the space and time for their positively inflected synchronous selves.

In each of these graveyard narratives, young people have developed their personalities intertwined with an Other, and the cemetery has been the site of this relationship. As a liminal space in which life and death intermingle, in which time exists in the present, extends backwards into history and reaches forward into optimistic futures, the graveyard is no longer horrific. Instead of being a place of sadness, it facilitates love. Rather than being a site of terror, it offers peace. For young people who are ostracised for being weird or different or for challenging adult authority, the graveyard provides a space in which they learn to understand themselves more fully. Like many of the liminal spaces in YA Gothic narratives, the graveyard provides a place for young people to transform their sense of self. If, as Chloé Germaine Buckley argues, Gothic fiction in the twenty-first century refigures the child 'as a nomad, whose journey across an expansive terrain engages with, rather than rejects, an irredeemably corrupt world' (2017: 199), then the fiction I analyse in this chapter continues these journeys and suggests the graveyard is a place in which to repose and reflect along the way. As stories that anticipate a flourishing future for their protagonists, these narratives resist closed endings. Rather, they feature young people in action – playing music, reading letters, writing stories, embracing and being embraced by friends. Graveyards, like adolescence, may be characterised by their liminality, but they are places in which to linger rather than to rush.

References

Bakhtin, Mikhail M (1990) [1981] 'Forms of Time and of the Chronotope in the Novel: Notes toward a Historical Poetics', in Michael Holquist (ed.), *The Dialogic Imagination: Four Essays*, trans. Caryl Emerson and Michael Holquist (Austin: University of Texas Press), pp. 84–258.
Buckley, Chloé Germaine (2017) *Twenty-First-Century Children's Gothic: From the Wanderer to the Nomadic Subject* (Edinburgh: Edinburgh University Press).
Cohen, Sigi (2015) *My Dead Bunny*, illus. James Foley (London: Walker Books).
Erickson, Anne K. Burke (2022) 'Liminality in Neil Gaiman's *The Graveyard Book* (2008)', in Aoileann Ní Éigeartaigh (ed.), *The Graveyard in Literature: Liminality and Social Critique* (Cambridge: Cambridge Scholars Press), pp. 189–204.
Gaiman, Neil (2008) *The Graveyard Book* (London: Bloomsbury).
Matthews, Martin (2017) *The Graveyard Girl and the Boneyard Boy* (Castroville: Black Rose Writing).
McCaw, Amy (2021) *Mina and the Undead* (Preston: uclanpublishing).
Moruzi, Kristine and Michelle J. Smith (2021) 'Introduction', in Michelle J. Smith and Kristine Moruzi (eds), *Young Adult Gothic Fiction: Monstrous Selves/ Monstrous Others* (Cardiff: University of Wales Press), pp. 1–14.
Ocker, J. W. (2017) *Death and Douglas* (New York: Sky Pony).
Sainsbury, Lisa (2021) *Metaphysics of Children's Literature: Climbing Fuzzy Mountains* (London: Bloomsbury).
Smith, Michelle J. (2017) 'Dead and Ghostly Children in Contemporary Literature for Young People', in Carol Margaret Davison (ed.), *The Gothic and Death* (Manchester: Manchester University Press), pp. 191–203.
Spooner, Catherine (2017) *Post-Millennial Gothic: Comedy, Romance and the Rise of Happy Gothic* (London: Bloomsbury).

Terry, Laura (2017) *Graveyard Shakes* (London: Scholastic).
Thomas, Aiden (2020) *Cemetery Boys* (New York: Macmillan).
Thompson, Lisa (2021) *The Graveyard Riddle* (London: Scholastic).
Wills, Deborah and Amy Bright (2011) ' "On the Cusp": Liminality and Adolescence in Arthur Slade's *Dust*, Bill Richardson's *After Hamelin*, and Kit Pearson's *Awake and Dreaming*', *Studies in Canadian Literature/Études en littérature canadienne*, 36:1, 100–23.

17

The graveyard level: anachronism, Anglo-Japanese semiotics and the cruel nightmare of resurrection in early horror video games

James T. McCrea

As each chapter in this collection demonstrates, graveyards have influenced cultural expressions throughout various media on a global scale. The arena of video gaming is no different, as indicated by several pop-culture websites that rank the noteworthy appearances of video game graveyards from the 1980s to the 2010s (Barr, 2016; Erhard, 2022; Nuan, 2015; Turi, 2014; Wolfman, 2020). Affectionately, Roger Barr of I-Mockery.com (2016) recounts his love of seeing graveyards in any video game, claiming, 'Sometimes it's unexpected, other times the graveyard fits in perfectly with the atmosphere with the rest of the game, but regardless, the spooky visuals have made for some truly memorable gaming moments over the years.' As video games gradually permeate critical discourse, the myriad representations of graves within them offer rich resources for criticisms dealing with intermediality and transnationality, as well as a salient opportunity to examine the global and postmodern Gothic of the last forty years.

Although there are indeed numerous depictions of graves throughout the history of video gaming, the graveyards detailed here illustrate the development of a distinctly Gothic environment in Japanese-designed games and its subsequent integration into Western reception. Japanese designers used imagery that would have been familiar to Western audiences to create anachronistic depictions of medieval Europe, decorating their medieval graveyard scenes with post-medieval tombstones. This phenomenon echoes the deliberate anachronisms of early Gothic novelists such as Horace Walpole, Ann Radcliffe and Clara Reeve, who placed their contemporary eighteenth-century narratives against medieval backdrops (Baldick and Mighall, 2012; Farnell, 2011). Such graveyards first appeared in arcades and home consoles in the 1980s, manifesting well into games released in 2022. Conceptually, these graveyard levels pertain to the functions of death and resurrection in gameplay narratives signified by Western tombstones. Accordingly, this chapter examines *Makaimura* (*Ghosts 'n Goblins*, 1985–2022), the early *Akumajō Dracula* games (*Castlevania*, 1986–91) and the *Dark Souls* series (2011–16), all of which feature anachronistic graveyard environments populated with endlessly spawning monsters and ever-mounting gameplay difficulty leading to frequent player death, which is often negated by the player's own inevitable reappearance within the graveyard environment. For ease of readership, the games in the discussion that follows will be referred to by their English name.

All these games take place in settings that depict or suggest medieval Europe, complete with ruined castles, armoured knights and antiquated weaponry. Inevitably, players encounter graveyards that often appear at or near the start of the game. These areas are populated with upright-standing headstones that often bear crucifixes engraved on their face or projecting from the top of the stone. Such headstones would be familiar to English-speaking audiences, as they have been used in burial grounds throughout Western Europe and North America consistently from the seventeenth century onwards (Ariès, 2008: 268; Laqueur, 2015: 141). Ergo, vertical headstones and crucifixes readily evoke an atmosphere of death, burial and commemoration to Western audiences.

However, the appearance of post-medieval tombstones in narratives based on medieval Europe is historically inaccurate. Contrasting with their modern counterparts, medieval graveyards featured bare commemoration, occasionally consisting of wooden crucifix-like markers (Gilchrist, 2012: 204). These markers were likely temporary indicators of burials within the churchyard, preventing new inhumations from disturbing existing graves (Daniell, 1997: 146–7). Medieval graves were largely temporary in and of themselves, as gravekeepers would routinely exhume fully decomposed corpses and place them in ossuaries or elsewhere throughout the church grounds (Ariès, 2008: 54). The inhumed body, cleansed of flesh with only bone remaining, may have signified the soul's successful passage through purgatory (Ariès, 2008: 54; Litten, 2007: 8). In other words, medieval graveyards were transient rather than commemorative, acting primarily as consecrated ground for dead parishioners to decompose in. They had no need for the densely clustered upright headstones that are more commonly associated with cemeteries from the eighteenth and nineteenth centuries, which were places intended to permanently memorialise the deceased (Laqueur, 2015: 279–80). A conceptual incongruity thus arises, rendering the depicted graveyard an ahistorical fusion of Western imagery that merges the medieval and the modern. Graveyards in the games discussed thus become anachronistic within the scope of the medievalist fantasy narratives that they occupy.

One of the earliest examples occurs in *Ghosts 'n Goblins* (1985), directed by Tokura Fujiwara, which follows a pseudo-Arthurian knight – whose name is in fact Arthur – in a quest to rescue his bride after she was kidnapped by a flying devil while they were relaxing in a graveyard. This graveyard functions as the opening stage of each game in the series, pitting the player against endlessly respawning zombies rising from the base of headstones, which closely resemble the post-medieval funerary sculptures previously described (Figure 17.1). Furthermore, the series is notorious for its brutal difficulty, which was initially intended for arcade audiences who were required to spend money to play the game (Hill, 2014). As such, any emotional investment players may experience becomes even more costly with the requisite financial transaction necessary to continue gameplay. Pursuant to this notion, *Ghosts 'n Goblins* features an advanced level of difficulty from the very beginning of the game, which is enhanced by a false ending forcing the player to complete the entire game a second time in order to unlock a true ending. Because of this, completing *Ghosts 'n Goblins* in its original arcade setting required not only tremendous skill but also adequate time and money. When *Ghosts 'n Goblins* was ported to home consoles,

Figure 17.1 Early horror video games like *Ghosts 'n Goblins* (1985) feature upright tombstones resembling modern graveyard architecture despite their medieval settings.

Fujiwara kept these challenging gameplay elements intact. Players could acquire the game and play it as much as they wanted without spending money, thus invalidating the functions originally served by the game's difficulty. Through the game's built-in repetition, gamers in the arcade and at home would experience the first level numerous times through any given playthrough, since both winning and losing the game would force players to restart the entire game in the graveyard. Failure and success are met with largely equal reward in *Ghosts 'n Goblins*, a feature that links to thanatological concepts of death and resurrection, as the player is very clearly killed on-screen by being reduced to skeletal remains, and yet always seems to rematerialise in a burial ground. These concepts, however, seem to be ancillary to Fujiwara's desire to create an arcade game with Western European horror themes (Shmuplations, 2015). Thus, the graveyard is essentially imported wholesale along with castles, armoured knights and bat-winged devils as neo-medievalisms of the 1980s video game scene.

Another early horror game featuring anachronistic graveyards is *Castlevania*, which concerns the intergenerational exploits of a family whose lineage is devoted to killing vampires. Although director Hitoshi Akamatsu incorporated several Western European elements in the first three games of the series, graveyards are absent from the first entry, which takes place entirely on the grounds of a semi-ruined medieval castle belonging to a fictionalised version of Count Dracula. However, its sequels *Castlevania II: Simon's Quest* (1987) and *Castlevania III: Dracula's Curse* (1989) used post-medieval, modern graveyards as treacherous environments featuring undead enemies that respawn in a similar manner to the zombies in *Ghosts 'n Goblins* (Figure 17.2). In contrast to its pseudo-Arthurian counterpart, *Castlevania* takes place in a real-world location, with each entry depicting a specific historical era of Transylvania – the first two games take place in 1691 and 1698 respectively, while *Castlevania III* is set in 1476. Hence, the first two games evince no anachronism in terms of tombstone aesthetics. However, *Castlevania III* places the player in graveyards with nearly identical headstones at the end of the first level, a location featuring constant streams of zombies and a large skeleton blocking the player's progress. This displays the ease with which Japanese designers reuse similar Western imagery despite the centuries-long historical gap in their narratives. Moreover, the ahistoricity of its graveyards seems to have made the *Castlevania* series more memorable than erroneous, as indicated by its frequent appearance in gaming journals' best-of lists (Barr, 2016; Wolfman, 2020). Similarly, *Castlevania* further reinforces the association between graveyards and infinite undead foes originally witnessed in *Ghosts 'n Goblins*.

Regarding transnationality, Martin Picard (2009) effectively delineates the intercultural exchanges taking place between Japanese and English-speaking

Figure 17.2 The skeletal enemies in *Castlevania II: Simon's Quest* (1987) populate graveyards, adding a sinister element to an environment formerly associated with piety and ancestor worship.

cultures in the video game marketplace, nullifying antiquated interpretations of Orientalism that have long plagued assessments of Japanese cultural expressions. Essentially, by attempting to isolate distinct qualities in Japanese cultural expressions that embody certain aspects of 'Japaneseness', one risks overlooking the ways in which foreign culture influences Japanese creators. Moreover, Picard reminds us that many horror games made in Japan are specifically intended for foreign markets, attesting to a sense of globality demonstrated by Japanese game designers (2009: 99) To this end, Picard emphasises the danger in examining video games for these qualities, considering the agency Western audiences have on the development of such commodities:

> To this day, people outside Japan maintain a great interest in its culture, specificity, and originality. Since the early twentieth century, both Westerners and Japanese scholars have tried to define this specificity, in order to characterize what they called the 'Japaneseness.' This concept continues to be valued by people interested in Japanese (popular) culture. It is the idea that brings many video game fans and critics to talk about true 'Japanese' video games or films (as for JRPG and J-Horror) and to be inclined to think that video game designers can create a game 'Japanese style' – even if the game has been created by a Western studio ... Part of this characterization came from the alleged

originality or 'uniqueness' of Japanese culture ... This has led to a specific perception of a cultural and national Japanese identity.

(Picard, 2009: 101)

Paradoxically, the unique quality of Japanese cultural expression seems to rely on creators' willingness to incorporate signifiers and aesthetics from foreign countries in their own output. Wendy Siuyu Wong (2006: 36–40) describes the deliberate attempt by Japanese industries to market media that could better appeal to foreign countries by fostering a sense of cultural vacancy in their own products. In other words, by omitting as many Japanese signifiers as possible from creative expressions such as manga and anime, Japanese distributors would enter foreign markets with greater ease. This process began with neighbouring countries China and the Koreas before shifting to a global scale, having first tested their culturally indistinct output with cultures whose proximity indicated similar values compared to Western audiences (Wong, 2006: 29–37). Picard (2009: 102–3) posits a similar globalised trajectory for video game distribution, seeing Japanese companies develop games with as few internal cultural signifiers as possible so as to better engage with, and facilitate, reception among English speakers. Consequently, the search for 'Japaneseness' in Japanese media risks becoming reductive via disregarding Japan's history of syncretism with global audiences.

As the graveyard level's anachronisms illustrate, the attempt to produce material that belies Japanese influence can lead to incongruous clashes of imagery and concept. Paul Martin (2011) further describes the process by which Japanese game designers utilise aspects of foreign cultures in order to eschew 'Japaneseness', resulting in complex semiotic instances that create polyvalent signifiers:

> At the level of representation, designers may use representations of space and place that already carry with them expressive baggage which, when used as part of a game, combines with other aspects of the game and with the context of consumption to give rise to unpredicted possibilities of interpretation ... Games are particularly prone to taking characters, images and generic conventions from different media and combining them in sometimes unusual ways. Each of these images carries with it its own political and interpretive baggage. This baggage is not jettisoned due to its new context, though it is transformed as it sparks off and reacts to the other images, themes and mechanics that make up the game. What emerges in this process is the potential for readings that the designers may not have intended and may or may not subscribe to, but are no less legitimate for that.
>
> (Martin, 2011: 18–19)

Martin describes a form of aberrant decoding – a semiotic phenomenon occurring during the transmission of meaning through different contexts and/or audiences (Munteanu, 2012: 230–7). In other words, unique meanings accrue arbitrarily as viewers encounter images and scenarios without knowing anything about their original context, leading them to interpret the arrangement of symbols on a purely independent, if not idiosyncratic, basis. Reinforcing Martin's claim, the results of such uninformed readings are not necessarily illegitimate due to the unintentional nature of the accrued meanings, as the viewer and the recipient may not have access to contextual information informing them of intended significance. Effectively, they do the best they can with what they are shown. This appears to be what governs Japanese creators utilising Western graveyard imagery in their game design, given the propensity for chronological inaccuracy.

Considering the ahistorical nature of these game environments, Gothic themes develop automatically through a comingling of anachronism, recursion and thanatological themes. However, not every Western graveyard appearing in a Japanese-developed game is inherently anachronistic or Gothic by association. For instance, *The Simpsons* arcade game (1991) features a graveyard level that borrows from the show itself, whose Halloween-themed episode 'The Treehouse of Horror' (2.3, 1990) features the names of cast and crew emblazoned upon weathered headstones during the opening title scrawl. Furthermore, the game displays visual cues from John Landis's music video for Michael Jackson's song 'Thriller' (1982), featuring zombies that mimic Jackson's distinctive choreography. When Sega developed video game versions of Michael Jackson's film *Moonwalker* (1988), each game contained graveyard levels referencing Landis's music video. These are cases where anachronism is not a factor, as Western audiences would be accustomed to seeing the types of tombstones displayed in each game just as they exist in everyday life. Rather, such examples warrant further enquiry into the role of video games in intermediality, as they display how several forms of media can interact with and influence one another. The fact that the graveyard informs these correlations may be tangential in the overall arena of intermedial criticism, but it is worth noting how it functions as a connective tissue that effectively binds several unrelated media expressions.

Japan's unique position as a fairly recent negotiator in global culture has been assessed by several scholars in terms of relevance in contributing to what Glennis Byron calls the 'globalgothic' (2013: 4–10). Rather pertinently, James Campbell examines the aesthetic interchanges occurring in the *Silent Hill* (1999–) games, which comfortably incorporate fog-shrouded aesthetics of North American horror writers Washington Irving and Stephen King into a narrative with equal basis in Japanese horror literature (2016: 169–72). As a result, *Silent Hill* represents an intentional blend of transnational horror elements that blurs the distinction between North American and Japanese Gothic. A similar assessment of the graveyard level reveals similar indicators of Japan's participation in the global Gothic, with the major difference being a mythical reinterpretation of medieval Europe. This conflation of medievalist and modern imagery in Japanese game design may be linked to Japan's lengthy isolation from the rest of the world, but cultural isolation is only partially responsible given the profusion of Western influence that has been flooding into Japanese culture since the isolation of the country ended in 1854 (Iguchi, 2010: 65–6). A thorough understanding of medieval Europe was largely absent from Japanese scholarship until the early twentieth century, when Noburu Orui introduced the study of Western medieval art to Japan with the establishment of Tohoku University's medieval history department in 1924 (Kido, 1995: 80). Orui's first major contribution to Western medieval studies, *Seiyo-Chusei no Bunka* (*A Culture of Western Middle Ages*, 1952), focused on the artistic, literary and intellectual aspects of medieval life. Prior to Orui, Japanese historians assessed Europe rather brusquely as a sequence of economic triumphs, which fostered an academic understanding of the Western Middle Ages as a geography of success without depicting the human element (Kido, 1995: 79–80). Thus, the aesthetic qualities of Western medievalism were rendered invisible within this academic sequence of fiscal and industrial assessments on the part of Japanese scholars. Japanese scholarship was largely bereft of widespread, viable descriptions of medieval Europe prior to Orui's contributions in the mid twentieth century. Given very recent attention paid to historically accurate Western medieval aesthetics in the history of Japanese scholarship, the anachronistic conflation of modern-era graveyards and medievalist imagery becomes understandable. Chronological distinctions throughout Western art and history could easily become blurred in the perspective of Japanese game designers whose exposure to medieval European history may have been limited.

Anachronisms warrant critical enquiry since they may indicate aberrant decoding rather than simple historical error. Cristinel Munteanu (2012: 233) asserts that misinterpretation also occurs when signifiers are removed from their original context and subsequently lost in a new contextual arena. The transmission of Western horror and medieval iconography from English-speaking reception to Japanese audiences and back again breaches language barriers, which most likely results in aberrant semiosis. Similarly, Fujiwara's wholesale importation of Western aesthetics in *Ghosts 'n Goblins* suggests that this phenomenon is at play, as does Akamatsu's conflation of vampires and graveyards in *Castlevania*. However, Japanese game designers may have inherited anachronisms by virtue of adopting Gothic themes that have long been subject to deliberate ahistoricity. Chris Baldick and Robert Mighall refer to the anachronism as a salient element of the Gothic that is often misunderstood as erroneous and thus warrants critical re-examination:

> Gothic Criticism here disastrously misunderstands the motivations of Gothic fictional historicity and its purposeful deployment of anachronistic emphases to structure its narrative effects. The anachronism resides principally in the evident 'modernity' of the typical heroes and heroines who feature in novels with 'historical' settings. As has often been remarked, these characters think and feel very much like their original readers and are manifestly out of place in their purportedly 'historical' settings ... Far from indicating negligence or somnambulism, this chronological discrepancy is the prime motivation of these narratives, and that which provides their central dramatic interest.
>
> (Baldick and Mighall, 2012: 378)

The graveyard as a Gothic aesthetic thus becomes a source of drama via anachronism, but the situations described by Baldick and Mighall are altered by the context of the graveyard level through aberrant decoding as well as the narrative limitations of early video games. The protagonists of *Ghosts 'n Goblins* and *Castlevania* are largely blank slates, bereft of even the most minimal dialogue to communicate internal thoughts. Unlike the protagonists of Gothic novels, they cannot directly communicate their own modernity – that is, if any exists in their character to begin with. Hence, the actions of these player-characters largely determine their relationship with the environment and the narrative itself, which become necessary indicators of anachronism. Perron describes the actions available to players of early examples of horror games as limitations that separate them from the psychological terror of the survival horror games they would inspire in decades to follow:

> The player-characters can punch, kick, throw knives and lances, use a whip, or wield the sword to eliminate the opponents. The main actional modality is the execution, especially since rolling, falling, and flying objects must be dodged, pits must be crossed, moving platforms might be reached via coordinated jumps, etc. But none of that promotes fear.
>
> (Perron, 2018: 164)

Perron's approximation of gameplay in early horror games demonstrates the relevance of Gothic aesthetics in communicating horror, as according to him nothing within the gameplay itself is capable of creating a sense of horror. In a way, anachronism forces the hand of creating Gothic horror in early video games, much in the same way anachronism defined the early Gothic novels of the late eighteenth century. Therefore, Western Gothic becomes a product of anachronism, and influences its reception by normalising the synthesis of historically distinct aesthetics. This is no different regarding the Japanese video games described, all of which utilise prominent anachronisms to maintain identifiable Gothic atmospheres.

The placement of medieval characters in a graveyard setting only further refines the Gothic's potential thanatological gravity, since the past is reinforced by close symbolic proximity to the dead, buried and resurrected. *Castlevania* shares this similarity with *Ghosts 'n' Goblins* in that both feature monsters perpetually attacking players in their respective graveyard levels. However, *Castlevania* contains far more undead creatures than *Ghosts 'n Goblins*, and this results in many of its monsters displaying overtly skeletal qualities. Even corporeal zombies and incorporeal phantoms bear obvious skeletal features, with ambulant human skeletons appearing throughout most of the games hurling their own bones at the player. The skeleton's proximity to the grave is palpable, as the decomposed body will almost invariably leave behind a clean skeleton so long as the environmental conditions of the burial support proper bodily decomposition (Mays, 2010: 22). Such representations of the reanimated body distort the ancestral significance of the Western churchyard while tacitly mocking Christian resurrection, creating not only a salient enemy to *Castlevania's* vampire hunter protagonist, but also placing the action in a distinctly European climate rife with cognates of the Christian churchyard while visually citing the *danse macabre*. Since many of these skeletal enemies respawn indefinitely, the concept of resurrection becomes linked to advanced stages of corporeal decay, thus bolstering the Gothic horror atmosphere of the graveyard level. Furthermore, Dracula's own reanimation in each game acts as the tacit catalyst for the plagues of skeletal undead, reinforcing the inversion of divine resurrection by positing Dracula as the antithesis of Christ in a videoludic cognate of Stoker's novel – itself a product of intentional ahistoricity. Hence, the Gothic manifests in the pixelated shadow cast by *Castlevania's* Dracula, revealing itself through anachronism, threat of (un)death and the aura of the grave.

Resurrection becomes an integral story element in a twenty-first-century update on the Gothic in *Dark Souls*, a series that utilises graveyard aesthetics and unending recursion in a way that integrates the funerary motifs from early horror games as intentional design elements reinforcing the design of the game universe. Instead of being design limitations stemming from the context of arcade game development, player death and recursion evoke philosophical narratives focusing on eschatology, futility and individual agency that encourage repeated player failure. It is also crucial to note that the player-character is undead in each game, and thus also subject to unending resurrection. Rather than ending the game after several deaths, players are invited to continue gameplay until they overcome the game's ever-mounting difficulty. In *Dark Souls*, players encounter headstones at the precipice near the end of the opening stage, a medieval prison populated with other undead humans and guarded by enormous demons. Players are then transported to a central hub linking several areas together, one of which is a graveyard strewn with headstones and scattered human bones. Wandering too close to the bones causes them to reassemble into animated skeletons which follow and attack the protagonist. Destroying the skeletons offers fleeting relief, as they reassemble again to continue their assault in a similar fashion to the undead enemies infesting the graveyards in *Ghosts 'n Goblins* and *Castlevania*. The feature reappeared in *Dark Souls III* (2016), where a graveyard filled with zombie hordes is located outside the Cathedral of the Deep. Interminable resurrection for the player-character persists throughout the series but also applies to the benevolent non-player characters in *Dark Souls II* (2014), who are replaced with an upright headstone when killed. Players can engage with the phantom of deceased non-player characters when interacting with their tombstones as though they remain alive. Through these unique gameplay constructs, the *Dark Souls* series reinvents player death as a conceptual element endemic to the home console rather than a relic of the arcade era, transforming a gameplay mechanic that is merely expected into a conceptual reinforcement of the series' fixation on death and resurrection.

This distinctly thanatological narrative reaches a pitch in *Dark Souls III*, where funerary sculpture proliferates throughout the entire setting. Headstones protrude from the architecture in clusters throughout the opening and surround the game's central hub, while every subsequent level features headstones, coffins and other funerary objects scattered throughout. These objects underline the game's plot involving the resurrection of several powerful entities known as Lords of Cinder, whose deaths are necessary to stave off a cataclysmic event that has already begun – and may have been occurring since time immemorial (Figure 17.3). The player is also resurrected for the sole purpose of slaying the Lords of Cinder, and each of these entities – including the player – can be seen emerging from coffins during the game's opening cinematics. From the outset, *Dark Souls III* establishes a systemic cycle of life and death wherein resurrection and murder become opposing forces that maintain the persistence of the universe. The omnipresent tombstones reflect the narrative's thanatological gravity by effectively signifying that the game world itself is a symbolic graveyard rife with the dead, the dying and the resurrected coexisting forever in dismal recursion.

In each of the video game series discussed, players originate within or near environments evoking a readily identifiable graveyard aesthetics. This pattern becomes noteworthy considering the notorious difficulty associated with each series, effectively increasing the likelihood of player death through repeated engagement. Ludologist Jesper Juul describes a rather utilitarian approach to death in video games as an essential element providing players

Figure 17.3 Tombstones permeate the world of *Dark Souls III* (2016), depicting a universe reliant on death and resurrection replete with corpse-like foes.

with an obstacle to overcome (2009: 237–40). However, Dawn Stobbart posits the value of player death in horror video games as a conceptual storytelling device, allowing players to re-examine their own participation in a given narrative through their own death or the deaths of other in-game entities (2019: 176–87). *Dark Souls* explores this directly through its narrative of players perpetuating a doomed form of existence via constant death and resurrection, but a retroactive assessment of *Ghosts 'n Goblins* and *Castlevania* leads to similar concerns about the role of dying players. In *Ghosts 'n Goblins*, how does Arthur's corpse contribute to the undead-infested graveyard in which he dies repeatedly? How many of the player's ancestors haunt the burial grounds of *Castlevania*? What is the nature of a world where dying is temporary? While most video games feature failure states and player death, the games in question effectively establish a digital necrogeography that allows death to be questioned as a conceptual element rather than a gameplay function.

Although this chapter has considered only three video game series, it is important to note that the relevance of graveyard levels persists even in the newest crop of independent games on a global scale. Revisiting his love for video game graveyards, Barr worked with Jacob West to develop *Grave Chase* (2017), which combines numerous elements of gaming culture, cinematic horror and science fiction in a narrative that takes place entirely in graveyards. Brazilian designers Danilo Dias and Thais Weiler incorporate ruined graveyards with nightmarish-looking respawning zombies in their dark fantasy/medievalist *Odallus: The Dark Call* (2015), mirroring the aesthetics and gameplay style of early *Castlevania* entries. In retelling the Albigensian Crusade in *L'Abbaye des Morts* (2010), Spanish developer Juan Antonio Becerra surrounds the game's titular abbey with upright headstones, further fictionalising the plight of the Cathars in thirteenth-century France while skeletal monks wander restlessly in tunnels below the burial grounds. Most tellingly, Russian developer Sviatoslav Cherkasov's *Graveyard Keeper* (2018) self-referentially touts itself as 'the most inaccurate medieval cemetery management sim of the year'. Cherkasov bolsters this claim by constructing a time travel simulation game placing a modern-day man in the role of a sexton within a fabricated vision of medieval Europe replete with post-medieval tombstones and a talking skull companion. Each of these games advances the cultural significance of intentionally anachronistic graveyards while revealing how Japanese game design has permeated global gaming culture. Rather saliently, these games are also anachronistic in their own design, as they faithfully replicate aesthetics from games developed in the 1980s using modern development tools. By releasing video games well into the late 2010s that intentionally resemble games made nearly forty years prior, developers register the cultural impact that designers such as Fujiwara and Akamatsu made upon a global audience, perhaps even unintentionally creating a recurring neo-Gothic format predicated upon games featuring graveyard levels. The cultural syncretism demonstrated in graveyard aesthetics manifests in developers comfortably incorporating anachronism and recursion in order to evoke Gothic horror throughout both independent and mainstream games.

Current developments reveal an intensification of this influence, as showcased in *Elden Ring* (2022) – a joint effort between *Dark Souls* developer Hidetaka Miyazaki and author George R. R. Martin – which features a post-medieval graveyard occupied by skeletons armed with medieval armaments (Figure 17.4). This collaboration between two noteworthy creators of medieval dark fantasy narratives expounds upon the eschatological content Miyazaki infused into *Dark Souls* through his usage of Western European funerary sculpture. Elden Ring's starting location of Limgrave takes its namesake quite literally, as colossal fragments of upright headstones are seen throughout the entire continent, embedded into mountains and jutting out from cliffsides. Moreover, normal-sized tombstones in scattered graveyards throughout the expansive game universe signal the presence of reanimated skeletons known as 'Those Who Live in Death', whose consistent corporeal revival acts as a desecrated foil to the resurrective powers that keep players from permanently dying in-game. Ultimately, the player, having been resurrected by the matriarchal goddess Queen Marika the Eternal, embodies an

Figure 17.4 Skeletal enemies resurface in *Elden Ring* (2022), reinforcing the graveyard's agency in warping negotiations between the living and dead.

expected rebirth, while the reanimated skeletons seem to occur by proxy to decay itself, rising from the slain corpse of Queen Marika's son Godwyn the Golden. Several non-player characters in *Elden Ring* devote themselves to obliterating these aberrant undead, whose source of unlife is the festering corpse of a deity whose body is actively spreading throughout the world like a fungus. Others, like Fia the Deathbed Companion, posit that these forms of undead are no different from the player-characters themselves, and have every right to benefit from being able to resurrect themselves. The main difference between these undead and the player is the player's role in maintaining a perpetual cycle of dying and resurrecting to keep the world moving. In contrast, 'Those Who Live in Death' exist outside the expected cycle, which is enough to construct and figure them as atrocities. In *The Hour of Our Death* (2008), Phillipe Ariès devotes much of his text to cultural attitudes to death in terms of expectation, with an expected death via old age being easier to handle than an unexpected death such as a murder. *Elden Ring* takes a step in a different direction by examining the reactions to expected and unexpected resurrections after death, using the graveyard as a crucible for such reactions. Consequently, the inversion of resurrection associated with undead in early horror games becomes an investigation of the nature of existence in a universe where dying is merely a setback. The world, embodying death itself, becomes a graveyard.

If nothing else, this examination should demonstrate how readily cultures with few shared similarities will communicate in visual media, demonstrated here by Japan's integration of Western imagery and the West's own unquestioning embrace of that very integration. Pertinent to this volume, the specific focus on funerary aesthetics reveals the development of a uniquely transnational Gothic that emerged from Japan in the 1980s and became an international phenomenon following the turn of the millennium. Ultimately, the development of the graveyard level from an incidental environment and a treacherous inversion of Christian resurrection in early horror video games into an intentional signifier of recursion and thanatology effectively mirrors Gothic narratives in a uniquely postmodern way that seems dependent upon anachronism to flourish. The graveyard accomplishes this twofold: primarily by being doubly familiar in cultural reception as both a Gothic icon and a classic video game motif, but also through its inherent association with death and commemoration in real life. Therein, the dead lie beneath the surface in one way or another, whether in body, in soul or in memory alone. Philosophical concerns about the nature of death and rebirth have the capacity to spring from video games as a medium dependent upon repeated engagement punctuated by failure, and the proximity to burial grounds only encourages such thought. In the Gothic graveyard, the nature of life and death might just be reversed. Watch your step.

References

Ariès, Philippe (2008) [1981] *The Hour of Our Death*. trans. Helen Weaver (Oxford: Oxford University Press).
Baldick, Chris and Robert Mighall (2012) 'Gothic Criticism', in David Punter (ed.), *A New Companion to The Gothic* (Sussex: Wiley-Blackwell), pp. 267–87.
Barr, Roger (2016) 'The Greatest Video Game Graveyards: Part 1', I-Mockery.com, www.i-mockery.com/minimocks/greatest-video-game-graveyards/ (accessed 19 November 2023).
Byron, Glennis (2013) 'Introduction', in Glennis Byron (ed.), *Globalgothic* (Manchester: Manchester University Press), pp. 1–10.
Campbell, James (2016) 'From *Sleepy Hollow* to *Silent Hill*: American Gothic to Globalgothic', in Glennis Byron (ed.), *Globalgothic* (Manchester: Manchester University Press), pp. 157–74.
Daniell, Christopher (1997) *Death and Burial in Medieval England 1066–1550* (London: Routledge).
Erhard, Via (2022) 'The 7 Spookiest Video Games Set in Graveyards', Gamerant, 21 July, https://gamerant.com/best-video-games-set-in-graveyards/ (accessed 19 November 2023).
Farnell, Gary (2011) 'Gothic's Death Drive', *Literature Compass*, 8:9, 592–608.
Gilchrist, Roberta (2012) *Medieval Life: Archaeology and the Life Course* (Woodbridge: Boydell Press).

Hill, Giles (2014) 'One Hard Ghoulie: 1985's *Ghosts 'n Goblins*', *The Register*, 31 October.

Iguchi, Atsushi (2010) 'Appropriating the Other on the Edge of the World: Representations of the Western Middle Ages in Modern Japanese Culture', *Journal of the Open University of Japan*, 28:1, 63–9.

Juul, Jesper (2009) 'Fear of Failing? The Many Meanings of Difficulty in Video Games', in Bernard Perron and Mark J.P. Wolf (eds), *The Video Game Theory Reader 2* (New York: Routledge), pp. 237–52.

Kido, Takeshi (1995) 'The Study of the Medieval History of Europe in Japan', *Journal of Medieval History*, 21:2, 79–96.

Laqueur, Thomas (2015) *The Work of the Dead: A Cultural History of Mortal Remains* (Princeton: Princeton University Press).

Litten, Julian (2007) *The English Way of Death: The Common Funeral since 1450* (London: Robert Hale).

Martin, Paul (2011) 'Space and Place as Expressive Categories in Video Games', PhD thesis (London: Brunel University).

Mays, Simon (2010) *The Archaeology of Human Bones* (Abingdon: Routledge).

Munteanu, Cristinel (2012) 'Aberrant Decoding and Its Linguistic Expression: An Attempt to Restore the Original Concept', *Procedia – Social and Behavioral Sciences*, 63, 229–41.

Nuan, C. (2015) 'Top 10 Video Game Graveyards' (online video), WatchMojo.com (accessed 19 November 2023).

Perron, Bernard (2018) *The World of Scary Video Games: A Study in Videoludic Horror* (New York: Bloomsbury).

Picard, Martin (2009) 'Transnationality and Intermediality in Japanese Survival Horror Video Games', in Perron, Bernard (ed.), *Horror Video Games: Essays on the Fusion of Fear and Play* (Jefferson: McFarland), pp. 95–120.

Shmuplations (2015) 'Makaimura Series – Interview Collection", www.shmuplations.com/makaimura/ (accessed 19 November 2023).

Stobbart, Dawn (2019) *Video Games and Horror: From Amnesia to Zombies, Run* (Cardiff: University of Wales Press).

Turi, Tim (2014) 'Rest in Pixels: The Top 10 Video Game Graveyards', Game Informer, 29 October, www.gameinformer.com/b/features/archive/2014/10/29/rest-in-pixels-the-top-10-video-game-graveyards.aspx (accessed 19 November 2023).

Wolfman, J. (2020) 'Halloween: Our Favorite Gaming Cemeteries', Source Gaming, 29 October, https://sourcegaming.info/2020/10/29/halloween-our-favorite-gaming-cemeteries/ (accessed 5 December 2023).

Wong, Wendy Siuyi (2006) 'Globalizing Manga: From Japan to Hong Kong and Beyond', *Mechademia*, 1, pp. 23–45.

Coda: the futures of graveyard Gothic

Eric Parisot, David McAllister and Xavier Aldana Reyes

This collection has sought to establish the graveyard, both real and imagined, as a key site for the Gothic imagination and made a strong case for the consistency and value of the cultural work it has carried out for all manner of artists – from poets and novelists to creators of audiovisual content and video game designers – across national and religious boundaries. Because chronotopes are context-sensitive, their meanings are not static but rather evolve and morph over time. Although a number of universal concerns around mortality and the afterlife, memorialisation and the legacy of colonial domination have recurred throughout the case studies and countries covered in this collection, it is pertinent to ask at this point what the future of graveyard Gothic may look like in a twenty-first-century landscape transformed by developments in the management and mourning of the dead as well as by a growing secularism. The graveyard has historically been present in the Gothic and mediated several individual and collective preoccupations, but does it still have a role to play in a digital milieu and a world where physical space is becoming a scarce commodity? This coda considers the possible ways in which the Gothic may continue to revisit the graveyard and what new avenues may open for research at the juncture between burial practices, commemoration and the Gothic tradition. Paradoxically, the picture that emerges shows that, for all the social, economic and medical changes wrought by vicious pandemics, our awareness of the human impact on the natural world, the digital curation of human experience and a renewed social activism and decolonial effort, the post-millennial period is still dealing with anxieties that are in consonance with, even extensions of, those explored by the Gothic's long engagement with the graveyard.

The idea for this volume started in the spring of 2020, as the first wave of COVID-19 infections spread across the globe, disrupting every area of life and temporarily reshaping the rituals and routines associated with death and burial. In the following months, as the essays were being commissioned and planned, a rapid increase in the death rate in some countries overwhelmed the infrastructure which keeps the dead body safely out of sight of the living. In the United Kingdom, temporary morgues were set up to store the dead in a range of unlikely locations: international airports, landfill sites, industrial parks, a council gritting depot. In the United States, thousands of dead bodies were buried in mass graves on New York's Hart Island, which sits in the Long Island Sound, in the north-eastern Bronx. These were often poor or indigent victims of the pandemic: those whose families could not be traced by overwhelmed city authorities, who had died on the streets or in hospitals without anyone to claim their bodies, who had to be moved from morgues and mortuaries in which space was desperately needed as the death toll mounted. Their remains were placed in identical pine coffins, stamped with a distinguishing serial number, and buried in gigantic pits, to be disinterred, identified and reclaimed later, when things had – it was to be hoped – returned to 'normal', or at least to something that more closely resembled how burial was organised before the virus. These scenes echoed any number of historic crises and calamities which have required the suspension of normal burial practices, particularly those that recognise the individuality and distinctiveness of those who have died. As René Girard noted long ago, '[t]he distinctiveness of the plague is that it ultimately destroys all forms of distinctiveness … All life, finally, is turned into death … the supreme undifferentiation' (1974: 834). The scenes visually recalled the over-crowded churchyards and cemeteries of nineteenth-century London, and the contagion discourse used to refer to the dead by journalists was reminiscent of the miasmatic theories of disease explored in Chapter 3 of this collection. The dehumanising clustering of COVID graves and the relentless nature of a fatal outbreak, at that time still poorly understood by health authorities and the media, manifested a form of real-life, politicised graveyard Gothic that exposed the ugly reality of social inequalities, especially how geosocial divisions translate into the organisation and disposal of human remains and how burial practices are inextricable from wealth and privilege.

A comparable form of graveyard Gothic materialised out of Russia's invasion of Ukraine in February of 2022. The conflict – ongoing at the time of writing – has claimed tens of thousands of lives, sent shock waves across global markets, effectively slowing down economic growth, and awakened the dormant ghost of nuclear threat.[1] Yet the true horror surfaced after the discovery of mass graves in Izyum, a city seized by Russia in March of 2022 and subsequently recaptured by Ukrainian forces in September of the same year. Haunting images depicted the trench-like, dug-out forests where victims had been hastily interred as officials claimed that the bodies of the executed civilians showed 'signs of torture' and 'violent death' (Harding, 2022). Once again, graves had become evidence of war atrocities, proof to validate the reports of 'crimes against humanity ... even genocide' (Ochab, 2022) that followed the country's invasion. The symbolism of these encounters with the war's dead gains counter-ideological resonance when one considers Russia's efforts to frame its actions as a 'special military operation' intended to free Ukraine from neo-Nazis. The country's authorities' repeated attempts to use the past to justify the present was also on display in Moscow's Victory Museum, where direct parallels were drawn between Soviet victory over Nazi Germany and the occupation of Ukraine (Vagner, 2023). This propagandist attitude contrasted starkly with Russia's own looting of Ukrainian art, itself more than reminiscent in scale to the Nazi plunder of European art during World War II, as commentators noticed at the time (Salam and De Luce, 2023). In this light, graveyard Gothic emerging from the twenty-first century's most heavily mediated war resonated with the diagnostic and testimonial roles of the dead in traditional Gothic texts as tell-tale signs of buried secrets and sins, and was a stern warning that some national wounds scar over but never truly close.

Naturally, there is some distance between a Gothic reading of actual mass graves and their fictional Gothicised treatments, and the line separating the two must be trodden with care. Yet the fictional can often valuably reinforce the real, especially when art acts as an outlet for otherwise silenced histories. In the case of Spain, the country's gradual recuperation of historical memory in the late twentieth and early twenty-first centuries went hand in hand with a literary and filmic boom during which novelists and filmmakers frequently returned to the visual language of the Gothic to tell stories about justice, discovery and reparation. As mentioned in Chapter 8, the 'Pacto del Olvido' (Pact of Forgetting), given legal basis in 1977, imposed a moratorium on the crimes committed during the Spanish Civil War (and the dictatorship that followed) to facilitate a swift transition to democracy. The consequences of this decision on the Spanish psyche are myriad and active in contemporary geopolitical tussles, especially the fractious relationships between regions like Catalonia or the Basque Country and the central government (Aldana Reyes, 2021). The symmetries between life and fiction were particularly apparent at the turn of the century. The year 2000 saw the foundation of the Asociación para la Recuperación de la Memoria Histórica (Association for the Recovery of Historical Memory), an organisation dedicated to collecting war testimonies and digging up the mass graves of the Civil War for the purposes of identifying the war dead and returning remains to their respective families. Carlos Ruiz Zafón published his *The Shadow of the Wind* (*La sombra del viento*), the first book in his best-selling tetralogy about the Civil War and its aftermath, only a year later. Its mixture of historical melodrama and Gothic formulae found a quick successor in Guillermo del Toro's much-celebrated *The Devil's Backbone* (*El espinazo del diablo*, 2001) and

Pan's Labyrinth (*El laberinto del fauno*, 2006) and in later films like *Painless* (*Insensibles*, 2012), in which two separate timelines merge to offer an astute Gothic study of the impact of the Spanish Civil War. Even Pedro Almódovar, who had largely avoided war mentions in his critically acclaimed films, felt the time was right to tackle the issue head-on in 2021. The climax of *Parallel Mothers* (*Madres paralelas*) takes place in a mass grave, where, without explanation, the relatives of the victims lie down in the positions in which the bones are found. This practice, which apparently takes place during real exhumations, is intended as 'a homage to the dead' (Almódovar, quoted in Delgado, 2022: 45) and passes comment on the still provisional state of the war and its associated mourning. Spain's case speaks to graveyard Gothic's ability to function as solace and reparation, as creative counterpart to the real-life excavation of the submerged past.

The power of graveyard Gothic is not limited to the work of revisionist war art and fiction, and clearly aligns with the liberal, destigmatising agendas of contemporary critical movements in the broader humanities and of the growth of Death Studies in particular. As this collection has demonstrated, the study of death is hardly new, but Death Studies as a discipline has intensified and pluralised since the late twentieth century. Significant milestones, such as the publication of the first issue of *OMEGA – Journal of Death and Dying* (1970–) and of Ernest Becker's *The Denial of Death* (1974), as well as the foundation of the Association for Death Education and Counseling (ADEC) in 1976 and its sponsored journal *Death Studies* (1977–), paved the way for further scholarly initiatives seeking to study death, dying, bereavement and mourning from interdisciplinary perspectives. Some of these later developments include, but are by no means limited to, the challenge to the traditional grief model of detachment mounted by 'continuing bonds' in the 1990s (Klass, Silverman and Nickman, 1996) and the establishment of the journal *Mortality: Promoting the Interdisciplinary Study of Death and Dying* (1996–), of the Centre for Death and Society (2005) at Bath University (UK), of the Association for the Study of Death and Society (ASDS) in 2009 (UK), of the Death Online Research Network in 2013 (Copenhagen) and of the Death Studies Podcast in 2021. The phenomenon is not limited to the academic world either. Since the first non-profit death cafe opened in 2011 (Tucker, 2014), the prospect of discussing death over tea and cake among like-minded people in a non-judgemental context where grief is not pathologised has become attractive to many.

Death Studies has also pluralised thanks to activism. The foundation of the Collective for Radical Death Studies, a group composed of 'Scholars, Funeral Directors, Death Work Practitioners, Activists, and Students of Death Studies' (CRDS, 2020) is an important case in point. Their mission doubles as their view on death and the importance of death work, which they see as 'as synonymous with anti-racism work, synonymous with actively dismantling oppression, and as a way to validate cultural and social life among marginalized groups' and thereby 'achieve the goals of decolonizing death studies in theory and in practice from a variety of angles' (CRDS, 2020). With this goal in mind, the group develops provision and resources for Death and Dying courses and promotes an academic standpoint that offers an alternative to the white and Euro-centring of Death Studies. One of the publications coming out of this approach, *Till Death Do Us Part: American Ethnic Cemeteries as Borders Uncrossed* (2020), edited by Allan Amanik and Kami Fletcher, explores the fault lines between ethnicity, social standing and race at play in North American cemeteries. As the collection demonstrates, the separate interment of African Americans, Chinese, Indians, Muslim, Jews and Christian Arabs, among other communities, can sometimes be explained as an internal preference by those groups but is also largely an expression of the type of racial and religious prejudice and anti-immigrant sentiment that became palpable during the many tensions generated by the Trump administration (2017–21).[2] This critical work, with its focus on the intersections between society and death rites and its ambition to expose and debunk the epistemological and ideological biases attendant upon cultural rituals, spells the possible decolonial future of a branch of graveyard Gothic that would, much like some chapters in this collection, begin to ask questions about the colonial monsters that plague the representation of cemeteries and the disruptive affordances of the Gothic. One question it might endeavour to ask is whether artists stemming from underrepresented ethnic, religious and economic communities may be producing fundamentally different forms of Gothic representation of death and burial. And in the spirit of collections that have tackled the Gothic as a global phenomenon, such as Rebecca Duncan's *The Edinburgh Companion to Globalgothic* (2023), it might also investigate how representations of graveyards in the Global South can be read as negotiations of the legacy of imperialism, both ideological and economic.

Finally, it seems impossible to end this volume without a wider consideration of the possible redundancy of graveyard Gothic at a time when traditional interments are falling out of favour and could soon become an old-fashioned and even obsolete practice. The history of burial shows a pattern of long periods of calm followed by sudden upheaval: rites and practices remain fixed, seemingly permanently, in settled forms often for hundreds of years, before radically changing at moments of flux in politics, religion or public health (McAllister, 2018: 9–12). The multiple, overlapping crises of the current era make this seem like a moment pregnant with similarly transformative potential. In the United States, the national cremation rate surpassed that for burials in 2015 (Marsden-Ille, 2023) and, according to the National Funeral Directors Association (2018), is expected to exceed 80 per cent by 2035. The United Kingdom, Canada and Australia are way ahead, with cremations in 2021 accounting for 78.40 per cent, 74.8 per cent and approximately 75 per cent of all funerals, respectively (The Cremation Society, 2022; Funeral Guide, 2019; Cremation Association of North America, 2022). There are multiple reasons for this decrease in conventional practices, the most commonly cited are the lower cost of cremations, a gradual move away from religious institutions and, most importantly, environmental concerns about burials, from the chemicals involved in the embalming process to the diminishing amount of available land. While, by comparison, still in their infancy, 'green' or natural burials, whereby bodies are not chemically treated and are buried in approved, often conservationist, areas, as well as other eco-friendly alternatives like burial at sea, could soon become just as popular. The Capsula Mundi project, still in development at the time of writing, involves enclosing the dead or their ashes in 'an egg-shaped pod, an ancient and perfect form, made of biodegradable material', on top of which '[a] tree, chosen in life by the deceased, will be planted ... and serve as a memorial for the departed and as a legacy for posterity and the future of our planet' (Capsula Mundi, n.d.). Part of the company's mission is to rethink '[c]emeteries', which 'will acquire a new look and, instead of the cold grey landscape we see today ... will grow into vibrant woodlands' (Capsula Mundi, n.d.). Given that a significant proportion of people who choose cremation also specify that they would like to have their ashes scattered, it is safe to diagnose a sea change in our thinking that has weakened the once 'natural' link between the dead and physical cemeteries. What of graveyard Gothic in a brave new organic world in which the dead are potentially unnoticeable, their traceability reduced to GPS locations?

Before we attempt an answer, it is worth highlighting that the information offered above is not intended to suggest that new methods of disposal and memorialisation of the dead have resulted in a concomitant disuse of cemeteries. 'Sustainability' and 'climate change' are contemporary buzzwords that speak to very real fears about the effects of the Anthropocene, the decimation of the world's resources, rising temperatures and the inevitable climate migrations to follow.[3] Two hundred years of exponential population growth and lower infant mortality rates (Ritchie et al., 2013) have led to more annual deaths than ever before. In urbanised countries like the United Kingdom, where most of the population live in cities (84 per cent in 2021, according to online platform Statista), this has put major pressure on cemeteries, whose 'limited profitability' is to blame for a lack of investment in their growth (de Sousa, 2015). Projections based on research published in 2021 suggested that a quarter of all council-owned cemeteries would be full within ten years and one in six within only five years (Howard, 2021).

Much as the ubiquity of the 'zombie mass' can be interpreted as a symptom of the 'statistical society', where individuals are replaced by 'abstracted populations', and of the pressing issue of 'bodies crammed into super-cities and suburban sprawls, demanding satiation beyond any plan for sustainable living' (Luckhurst, 2015: 10–11), graveyard Gothic is doomed to record our panics about an overcrowded world in which persons become de-individualised, flattened into the benumbing peaks and flows of death counts and graphs like those that marked the first year of the COVID-19 pandemic. In December 2022, the Law Commission of England and Wales launched a project to review the laws governing burial and the disposal of the dead, which it described as 'unfit for modern needs' (Law Commission, 2022). One likely outcome could be to ensure graves can be reused after seventy-five years, overturning nineteenth-century legislation that established them as being the possession of the dead in perpetuity. Such a move would ease pressure on limited land and echo an approach that is already being taken by some European countries (Ferraz, 2018). These dramatic changes will affect the public perception of graveyards and cemeteries, long held as places of immutability, perpetuity and even transcendence. As funereal plots become transitory and subject to the same stresses of the living (time and rents), graveyard Gothic will surely grow more preoccupied with precarity and transience. The displacement of the cemetery as the primary setting for mourning and commemoration will necessitate a similar move and expansion of the coordinates of graveyard Gothic.

The turning point may, in fact, have already been reached. It makes perfect sense that, at a time when the (im)materiality of death and our engagement with grief have been comprehensively rethought by modern funereal practices, we should be looking for graveyard Gothic in a ubiquitous, intangible place: the World Wide Web. As Jeffrey Sconce has argued, all new forms of media, from nineteenth-century telegraphy to the radio and on to television and computers, have been consistently associated to paranormal or supernatural phenomena because of their seemingly magical properties and ability to conjure up a form of 'telepresence' reminiscent of popular configurations of a possible afterlife (2000: 21). Since the 1990s, when Carla Sofka coined the term 'thanatechnology' (1997) to refer to the inevitable entanglement of death and technology that followed the digital revolution, the gradual encroachment of the internet on all aspects of leisure and our working lives, the dead have been remembered by means of digital media, first through commemorative pages, bulletin boards, news groups and chat rooms, and then through social media and networking apps (Arnold et al., 2018: 5–6).[4] Online pages and profiles, which can continue to be curated by friends and/or relatives of the deceased, have been interacted with in forms that recall and, in some cases mirror, the intimate functions of cemeteries and gravestones: they do not just allow the bereaved to communicate their pain and loss but act as conduits between them and their dead (de Vries and Rutherford, 2004), facilitating a form of ritualistic 'returning' (Socolovsky, 2004: 474) and intended contact with what lies beyond. From 2003, the year when digital cameras outsold film ones, photographic online banks have gradually replaced photo albums, allowing platforms like Facebook and Instagram to double as image repositories chronicling vast swathes of a person's life. Have digital media become a new form of graveyard Gothic? The swelling numbers of texts that situate hauntings and ghostly revenges online, manifesting through the same telecommunication services that enable social and professional exchanges – Skype in *Unfriended* (2014), Facebook in *Friend Request* (2016), Zoom in *Host* (2020) – would certainly seem to indicate as much. The proliferation of internet ghosts opens up yet another future for graveyard Gothic. If Marc Olivier is right in his view that 'the jarring spectacle of data ruins' is the contemporary equivalent to the nineteenth-century Gothic mansion, 'the privileged space for confrontations with incompatible systems, nostalgic remnants, and restless revenants' (2015: 253), graveyard Gothic can be productively situated in the interstices between hypermediated, viral users and the computerised, synergistic traces of their dead. Computers, laptops, tablets and phones might thus be reconceptualised as gates that open up onto the unconsecrated grounds of the digital graveyard, full of the *memento mori* of the data age, and rogue, demanding technoghosts as another intimation of the tragedy of human finitude, the fear that one day we could be irretrievably forgotten.

Notes

1 As of April 2023, Ukraine has reportedly suffered '124,500–131,000 total casualties, including 15,500–17,500 killed in action and 109,000–113,500 wounded in action', and Russia has suffered '189,500–223,000 total casualties, including 35,500–43,000 killed in action and 154,000–180,000 wounded' (Faulconbridge, 2023).
2 We are referring specifically to the US–Mexico barrier commonly termed the 'Trump wall', which was crucial to Donald Trump's election, and the critical attention garnered by the Black Lives Matter movement following the murder of George Floyd on 25 May 2020.
3 Researchers predict that, by 2070, 19 per cent of the planet will be inhabitable due to rising temperatures and that this will lead to the death of billions of people and mass-scale displacements. It is estimated that, as soon as 2050, climate change could force around 86 million people to move (Lustgarten, 2022: 166–7).

4 Holographic technology, virtual reality (VR) and artificial intelligence (AI) are also being utilised to orchestrate resurrective encounters with the dead through the use of digital remains (surviving conversations, photos, videos and audio). Two notable cases are those of the interactive Holocaust survivor, Pinchas Gutter (McMullan, 2016), and the VR-assisted reunion of a South Korean mother with an aged digital avatar of her dead daughter (Park, 2020). HereAfter AI is one of many companies whose services specialise in building personalised, responsive avatars for the bereaved.

References

Aldana Reyes, Xavier (2021) 'Spanish Civil War Horror and Regional Trauma: The Politics of Painful Remembrance in Juan Carlos Medina's *Insensibles* (*Painless*, 2012)', *English Language Notes*, 59:2, 20–34.

Amanik, Allan and Kami Fletcher (eds) (2020) *Till Death Do Us Part: American Ethnic Cemeteries as Borders Uncrossed* (Jackson: University Press of Mississippi).

Arnold, Michael, Martin Gibbs, Tamara Kohn, James Meese and Bjorn Nansen (2018) *Death and Digital Media* (Abingdon: Routledge).

Becker, Ernest (1974) *The Denial of Death* (New York: Free Press).

Capsula Mundi (n.d.) 'Capsula Mundi. Life Never Stops', www.capsulamundi.it/en (accessed 5 May 2023).

Collective for Radical Death Studies (2020) 'Our Mission', www.radicaldeathstudies.com/our-mission (accessed 5 May 2022).

Cremation Association of North America (2022) 'Industry Statistical Information', www.cremationassociation.org/page/IndustryStatistics (accessed 5 May 2023).

Cremation Society, The (2022) 'Process of Cremation in the British Isles, 1885–2021', Cremation.org.uk, www.cremation.org.uk/progress-of-cremation-united-kingdom (accessed 5 May 2023).

de Sousa, Ana Naomi (2015) 'Death in the City: What Happens When All Our Cemeteries Are Full?', *The Guardian*, 21 January, www.theguardian.com/cities/2015/jan/21/death-in-the-city-what-happens-cemeteries-full-cost-dying (accessed 5 May 2023).

de Vries, Brian and Judy Rutherford (2004) 'Memorializing Loved Ones on the World Wide Web', *Omega: Journal of Death and Dying*, 49:1, 5–26.

Delgado, Maria (2022) 'Pedro Almodóvar', *Sight and Sound*, 32:2, 38–42, 45.

Duncan, Rebecca (2023) *The Edinburgh Companion to Globalgothic* (Edinburgh: Edinburgh University Press).

Faulconbridge, Guy (2023) 'Ukraine War, Already with up to 354,000 Casualties, Likely to Last Past 2023 – U.S. Documents', Reuters, 12 April, www.reuters.com/world/europe/ukraine-war-already-with-up-354000-casualties-likely-drag-us-documents-2023-04-12/ (accessed 19 November 2023).

Ferraz, Rafaela (2018) 'Cemetery Overcrowding is Leading Europe to Recycle Burial Plots', Talk Death, 18 July, www.talkdeath.com/cemetery-overcrowding-leading-europe-recycle-burial-plots/#:~:text=France%2C%20like%20Portugal%2C%20still%20allows,been%20touched%20in%202075%20years (accessed 5 May 2023).

Funeral Guide (2019) 'A Guide to Cremation Costs and Arrangements: Information on Arranging a Cremation and the Costs Involved', www.funeralguide.net/help-resources/arranging-a-funeral/funeral-guides/a-guide-to-cremation-costs-arrangements (accessed 5 May 2023).

Girard, René (1974) 'The Plague in Literature and Myth', *Texas Studies in Literature and Language*, 15:5, 833–50.

Harding, Luke (2022) 'Ukraine Says Victims from Izium Mass Grave Show Signs of Torture', *The Guardian*, 16 September, www.theguardian.com/world/2022/sep/16/ukraine-mass-grave-with-440-bodies-discovered-in-recaptured-izium-says-police-chief (accessed 5 May 2023).

Howard, Jules (2021) 'Here's What Will Happen When We Run Out of Space to Bury the Dead', *Science Focus*, 31 October, www.sciencefocus.com/the-human-body/deal-with-the-dead (accessed 5 May 2023).

Klass, Dennis, Phyllis R. Silverman and Steven L. Nickman (eds) (1996) *Continuing Bonds: New Understandings of Grief* (Philadelphia: Taylor & Francis).

Law Commission, The (2022) 'A Modern Framework for Disposing of the Dead', www.lawcom.gov.uk/project/a-modern-framework-for-disposing-of-the-dead/ (accessed 23 May 2023).

Luckhurst, Roger (2015) *Zombies: A Cultural History* (London: Reaktion Books).

Lustgarten, Abrahm (2022) 'Climate Refugees', in Greta Thunberg (ed.), *The Climate Book* (London: Allen Lane), pp. 165–8.

Marsden-Ille, Sarah (2023) 'What Is the 2023 Cremation Rate in the US? How Is This Affecting Prices?', US Funerals Online, www.us-funerals.com/2023-us-cremation-rate/#:~:text=The%20N.F.D.A%202022%20report%20indicated,opting%20for%20a%20casketed%20service (accessed 5 May 2023).

McAllister, David (2018) *Imagining the Dead in British Literature and Culture, 1790–1848* (Basingstoke: Palgrave Macmillan).

McMullan, Thomas (2016) 'The Virtual Holocaust Survivor: How History Gained New Dimensions', *The Guardian*, 18 June, www.theguardian.com/technology/2016/jun/18/holocaust-survivor-hologram-pinchas-gutter-new-dimensions-history (accessed 5 May 2023).

National Funeral Directors Association (2018) 'Cremation on the Rise: NFDA Predicts the National Cremation Rate Will Climb by a Third Within 20 Years', 12 July, https://nfda.org/news/media-center/nfda-news-releases/id/3526/cremation-on-the-rise-nfda-predicts-the-national-cremation-rate-will-climb-by-a-third-within-20-years (accessed 5 May 2023).

Ochab, Ewelina U. (2022) 'New Mass Graves Found In Ukraine As Putin's Atrocities Continue', Forbes, 22 September, www.forbes.com/sites/ewelinaochab/2022/09/22/new-mass-graves-found-in-ukraine-as-putins-atrocities-continue/?sh=7604746258ba (accessed 5 May 2023).

Olivier, Marc (2015) 'Glitch Gothic', in Murray Leeder (ed.), *Cinematic Ghosts: Haunting and Spectrality from Silent Cinema to the Digital Era* (London: Bloomsbury), pp. 253–70.

Park, Minwoo (2020) 'South Korean Mother Given Tearful VR Reunion with Deceased Daughter', Reuters, 14 February, www.reuters.com/article/us-southkorea-virtualreality-reunion-idUSKBN2081D6 (accessed 5 May 2023).

Ritchie, Hannah, Lucas Rodés-Guirao, Edouard Mathieu, Marcel Gerber, Esteban Ortiz-Opsina, Joe Hasell and Max Roser (n.d.) 'Population Growth', Our

World in Data, https://ourworldindata.org/population-growth (accessed 5 May 2023).

Salam, Yasmine and Dan De Luce (2023) 'Just the Way the Nazis Did': Evidence Suggests Russians Are Stealing Art from Ukraine on a World War II Scale', NBC News, 6 April, www.nbcnews.com/news/world/russia-stealing-art-ukraine-nazi-level-world-war-2-rcna77879 (accessed 5 May 2023).

Sconce, Jeffrey (2000) *Haunted Media: Electronic Presence from Telegraphy to Television* (Durham: Duke University Press).

Socolovsky, Maya (2004) 'Cyber-Spaces of Grief: Online Memorials and the Columbine High School Shootings', *A Journal of Composition Theory*, 24:2, 467–90.

Sofka, Carla (1997) 'Social Support "Internetworks," Caskets for Sale, and More: Thanatology and the Information Superhighway', *Death Studies*, 21:6, 553–74.

Statista (2023) 'United Kingdom: Degree of Urbanization from 2011 to 2021', www.statista.com/statistics/270369/urbanization-in-the-united-kingdom/ (accessed 5 May 2023).

Tucker, Eleanor (2014) 'What on Earth Is a Death Cafe?', *The Guardian*, 22 March, www.theguardian.com/lifeandstyle/2014/mar/22/death-cafe-talk-about-dying (accessed 5 May 2023).

Vagner, Volodya (2023) 'This Moscow Military Museum Blurs History and Propaganda. We Visited It', openDemocracy, 18 April, www.opendemocracy.net/en/odr/victory-museum-moscow-ukraine-russia-nazi-history-great-patriotic-war/ (accessed 5 May 2023).

Index

Abbey of St. Asaph, The (Kelly) 41, 43
'Aboriginal Mother, The' (Dunlop) 104
Aboriginal people
   grave robbery 104–7
   massacre sites 101–4
Adams, Robert Dudley 104
Addams Family, The (TV) 157–9
Addison, Joseph 32–3
adolescence 238–40
aesthetics, graveyard
   Dracula (Stoker) 71–2
   Lovecraft 113–23
   Medieval 252–3
   new cemeteries 63–8
Akamatsu, Hitoshi 255, 259
Alcoriza, Luis 200
Aldana Reyes, Xavier 188
Almodóvar, Pedro 131, 271
American Gothic 223, 230, 233, 235
American Horror Story: Hotel (TV) 161
Amityville Horror, The (Anson and films) 229–31, 232
anachronisms in Japanese games 252–3, 259–60, 263–4
Ancuta, Katarzyna 184
Anson, Jay 229–31, 232
'Anthem for Doomed Youth' (Owen) 149
Arabian Nights 122
As Above, So Below (Dowdle) 134
Asian Games, the 183, 193
associationist psychology 62–4, 68
'At the Mountains of Madness' (Lovecraft) 120–1
Austen, Jane 5
Australia
   Aboriginal people 101–8
   settlers 96–101

Babel, Isaac 217
'Bad Place,' the 230
Bakhtin, Mikhail 210, 239
Baldick, Chris 2, 259
Barker, Clive 134–6
Bataille, Georges 121
Baudelaire, Charles 115, 116
Bazin, André 136
Bell, Michael Mayerfield 203
Benjamin, Walter 86, 219
Bentham, Jeremy 50–2, 80
Bhandari, Rajika 185
biopolitics 50–1
Blackwood, Algernon 227
Blair, Robert 21, 22, 24–5, 27–9, 32–3
Bleak House (Dickens) 57
Blunden, Edmund 148, 149
bodies
   emerging from the grave 165–8
   The Grave (Blair) 27–9
   Lucy Westenra 68–71
   paradoxical nature 128
   reanimated 47–9, 128–32, 211–12, 226–7, 261
   relics 79–80
   wartime 141–3
bodysnatchers 47–9
bombing, Home Front 149–51
Botting, Fred 6
Bride of Re-Animator 129
Bright, Amy 239
Brooke, Rupert 144
Buffy the Vampire Slayer (TV) 159, 164, 165, 166–8, 238
Bundy, Mark W. 162
bungalows, *dak* 185–6

Bunhill Fields 19–20, 52
burial
  alive 198–9
  Home Front bombing 149–51
  in trenches 147–9
burial practices, changing 171–2, 272–5
  See also cremations
burial reform 52–7, 61–8
Burnt Offerings (Marasco) 232–3
'Bush Undertaker, The' (Lawson) 106–7
Byron, Lord 70

'Call of Cthulhu, The' (Lovecraft) 120, 122
Calvinism 27
'Cancerous Image, The' (Guibert) 89–91
cannibalism 227
Carlyle, Thomas 80
Carrie (De Palma) 130
Carter, David 97
cassette culture, Indian 183
Castle of Otranto, The (Walpole) 3–4, 228, 231
Castlevania (video game) 255, 259, 261, 263
Cathcart, Michael 96
Cave, Alfred A. 233
Cawelti, John 44
Cemetery Boys (Thomas) 248–9
censorship, wartime 143, 150
Chadwick, Edwin 55, 62, 64
Cherkasov, Sviatoslav 264
chernukha 217–18
Chevalier, Tracy 177–80
children
  associationist psychology 62–3
children, ghostly 241
Chomón, Segundo de 127
Christianity 3
chronotope
  Gothic castle 210, 219–20
  graveyards 6–7, 210, 219–20, 239
churches 23–6
churchyard poetry 20
churchyards 2, 3, 19–20
Cien gritos de terror (Obón) 198
cinema
  Indian 183–94
  Mexican 198–201

  Polish 209, 211–12, 214–16
  Soviet and post Soviet 208–21
  Spanish 130–1, 270–1
  Western 125–37
clearance, graveyard 171
Coco (Unkrich) 196–7, 201–6
Coleridge, Samuel Taylor 38
Collective for Radical Death Studies 271
colonialism
  Aboriginal massacre sites 101–4
  Australian weird 108
  grave robbery 104–7
  Indian domestic buildings 184–6
  Native Americans 223–36
  racial prejudice 271–2
  Ramsay Brothers films 192
  settler graves 96–101
commemoration of war dead 141–2, 143–5
communication between living and dead 196–9, 200–6
communities, place of graveyards in 2–3, 201–6
Connolly, Cyril 150
consecrated ground 19–20
corpselessness, wartime 143, 150
corpses *see* bodies
Coscarelli, Dan 134
COVID-19 268–9
Cowley, Hannah 18
'Creek of the Four Graves, The' (Harpur) 100–1
cremations 179–80, 272–3
crime and burial 187–8
crime scene photographs 191
Cullen, Stephen 41

Dahshat 190
Dak Bangla (Ramsay brothers) 186–9, 192
dance sequences 193–4
Dark Shadows (TV) 157, 159–60, 163
Dark Souls (video game) 262
Davison, Carol Margaret 60
Day of the Dead 196–7, 201–6
De Palma, Brian 130
Dead Souls (Gogol) 208
Death and Douglas (Ocker) 244–6
Death Studies 271–2

'Death-Bed, The' (Hood) 69–71, 72
Decadence 72–3, 113–19
decay
 fin de siècle 72–4
 memorials 81–6
de-Gothicisation 61–8
Dellamorte Dellamore (Soavi) 132
democratic nature of graveyards 220
Derrida, Jacques 196
'Desecration of the Gravestone of Rose P.' (Pinsky) 91–3
DeSilvey, Caitlin 87
destruction of graveyards 220
'Devil and Tom Walker, The' (Irving) 234
Devil, Native Americans and the 233–4
Devil, The (Żuławski) 214
Dhansey, Iqbal 188
Día de difuntos (Alcoriza) 200
Dickens, Charles 57–8
Dickey, Colin 225
digital technology 274–5
disturbance of the dead
 Aboriginal graves 104–7
 grave robbery 47–9, 104–7
 Medieval exhumations 253
 Native Indian graves 228–9, 232
 reuse of graves 274
 urban graveyards 52–6
domestic settings in Western TV 155–9
Dracula (game character) 255, 261
Dracula (Stoker) 58, 68–74
Dracula (TV) 165–6
Dunlop, Eliza Hamilton 104

Earl Strongbow (White) 4–5
Elden Ring (video game) 266–5
'Elegy Written in a Country Churchyard' (Gray) 21–2
entertainment, graveyard visits as 32–3
environmental concerns about burial 273
epitaphs, war grave 145–6
Essay on Sepulchres (Godwin) 47, 80–1
Eunapius of Sardis 3
'Evil of Yelcomorn Creek, The' (Walker) 107–8
evil, ancient 227–8, 230–1, 232–3

exhumations of mass graves 271
explorers, Australian 100

Falling Angels (Chevalier) 177–80
family
 Day of the Dead 201–6
 dynastic tombs 42–4
fear, salvation through 27–9
Fée Carabosse ou le poignard fatal, La (Méliès) 127
Féeries 127
Field, Barron 99
fin de siècle and decay 72–4
'Fisher's Ghost: A Legend of Campbelltown' (Lang) 99
Foucault, Michel 5–6, 50–1, 79, 170
Fox, Hester 171
Frankenstein (Shelley) 47–8
Frankenstein (Whale) 47–9, 125–6
Freneau, Philip 233
Fujiwara, Tokura 255, 259
Fulci, Lucio 129
Fussell, Paul 148, 149

Gaiman, Neil 238
Galindo Jr, Rubén 199
garden cemeteries 67–8, 170, 171
Gatherings from Graveyards (Walker) 52
ghost literature, colonial 98–9
ghosts
 children 241
 and place 203
 Woman in Black, The (Hill) 172–7
Ghosts 'n Goblins 255, 259, 263
'Giaour, The' (Byron) 70
Gilfillan, George 28
Gillray, James 39
Girard, René 269
Goddu, Teresa 232, 235
Godwin, William 47, 80–1
Gogol, Nikolai 208
grave robbery 47–9, 104–7
Grave, The (Blair) 21, 22, 24–5, 27–9, 32–3
graves
 covered 163
 open 164–5
Graves, Robert 148

gravestones
    ephemeral markers 81–6
    imagery on 89, 128
    Medieval 252–3
    video games 253
    war graves 145–6
Graveyard Book, The (Gaiman) 533
Graveyard Girl and the Boneyard Boy, The (Matthews) 246–7
graveyard poetry 18–30, 84–6
Graveyard Riddle, The (Thompson) 243–4
Graveyard Shakes (Terry) 241–3
graveyard, lexical origins of the term 19–20
Gray, Thomas 21–2
grief 35–6, 68–72
Grimstone, Mary 98
Guibert, Hervé 89–91
guilt, American 223–5, 232

Hamilton, Elizabeth 63
happy Gothic 240
Hardy Tree, the 86
Hardy, Thomas 84–6 72
Harpur, Charles 100–1, 103–4
Harrison, Robert Pogue 1
haunted house stories 229–31
Haunted Priory, The (Cullen) 41
Haunting of Hill House, The (Jackson) 229
haveli 184–5
Hawthorne, Nathaniel 223, 233
'Herbert West - Reanimator' (Lovecraft) 114–16
Herbert, George 91–3
heroes and heroines in Japanese games 259–60
Hervey, James 20, 25–6, 32–3
heterotopias 5–6
Highgate Cemetery 177–8
Hill, Miranda and Octavia 58
Hill, Susan 172–7
histories, collective 86–8, 209, 220
Hollywood Forever Cemetery 161
Holmes, Isabella 50, 57
Hood, Thomas 69–71, 72
'Hound, The' (Lovecraft) 117–18
Humble Cemetery, The (Itygilov) 210, 216–19

Imperial War Graves Commission, the 145–6
'In Flanders Fields' (McCrae) 332
In Parenthesis (Jones) 149 120–3
'In the Cemetery' (Hardy) 202
In the Flesh (TV) 166–8
Indian (Native American) burial grounds 223–36
'Indian Burying Ground, The' (Freneau) 233–4
Indian cinema 183–94
interment, wartime
    Home Front bombing 147, 149–51
    in trenches 147–9
'Invocation: To Horror' (Cowley) 18
Irving, Washington 234
Itygilov, Aleksandr 209–10, 216–19

Jack, J. L 148
Jackson, Michael 193–4, 258
Jackson, Shirley 229
Japan
    and Medieval Europe 259
    and Western aesthetics 255–8
    video games 252–66
Jones, David 148, 149
Jones, Steven Graham 236
jouissance, Lovecraft and 113–19

Kamińska, Magdalena 211
Kelly, Isabella 41, 42
Kendall, Henry 99
Kensal Green Cemetery 66–7
Kenyon, Sir Frederic 146
King, Stephen 224–8, 230, 232, 258
Kipling, Rudyard 145, 146
Knapp, Henry 101–2
kothi 185

Lacan, Jacques 113–14
Lake Shawnee Amusement Park 235
land ownership, Native Indian 224–6
Lane, William 40
Lang, John 99
Laqueur, Thomas 19, 171
Lawrence, D. H. 72
Lawson, Henry 106–7
Légende du fantôme, La (de Chomón) 127

'Levelled Churchyard, The' (Hardy) 199
Lewis, Matthew 30, 36–9
'limit experience' in Lovecraft 113–14
Locke, John 63
London burial grounds 52–8
London Burial Grounds (Holmes) 50
Loudon, John Claudius 62, 170
Lovecraft, H.P. 111–23
Luckhurst, Roger 119, 157
Luki, Marko 30
'Lurking Fear, The' (Lovecraft) 116

Macaulay, Rose 151
Machen, Arthur 119
Madres paralelas (Almódovar) 131
Manitou, The (Masterton) 224
Manning, Frederic 148, 149
Marasco, Robert 232
marginalised groups
   Humble Cemetery, The
     (Itygilov) 216–19
   places of inclusion 134–6
   See also young adult (YA) fiction
Martin, Paul 257–8
Marx, Karl 2
mass graves 268–71
   See also massacres of
     Aboriginal people
massacres of Aboriginal people 101–4
Master Designer (Teptsov) 210, 212–14
Masterton, Graham 224
Matthews, Martin 246–7
Mazierska, Ewa 209
McCombie, Thomas 100
McCrae, John 143
Medieval Europe, Japanese scholarship and 259
Medieval graveyards 252–3
Meditations among the Tombs (Hervey) 20, 25–6, 32–3
Méliès, Georges 127
memento mori 8, 19, 23, 30, 32–3, 44, 65, 79–80, 125–6, 157, 275
memorials
   Aboriginal massacres 104
   digital technology 274–5
   ephemeral 81–6
   Frankenstein (Whale) 125–6
   The X-Files (TV) 161–2
   See also gravestones

memory, communal 201–6
memory, historical 86–8, 209, 220
Mexico
   cinema 198–201
   Coco (Unkrich) 196–7, 201–6
   literature 197–8
Mighall, Robert 260
Mikołajczyk, Maja 211
Minerva Press 40
'Miss Anstruther's Letters'
   (Macaulay) 359
Miyazaki, Hidetaka 264
Modernist graveyard aesthetic 120–3
Monk, The (Lewis) 36–9
monsters in Ramsay brothers
   films 189–92
Morales, Orquidea 204
More Ghosts! 41
Morrison, Susan Signe 216
Moruzi, Kristine 240
mourning 35–6, 142
Mudford, William 66
Munsters, The (TV) 157–9
Murdering Flat 101–3
Myall Creek Massacre 103–4
Mysteries of London, The
   (Reynolds) 57
Mysteries of Udolpho, The (Radcliffe) 4, 34–6, 39–40, 43

'Nameless City, The' (Lovecraft) 121–2
Native American Indians
   burial grounds 223–8, 230–1, 232, 235–6
   the Devil 233–4
   rights 224–6, 231–2
'Native's Lament, The' 104
nature
   churchyard poetry 20–3
   garden cemeteries 67
necromanticism 48, 80–1
necronationalism 97
neo-Edwardian novels 169–81
Netley Abbey (Warner) 41, 42
Night of the Living Dead (Romero) 129
Night Thoughts (Young) 22–3, 25
Nightbreed (Barker) 134–6
'Night-Piece on Death, A' (Parnell) 20, 21, 23–4, 26–7, 32–3

noche del terror ciego, La
  (Ossorio) 130–1
Nora, Pierre 146
novels
  early Victorian 57–8
  Gothic 3–5, 6, 32, 34–45
  Mexican 197–8
  neo-Edwardian 169–81
  neo-Victorian 170–1
  young adult 238–50
Novodevichie Cemetery 208

'Obliterate Tomb, The' (Hardy) 197
Obón, Ramon 198–9
Ocker, J.W. 244–6
Olivier, Marc 275
'On Passing the New Menin Gate'
  (Sassoon) 143
On the Silver Globe (Żuławski) 214
'On Visiting the Cemetery in Hobart
  Town' (Grimstone) 98
'On Visiting the Spot where Captain
  Cook and Sir Joseph Banks First
  Landed in Botany Bay' (Field) 99
Only Good Indians, The (Jones) 236
Orphan of Cemetery Hill, The
  (Fox) 399
Orui, Noburu 259
Ossorio, Amando de 130–1
Ousby, Ian 18
overcrowding, graveyard 50, 52–7,
  268–9, 273–4
Owen, Wilfred 149

Pair of Blue Eyes, A (Hardy) 204
Parezanovi, Tijana 30
Paris Catacombs, the 133
Parnell, Thomas 20, 21, 23–4, 26–7,
  32–3
parodies
  of Gothic fiction 4–5, 41–2
  of Indian burial ground trope
    224–5
Past and Present (Carlyle) 80
Peake, Mervyn 151
Pedro Páramo (Rulfo) 197–8
Perestroika 208–9
Perron, Bernard 260
Pet Sematary (King) 224–8, 232
Phantasm (Coscarelli) 134
'Photograph, The' (Hardy) 212

photographs 88–91, 191
Picard, Martin 255–7
'Pickman's Model' (Lovecraft) 118
picturesque, charnel 116–17
Piestrak, Marek 209–10, 211–12
Pinsky, Robert 91–3
Piper, John 151
pleasure, Gothic novels and 34–45
Pliny the Younger 231
Poe, Edgar Allan 112, 198
poetry
  churchyard 20
  colonial epitaphic 99–100
  deathbed 69–71
  graveyard 18–30, 32–3
  Hardy 84–6
Polish cinema 209, 211–12, 214–16
Poltergeist (Hooper) 228–9
Porter, Joy 227, 235
posthuman graveyards 120–3
'Premature Burial, The' (Poe) 198
privacy, burial vaults and 34–8
Profanadores de tumba (Morales) 199
protests, American Indian 231–2
psychological dangers 62–8
public health 52–7, 268–9
pulp modernism 111
Purana Mandir (Ramsay brothers)
  187, 191
Putney, Christopher 220

Quakers 19–20
Quella villa accanto al cimitero
  (Fulci) 129

racism 158–9, 271–2
Radcliffe, Ann 4, 30, 34–6, 39–40, 43
Ramsay brothers 183–4, 186–93
Ramsey, Winston 150
readers and Gothic novels 38–41
reform, burial 52–7, 61–8
refuges, graveyards as 238, 243–6
relics
  photographs 88–91
  sacred 79–80
religious contemplation 18–30
Restless Matron, The 42
resurrection
  Christian 261
  Gothic TV 165–8
  Japanese games 261–3, 264–5

'Resurrection' (Wagner) 77–8
Return of the She-Wolf, The (Piestrak) 210, 212
reuse of graves 274
Reyez-Cortez, Marcel 203
Riding In, James 232
roadside memorials 81–4
Rod Serling's Night Gallery (TV) 156
Roger Barr 252
Rollin, Jean 133
Romero, George A. 128–9
Rose de fer, La (Rollin) 133
Rosewarne, Vivian 140
ruin
    destructive 91–3
    slow 81–8
Ruins of Avondale Priory, The (Kelly) 42, 43
Rulfo, Juan 197–8
Russia
    cinema 212–14
    video games 264
    war with Ukraine 269–70

Sainsbury, Lisa 241
salvation through fear 27–9
Sassoon, Siegfried 143
Scutts, Joanna 145
secularisation of funeral customs 172
self, death and sense of 201
Sen, Meheli 190
sentimentalism 63–5, 68–72
sentinels, graveyard 21, 24, 134, 247
settler graves, Australian 96–101
sexual transgression 36–8
shamans 214–16, 224
Sharma, Jyoti Pandey 185
Shelley, Mary 47–8
'Shepherd's Grave, The' (Knapp) 101–2
Sherlock (TV) 165
She-Shaman 210, 214–16
She-Wolf 210, 211–12
Silent Hill (video game) 258–9
Simpsons, The (TV) 258
sitcoms 157–9
Six Feet Under (TV) 162–3
skeletons 261
Smith, Andrew 169, 201
Smith, Michelle J. 240, 241
social dislocation 86–8

social interaction between living and dead 196–9, 200–6
solace, places of 134–6, 249–50
'Soldier, The' (Brooke) 144
sound and dread 24
South Asian Gothic 184
Soviet and post Soviet cinema 208–21
Spain
    Civil War 130–1, 270–1
    film 130–1, 270–1
    video games 264
spiritualism 142–3
Spooner, Catherine 240
Sprackland, Jean 128, 169
Stableford, Brian 115
'Statement of Randolph Carter, The' (Lovecraft) 114
Stoker, Bram 68–74
Story, Joseph 64
storytelling, collective 86–8
Strang, John 62, 64, 65, 67
sublime in Gothic novels 39
suburbia in Gothic TV 157–9
Sundaram, Ravi 183
'Sutherland's Grave (The first white man buried in Australia)' (Kendall) 99

Tales of Terror 39
Taylor, William M. 67
tehkanas 184–92, 194
television, Western 155–68
temporality 1, 6–7
Teptsov, Oleg 209–10, 212–14
Terry, Laura 241–3
Thacker, Eugene 118, 121
Thomas, Aiden 248–9
Thompson, Lisa 243–4
thresholds 7, 133–4, 220
Thriller (music video) 193–4, 258
'Tomb, The' (Lovecraft) 112–13
Tombs of Unknown Warriors 144
Toro, Guillermo del 270
tourism, graveyard 32–3
Townshend, Dale 63
trade Gothic 40–4
trash, history as 216–17
trenches, World War I 147–9
Trowbridge, Serena 147, 163
'Trucanini's Dirge' (Adams) 104–5

'true stories' 229–31
Truganini 104–6
Twin Peaks (TV) 164–5

Ukraine, Russian war with 269–70
'Unnamable, The' (Lovecraft) 119
Unquiet Grave, The (Connolly) 150–1
urban graveyards 52–8
Utilitarianism 50–2

Valančiūnas, Deimantas 184
vampires
    Dracula (character) 58, 68–74, 165–6, 255, 261
    Gothic TV 159–61
Vasser, Shea 235
vaults, burial 34–8, 40–4
    See also tehkanas
vengeance, Native American 223–5, 232
ventriloquised corpses, wartime 141–3
video games 252–66

'Wail from the Bush, A' (Harpur) 103–4
Walker, George Alfred 52–7
Walker, William Sylvester 107–8
Walpole, Horace 3–4, 228, 231
war
    First World War 140–9
        Imperial War Graves Commission 145–7
    mass graves 269–71
    Second World War 140–3, 151
    Spanish Civil War 130–1, 270–1
    See also Aboriginal people: massacre sites; settler graves, Australian
Warton, Thomas 33
Watts, Isaac 27
weird tales, Lovecraft and 111
weird, Australian colonial 104–8
Wendigo, the 227–8
werewolves 210, 211–12
Westmacott, Charles Molloy 65, 66
Whale, James 47–9, 125–6
Wheatley, Helen 155
White, James 4–5
Wild Hunt of King Stakh, The (Rubinchik) 208
Wills, Deborah 239
Woman in Black, The (Hill) 172–7
Wood, Nancy 147
wooden crosses 80–4
Wordsworth, William 2

X-Files, The (TV) 161–2

yew trees 22
young adult (YA) fiction 238–50
Young, Edward 22–3, 25
Yuzna, Brian 129

zombies 128–32, 165, 166–8
Żuławski, Andrzej 209–10, 214–16

EU authorised representative for GPSR:
Easy Access System Europe, Mustamäe tee 50,
10621 Tallinn, Estonia
gpsr.requests@easproject.com

www.ingramcontent.com/pod-product-compliance
Lightning Source LLC
LaVergne TN
LVHW091731200625
814311LV00002B/5